Teen Genreflecting

Genreflecting Advisory Series

Diana Tixier Herald, Series Editor

Genreflecting: A Guide to Reading Interests in Genre Fiction, 5th Edition, by Diana Tixier Herald

Teen Genreflecting by Diana Tixier Herald

Romance Fiction: A Guide to the Genre by Kristin Ramsdell

Fluent in Fantasy: A Guide to Reading Interests by Diana Tixier Herald

Now Read This: A Guide to Mainstream Fiction, 1978–1998 by Nancy Pearl with assistance from Martha Knappe and Chris Higashi

Now Read This II: A Guide to Mainstream Fiction, 1990–2001 by Nancy Pearl

Hooked on Horror: A Guide to Reading Interests in Horror Fiction by Anthony J. Fonseca and June Michele Pulliam

Junior Genreflecting: A Guide to Good Reads and Series Fiction for Children by Bridget Dealy Volz, Cheryl Perkins Scheer, and Lynda Blackburn Welborn

Christian Fiction: A Guide to the Genre by John Mort

Strictly Science Fiction: A Guide to Reading Interests by Diana Tixier Herald and Bonnie Kunzel

Hooked on Horror: A Guide to Reading Interests in Horror Fiction, 2d Edition, by Anthony J. Fonseca and June Michele Pulliam

Teen Genreflecting

A Guide to Reading Interests

Second Edition

Diana Tixier Herald

LIBRARIES
U N L I M I T E D
A Member of the Greenwood Publishing Group

Westport, Connecticut • London

Library of Congress Cataloging-in-Publication Data

Herald, Diana Tixier.
    Teen genreflecting : a guide to reading interests / Diana Tixier Herald—2nd ed.
        p. cm.
    Includes bibliographical references and indexes.
    ISBN 1-56308-996-3 (paper)
    1. Young adult literature, American—Bibliography. 2. Young adult literature—Stories, plots, etc.
3. Popular literature—Stories, plots, etc. 4. Fiction genres—Bibliography. 5. Teenagers—
Books and reading. 6. Fiction—Bibliography. 7. Reading interests. I. Title.
    Z1232.H47 2003   [PS490]
    016.813008'09283—dc21   2003054610

British Library Cataloguing in Publication Data is available.

Library of Congress Catalog Card Number: 2003054610
ISBN: 1-56308-996-3

First published in 2003

Libraries Unlimited, Inc., 88 Post Road West, Westport, CT 06881
A Member of the Greenwood Publishing Group, Inc.
www.lu.com

Printed in the United States of America

∞™

The paper used in this book complies with the
Permanent Paper Standard issued by the National
Information Standards Organization (Z39.48–1984).

10   9   8   7   6   5   4   3

*To Deborah Steinke, Ray Glauner, and Mark Glauner—
the earliest victims of my readers' advisory obsession.*

Contents

Acknowledgments ix
Introduction xi

1. Serving Teen Readers 1
2. Issues 15
3. Contemporary Life 45
4. Adventure 65
5. Mystery and Suspense 73
6. Fantasy 85
7. Science Fiction 111
8. Paranormal 127
9. Historical Novels 139
10. Multicultural Fiction 159
11. Alternative Formats 169
12. Christian Fiction 185

Appendix I: Resources..193
Appendix II: Epic Fantasy 199
Appendix III: Genre Fiction for Reluctant Readers.......................203
Title Index...209
Subject Index 225
Author Index 245
About the Author 251

Acknowledgments

The Young Adult Library Services Association, a division of the American Library Association, is always available with great support for endeavors that attempt to help put teens and books together.

Bonnie Kunzel, Diane Monnier, Caryn Sipos, Mary Arnold, Lynn Evarts, Cindy Dobrez, Michael Cart, and Joel Shoemaker have all been sources of inspiration, suggesting terrific young adult books to read.

Barbara Ittner's editing makes all the difference in the world, but any mistakes that did sneak through are solely my own.

Introduction

No one disputes that the young adult population is growing, although there is some disagreement as to how fast and by how much. According to Mark L. Alch (2001) in the article "Echo-Boom May Keep U.S. Booming," today's young adult generation is the largest ever, with 80 million people born between 1977 and 1996. In an article of July 24, 2000, "Meet the Future," *Fortune* magazine calculated the numbers differently, considering this generation to have started in the early 1980s with some of its members just then entering the world. Nevertheless, they certainly agreed that the numbers rival or surpass those of the baby boom generation. Yet a third take on this issue is put forth by Peter Zollo (1999), author of *Wise Up to Teens: Insights into Marketing and Advertising to Teenagers.* According to Zollo, the teen population will reach 24 million by the year 2010.

The business world has taken note of the demographic swell, and we see evidence of new marketing strategies aimed at teens everywhere. There are new products for teens and new magazines aimed at teen audiences (e.g., *Teen People*), and advertising to teens is inescapable, with large companies such as Nike launching television and print promotions targeted specifically to teens. There are new teen sections in bookstores, such as Barnes & Noble and Borders, and the number of books published for teen readers continues to grow.

Libraries cannot afford to disregard these demographics, nor can they afford to cling to the assumption that teens don't read or use libraries. Another study shows that nearly one of every four individuals who enters a library is a teen (U.S. Department of Education 1995). Yet until recently, teens were frequently overlooked as library consumers, and sometimes even consciously discouraged from using the library. Even today, although some libraries and bookstores make an effort to attract teens as clientele, others seem to actively dissuade the teen trade through unfriendly, condescending, or even repressive attitudes and policies.

In fact, many libraries are turning their attention to teens. Libraries that abolished their YA librarian positions and teen centers decades ago are now restoring them. Along with special spaces, libraries are developing special collections, Web pages, and other services for teen users. For example, Phoenix Public Library's Teen Central features homework help, a teen 'zine, and a teen council. Library schools are beginning to offer course work in young adult services once again as well.

Meanwhile, membership in the Young Adult Library Services Association (YALSA), a division of the American Library Association, has burgeoned; its membership is projected to reach 4,000 by 2005. Its annual event, Teen Read Week (TRW), has proved to be a tremendous success. In 2001 more than 1,400 schools, public libraries, and bookstores that celebrate Teen Read Week registered on the TRW Web site.

New awards for teen literature have been established, including YALSA's Michael L. Printz award, which recognizes literary excellence in young adult literature, and the Alex Awards, which are given to adult books that young adult readers will enjoy as well.

As librarians, we have learned the value of reading and books, and we seek ways to promote reading in our communities. It is widely known that avid reading develops good reading skills. Avid readers, however, are often devoted to types of literature that do not receive much respect from educators and the literary establishment—that is, genre fiction.

The key to motivating teens to read is to provide them with the reading material in which they are most interested. Even reluctant readers can become avid readers if they find the right material. Patrick Jones, author of *Connecting Young Adults and Libraries* (1998), recommends that libraries stock plenty of magazines for their teen clientele—including *WWF, Teen People, Transworld Skateboarding,* and *Weekly World News.* These magazines may look ephemeral or even trashy, but legions of teens read and enjoy them.

As individuals, teenagers have unique needs—physically, intellectually, and emotionally. Thus, their reading tastes and habits differ from those of children and adults. Teens are struggling to define themselves as individuals, to redefine their relationships with family members, and to find out how they fit into the larger world. Because they are involved in this identity search, teens enjoy exploring different roles and personae that help them come to terms with who they are. Coming-of-age stories are particularly pertinent to teens, as are stories that address issues of family, friends, and society.

Teens are curious—they are very interested in the latest trends and hottest issues, so books with a current, topical focus intrigue them. As teens stretch their intellectual abilities, they enjoy practicing their problem-solving skills through mystery stories and stretching their imaginations through fantasy and science fiction tales.

Today's teens are also under tremendous stress, and reading can provide a soothing retreat from youthful angst. A gentle romance with a happy ending or a nostalgic historical novel provides relief to some readers, whereas the successful resolution of an action-packed survival story, with a strong definition between good and evil, reassures others.

Genre fiction fits various needs of young adult readers. Teens like to know what they are getting, and genres organize the world of literature into understandable segments. They want an identifiable product from which they will receive a certain something that they desire. Teens often identify themselves by what they read, and they can be very definite about that—"I only read romances," "I never read science fiction," or "I love fantasy the most."

Teens are also brand-name conscious, and they pay attention to the labels on the books they read—just as they do with FUBU or Hurley jerseys and Nike visors. I have even heard teens ask for books not by author or title, but by imprint.

Developing and marketing a YA genre collection is one way to provide teens with access to the books they want and most enjoy. By grouping similar books together, whether through spine labeling, shelving, and display or by creating and distributing lists, you can make it easier for teen readers to find what they want. Readers can browse a genre they know and like, and they are likely to find new authors in that area in addition to authors they already know and enjoy. By grouping books according to their appeals, the genre approach and passive readers' advisory techniques also make your job easier.

Many individuals enter adolescence as readers and regular library users, but they quit some time before entering adulthood. Teen years are busy years, with many distractions and new experiences, and whatever it was that got them hooked on books is too often not strong enough to keep them reading.

Mary Beth Curtis of Lesley University, speaking at the Second Workshop on Adolescent Literacy, said that up until starting secondary school, kids read for intrinsic reasons—in other words, they read for themselves; upon starting middle school or junior high school, however, they read for extrinsic reasons—because they are required to do so, or because they need to find specific information for school assignments.

Yet teens needn't lose interest in reading. Often all they need is support and encouragement—and help in finding the right reading material. Librarians and booksellers are in the perfect position to make the difference. By supplying teens with the books they like to read in friendly surroundings, we can encourage reading in the teen years and make friends for life. Identifying those books is what this guide is all about.

Purpose and Audience

This guide is intended to help readers' advisors connect teens with the books they most enjoy. It organizes and describes more than 1,500 fiction titles by genre, subgenre, and theme—grouping them according to specific appeals and reading tastes. In addition to the annotations, you will find notes on the genres—their distinctive features, characteristics, and tips for advising readers.

This guide is not intended to be an all-inclusive compendium of authors who write genre fiction for teens. It is not a scholarly or historical treatise on the subject of young adult genre fiction. Nor is it intended to provide comprehensive lists of titles by specific authors. It is not intended to identify "safe" or "clean" books for inclusion in censored collections, or even to identify the "best" teen fiction according to literary standards. It is merely a guide to assist readers' advisors in understanding genre fiction, and in filling reading requests of young adults. It is hoped that public and school librarians, educators, booksellers, and other adults who work with teen readers will find this a valuable professional tool and readers' advisory aid.

New subgenres, authors, and titles appear constantly, and it is impossible for a book such as this one to remain completely up-to-date. Users are encouraged to supplement this guide with further reading. Scanning reviews, talking to teens, and reading new genre titles are good ways to keep current.

Changes and Revisions

This edition differs a great deal from its predecessor, which was published in 1997. Most titles included are new to this edition, having been published since the mid-1990s. In addition to covering newer titles, this edition provides more explanatory text about the genres, as well as plot summaries for most titles. Furthermore, publication dates and reading levels are cited for most titles, and awards and other recognitions are noted.

Reflecting recent publishing trends and changes in teen reading taste is the complete chapter in this edition devoted to issue novels (which were contained in the "Contemporary" chapter in the last edition, under the heading "Problem Novels"). Because straight "horror" is less common, while elements of the genre have been blended into other genres, these titles are now covered in a new "Paranormal" chapter. There are also new chapters—"Alternative Formats," "Multicultural Fiction," and "Christian Fiction." It is hoped that these additions and changes will help readers' advisors more effectively address the needs of their teen clientele.

Scope, Selection Criteria, and Methodology

All major genres popular with teens are represented in this book. It contains titles published specifically for the teen audience, as well as books published for adult readers that are also popular with teens. Most of the titles in this book were published in the last decade, but some classics and older but highly popular titles are included if they are commonly available in library collections. Selections are based on popularity with teen readers and, in some cases, because the titles help to define a genre. Award and recommendation lists from library and educational associations, genre writer's organizations, and public libraries with active services to teens were consulted in making the final selections. Personal reading and consultation with teen readers were also sources of information.

Genre fiction can be timeless, but teens are far more conscious of the age of a title than adults are. Yet even though many teens are adamant about only wanting to read "new" books, often they have not noticed the original publication date—instead they base their judgment on the look of the cover art. For example, Diana Wynne Jones's fantasy titles written in the 1980s remain popular, but only the titles that have been recently reissued with new cover art are borrowed frequently from the library. In response to this phenomenon, publishers of YA fiction commonly reissue titles with updated covers, and sometimes they even give the books new titles! Genre fiction with high author recognition allows some books to remain popular long after the time that most of their age mates have been retired from the collection.

Many of the authors represented in this guide are prolific and well established, but readers will also find new authors who are expected to grow in popularity. There are some authors of great stature whose output is limited. For example, Terry Davis has written only two books for teens—*Vision Quest* and *If Rock and Roll Were a Machine*—but both are gems and highly popular with young adult readers. Of course, exciting new genre authors are constantly exploding onto the scene. Who, in 1995, had ever heard of J. K. Rowling or Lemony Snicket—two of today's most popular authors?

The author reviewed all annotated titles in this guide, with the exception of some graphic novels and some series titles. In the case of series, sample titles were reviewed as deemed appropriate. The annotations are therefore based on the author's impressions and understanding of the books.

Organization and Features

As noted previously, the titles in this book are arranged according to genres, subgenres, and themes. The chapters, sections, and subsections are meant to group books with similar appeals together, so users can identify read-alikes. Chapters include broad sections for "types," "themes," or both. Types represent distinct genres and subgenres with titles that share a number of common features and characteristics. Other titles may share a single, appealing theme. While "types" represents a stronger and more multifaceted unity among titles, many readers are interested in specific themes.

In many cases an argument can be made to place a specific title in more than one category. Obviously, the final decision involves some subjectivity. The judgments made here are based on publisher information and personal experience in the field of readers' advisory. Appendixes with special lists and a detailed subject index provide additional access points for users.

Books in series are listed in one paragraph under the author's name. In cases in which multiple authors have contributed to a series, the series is placed alphabetically by series title. Individual titles within the series are placed in series (chronological) order, rather than alphabetical order, because readers commonly wish to read the titles in series order.

Author, title, and publication date are provided for all titles, along with an indication of reading level. Designations used are as follows:

M = middle school, grades 6–8

J = junior high school, grades 7–9

S = senior high school, grades 9–12

These designations are based on reviews, library catalogs, and, again, personal experience and judgment. The overlap reflects the developmental pace of readers and the rapidity of change at the younger end of adolescence. Users should also keep in mind that these designations are somewhat subjective. Often one resource will recommend a title for grades 5–8, whereas another will recommend the same title for ages 14 and up. It cannot be overemphasized that teens should read what they are comfortable with and what they find interesting and exciting, regardless of the assigned grade range.

Major awards and honors are discussed in the next chapter. The following awards and honors, noted with annotations where they apply, are included:

BBYA = Best Books for Young Adults, a list created by a committee of the Young Adult Library Services Association, a division of ALA

IRA = International Reading Association Award

IRAYAC = The Young Adult Choice list of books selected by teen readers for the International Reading Association Award

VOYA = Outstanding books for middle school readers selected by the reviewers and editors of *Voice of Youth Advocates*

YALSA 100 Best Books = Retrospective list covering the years 1950–2000, which includes some titles published before the inception of the BBYA list and some that were missed in the year they were published

Other pertinent awards are noted as deemed appropriate. Icons are used to denote books that have been made into movies, titles published for adults but read by teens, and classics.

In addition, most titles are annotated with a brief description. Annotations are purposefully descriptive rather than critical because the philosophy of this book is to support readers in their choices rather than to dictate what is "good literature." Annotations focus on the story line and on the most important aspects and appeals of the titles. They often contain the name and age of the protagonist, as well as the names of other major characters. When setting plays a prominent role in the story, it is described in the annotation. The plot, usually important in genre fiction, is almost always summarized or alluded to in the annotations.

How to Use This Guide

This guide can be used in a number of ways. Perhaps the most common is in identifying read-alikes. Books with similar characteristics and themes are grouped together, so if a reader is looking for "another book just like the last one I read," the reader advisor can look for the said title in the title index and find similar titles grouped around it in the text. Once the user finds the genre or subgenre of interest, a quick scan of the plot summary gives indication on whether a specific title is of interest to the reader. Grade levels, awards, the age of the protagonist, setting—all provide clues to finding the best choice for the reader. Some teens may wish to consult the book directly, and librarians are encouraged to share the guide, rather than hiding it behind the reference desk.

Of course, the book can also be used to simply familiarize readers' advisors with genre fiction for young adults. Book lists and narrative material will help clarify what the genres are and which books and authors they contain.

Librarians wishing to expand their genre fiction collections can consult this guide to find some of the newest and more popular titles. The guide can also be used as a source for book lists, displays, and other passive readers' advisory techniques.

Whatever the specific application, this book should be used to share the joy of reading and books. Happy reading.

References

Alch, Mark L. "Echo-boom may keep U.S. booming." *World and I* 16 (February 2001): 46.

Jones, Patrick. *Connecting Young Adults and Libraries*. 2d ed. New York: Neal Schuman, 1998.

O'Reilly, Brian, and Karen Vella-Zarb. "Today's kids meet the future." *Fortune,* July 24, 2000, pp. 144+.

U.S. Department of Education, Office of Educational Research and Improvement, National Center for Education Statistics. *Services and Resources for Children and Young Adults in Public Libraries.* Washington, D.C.: GPO, 1995.

Zollo, Peter. *Wise Up to Teens: Insights into Marketing and Advertising to Teenagers.* 2d ed. Ithaca, N.Y.: New Strategist Publications, 1999.

Chapter 1

Serving Teen Readers

Teens are an important and growing market for libraries and bookstores. Because teens have unique needs and reading habits, serving teen readers requires special efforts and techniques. Using a genre approach to readers' advisory is a highly effective way to serve teens' needs. As stated in the introduction to this book, genre fiction holds great appeal to teen readers, and recommending titles according to genres and themes eases the readers' advisory transaction for the reader and the advisor. This book is meant to guide you in using the genre approach to advise and build collections for teen readers.

It is important, however, for you also to keep abreast of new titles and trends in genre fiction and to continue improving and refining your services for teens. In this chapter, I address some of the ways that librarians and other professionals who work with teen readers can establish and improve their YA collections and services.

Understanding Teen Genre Fiction

The first step to serving teen readers is understanding genre fiction. Readers, whether adults or teens, usually look for titles by genre, often favoring one genre over others. The publishing industry supports and encourages this approach, routinely categorizing titles by genre. Looking at books through genres is merely a way of categorizing literature according to the general characteristics and conventions that are reflected in reader preferences, thus making a huge body of fiction more manageable. Genre is not synonymous with generic. Genres group together books with similar appeal factors. *Merriam-Webster Collegiate Dictionary,* 10th edition, defines a genre as "a category of artistic, musical, or literary composition characterized by a particular style, form, or content."

When one considers it, all fiction can be put into one genre or another—or even into several genres. Many people tend to perceive genre fiction as encompassing only the most established, easily identifiable, or often described genres, such as mysteries and romance, but genres can also be broader, narrower, or more elusive. For example, graphic novels can be considered a genre, even though some would argue that these titles simply share a specific format. As I discuss in Chapter 11, "Alternative Formats," the specific format of graphic novels results in a cluster of common convention characteristics—from pacing and action to the use of dialogue balloons and sound effects. More important, publishers and bookstores recognize the unique appeals of graphic novels, and readers specifically seek out novels in this format. Likewise, Latino fiction can be considered a genre because these novels share a vision of a common milieu, and their characters generally share qualities imparted by Latino culture. Literary and mainstream fiction can also be viewed as genres—genre in which "voice" and "language" predominate over story line. Some even consider YA fiction a genre. Certainly, publishers recognize the unique needs and desires of young adults, developing entire product lines specifically for the teen reader. These novels are likely to feature teen protagonists and have shorter chapters; the average overall length of the typical YA novel is substantially less than its adult counterpart. The term "genre," then, is broadly defined in this book for the purpose of practicality.

The genres and subgenres in teen fiction, like the readers themselves, are far more volatile than adult genre fiction, even though teen genre fiction has many similarities to adult genre fiction. With some genres, fantasy and science fiction in particular, teens and adults read many of the same authors and titles.

You'll find more information about specific genres and themes in the chapters that follow. It may seem obvious, but the best way to learn about genre fiction is to read it. Readers' advisors are encouraged to read about the genres in this guide, select a sampling of titles from each of the sections, and enjoy.

Publishing Trends

Understanding publishing trends gives readers' advisors a broader perspective on the world of genre fiction. Michael Cart's (1996) *From Romance to Realism: 50 Years of Growth and Change in Young Adult Literature* offers a fascinating history of YA literature. As Cart notes, in the early 1990s, it appeared that fiction for older teens was disappearing, and the label "YA" was appearing on titles with more appeal to preteens than to teens. But what's happening today? Fortunately, that trend has reversed itself, and in the early twenty-first century we see the strong presence of books aimed at mature teens. Many publishers have resurrected or re-created lines of genre fiction specifically geared to teen readers. This young adult fiction, as it is called, tends to be shorter than fiction written for adults, averaging two hundred pages. Of course, the protagonists in YA fiction are almost always teenagers.

Like authors of adult genre fiction, many authors of teen genre fiction are prolific. Meg Cabot, author of the Princess Diaries series, seems to turn out several series books a year under her various pseudonyms; Gary Paulsen can always be counted on for at least a couple of new titles each year.

Some of the genres and subgenres most popular with teens are unique to that market (e.g., issues, sports), whereas others, such as adventure and science fiction, are similar to or the same as their adult counterparts. As in adult genre fiction, genreblending is on the rise in YA fiction. It is not uncommon to find mysteries with a touch of the paranormal, fantasies that also feature romance, or historical fiction combined with Christian themes.

Currently, two of the hottest genres for teens are issues and fantasy. Issues novels have evolved from what was called the "Problem" novel back in the seventies, but today's issues novels are far less preachy than their predecessors. They tell it like it is. For the most part, these books are read solely by teens.

Fantasy, extremely popular in the seventies, is also back with a vengeance. Much of this can be attributed to a new generation of fans spawned by the Harry Potter craze. The *Lord of the Rings* films have also played a part in introducing teens to the joys of fantasy. Fantasy is a unique genre in that the books read by teens, adults, and children are often the same. Fantasy readers do not care which audience a book was written and published for—if it's good fantasy, they will read it.

Mysteries are also making a comeback with teen readers. In the 1990s, Joan Lowery Nixon dominated YA mysteries, and few other mystery authors were popular with teens. Today increasing numbers of teens identify themselves as mystery readers. This is reflected in (and perhaps a result of) publishing trends, with new mystery series by the Hooblers, Zindell, and Delaney.

Although romance is the best-selling genre in adult fiction, and true-life romance plays a major role in teen lives, the recent trend in YA reading and publishing has been away from pure romance, with the emphasis moving to other types of peer relationships and genreblends. Romantic themes occur in all genres of teen fiction, but usually take a back seat to the fantasy, mystery, or paranormal events.

Horror, the hot genre of a decade ago, has recently waned in popularity—or at least it has changed dramatically. As with romance, the trend has been away from pure horror to hybrids and genreblends, with paranormal elements appearing in other popular genres. Paranormal themes are often combined with mystery, as in Silver Ravenwolf's Witches Chillers series, or with romance, as in the Enchanted Hearts series. Books about witches or girls with extraordinary powers, such as Isobel Bird's Circle of Three series and Lynn Ewing's Goddess of the Night series, are extremely popular with teen readers.

Historical fiction has had a consistently faithful following with teen readers. When combined with a diary format, it has emerged as a very popular genre. Cart (1996) discusses a "historical fiction renaissance." It is true that more historical fiction titles are being published for teens. In addition, the topics they cover are becoming more diverse; they now present a grittier, more realistic view of life in other times.

The multicultural experience is a growing phenomenon in our society, and books featuring characters from other cultures—minority populations in the United States, recent immigrants, and Third World citizens—are becoming increasingly common. Although these novels are not formally a distinct genre, many readers seek out books with these themes and motifs, so a chapter is included for them.

Alternative formats are not a genre in the strict sense of the word, but they have become one of the hottest trends for teen readers. Epistolary novels, diaries, graphic novels, and illustrated stories, as well as verse novels and connected short stories, are popular and growing in number. These titles fall into other genre categories within this guide, but they also abide by certain conventions and have specific features that appeal to teen readers. Thus, an entire chapter is devoted to alternative formats.

Inspirational and Christian fiction have loyal followings among some teens and a strong backing by evangelical publishers, such as Bethany House and Zondervan. A few years ago teens who read in this genre often sought adult titles with historical settings, such as the series written by Brock Thoene and Bodie Thoene and Gilbert Morris. At the turn of the millennium, the Left Behind series (science fiction) reached best-seller status and became the Christian fiction most often requested and talked about among teens. Today themes of Christian redemption can be found in many other teen genres—from mystery and historical to contemporary teen life. A sampling of YA Christian fiction appears in Chapter 12. Teen fans of this genre also read many adult Christian fiction titles. John Mort's (2002) *Christian Fiction,* which covers reading tastes in this genre, tags adult titles that appeal to teen readers and includes a chapter devoted to young adult literature.

Advising Teen Readers

Respect is the most important component in providing excellence in readers' advisory services to teens. These readers should be treated as seriously and thoughtfully as any other library user. A good article to read on readers' advisory for teens is Benedetti's (2001) "Leading the Horse to Water."

Here are some other specific tips for working with teen readers.

Dos and Don'ts for Teen Reader Advisory

- Do treat teen readers as you would like to be treated.

- Do not make assumptions. Appearances can be deceiving, and one cannot tell which books will appeal to a reader without establishing a dialogue.

- Do ask teens about their reading preferences. Use standard readers' advisory techniques such as asking the reader to describe a book that he or she likes or even asking which movies or video games he or she enjoys.

- Do listen to what teens have to say. Pay attention. Sometimes parents accompany younger teens, but if the teen will be reading the book, it is important to make eye contact with and address questions to the teen rather than the parent.

- Don't patronize. Teens are entitled to be treated as the individuals they are.

- Don't oversell. Just because something is your favorite doesn't mean it is perfect for every teen reader. Try to give the reader several titles to choose from and permission to reject a title that, for any reason, does not hold appeal.

- Don't try to act like a teen. Teens hate fakes.

- Do be honest. You don't need to have loved every book you recommend, and not every teen is going to like the books you love. Be truthful, but don't go on and on.

- Don't pretend to know all about a book you haven't read. It is OK to recommend books based on reviews or what other readers have said. Just be sure to tell the teen that you are recommending the title because of what you have heard about it rather than from personal experience. Nobody can read everything, and teens know this.

- Do read young adult literature. It will give you a solid basis for making recommendations and the background needed to discern books that the reader may enjoy. Young adult literature is great reading.

Besides following these guidelines, it is important to have a general understanding of what appeals to teen readers.

What Appeals to Teen Readers?

Like adults, teens have diverse reading tastes, and no two teen readers have exactly the same likes or dislikes. Some general principles, however, do apply when discussing teen reader preferences. First of all, teens enjoy reading about characters with whom they can identify, characters who are dealing with the same issues that they face—belonging, relationships, finding strengths, and mastering skills. The age of the protagonist is often important to teen readers, with most teens preferring books that feature characters as old or older than their own age. Gender can also be an issue, but more with male than female readers.

Teens in my book groups have said that they like interesting plots with fast pacing. Genre fiction, in general, features strong, fast-paced stories. There are many genres that appeal to certain groups of teens. Those genres and their special characteristics are discussed in the individual genre chapters.

In addition, as noted previously, appearances and formats are important to teens. Teen readers often prefer paperbacks, because they often look cool and current. And if one does not want to be seen with a book, a paperback is more easily hidden than a hardcover. In fact, the look of a book is far more important to teens than to any other group. Teens are especially conscious of the appearance of people depicted on the cover. If the people in the cover illustrations appear too young or are wearing outdated apparel, forget it! Sometimes it seems that the cover is the most important appeal factor for teen readers. Fortunately, publishers usually pay attention to the covers, and often a book that didn't hook teens with its hardcover dust jacket hooks them with an appealing paperback cover.

Unfortunately, in libraries paperbacks can get pretty ratty after just a few circulations. Covering them with clear vinyl or purchasing prebound copies can improve the durability and preserve the appearance. Some libraries do not catalog their paperback collections. This is a big mistake with teen paperbacks. Because paperbacks are the preferred format of most teens, it only makes sense to provide teens with easy access to them. Many times teens will want to read everything by an author or read a series in order. The ability to find the title in the catalog and place a hold is important to the patron. Also, if a book that teens frequently request is not in the catalog, it is usually an indication that perhaps it should be placed on order.

Building a Teen Fiction Collection

Creating and cataloging a collection that fits teen needs and reading tastes is a fundamental step in serving teen readers. A collection of teen fiction must be continuously maintained to make it easy for readers to find the right book at the right time. Librarians must select and purchase the books that best meet the needs of the library's users; they must also weed the collection to keep it fresh and not overwhelm the user with books that no longer have appeal. Cataloging teen fiction is imperative, as it provides a point of access for readers.

To make the best book selections for teens, you should establish a relationship with these library users and ascertain their reading tastes and needs. This can be done informally, through one-on-one discussions and with book groups; or through a more formal process—for example, with a focus group or a teen advisory group, as discussed later in this chapter. You can also find information about YA fiction in journals and publishers' catalogs.

Reviews of Teen Genre Fiction

Traditionally, most libraries have based their collections on reviews, but reviews of teen genre fiction can be difficult to find. The major young adult review sources, with the exception of *Voice of Youth Advocates* (*VOYA*), do not separate reviews of genre fiction from those of mainstream and literary fiction. Often, a book's genre is not even mentioned in a review. *VOYA,* the most comprehensive review source of young adult materials, groups science fiction, fantasy, and horror together, separate from the other fiction reviews. Although it does not separate out other genres in the reviews, it often publishes bibliographies for the other genres and feature specific themes. *VOYA* also does an excellent job of reviewing paperbacks. Many of the books teens want to read are paperback originals that are seldom reviewed in other resources.

You'll find more reviews of YA fiction in *Booklist, Library Journal, School Library Journal, Bulletin of the Center for Children's Books, Horn Book, Kirkus Children's Reviews,* and even some issues of *Publishers Weekly*. These are reputable and reliable review sources. With some of these periodicals, however, you must plow through pages and pages of children's book reviews to glean the few reviews of teen books. Some of the other review sources commonly used by libraries are *Kliatt* and *ALAN Review,* both providing good coverage of books for teens.

Awards

Keeping track of awards for young adult books is a good way to find some of the best and most recent titles for teen readers. This guide notes award-winning titles. Here is a sampling of some of the more important organizations and the honors they award to teen literature.

- ALAN (Assembly on Literature for Adolescents). Each year, this special-interest group of National Council of Teachers of English, recognizes an outstanding individual in the field of adolescent literature with the ALAN Award. Authors Gary Paulsen, Chris Crutcher, and Walter Dean Myers are recent honorees.

- ALA and YALSA (American Library Association and Young Adult Library Services Association). ALA and its YALSA division annually issue three lists of particular interest to those advising teen readers: the Best Books for Young Adults list, the Quick Picks for Reluctant Young Adult Readers List, and the Popular Paperbacks list. Titles in this guide that have won the honor of inclusion on these lists are denoted by "BBYA," "Quick Picks," or "Popular Paperbacks." These designations follow the annotation. In addition, a YALSA preconference selected a list of the 100 Best Books from 1950–2000 and those are indicated by "YALSA 100 Best Books."

- YALSA also awards the Michael L. Printz Award, given to a book that exemplifies literary excellence in young adult literature. The award was named for a Topeka, Kansas, school librarian who was a long-time active member of the Young Adult Library Services Association. Printz Award winners and Honor Books are marked in this guide, denoted by "Printz." Like the Newbery Medal for children's books and the Coretta Scott King Award, the Printz committee also has the discretion to name up to four Honor Books each year.

- The Alex Awards are given annually to ten adult books that will be enjoyed by young adults, ages twelve through eighteen years.

- The Margaret A. Edwards Award, established in 1988, honors an author's lifetime achievement for writing books that have been popular over a period of time. The annual award is administered by YALSA and sponsored by *School Library Journal.* It recognizes an author's work in helping adolescents become aware of themselves and addressing questions about their role and importance in relationships, society, and in the world.

- The Coretta Scott King Award is presented annually by the Coretta Scott King Task Force of the American Library Association's Social Responsibilities Round Table. Recipients are authors and illustrators of African descent whose distinguished books promote an understanding and appreciation of the "American Dream" (see http://www.ala.org/Content/NavigationMenu/Our_ Association/Round_Tables/SRRT/Coretta_Scott_King_Book_Awards/ Coretta_ Scott_King_Book_ Awards.htm).

- CLASP (National Consortium of Latin American Studies Programs). This organization sponsors the Américas Award for Children's and Young Adult Literature. This award is "given in recognition of U.S. works of fiction, poetry, folklore, or selected nonfiction (from picture books to works for young adults) published in the previous year in English or Spanish that authentically and engagingly portray Latin America, the Caribbean, or Latinos in the United States."

- IRA (International Reading Association; http://www.reading.org/awards/children .html). The IRA established its Children's Book Awards in 1975 to recognize an author's first or second published book. One award is given for fiction for older readers (ages ten to seventeen). Books from any country and in any language copyrighted during the previous calendar year are considered. IRA also sponsors the Young Adult Choice Poll for which teens read and evaluate books from the previous year that received at least two favorable professional reviews. Young Adult Choice was begun in 1987, as an annual project of the IRA. Each year thirty titles are chosen by approximately 4,500 students in grades 7–12 from different regions of the United States. Books are selected from new publications donated by North American publishers. The annotated list is printed in the November issue of the IRA's *Journal of Adolescent and Adult Literacy* and is available as an offprint in mid-November. Books that made this list are indicated in this guide by the designation "IRAYAC."

Other awards that are sometimes given to titles popular with teens include the following:

- Bram Stoker Award from the Horror Writers Association

- Edgar Award from the Mystery Writers of America

- Hugo from the World Science Fiction Convention

- Nebula from the Science Fiction and Fantasy Writers of America

- Spur Award from the Western Writers of America

Canadian awards include the following:

- Arthur Ellis Award from the Crime Writers of Canada

- Book of the Year for Children Award given by the Canadian Library Association

- Geoffrey Bilson Award for Historical Fiction for Young People awarded by the Canadian Children's Book Centre for the best historical fiction book

- Governor General's Award

- Young Adult Canadian Book Award awarded by the Canadian Library Association

Distributor and Publisher Catalogs

Although reading reviews and tracking awards helps keep you apprised of new titles and developments, when it comes to genre fiction, you often need more. Publications from large book distributors are by far the most up-to-date resources for discovering the latest paperback genre titles for teens. *Hot Picks* is the name of the prepublication catalog from Baker and Taylor and *Paperback Advance* is Ingram's catalog. Another source of information on teen genre titles comes from the prebound distributors. Catalogs from both Permabound and Sagebrush (formerly Econoclad) hold a wealth of information for the readers' advisor. They are often excellent sources for the books that teens have been asking for, but which you have never heard of. Publisher catalogs can also be helpful, especially when looking for forthcoming books by the most popular authors or in the most popular series in paperback.

The online catalogs of booksellers such as Amazon and Barnes & Noble also provide a wealth of information.

Young Adult Library Services Association

YALSA offers wonderful support for YA librarians, with conference workshops, a listserv, and other services. This is the division of the American Library Association for young adult librarians. It develops and publishes the Best Books for Young Adults, Quick Picks for Reluctant Young Adult Readers, and Popular Paperbacks lists each year. Check ALA's Web site (http://www.ala.org) for information on how to join YALSA.

Programs for Teens

Having teen summer reading games or teen participation councils are excellent ways to meet face-to-face with the teens who use your library. One of the best ways to know what's going on in teen genre fiction is to talk to teens and find out what they are reading. The really hot authors will come up in conversation again and again. Teens see and seek out paperback books in game stores and bookstores that may not have been reviewed in library selection resources.

By offering programs in which you can interact with teens, you will learn a lot and be able to provide teen readers with a larger range of what they want to read. *Excellence in Library Services to Young Adults: The Nation's Top Programs* (Chelton 2000) is a good resource for inspiration and ideas.

Teen Advisory Boards

Teens and libraries can work together in many ways. Teen advisory boards have proved to be a good way for libraries to obtain feedback successfully from teens on programs and resources. Some teen advisory boards plan programs from start to finish; others identify areas in which they would like to see programming; and still others advise librarians on aspects of programs conceived and implemented by the library staff. A teen advisory board can also work as a book discussion group, giving librarians an up-close and personal look at what teens think about what they are reading.

Often teen advisory boards provide willing and able teen volunteers to fulfill various tasks. "Buy More Books" (Herald 1996) outlines how one library made it work.

Teen Summer Reading Games

Because they are fun and provide a forum to meet and spend time with peers, reading games can be a great way to keep teens coming into the library (and bookstore), when school is out for the summer. Libraries in various parts of the country have provided teen summer reading games for their young adult patrons. The secret to having a good game is to structure it specifically for teens, making it different from summer reading games for children.

A teen advisory board provides an excellent place to start planning and promoting a teen reading game. Find out what the teens who use your library would like in a game and proceed from there.

Many libraries currently allow the teens great latitude in determining what kinds of programs will be offered. In the past, some states sponsored statewide teen reading programs, and specific libraries created intricate programs with guides that are filled with ideas. Often the participants are given incentives for attending library programs, volunteering, reading magazine articles, and watching videos or listening to books in an audio format, as well as for reading books.

Author and young adult librarian Patrick Jones put up a page of links to teen summer reading programs on his Connecting YA Web page (http://www.connectingya.com). It provides a terrific overview of how teen summer reading is handled in different parts of the country.

Teen Read Week

Teen Read Week, an initiative of YALSA, has been making inroads into the American consciousness with radio and television spots as well as colorful posters, bookmarks, and postcards. Libraries all over the United States have jumped on the bandwagon, creating innovative programs for Teen Read Week. In 2001, more than 1,400 schools, public libraries, and bookstores celebrated Teen Read Week and registered on the Teen Read Week Web site. The theme that year was "Make Reading a Hobbit," tying in with the popularity of the *Lord of the Rings.* The 2002 Teen Read Week theme was "Get Graphic@Your library," which put an emphasis on graphic novels. The 2003 theme, "Slammin'!@ Your Library," highlighted poetry. Teen Read Week always uses the overlying theme "Read for the Fun of It"—a truly appropriate sentiment.

Author Visits

All readers, no matter what age, love to hear from and about their favorite authors, and teens are no exception. Author visits can take place in cooperation with other organizations and businesses, such as secondary schools or bookstores. Be forewarned, though, that the visits seem to escalate the popularity of the author's books and frequently other books in the same genre, so be sure to have plenty of extra copies on hand. Toni Buzzeo and Jane Kurtz, authors of *Terrific Connections with Authors, Illustrators, and Storytellers* (1999), provide helpful information on author visits. This is also a topic discussed with some frequency on YALSA-BK and YALSA-L, two Internet list groups. Subscription information is in Appendix I.

Teen Volunteers

Many high schools have instituted service learning requirements for graduation requiring teens to volunteer at community organizations. This provides an excellent opportunity to get teens into the library and to build relationships with them. The National Honor Society also has a service requirement that can provide a source of bright, interesting teen volunteers to libraries and teen reading programs.

In addition to asking teens to help in the library's teen center, many libraries offer their teen volunteers the opportunity to help with programming for younger children or with tutoring library patrons on how to use electronic resources. Teens may even produce articles for your library newsletter or Web site, help at the annual used book sale, or design a book club T-shirt. There are many possibilities for teen participation—use your imagination. By taking the time to learn about teen interests and skills and offering opportunities beyond the usual clerical tasks, you will find you have a wonderful new resource.

Booktalking

Booktalking—giving promotional presentations on specific book titles—is a great way to broaden the horizons of teen readers and let them know about some of the wonderful books in your collection. There are many helpful resources on booktalking. If you're new to booktalking or need a refresher course, *The Booktalker's Bible* by Chapple Langemack (2003) is a good place to start. It has a chapter on teens, complete with sample booktalks. Other excellent examples of booktalks can be found in The Booktalker series by Joni Richards Bodart (published by Wilson). Bodart also hosts an e-mail discussion group where members discuss booktalking, providing a constant source of new booktalks (http://groups. yahoo.com/group/booktalking). Nancy Keane's *Booktalking across the Curriculum* (2002) focuses on books that tie into the middle school curriculum, offering booktalks and activity ideas to extend learning. In *Connecting Young Adults and Libraries,* Jones (1998) provides examples of booktalks and a comprehensive outline of how to plan and execute booktalking programs. Finally, Scholastic Books offers an Internet mailing list that e-mails booktalks to subscribers for free. To subscribe to the Scholastic mailing list, go to www.scholastic.com/bookupdate.

One of the best ways to demonstrate your book savvy to teens is to booktalk a genre title that is wildly popular. Talking about the newest Harry Potter or Louise Rennison book may not introduce anything new to the listeners, but it does help establish your credibility. If teens see that the booktalker knows and likes the books they enjoy, they are more inclined to think that some of the other books discussed are worth looking at.

Other Ways to Market to Teens

If you wish to build your teen clientele and increase circulation of teen materials, you need to market your services and collection actively in every way you can. Whether this means putting up book displays, creating reading lists, establishing a homework club or book discussion group, or hosting a Web page for teens will depend on your resources and the needs of your community. That said, there are a few guidelines to keep in mind when marketing to this audience.

Teens' main (and most trusted) source of information is word of mouth—from their peers. Teen pages or shelvers who like to read and informally booktalk can increase library use of teen collections dramatically. An enthusiastic recommendation from another teen about a book invariably makes it more desirable. Even reluctant readers may start asking for books if a friend or other peer (not an adult) mentions his or her enjoyment of a particular title.

Because word of mouth is so important in the teen world, sometimes a book's popularity will really take off in a specific locale because it somehow got hooked into the local network of teen readers. One of my foster kids, a popular high school boy, had dozens of macho reluctant readers special ordering Jonah Black's The Black Book: Diary of a Teenage Stud series after he mentioned to his friends that it was really good.

As noted in the previous section, booktalking is an effective way to promote books and reading. Booktalking visits to schools, juvenile correctional facilities, shelters, and many other places where teens can be found in supervised groups are excellent places to market your library's offerings. And of course, by booktalking, you are marketing specific titles. By taking your show on the road, you will be able to demonstrate the attitudes and resources available at the library.

Making Room for Teen Genre Fiction

Where do teens find their reading material at your library? Teen sections vary widely from library to library. Some libraries have well-established and heavily used teen sections. In other libraries, even a well-stocked and well-defined teen area does not seem to attract teen readers. Libraries that do not have sections specifically devoted to teens often house their young adult collections in children's departments or the adult services area. Teens who have so recently left their childhood behind do not like to be regarded as children. Without an exceptional marketing program, teen collections in close proximity to children's sections have a difficult time attracting readers. Locating the collection too close to adult authority figures can also be a deterrent.

Paying attention to the particular needs of your community cannot be overstressed. Because of the various idiosyncrasies of the populations served, you need to analyze what works best in your own situation. Of course, it never hurts to query local teens on their preferences.

Libraries deal with the physical aspects of managing genre collections in different ways. What is the best way to manage them? That answer varies from library to library. The size of the collection plays an important role. According to Sharon Baker (2002), who speaks and writes on the subject of reducing information overload for fiction-reading library users, physically separating genre fiction in large collections helps readers find what they want to read. In other libraries, the teen collections are small, and information overload may not present a major problem. Different methods of identifying genre fiction work for different sized collections. In large collections, separating genres generally works best; in smaller collections, genre spine labels and book lists may suffice. Teens who enjoy genre fiction are always happy to find what they want to read, so the library should do whatever it can to accommodate them.

As mentioned earlier, appearances are important to teens and many teens really do judge a book by its cover, which is possibly one of the reasons that paperbacks are so popular. If a reader selects a book because of its cover, it makes sense to display that book with the cover showing. Many manufacturers of library shelving are now producing slanted shelving for face-out display. Video display shelving offers a low-cost alternative for paperback collections.

Another effective way to make genre fiction attractive and enticing to readers is to use "dumps," the cardboard displays used in bookstores. A friendly bookseller may be willing to pass on some of these cardboard displays to your library. Another source is to watch the major book jobbers' catalogs for dumps featuring assorted titles. Even though the dumps are usually sold stocked with only one title or perhaps a few titles by a single author, occasionally a dump featuring mixed titles is available. Tor Books has produced dumps specifically for the teen market. One of their dumps features assorted classics for teens, for example. The cover illustrations range from nothing special to attractive and enticing. The headers often apply specifically for use in schools, but in a public library the dumps can be used without the headers. This is an excellent way to display teen books.

Resources for Librarians

There are many useful resources for those who wish to learn more about YA literature and serving teens. You'll find a list of resources at the end of this guide, but it is especially worth noting that the Young Adult Library Services Association, a division of the American Library Association, provides support to librarians working with teens by sponsoring programs at the ALA annual conference, and publishing the annual book lists Best Books for Young Adults, Popular Paperbacks, and Quick Picks. They also offer a register of speakers who are available to present workshops on young adult library services topics including genre fiction.

Of course, the greatest resource for teen readers is a librarian who really cares that teens find the books they want and enjoy. Never underestimate your power. It is my belief that whatever the size of your budget, your collection, and your community, you can find ways to connect teen readers with the books they love; it is my sincere hope that this guide supports you in that endeavor. Genre fiction is a vital and rich field of teen literature. Many adults enjoy reading YA genre fiction as well. If you work with teen readers, I strongly recommend you acquaint yourself with the many facets of teen genre fiction. You may find, as I did, that once you get started, you're hooked for life.

References

Baker, Sharon, and Karen Wallace. *The Responsive Public Library: How to Develop and Market a Winning Collection.* 2d ed. Englewood, Colo.: Libraries Unlimited, 2002.

Buzzeo, Toni, and Jane Kurtz. *Terrific Connections with Authors, Illustrators, and Storytellers.* Englewood, Colo.: Libraries Unlimited, 1999.

Cart, Michael. *From Romance to Realism: 50 Years of Growth and Change in Young Adult Literature.* New York: HarperCollins, 1996.

Chelton, Mary K., ed. *Excellence in Library Services to Young Adults: The Nation's Top Programs.* 3d ed. Chicago: American Library Association, 2000.

Herald, Diana Tixier. "Buy more books." *School Library Journal,* July 1996, p. 26.

Jones, Patrick. *Connecting Young Adults and Libraries: A How to Do It Manual.* 2d ed. New York: Neal Schuman, 1998.

Keane, Nancy. *Booktalking across the Curriculum.* Greenwood Village, Colo.: Libraries Unlimited, 2002.

Langemack, Chapple. *The Booktalker's Bible.* Westport, Conn.: Libraries Unlimited, 2003.

Mort, John. *Christian Fiction.* Greenwood Village, Colo.: Libraries Unlimited, 2002.

Chapter 2

Issues

All teens struggle with issues and problems. In the 1970s, they seemed to dominate YA fiction. By the 1990s, problem novels—often called "bleak books," "teen angst books," or "realistic fiction" as well—were still going strong. These are the novels that confront contemporary issues such as homelessness, abuse, and addiction. Even now, problem novels endure, simply because if teen characters are present, so are problems. But not all issues are problems. Sometimes, as in the novels in the Activism section of this chapter, teens see a way to make the world a better place and strive to change it. Over the past decade, the tone of this popular subgenre has shifted from the dark, tragic sufferings and raw honesty of innocent victims to take-charge endeavors of feisty protagonists with a cause, even if the cause is dealing with tragedy. Hence, the term "problems" has been changed to "issues," reflecting that shift in focus and tone.

It is also interesting to note how the specific issues that teen fiction deals with have changed since the first volume of *Teen Genreflecting*. In 1997, there were enough recent releases about AIDS and missing teens to create subcategories for each. In 2002, the focus on issues has swung in the direction of school violence and activism. Of course, some themes, such as death and deadly diseases, are timeless.

Issue novels address the real-life problems and concerns of teens. They give readers insights into the lives of other teens and help them understand issues in their own lives or the lives of their peers. They satisfy the curiosity that teens often have about serious problems. In some cases, they might make the reader feel fortunate and well centered in comparison with a book's characters. Most titles in this genre show how the issue in question affects the protagonist and those around him or her, then how the protagonist resolves the issue or learns to live with it. Today's issue novels are truly descendents of the old problem novels—the same, but different. Although problem novels dealt with a small core of problems, issue novels address a broader spectrum of considerations, with teens being more proactive in solving them.

But what is it exactly that teens enjoy about issue novels? Usually set in contemporary times, these books address the real-life issues that teens hear about in the media, may witness in the lives of friends or family, or may even face in their own lives. Teens relish the brutally honest, often gritty portrayals of contemporary life—books that "tell it like it is," and "get real." These stories are often character driven. Teens can identify with protagonists who, like themselves, have inherited an imperfect world and are struggling to change it. Adults and other secondary characters are sometimes cast in negative terms—the alcoholic father, the abusive teacher, the dysfunctional family.

Although the tone may range from deadpan humorous or reflective to heavy or downright bleak, issue novels also contain a good share of passion and drama to which teens can relate. This is often accompanied by the messages most teens want to hear: there is hope, you can make a difference.

Teens who read these novels gravitate to books about specific issues and problems, which function as the focus and themes of the books. Thus, this chapter is organized thematically. Teens who enjoy reading about less serious contemporary life and issues and desire a more lighthearted treatment should consult the following chapter, "Contemporary Life." Issues often play a part in other genres, such as historical and mystery titles, and users are encouraged to consult the index for additional issue-related titles.

Themes

The themes in this section have been divided into three major categories. The first, "Physical, Mental, and Emotional Concerns," covers novels involving health of all types. "Social Concerns" includes books about issues that occur in the larger world and affect teens. "Life Is Hard" focuses on stories about other problems, often several in one book, and how the teen protagonists deal with them.

Physical, Mental, and Emotional Concerns

The problems addressed in the following sections are of a personal nature—that is, they mainly affect and challenge an individual, usually the protagonist of the book. How characters overcome obstacles and meet challenges is a topic of great interest to teen readers.

Physical Challenges

The general North American view of teens as carefree, healthy, and strong does not always apply. There are teens with physical disabilities and challenges resulting from genetics, disease, or accidents. Coming to terms with these conditions while coming of age is a double challenge—and a popular theme in YA fiction. The stories in this section cover issues ranging from obesity to paralysis to dwarfism. Teens, hyperaware of body image, can relate to the difficulties imposed by physical limits. Reading about peers who come to terms with challenges that are beyond their control is appealing to teens.

**Bennett, Cherie. *Life in the Fat Lane.* 1998. *MJS.* Life changes dramatically for Lara, homecoming and beauty pageant queen, when she mysteriously starts gaining weight and can't seem to lose it. (BBYA)

Bloor, Edward. *Tangerine.* 1997. *MJS.* Although legally blind, twelve-year-old Paul Fisher is a kick-butt soccer goalie who comes of age in this hauntingly realistic tale set in a surrealistic town (Tangerine, Florida) where muck fires burn continuously, plagues of mosquitoes and termites harass the populace, and Paul's older brother, the football hero, is the embodiment of evil. This book is so skillfully written that the reader smells the fires and the citrus groves, feels the ice of a killer freeze and the viscous mud that sucks a middle school into the bowels of the earth. (IRAYAC; YALSA 100 Best Books; BBYA; Popular Paperbacks.

Froese, Deborah. *Out of the Fire.* 2002. *JS.* A drunken party leaves a teen girl badly burned and hospitalized. (BBYA)

Hautman, Pete. *Sweet-Blood.* 2003. *JS.* Sixteen-year-old Lucy finds meaning, friendship, and possible danger in her Goth lifestyle as she tries to deal with her out-of-control diabetes.

Ingold, Jeanette. *The Window.* 1996. *JS.* Blinded and orphaned after an accident, Mandy, age fifteen, moves in with relatives in Texas—relatives she has never met. There, she confronts her limitations and a mysterious family history. (BBYA; IRAYAC)

Jordan, Sherryl. *The Raging Quiet.* 1999. *JS.* In the Middle Ages, sixteen-year-old Marnie is accused of witchcraft when she establishes communication with Raven, who is actually deaf and not possessed as others claim. (BBYA; IRAYAC)

Orr, Wendy. *Peeling the Onion.* 1996. *JM.* Coming home after winning a karate competition, seventeen-year-old Anna's life and body are shattered when another car crashes into the one her new boyfriend is driving. As Anna's body slowly heals, she finds she must rethink her ambition to become a P.E. teacher, as well as her relationship with the steadfast Hayden. (BBYA; YALSA 100 Best Books)

Philbrick, Rodman. *Freak the Mighty.* 1993. *MJ.* (Film: *The Mighty*) Kevin is tiny and unable to walk because of his disabilities; Max is hulking, alienated, and depressed. Together they are much more. They are Freak the Mighty. More in the Heroism section of Chapter 4, "Adventure." (Popular Paperbacks; BBYA)

Trueman, Terry. *Stuck in Neutral.* 2000. *MJS.* Because of severe cerebral palsy, fourteen-year-old Shawn McDaniel is unable to let the world or even his family know that he thinks, that he knows what is going on around him—and that he is afraid his father may want to kill him to end his suffering. (BBYA; Quick Picks; Printz-Honor)

Death and Deadly Disease

Lynne Evarts, the librarian at Sauk Prairie High School in Prairie du Sac, Wisconsin, has made the term "crying girls" popular in groups discussing teen books. Books for the "crying girls" are those that, in less sensitive terms, could be called "tearjerkers." This is the section of books for those crying girls. Although it includes many titles that will bring tears and sobs to those readers who like a cathartic experience, the full range of teen experience with death, with losing those near and dear, and with the grief of facing serious diseases is included.

Abelove, Joan. *Saying It Out Loud.* 1999. *S.* High school senior Mindy has to face the fact that her mother is not going to recover from a brain tumor. (BBYA)

Almond, David. *Skellig.* 1998. *MJ.* While his little sister suffers from a possibly terminal disease and his parents focus their energies on her, Michael finds a strange creature in the dilapidated garage of the house into which his family has just moved. (Carnegie Medal; Whitbread Award; Printz-Honor)

Bowler, Tim. *River Boy.* 2000. *M.* Jess, a fifteen-year-old swimmer, has a deep bond with her grandfather, who wants to paint one last painting before he dies, so the pair travels back to Grandfather's boyhood home. (VOYA; Carnegie Medal)

Bradley, Kimberly Brubaker. *Halfway to the Sky.* 2002. *M.* Twelve-year-old Katahdin takes an epic hike on the Appalachian Trail after her brother dies and her parents divorce.

Bunting, Eve. *Blackwater.* 1999. *M.* Even as thirteen-year-old Brodie is hailed as a hero, he knows that his actions caused the death of two others. (Quick Picks)

Cook, Karin. *What Girls Learn.* 1997. *S.* Tilden and Elizabeth move from Atlanta to Long Island when their mother falls in love with Nick, but shortly after the move, they learn that their mom is dying from breast cancer. (Alex Award; BBYA)

Couloumbis, Audrey. *Getting Near to Baby.* 1999. *M.* After Baby dies, thirteen-year-old Willa Jo Dean and her little sister are sent to live with Aunt Patty. A touching, reflective, and sometimes funny story. (VOYA; Newbery Honor)

Draper, Sharon M. *Tears of a Tiger.* 1994. *JS.* Driving drunk, Andy Jackson, an African American high school student, kills his best friend in a car accident. Now no one seems to understand how he feels. This tragic story is told through journal entries, newspaper articles, and homework assignments. (BBYA; YALSA 100 Best Books)

Hawes, Louise. *Rosey in the Present Tense.* 1999. *S.* Romantic seventeen-year-old Franklin refuses to give up on Rosey, the Japanese American girl he loves—even after she dies. (Popular Paperbacks)

Hurwin, Davida Wills. *Time for Dancing.* 1995. *JS.* Two dancers, best friends, must deal with death when one becomes seriously ill. Definitely a five-hankie book. (BBYA; YALSA 100 Best Books)

Johnson, Angela. *Looking for Red.* 2002. *MJS.* The heart-wrenching tale of Mike (short for Michaela), a middle school girl who is trying to get over the loss of her brother Red while living with a terrible secret.

Johnson, Angela. *Toning the Sweep.* 1993. *MJ.* As fourteen-year-old Emily helps her dying grandmother pack up a lifetime of memories, the stories of three generations of African American women emerge. (BBYA; Coretta Scott King Award; Popular Paperbacks)

Lester, Julius. *When Dad Killed Mom.* 2001. *JS.* Jenna and Jeremy have to learn how to live again after their college psychologist father shoots their artist mother. Their narcissistic father had improperly started an affair with their mother when she was a client. It turns out he has been having affairs with students and clients for years, and now he is trying to blame his dead wife for inciting him to murder. (Quick Picks; IRAYAC)

Mazer, Norma Fox. *GirlHearts.* 2001. *MJ.* Thirteen-year-old Sarabeth Silver loses her mother to a sudden heart attack.

McDaniel, Lurlene. Having written more than forty teen "death novels," McDaniel is certainly the queen of this subgenre. Even though the stories elicit tears, they usually have an inspirational tone to them as well.

April and Mark Duet. Two teens with life-threatening conditions meet and fall in love.

> *Till Death Do Us Part.* 1997. *MJS.* Wealthy high school senior April, who has a brain tumor, and race car driver Mark, diagnosed with cystic fibrosis, would seem to have little in common until they meet in the hospital. Part of the April and Mark Duet. (Quick Picks)

> *For Better, for Worse, Forever.* 1997. *MJS.* April must figure out how to live with Mark gone, but just when it seems she may have found love again, her brain tumor reasserts itself. Part of the April and Mark Duet.

McDaniel, Lurlene. *Angel of Mercy.* 1999. *MJS.* Eighteen-year-old missionary Heather travels to Africa to help in a refugee camp. (Quick Picks)

McDaniel, Lurlene. *The Girl Death Left Behind.* 1999. *MJ.* Fourteen-year-old Beth loses her entire family and must go live with relatives. (Quick Picks)

Nelson, Theresa. *Earthshine.* 1994. *M.* Twelve-year-old Slim's father is dying from AIDS, and there is nothing she can do about it. (BBYA; YALSA 100 Best Books)

Park, Barbara. *The Graduation of Jake Moon.* 2000. *M.* Eighth-grader Jake realizes that Alzheimer's disease has completely stolen his beloved grand father away. (VOYA)

Ritter, John. *Over the Wall.* 2000. *MJ.* Tyler was only four years old when his father accidentally ran over and killed his baby sister, dramatically changing Tyler's life. Ten years later, living with relatives in New York and playing baseball in Central Park, Tyler is still filled with anger. He decides that to heal, he must reconnect with his father.

Shusterman, Neal. *What Daddy Did.* 2000. *JS.* Preston must not only try to rebuild his life after his mother is killed, he must also face the fact that his father was her killer. (BBYA)

Warner, Sally. *Sort of Forever.* 1998. *M.* Twelve-year-olds Cady and Nana have been friends forever, but now one of them is dying of cancer. (Quick Picks)

Mental, Emotional, and Behavioral Problems

Although some of the books in this section have humorous-sounding titles, all deal with the serious and disturbing issue of teens facing mental illness or disability—in a parent, sibling, or even themselves. The topics run the gamut from serious mental illness to attention-deficit disorders and life-impacting anger. Elective mutism is a common theme in this category. Attempted suicide, drug abuse, and self-mutilation are also included. Books dealing with mental illnesses that require hospitalization are listed in the Kids in the System section of this chapter.

Teens, coming to terms with their own mental capabilities, emotions, and behaviors, are intrigued by stories on these topics. Sometimes caught in extremes of emotion, they may even wonder if they have a problem.

Anderson, Laurie Halse. *Speak.* 1999. *MJS.* Outcast because she dialed 911 at her first drinking party, Melinda decides to stop talking in her first year of high school. (Printz-Honor; BBYA; Quick Picks; IRAYAC)

Brooks, Bruce. *Vanishing.* 1999. *M.* After a bout with bronchitis, eleven-year-old Alice wants to live with her dad and goes on a hunger strike to avoid going home from the hospital to live with her alcoholic mother and hateful stepfather.

Buffie, Margaret. *Angels Turn Their Backs.* 1998. *JM.* Agorophobic fifteen-year-old Addy is drawn into a mystery surrounding the death of someone who once lived in the apartment she can't leave. (IRAYAC)

Cadnum, Michael. *Edge.* 1997. *S.* High school dropout Zachary faces drastic life changes when he finds out that his beloved father has been shot in a car jacking and is in intensive care at the hospital. After the perpetrator is apprehended and then let go, Zachary remembers the gun he found after a street fight, now buried in the backyard.

Choldenko, Gennifer. *Notes from a Liar and Her Dog.* 2001. *M.* Sixth-grader Antonia (Ant) MacPherson is a female equivalent of Gantos's Joey Pigza (annotated later in this section). She is a compulsive liar, always in trouble for her behavior.

Connelly, Neil. *St. Michael's Scales.* 2002. *JS.* Keegan plans to kill himself before his sixteenth birthday because he thinks that his twin, who died at birth, wants him to. When he is drawn into wrestling for his 1970s parochial school, he discovers that wearing a wrestling helmet makes him invisible to his twin. He comes up with a plan to blow up the school's defective boiler and run away to a new life, rather than taking his own.

Fleischman, Paul. *Whirligig.* 1999. *JS.* After moving to a new community, Brent attempts suicide, believing he has made a total fool of himself in front of his peers. Instead of dying, he accidentally kills another teenager. As restitution, the girl's mother asks that he travel the country by bus for forty-five days to build and place whirligigs (pinwheel-type wind sculptures) to commemorate her daughter's life. The story jumps between Brent's story and those of people who are affected by the whirligigs. (BBYA; YALSA 100 Best Books)

Gantos, Jack. *Joey Pigza Loses Control.* 2000. *M.* Joey Pigza is off to visit his dad and grandmother. Grandma chain smokes and has emphysema, so Joey has to push her around in the shopping cart. Dad is as hyper as Joey but drinks and coaches a baseball team. Joey is an ace pitcher, but obsessive-compulsive, and he doesn't field or hit. It's going to be a strange summer. (Newbery Honor; VOYA)

Glenn, Mel. *Split Image.* 2000. *JS.* Lauri Li's world looks very different to observers at school, especially after she takes her own life. (BBYA; IRAYAC)

Hanauer, Cathi. *My Sister's Bones.* 1996. *JS.* Sixteen-year-old Billie worries about her older sister, who has come back with anorexia from her first semester of college. (BBYA)

Jenkins, A. M. *Damage.* 2001. *S.* It looks like high school senior Austin has it all—good looks, good grades, great athletic ability, and the girlfriend of his dreams. But he still contemplates ending it all. (BBYA)

Koja, Kathe. *Straydog.* 2002. *MJS.* As Rachel, friendless and strange, writes an essay from the viewpoint of Grrl, a feral Collie she is trying to rescue from an animal shelter, she finds herself and true friendship. Koja, an acclaimed author of cutting-edge horror for adults, presents a deceptively simple tale of anger, love, and acceptance. It is powerful and moving.

Lipsyte, Robert. *Warrior Angel.* 2003. *JS.* Starky, a teenage mental patient, believes he is a warrior angel and that his mission on Earth is to save heavyweight boxing champ Sonny Bear. Sonny is in a major funk; his new manager virtually keeps him a prisoner, and he feels as if he's nothing. The Warrior Angel's e-mail messages give him the impetus to escape his entourage and go back to Harlem, where he meets Starky, who has also escaped. Starky's obsession with the book written about Sonny enables him to be an excellent trainer for him, but others in the gym are wary of the white kid who seems to be growing more and more deranged.

McCormick, Patricia. *Cut.* 2000. *JS.* Fifteen-year-old Callie cuts herself. Because she refuses to talk, she is called ST, or Silent Treatment, by the other girls at the Sea Pines mental hospital where she lives. (BBYA; Quick Picks)

Nolan, Han. *Dancing on the Edge.* 1997. *S.* Miracle came into the world by being sliced out of the belly of a dead woman. Now with her father missing, the troubled teen attempts to find him in a way that threatens her life. (National Book Award; BBYA)

O'Keefe, Susan Heyboer. *My Life and Death, by Alexandra Canarsie.* 2002. *JS.* Alexandra could be the poster child for poor impulse control. New in her mother's old hometown, the fifteen-year-old has started attending strangers' funerals and has decided that a dead boy her age was murdered.

Plummer, Louise. *A Dance for Three.* 2000. *S.* Annotated in the Pregnancy and Teen Parents section of this chapter. (BBYA)

Quarles, Heather. *A Door Near Here.* 1998. *JS.* A family of three teens and one younger sister tries to keep things going and the family intact while their mother sleeps off a very long alcoholic binge. This involves trying to keep their remarried father and the school authorities in the dark. (BBYA; IRAYAC; Delacorte Press Prize)

Rosenberg, Liz. *Heart & Soul.* 1996. *JS.* This first novel by an award-winning poet is the coming-of-age, struggle-against-depression tale of Willie Steinberg, a talented seventeen-year-old musician. Willie has left an expensive private high school (for music students in Philadelphia) midyear to mope around the new family home in Richmond, Virginia.

Sones, Sonya. *Stop Pretending: What Happened When My Big Sister Went Crazy.* 1999. *MJS.* When Cookie's older sister is hospitalized for a mental illness, the thirteen-year-old must sort through her own powerful emotions. A poignant tale told in verse. (Popular Paperbacks; BBYA; Quick Picks; IRAYAC)

Sparks, Beatrice, ed. *Kim: Empty Inside: The Diary of an Anonymous Teenager.* 2001. *JS.* Kim, a high school senior, has issues with food that seem to be ruining her life.

Toten, Teresa. *The Game.* 2002. *JS.* While teen Dani (Danielle) Webster is in a mental hospital, she confronts the realities of her life with an abusive father and an emotionally absent mother. She gradually relates the tale of the magical place and the adventures she shared with her younger sister, Kelly. She also relates the stories of her two new friends—self-mutilating Scratch and Kevin, whose parents won't accept the fact that he is gay. (BBYA)

Trueman, Terry. *Inside Out.* 2003. *JS.* Sixteen-year-old Zach Wahhsted, who suffers from adolescent-onset schizophrenia, never knows what is real and what isn't. He becomes a hero when two teen gunmen take everyone in a coffee shop hostage during a failed robbery attempt.

Warner, Sally. *How to Be a Real Person (in Just One Day).* 2001. *MJ.* Sixth-grader Kara tries to hide her mother's descent into mental illness.

White, Ruth. *Memories of Summer.* 2000. *MJS.* In 1955, sixteen-year-old Summer and thirteen-year-old Lyric move from Appalachia to Flint, Michigan, so their Poppy (father) can work in the automobile plant. Soon Summer's peculiarities escalate into full-blown schizophrenia. (BBYA)

Williams, Carol Lynch. *The True Colors of Caitlynne Jackson.* 1997. *MJ.* In a *Homecoming*-type story, Cait and her sister travel to their grandmother's after being abandoned for the summer by their abusive, mentally ill mother. (BBYA; Quick Picks)

Sexual Identity

First love and coming of age for a gay boy, a lesbian, or a bisexual teen present problems different from those heterosexual teens face. The following books deal with individuals—heterosexual, bisexual, and gay—discovering their own sexual preferences and identities. The pain and issues surrounding coming to terms and coming out as well as the joy of first love and the confusing nature of crushes are found in this section. An excellent short story anthology, *Am I Blue?* edited by Marion Dane Bauer, deals with the same issues and includes stories by major YA authors. Teens often struggle with their own sexual identities, and no matter what their sexual orientation, they can relate to the challenges other teens face.

Block, Francesca Lia. *Baby Be-bop.* 1995. *JS.* The story of Dirk, Weetzie Bat's (from the book by the same title) best friend, who is gay. (BBYA; YALSA 100 Best Books)

Cart, Michael, ed. *Love & Sex.* 2001. *S.* (Short Stories) A collection of short stories that spans the breadth of teen sexuality. Leading YA authors tackle abstinence, crushes, gender identity, and homosexuality. (BBYA; Quick Picks)

Cart, Michael. *My Father's Scar: A Novel.* 1996. *S.* Andy, a college freshman, gets away from his abusive father and homophobic town and enters his first gay relationship. (BBYA)

Chambers, Aidan. *Postcards from No Man's Land.* 2002. *S.* Seventeen-year-old Jacob visits Oosterbeck in the Netherlands where his grandfather, a British soldier in WWII, was hidden after being wounded. While staying with the family of Geertrui, who had loved his grandfather, Jacob finds himself attracted to both a beautiful young woman and an openly gay young man. (Carnegie Medal; BBYA; Printz Award)

Ferris, Jean. *Eight Seconds.* 2000. *JS.* At bull-riding camp, eighteen-year-old John finds himself fascinated by Kit, a good-looking charismatic teen who he discovers is gay. (BBYA)

Freymann-Weyr, Garret. *My Heartbeat.* 2002. *JS.* Ellen has always hung out with her older brother Link and his best friend James, who many think are gay. But now the two boys are barely even speaking, and Link has started dating a girl. (BBYA; Printz-Honor)

Gantos, Jack. *Desire Lines.* 1997. *S.* Fancying himself a natural scientist, sixteen-year-old Walker observes the "mating habits" of a couple of lesbians from his school who meet in a deserted and overgrown golf course. Walker has a lot of fears—the local group of toughs who harass him are bad enough, but when an itinerant teen preacher and his evangelizing family pick Walker's school to clean up from what they consider to be the scourge of homosexuality, he is singled out. To turn the attention away from himself, he tells on the girls, which leads to tragedy.

Garden, Nancy. *Annie on My Mind.* 1982. *S.* Liza and Annie are in love, but it seems that no one wants them to be. (BBYA; YALSA 100 Best Books; Popular Paperbacks)

Jenkins, A. M. *Breaking Boxes.* 1997. *JS.* When Charlie Calmont is sent to in-school suspension for fighting with rich and popular Brandon Chase, he has no reason to suspect that a friendship will emerge that will change his life. Brandon seems to have it all—a nice house, nice clothes, a silver Corvette, and two parents—but he wants to hang out with Charlie, who lives in a cheap apartment with his older brother Trent, who works double shifts at a bookstore to make ends meet. Charlie slowly lets his barriers down and new people in his life, but when he tells Brandon something he thought was obvious, his world comes crashing down. (Quick Picks; Popular Paperbacks)

Kerr, M. E. *"Hello," I Lied.* 1997. *JS.* Spending the summer in the Hamptons where his mom is working for retired rock star Ben Nevada, seventeen-year-old gay Lang Penner finds himself drawn to a girl.

Peters, Julie Anne. *Keeping You a Secret.* 2003. *JS.* Class president Holland Jaeger finds herself curiously drawn to an openly lesbian new girl at her school and begins to wonder if there is a reason she has never felt passion for her boyfriend.

Reynolds, Marilyn. *Love Rules*. 2001. *JS.* Kit tells Lynn, her lifelong best friend and across-the-fence neighbor, that she is a lesbian. Lynn first doesn't believe it and then doesn't understand it. When she finally comes to accept it, she provides Kit with support as antigay and rainbow forces line up against each other at Hamilton High School.

Ryan, Sara. *Empress of the World*. 2001. *JS.* Fifteen-year-old Nicola, "Nic," goes to a summer program for gifted teens where she meets Battle and falls in love; but then Battle dumps her and starts going out with a boy. (BBYA)

Taylor, William. *The Blue Lawn*. 1999. *S.* Fifteen-year-old rugby star David and sophisticated Theo grapple with their intense attraction to each other. Do they dare act on their feelings? (Popular Paperbacks)

Wersba, Barbara. *Whistle Me Home*. 1997. *JS.* Independent and alcoholic, seventeen-year-old Noli has her own style that the new guy, the gorgeous TJ, finds fascinating. As Noli falls more and more in love, TJ tries to control her appearance and Noli begins to wonder whether TJ's hands-off policy is a matter of respect, or does she just not turn him on? (BBYA; Quick Picks)

Wittlinger, Ellen. *Hard Love*. 1999. *JS.* John, a high school junior, shuttles back and forth between his mom, who won't touch him, and his big-city playboy dad. He also wonders whether he's normal, because he has never fallen in love, never even been strongly attracted to anyone. He is involved in the 'zine scene, however, writing his own 'zine and admiring others, particularly Marisol's, who he contrives to meet on one of his lonely weekends in the city with dad. They mesh, having quite a bit in common even outside the 'zine world. Even though Marisol is a professed lesbian, John falls in love with her. (Printz-Honor; Popular Paperbacks; BBYA; Quick Picks; IRAYAC)

Yamanaka, Lois-Ann. *Name Me Nobody*. 1999. *JS.* Emi-Lou is a fat, Hawaiian middle-schooler who has one friend, Yvonne. Now people are saying that Yvonne is a "lez."

Pregnancy and Teen Parents

With the high rate of teen pregnancy and the prevalence of teens choosing to keep their babies, many teens want to read about how others cope with the situations early parenthood causes. Although most titles in this group feature girl protagonists, Bechard's *Hanging on to Max,* Johnson's *The First Part Last,* and Reynolds's *Too Soon for Jeff* see the situation from the young father's point of view.

Bechard, Margaret. *Hanging on to Max.* 2002. *JS.* Seventeen-year-old Sam takes on the responsibility of parenting his infant son, Max, but finds life as a single parent rough going even with the support of an alternative high school for teen parents. (BBYA; Quick Picks)

Dessen, Sarah. *Someone Like You.* 1998. *JS.* Halley, a high school junior, is summoned home from camp by a frantic late-night phone call from her best friend, Scarlett. Not long after her boyfriend dies, Scarlett finds that she is pregnant. Halley, formerly the quiet sidekick, shows true reserves of strength as she bolsters Scarlett through the difficult months ahead. (BBYA; Quick Picks)

Fienberg, Anna. *Borrowed Light.* 2000. *S.* At sixteen, Callisto, who thinks of everyone in astrophysical terms, faces some very real adolescent problems. A powerful coming-of-age tale that moves slowly but provokes much thought.

Hobbs, Valerie. *Get It While It's Hot. Or Not: A Novel.* 1996. *SJ.* Mia and Elain try to help their friend Kit, a high school junior who happens to be pregnant. How far will they go to prove their friendship? (IRAYAC)

Hrdlitschka, Shelley. *Dancing Naked.* 2002. *JS.* Sixteen-year-old Kia weighs the options and makes her own decision on what to do about her pregnancy. Fortunately, she has a supportive Filipina mother and Unitarian youth group counselor.

Johnson, Angela. *The First Part Last.* 2003. *JS.* The narrative flashes back and forth in Bobby Morris's seventeenth year, which is somewhat disorienting—but then so is Bobby's life. On his sixteenth birthday, his girlfriend, Nia, tells him she is pregnant. In alternating chapters, we see him fathering his baby girl, Feather, becoming a man, and how he got to where he is.

McDonald, Janet. *Spellbound.* 2001. *MJS.* A teen mother from the projects may be able to do something with her life if she can win a spelling bee that will get her a college scholarship. (BBYA)

Plummer, Louise. *A Dance for Three.* 2000. *S.* Fifteen-year-old Hannah, her widowed agoraphobic mother's link to the outside world, becomes pregnant by the egotistical Milo, who denies all responsibility. The stress lands her in a mental ward. (BBYA)

Reynolds, Marilyn. True-to-Life from Hamilton High series. *JS.* Although not truly a series because each title concerns the life of a different teen, these stories are connected by virtue of the characters' attendance at the same school and the fact that they all involve teen parenthood.

Baby Help. 1997. Annotated in the Physical and Emotional Abuse section of this chapter.

Detour for Emmy. 1993. Fifteen-year-old Emmy is an A student with grand ambitions who realizes her life will change when she becomes pregnant. (BBYA)

Too Soon for Jeff. 1994. Just when Jeff, who is planning to go off to college on a debate scholarship, decides to break up with Christy, she informs him that she is pregnant and planning to keep the baby. (BBYA)

Williams-Garcia, Rita. *Like Sisters on the Homefront.* 1995. *JS.* When fourteen-year-old Gayle becomes pregnant for the second time, her mother gets her an abortion and packs her off to live in Georgia with her uncle, a pastor, and her teenage cousin, whose life couldn't be more different from Gayle's. (Coretta Scott King Honor; BBYA; Quick Picks; Popular Paperbacks)

Social Concerns

No man is an island, and neither is any teen. Issues that teens face may be part of a larger context of the society and world around them. Awareness of social issues gathers momentum in teen years, and many teens look to social and political activism as a way to change the world.

Activism

Teens can feel very strongly about issues and are often willing to take a stance for what they believe is right, as do the protagonists in the following stories. Strong characters and clearly drawn lines between right and wrong resonate with teen readers.

Avi. *Nothing but the Truth: A Documentary Novel.* 1991. *MJ.* Ninth-grader Philip is suspended from school for humming the national anthem. The story is composed of school memos, news clips, dialogue, and diary excerpts. (BBYA; YALSA 100 Best Books)

Carvell, Marlene. *Who Will Tell My Brother?* 2002. *JSM.* Evan, whose Indian heritage does not show in his face, decides to carry on the battle started by his older brother—to change his school's offensive mascot. Deserted by people he once thought were friends, the high school senior comes up against a brick wall in the form of the school board. A visit to elder relatives reassures him that he is part of his family even though he doesn't look like his father or brother. When his brother's loyal and beloved dog is killed, those at school who had not actively supported him but were sympathetic to his cause rally around him. (Alternative Format)

Cooney, Caroline B. *Burning Up.* 1999. *JS.* Annotated in the Racism section of this chapter. (Quick Picks)

Goobie, Beth. *Sticks and Stones.* 2002. *JS.* (High-low) Jujube Gelb is not a slut, but when she refuses to put out for Brent Floyd in the backseat of his car at a school dance, rumors start flying. Somehow word got out that she *did* go all the way, and now her name and phone number are on bathroom walls throughout the school. She decides to fight back, banding together with the other girls who have been defamed by school graffiti.

Hobbs, Will. *Jackie's Wild Seattle.* 2003. *M.* Fourteen-year-old Shannon and her little brother Cody go to stay with their Uncle Neal in Seattle when their physician parents travel to Pakistan with the Doctors without Borders program. Uncle Neal is volunteering 24-7 as the ambulance driver for Jackie's Wild Seattle, a wildlife refuge and clinic for animals that have suffered from encounters with civilization. Shannon's unexpected summer at a wildlife rescue center thrusts her into adventure and self-discovery as she becomes an animal rescuer.

Howe, James. *The Misfits.* 2001. *M.* Four outcast seventh-graders start a campaign against labeling people and name calling.

Hyde, Catherine R. *Pay It Forward.* 1999. *JS.* (Film: *Pay It Forward*) When Trevor, an eighth-grader, comes up with the idea of doing three good deeds and telling the recipients to "pay it forward," his idea takes off in a big way. (BBYA) Adult

Keizer, Garret. *God of Beer.* 2002. *JS.* Kyle, Quaker Oats, and Diana, teen residents of a Vermont town, decide to start a protest movement to lower the drinking age, raise the drinkers' awareness, and destroy the nondrinkers' stigma.

Napoli, Donna Jo. *For the Love of Venice.* 1998. *JS.* When Percy's family spends the summer in Venice, the seventeen-year-old falls for Graziella, who is part of a movement working for the rights of Venetians and their city, which is being drowned by tourism.

Tashjian, Janet. *Gospel According to Larry.* 2001. *MJS.* At age seventeen, Josh, using the pseudonym Larry, creates an anticonsumerism Web site that takes off and starts up a worldwide movement, bringing him celebrity and a stalker who wants to unmask him. (BBYA)

Thomas, Rob. *Slave Day.* 1997. *JS.* Annotated in the Racism section of this chapter.

Politics

The following novels deal with political situations and issues that have an impact on teen characters either directly or through effects on their families or communities. These novels provide a connection point for teens who are interested in local, national, and global communities. As the world grows smaller, teens are increasingly aware of their role in the larger communities around them, and they are curious about lives of teens from different cultures and backgrounds. Many of the titles deal with teens taking a stand for what they believe and the conflict that arises from having done so.

Laird, Elizabeth. *Kiss the Dust.* 1991. *MJS.* Thirteen-year-old Tara and her middle-class Kurdish family must flee their home in Iraq. Based on real events. (BBYA; YALSA 100 Best Books)

Mikaelsen, Ben. *Red Midnight.* 2002. *MJ.* On the night that soldiers burned their village and killed almost everyone, twelve-year-old Santiago grabbed his four-year-old sister Angelina and ran into the Guatemalan jungle. His dying uncle had told him to go to his far-off village, take his *cayuco,* and sail to the United States. More in the Survival section of Chapter 4.

Peck, Richard. *The Last Safe Place on Earth.* 1995. *MJS.* Fifteen-year-old Todd's younger sister is terrorized by a baby-sitter's religious beliefs, which leads to a resurrection of parental responsibility and neighborliness. Censorship also becomes an issue. (BBYA; Quick Picks; Popular Paperbacks)

Staples, Suzanne Fischer. The Shabanu series. *JS.* Life in contemporary Pakistan is illuminated through the perspective of an eleven-year-old girl.

> *Shabanu: Daughter of the Wind.* 1989. A nomadic eleven-year-old girl is given to an older man to be his fourth wife in contemporary Pakistan. (BBYA; YALSA 100 Best Books; Popular Paperbacks)

> *Haveli.* 1993. Shabanu, now the teen mother of a little girl, must be ever vigilant to protect them both in treacherous times. (BBYA)

Temple, Frances. *Taste of Salt: A Story of Modern Haiti.* 1992. *JS.* Seventeen-year-old Djo has been beaten and burned by opponents to social reformer Father Aristide. (Popular Paperbacks; Jane Addams Award)

Racism

Racism continues to concern teens as a sociopolitical issue and a destructive force that often touches their lives. These titles clearly delineate right from wrong, and heroic protagonists are morally compelled to take action to resolve negative situations.

Bloor, Edward. *Crusader.* 1999. *JS.* Fifteen-year-old Roberta Ritter works in a family-owned arcade featuring games that promote racism. More in the Outsiders section of this chapter.

Cooney, Caroline B. *Burning Up.* 1999. *JS.* Macey, who has always thought her family, her town, and her state were close to perfect, unveils some ugly truths when she decides to research a barn fire that happened long before she was born on a property near her grandparent's beachside home. A few hours spent working at the church opens Macey's eyes to the disparity between her idyllic life and that of a girl from the church, with whom she feels an instant kinship. A suspenseful mystery that probes the topic of racism. (Quick Picks)

Fogelin, Adrian. *Crossing Jordan.* 2000. *MJ.* Two neighbors, twelve-year-old Cassie and Jemmie, have a lot in common. They both like to read and run, and they both have bigoted families who do not like it that the two girls, one white and one African American, have become friends. (VOYA; BBYA)

Hewett, Lorri. *Lives of Our Own.* 1998. *MJ.* When she moves to the South, Shawna uses the school newspaper to fight the mores that prohibit interracial dating and segregate community functions. (IRAYAC)

Krisher, Trudy. *Spite Fences.* 1994. *JS.* Thirteen-year-old Maggie, a white girl living in Kinship, Georgia, in 1960 observes the racism in her community through the lens of her camera. (IRA 1995; BBYA)

Les Becquets, Diane. *The Stones of Mourning Creek.* 2001. *MJS.* Only a few months after fourteen-year-old Francie loses her mother, she almost loses her life to a snake bite. Returning to consciousness in the home of a local black family, Francie finds friendship and belonging that eventually lead to ostracism at her all-white Alabama high school. As Francie and her friend Ruthie delve into the evil that pervades their segregated community, danger stalks them. (BBYA)

Qualey, Marsha. *Revolutions of the Heart.* 1993. *JS.* Some people in this small town in Wisconsin are willing to go to great lengths to keep apart seventeen-year-old Cory, a white girl, and Mac, who is Cree. More in the Romance section of Chapter 3. (BBYA; Quick Picks)

Spinelli, Jerry. *Maniac Magee.* 1990. *MJ.* In this tall tale, an exceptional twelve-year-old orphan, Jeffrey Lionel "Maniac" Magee, confronts racism in a divided small town. (Newbery Award; BBYA)

Thomas, Rob. *Slave Day.* 1997. *JS.* Slave Day, a traditional fundraiser at Robert E. Lee High, auctions off the student council and teacher volunteers to be slaves from the morning assembly until the Homecoming bonfire at the end of the evening. In one day—just a brief fourteen hours and fifty-two minutes, we see friendships begin, relationships end, and the story of a teacher's life gone wrong. Thomas's subtle voice takes a moral stand without preaching in any way, and his swift, sure characterizations take us intimately into the lives of a geek, a budding African American activist, a rich girl, a football player, and other students.

Gangs

What would it be like to be in a gang? Gangs are mysterious to outsiders, giving books about gangs and teens a tinge of mystery. Teens have a strong need to belong as well as a fascination with the "wild side," so it isn't surprising that readers in this age group are attracted to stories about peers who have joined gangs. The heavy action and dark violence typical of gang stories, along with the often thrilling suspense, appeal to many teen readers.

Cross, Gillian. *Tightrope.* 1999. *JS.* Ashley escapes her dutiful and dull life when she tags difficult spots in hard-to-reach places with her graffiti art. But now it has brought her to the attention of the local gang—and a stalker. (Popular Paperbacks; BBYA; IRAYAC)

Ewing, Lynne. *Party Girl.* 1998. *JS.* Kata's best friend got out of their gang the hard way—in a coffin. (Popular Paperbacks; Quick Picks)

Hinton, S. E. *The Outsiders.* 1967. *JS.* (Film: *The Outsiders*) Three parentless boys live in a part of Tulsa that is ruled by gangs. A classic title that teens still read and enjoy. (Newbery Award) [Classic]

Mowry, Jess. *Babylon Boyz.* 1997. *MJS.* Annotated in the Multiple and Unique Issues section of this chapter. (Popular Paperbacks)

Myers, Walter Dean. *Scorpions.* 1988. *MJ.* Jamal's brother has written from prison asking him to take over leadership of his gang. (BBYA; Newbery Honor)

Shusterman, Neal. The Shadow Club duo. *JS.*

> *The Shadow Club.* 1988. A group of high school second-bests join together to play pranks on the boys who are "unbeatable," but the seriousness of the pranks escalates into dangerous territory.
>
> *The Shadow Club Rising.* 2002. Even with the Shadow Club disbanded, fourteen-year-old Jared is suspected when new practical jokes are inflicted on a popular new boy.

Crime and Criminals

The appeal of stories about crime and criminals is similar to those specifically about gangs—a fascination with the darker side of society, action, and suspense. These titles address crimes that range from theft, to drug dealing, to murder.

Cadnum, Michael. *Redhanded.* 2000. *J.* Steven loves to box, but to obtain the money he needs for a big tournament, he turns to crime.

Cormier, Robert. *The Rag and Bone Shop.* 2001. *MJS.* Cormier, in great form for his final novel, describes the hours in the life of twelve-year-old Jason following the death of his seven-year-old friend. The police bring in an expert interrogator, who specializes in manipulating the setting to elicit confessions. Can he uncover the real truth? (BBYA)

Cormier, Robert. *Tenderness.* 1997. *S.* Eric Poole, an eighteen-year-old serial killer, is released from a juvenile correction facility, while an aging detective tries to put a stop to his heinous avocation. A fifteen-year-old runaway girl, Lori, controlled by obsessions, stalks Eric and eventually hits the road with him. (BBYA; Popular Paperbacks)

Ferris, Jean. *Bad.* 1998. *JS.* Sixteen-year-old Dallas ends up in a rehabilitation center after her dad gives up on her. (BBYA; Quick Picks; IRAYAC)

Flinn, Alex. *Breaking Point.* 2002. *JS.* Paul Richmond's life is hell. His recently divorced mother has taken a job at a private school so that he can attend for free, but it is not just the adjustment of switching from home school that's so bad—the mostly wealthy students are downright mean. His only friend is Binky, a girl who has refused to kowtow to popular Charlie, who runs the school. But Paul is quick enough to dump her when he becomes Charlie's new best friend. As best friend, it falls on Paul to do things for Charlie, things that he never would have done otherwise. A shockingly realistic view of what can lead a good kid to do very bad things.

Hobbs, Will. *The Maze.* 1998. *MJ.* When fourteen-year-old Rick escapes from a juvenile correction facility, he ends up in a remote canyon in Canyonlands National Park, where he meets a wildlife biologist and learns to hang glide. (BBYA; Popular Paperbacks; Quick Picks)

McDonald, Joyce. *The Shadow People.* 2000. *S.* Four alienated teens band together, and the crimes they commit rapidly escalate in severity.

Mikaelsen, Ben. *Touching Spirit Bear.* 2001. *MJS.* After Cole beats another boy so severely that the victim sustains brain damage, Cole is sent to a remote northern island as part of a circle of justice, an alternative to incarceration. Angry and determined to escape, Cole burns the fully provisioned cabin to the ground before trying to swim away, only to be turned back by the tide. When a bear looks at him, he gets in its face, only to be taught a painful lesson. (BBYA)

Myers, Walter Dean. *Monster.* 1999. *S.* (Alternative format) As Steve Harmon sits in jail awaiting trial for murder, he writes a screenplay about his situation. (Printz Award; BBYA; Quick Picks; Coretta Scott King Honor)

Salisbury, Graham. *Shark Bait.* 1997. *M.* Annotated in Chapter 3, "Contemporary Life."

Woodson, Jacqueline. *Miracle's Boys.* 2000. *MJS.* When Charlie is released from a detention facility, he blames twelve-year-old Lafayette for the death of their mother. (BBYA; Coretta Scott King Award; VOYA)

Life Is Hard

Some difficulties that teens face seem almost insurmountable—physical and sexual abuse by parents or peers, racism in the community, homelessness—situations often not chosen, but that life has simply dealt them. At this age, when teens are trying to figure out where they belong, many feel like outsiders, and some turn to substance abuse or decide to disappear altogether. The titles in this section center on tough issues. These are the books often classified as "bleak books," and their harsh depictions of reality, which stand in stark contrast to the sugar-coated versions often portrayed in the media, make for compelling reading. A feeling of being "out of control" dominates, and tragic endings are common.

Multiple and Unique Issues

The titles here deal with teens who confront multiple or unique issues (themes not found in other titles).

Dean, Carolee. *Comfort.* 2002. *JS.* His mother altered his birth certificate so that fourteen-year-old Kenny can get a driver's license to drive his ex-con dad to AA meetings. She made him quit the football team and is just waiting for him to be old enough to drop out of school. But Kenny wants other things in life, and winning a poetry competition may be his ticket out.

Draper, Sharon M. *Forged by Fire.* 1997. *JS.* Gerald's life changed for the better when his doper mom was sent to jail and he went to live with his loving great-aunt. Tragically, the aunt dies just when Gerald finds out that his mother wants him back—and now he has a younger half-sister and a vile abusive stepfather. Coping magnificently, Gerald Nickleby makes lots of good decisions in a world fraught with peril. A sequel to *Tears of the Tiger.* (Coretta Scott King Award; Popular Paperbacks; BBYA)

Flinn, Alex. *Breaking Point.* 2002. *JS.* Annotated in the Crime and Criminals section of this chapter.

Frank E. R. *Life Is Funny.* 2000. *JS.* (Short Stories) The connected stories of eleven Brooklyn teens give a realistic and gritty view of teen life. (Quick Picks)

Fraustino, Lisa Rowe, ed. *Dirty Laundry: Stories about Family Secrets.* 1998. *JS.* All families have secrets, and eleven authors, including Chris Crutcher, Graham Salisbury, and Bruce Coville, bring some to light in this anthology where the secrets range from child abuse to a transvestite uncle. (Quick Picks)

Haddix, Margaret Peterson. *Don't You Dare Read This, Mrs. Dunphrey.* 1996. *JS.* Sixteen-year-old Tish is trying to support her brother and herself. Her only outlet is the diary her teacher has promised never to read. (IRA 1997; BBYA; Quick Picks; IRAYAC)

Hartnett, Sonya. *Thursday's Child.* 2002. *S.* Life in Australia during the depression is grim for seven-year-old Harper Flute and her family, which includes younger brother Tin, who spends all his time burrowing through the earth.

Heneghan, James. *Flood.* 2002. *MJ.* When eleven-year-old Andy Flynn loses his mother and stepfather in a Vancouver flood, his aunt takes him back to Toronto. On the way, he learns that the father his mother had told him was "killed in the war" is actually still alive and living in Toronto. Upon arrival, Andy gives his aunt the slip and sets out to the seedier parts of the city to find his father, who, it turns out, sells packs of stolen cigarettes in bars and lives in a vermin-infested hotel room. Andy settles into a life of hunger and boredom as he tries to convince his father to find a job and a decent place to live—not to mention a change of clothes.

Holt, Kimberly Willis. *My Louisiana Sky.* 1998. *MJ.* Twelve-year-old Tiger Ann Parker's parents are very different from other parents in 1950s Louisiana. They are developmentally disabled. (BBYA; IRAYAC)

Kessler, Cristina. *No Condition Is Permanent.* 2000. *JS.* Reluctantly accompanying her anthropologist mother to Sierra Leone, fourteen-year-old Jodie meets Khadi, who becomes her best friend. But the friendship is imperiled when Khadi joins a secret society that practices female circumcision, and Jodie decides she must try to stop her. (BBYA)

Lynch, Chris. *Whitechurch.* 1999. *J.* (Alternative format) Pauly, Lilly, and Oakley are trapped in the small town of Whitechurch—and in a triangular relationship.

McDonald, Joyce. *Swallowing Stones.* 1998. *JS.* On his seventeenth birthday, the fourth of July, Michael MacKenzie seemingly has it all—a cool girlfriend, a buddy who hooks him up with the school slut, a good job as lifeguard at the pool, and the respect and affection of all who know him. He also has an antique Winchester rifle that he received for his birthday from his grandfather. As he shoots it into the sky amid the sounds of revelry and firecrackers, he doesn't realize that he has just ended the life of another human being and drastically changed the lives of many. Sensitive and thought provoking, this story helps us grow to know the people beneath the images they project. (BBYA)

Nolan, Han. *Born Blue.* 2001. *S.* Janie/Lashaya is a blond-haired blue-eyed foster child being raised in a smelly home with her African American foster brother Harmon, who introduces her to his "ladies," cassette tapes of the greatest women blues singers.

Janie has a phenomenal voice, and her experiences—from the kidnapping by her heroin-addicted mother, who sells her to a drug dealer, to the abandonment of her own infant—infuse her singing with the pain that makes the blues resonate. (BBYA; YALSA 100 Best Books; IRAYAC)

Miller, Mary Beth. *Aimee.* 2002. *S.* A high school senior agonizes over the death of her best friend, Aimee, which led to her trial for murder and the loss of her entire group of friends. (BBYA)

Mowry, Jess. *Babylon Boyz.* 1997. *S.* Gay Pook, sickly Dante, and fat Wyatt are outcasts in Babylon, an inner-city Oakland neighborhood, who find a suitcase full of cocaine and think it may be their way out. (Popular Paperbacks)

Myers, Walter Dean. *Somewhere in the Darkness.* 1992. *JS.* When Jimmy's dad, who has been in prison, shows up, Jimmy takes off with him on a journey that lets them come to know each other. (BBYA; Coretta Scott King Honor; Popular Paperbacks; Newbery Honor; YALSA 100 Best Books)

Rottman, S. L. *Stetson.* 2002. *JS.* Abandoned by his mother and living with his alcoholic father, seventeen-year-old Stet has pretty much raised himself. One day he returns home from his junkyard job to find Kayla, a fourteen-year-old sister he never knew he had. The siblings discover a shared talent for art, but then tragedy strikes. (BBYA)

Soto, Gary. *Buried Onions.* 1997. *S.* Amid the violence and gangs of Fresno, nineteen-year-old Eddie just tries to get along, riding around on his bike, stenciling address numbers on curbs for a few bucks, and trying to avoid his aunt, who wants him to shoot his cousin's killer. (BBYA; Popular Paperbacks; Quick Picks)

Wallace, Rich. *Playing without a Ball.* 2000. *S.* Annotated in the Outsiders section of this chapter. (BBYA; Quick Picks)

Weaver, Will. *Claws.* 2003. *S.* Jed Berg's "perfect" life starts spiraling downhill when a pink-haired punk girl tells him that his father and her mother are having an affair. Jed's investigation takes him to Ely and a lakefront log home designed by his architect dad, where he discovers Laura (of the pink punk wig) is almost the perfect girl. As the two teens try to make sense of the situation and save their families, things go from bad to worse.

Wolff, Virginia Euwer. **Make Lemonade series.** *JS.* Annotated in the Poetry and Verse Novel section of Chapter 11, "Alternative Formats." (Popular Paperbacks; YALSA 100 Best Books; BBYA)

Zusak, Markus. *Fighting Ruben Wolfe.* 2001. *JS.* Underdog Cameron and Fighting Ruben Wolfe, both working-class Australian teens, are recruited by a shady guy to fight in unregulated, not-quite-legal fights. In the ring Ruben takes out his anger over their father's unemployment following a serious plumbing accident and their sister's worsening reputation as she starts drinking too much and running around. (BBYA)

Physical and Emotional Abuse

Abuse as a theme in teen literature has been a growing trend in the past decade. Sometimes a parent or other adult inflicts the abuse, but in more recent releases it often comes from a peer, whether a friend, an enemy, or a lover. In YA fiction, abuse is often just one of the issues characters face, and situations of abuse are also covered in the Multiple and Unique Issues section. Since the tragedy at Columbine High School in Colorado, several novels have been published that focus on the mental and psychological abuse of teens by peers. Some of those novels fit into the Outsiders section of this chapter.

Arnoldi, Katherine. *The Amazing True Story of a Teenage Single Mom.* 1998. *JS.* Annotated in the Graphic Novels section of Chapter 11, "Alternative Formats." (BBYA; Quick Picks)

Dessen, Sarah. *Dreamland.* 2000. *JS.* Caitlin's sister Cass was practically perfect, but when Cass runs off with her boyfriend instead of heading off to Yale, their parents don't turn their doting attentions to Caitlin. It doesn't even seem to matter that she made the cheerleading squad. Then Caitlin discovers the fascinating Rogerson, who turns her on to drugs and sex, and then begins to abuse her. (BBYA)

Flinn, Alex. *Breathing Underwater.* 2001. *JS.* Nick, a rich and handsome teen, falls for Caitlin, the formerly fat girl who has blossomed into the girl of his dreams. Finally having someone to love him, he begins to control her and isolate her from her friends, chipping away at her self-esteem to keep her. When he is placed under a restraining order and required to take domestic abuse classes, he remains in denial but writes a journal of their time together. This is an outstanding depiction of abuse from the abuser's point of view. (BBYA; Quick Picks; IRAYAC)

Howe, James. *The Watcher.* 1997. *JS.* In this atmospheric novel, a girl sits on the steps at a Long Island beach and watches. She sees the perfect family with the older brother who takes care of his little sister. She sees the virile lifeguard, safeguarding the swimmers. She sees life as she would like it to be, not as the nightmare it is. (BBYA)

Klass, David. *You Don't Know Me.* 2002. *JS.* Fourteen-year-old John regularly gets verbal and physical beatings from a man who is not his father and is victimized by a girl who is not his girlfriend. While at times laugh-out-loud funny, this book explores serious issues. (BBYA; IRAYAC)

Mazer, Norma Fox. *When She Was Good.* 1997. *JS.* Fourteen-year-old Em Thurkill is constantly terrorized by her older, abusive, and mentally ill sister. (BBYA)

McNamee, Graham. *Hate You.* 1999. *JS.* Her voice permanently ruined by her father's abuse, seventeen-year-old Alice Silvers grudgingly comes to the realization that her life and aspirations as a songwriter are not ruined. (BBYA; Quick Picks)

Na, An. *A Step from Heaven.* 2001. *MJS.* Young Ju moves from Korea to America with her mom and her dad. Her father later becomes abusive. (BBYA; Printz Award)

Philbrick, Rodman. *Max the Mighty.* 1998. *MJ.* Annotated in the Heroism section of Chapter 4, "Adventure."

Reynolds, Marilyn. *Baby Help.* 1997. *JS.* Independent two-year-old Cheyenne and her seventeen-year-old mom Melissa live with Melissa's abusive boyfriend Rudy. After a guest speaker at school talks about abusive relationships, Melissa realizes that her relationship with the father of her baby fits the definition, but she is not moved to take action until Rudy's violence terrifies Cheyenne. Melissa's attempt to extricate herself from a possibly fatal relationship is realistically and sympathetically told.

Stratton, Allan. *Leslie's Journal.* 2000. *S.* Leslie's home life isn't great, and school isn't any better. One of her friends has started hanging out with her enemies. When she brags that she knows the gorgeous new boy at the high school, she is taunted into proving it. When she goes out to "prove it," he kisses her, raising her status in the eyes of her nemesis, but starting a relationship that is both dangerous and sick. Her only outlet is a journal that her teacher has promised no one will read, where she records everything that Jason does to her. (BBYA; Quick Picks)

Sexual Abuse

What may be the most heinous crime against some children and teens is the conflict that propels the following novels. Sexual abuse adds another layer of anguish to physical and emotional abuse. The stories in this section are particularly intense.

Atkins, Catherine. *When Jeff Comes Home.* 1999. *S.* When Jeff returns after two years of physical, psychological, and sexual torture at the hands of his kidnapper, he finds his friends and family have become strangers. Trying to adapt to his old life becomes a nightmare. (BBYA; Quick Picks; IRAYAC)

Block, Francesca Lia. *I Was a Teenage Fairy.* 1998. *JS.* Barbie Marks, child model, finds a friend in pinky-sized Mab, a feisty fairy. Despite a manipulative and ambitious mom and a distant and uncommunicative dad who is a molesting photographer, Barbie, with the help of Mab, takes control of her own life and destiny. (Quick Picks)

Cole, Brock. *The Facts Speak for Themselves.* 1997. *S.* Told in a series of flashbacks, this powerful tale tells of thirteen-year-old Linda's life as she takes responsibility at a very young age for her mother, an elderly stepfather, and her two younger brothers. In graphic detail, she relates that she has been sexually assaulted—and that now two men are dead. (Quick Picks)

Crutcher, Chris. *Chinese Handcuffs.* 1989. *S.* Sixteen-year-old Dillon witnessed his older brother's suicide. Now he is worried about his girlfriend Jennifer, who has been sexually abused not only at the hands of her father, but of her stepfather as well. (BBYA; YALSA 100 Best Books)

Draper, Sharon M. *Darkness before Dawn.* 2001. *JS.* An African American high school senior, Keisha Montgomery, in the aftermath of the suicide of her ex-boyfriend Andy, falls for Jonathan Hardaway, the new track coach—who is also a rapist. While Draper's novels stand alone, the characters in the different titles all know each other at Hazelwood High. For other titles by this author, consult the index; the issues involved in each book are different. (IRAYAC)

Frank, E. R. *America.* 2002. *S.* Annotated in the Homelessness and Foster Living section of this chapter.

Lundgren, Mary Beth. *Love, Sara.* 2001. *JS.* Fifteen-year-old foster child Sara is happy with her widowed foster mom and her best friend Dulcie, but she fears being alone again. She suffers from PTSD (posttraumatic stress disorder) as the result of sexual abuse by her bio-dad, and she misses her younger sister, who she was trying to save by reporting the abuse.

Placide, Jaira. *Fresh Girl.* 2002. *J.* Annotated in Chapter 10, "Multicultural Fiction."

Rapp, Adam. *Little Chicago.* 2002. *JS.* Eleven-year-old Blacky Brown is sexually assaulted by his mother's boyfriend and then ostracized at school.

Rottman, S. L. *Head above Water.* 1999. *JS.* Skye swims to win a scholarship, takes care of her brother who has Down's syndrome, and tries to fend off the sexual advances of her boyfriend. (BBYA)

Sparks, Beatrice, ed. *Treacherous Love: The Diary of an Anonymous Teenager.* 2000. *JS.* Mom and Dad aren't much support for fourteen-year-old Jennie. She finds solace in fantasizing about the substitute teacher, but when fantasy starts becoming reality, disturbing problems begin to arise. (Quick Picks)

Williams, Lori Aurelia. The Shayla series. *JS.*

> *When Kambia Elaine Flew in from Neptune.* 2000. Twelve-year-old Shayla befriends her strange new neighbor, Kambia. Kambia fears the tigers and ghosts who come out from the wallpaper, but it is really her "mother's" customers who terrify her. When Shayla discovers the true source of Kambia's fears, she must decide what to do. (BBYA; VOYA)

> *Shayla's Double Brown Baby Blues.* 2001. Shayla, now thirteen, meets Lemm, a new boy in the 'hood who has his own set of problems. In the meantime, she finds that even with loving foster parents, and even though the abuse has stopped, her friend Kambia's problems will not disappear.

Woodson, Jacqueline. *I Hadn't Meant to Tell You This.* 1994. *MJS.* A middle-class African American girl befriends a lonely, abused "white trash" student new to her school. The twelve-year-olds find that they have much in common, including having to deal with the racism in their own families. (BBYA; Popular Paperbacks; Coretta Scott King Honor)

Kids in the System

Life in an institution offers readers another look at "the other side." Mental hospitals and correctional facilities are wrapped in a cloak of secrecy, causing outsiders to wonder what goes on in the lives of the teens who live in them. This air of mystery makes the following stories all the more enticing.

Bryant, Sharon. *The Earth Kitchen.* 2002. *MJ.* In 1963, a young girl in a mental hospital receives from a bird a magical gold key that opens a forest off of a solitary confinement cell. There she finds a kitchen buried under a huge tree and creates a garden of paper flowers.

Giff, Patricia Reilly. *Pictures of Hollis Woods.* 2002. *MJ.* Why has twelve-year-old Hollis Woods left the foster father she calls Old Man, the foster brother who is exactly perfect for a brother, and the foster mother who shares hard candy and understanding with her? What could she have done to have stripped herself away from the perfect family she has always wanted? (BBYA; Newbery Honor)

Konigsburg, E. L. *Silent to the Bone.* 2000. *MJ.* When Branwell is accused of causing an injury that has put his baby sister in a coma, he loses the ability to talk and is locked in a juvenile behavioral center. Now Branwell's best friend Connor must devise a way of communicating with him so that he can find out what really happened and who was really responsible. (BBYA; IRAYAC)

Marsden, John. *Checkers.* 1998. *JS.* An unnamed young woman, who has everything money can buy, tells of how she went from a life of privilege to a mental ward. When scandal breaks around her family, she clings to her dog Checkers, a mutt given to her when her dad closed a big business deal. A page-turning suspense story.

Rapp, Adam. *Buffalo Tree.* 1997. *J.* At age twelve, Sura is sent to a juvenile correctional facility for stealing hood ornaments.

Sacher, Louis. *Holes.* 1998. *MJS.* Annotated in the Heroism section of Chapter 4, "Adventure." (Newbery Award; Quick Picks; BBYA; YALSA 100 Best Books)

Outsiders

Outsiders—teens who don't fit in—have been featured in YA novels since J. D. Salinger's *Catcher in the Rye* and S. E. Hinton's *The Outsiders* defined YA literature decades ago, and both of these landmark titles remain popular today. *On the Fringe,* a collection edited by Don Gallo and published in 2001, features a broad spectrum of outsiders in short stories written by outstanding young adult authors including Ron Koertge, Graham Salisbury, Nancy Werlin, Will Weaver, Joan Bauer, and Chris Crutcher. The appeal of these titles is obvious—empathy with the protagonist. After all, what teen doesn't feel like an outsider at least on occasion? As part of the process of individuation and separating from their families, teens long to find peers who act and feel the way they do, but often they end up feeling left out. Although teens featured in the following books may not be victimized to the extent of those in other Life Is Hard subsections, the internal anguish is intense.

Bennett, Cherie. *Life in the Fat Lane.* 1998. *MJS.* Sixteen-year-old Lara, homecoming and beauty pageant queen, the ultimate insider, finds herself on the outside when she mysteriously starts gaining weight and can't lose it. (BBYA)

Block, Francesca Lia. *Violet & Claire.* 1999. *S.* Seventeen-year-old filmmaker Violet becomes friends with Claire, who wears fairy wings sewed to her shirts. But their friendship can't save them from the world. (Quick Picks)

Bloor, Edward. *Crusader.* 1999. *JS.* At age fifteen, Roberta Ritter is more or less a nonentity. With her androgynous looks and lack of a social life, she seems to blend into the background, spending most of her time outside of school, working in the family arcade in a decaying Florida mall. Her best friend is the elderly owner of a card shop in the mall who, on Sundays, accompanies her to the cemetery where Roberta visits her dead mother.

Brooks, Kevin. *Martyn Pig.* 2002. *SJ.* Poor Martyn—he has an awful name *and* an awful life. Well, he does have one friend, Alex, a girl who is a couple of years older than he is, and he also has an interest in mysteries. Martyn doesn't think his life can get much worse until his drunken dad is accidentally killed and he fails to report it.

Crutcher, Chris. *Whale Talk.* 2001. *MJS.* The Tao (TJ) Jones, a Black-Japanese-White high school senior, assembles a great swimming team consisting of a DD (developmentally disabled) kid, a fat kid, a kid who never talks, an extra-intelligent but pompous kid, and a one-legged sociopath. They are the rejects—the ones who don't go on a shooting spree. (BBYA)

Friel, Maeve. *Charlie's Story.* 1997. *JS.* Fourteen-year-old Charlie lives in Ireland with her dad, grandmother, and uncles, but at school she is friendless and picked on by the popular crowd once they discovered that she was abandoned at London's Victoria Station as a young child. A strange boy helps her out a few times, but the hatred and cruel tricks played on her at school have her contemplating suicide, especially after she begins to suspect that her dad knows her mother's whereabouts.

Giles, Gail. *Shattering Glass.* 2002. *SJ.* Simon Glass is the goat at his high school until Rob, the class favorite, decides to elevate him to cool status and make the once-popular Lance the new goat. With the help of four popular students and through diet, exercise, a new wardrobe, a driver's license, and hanging out with the right crowd, Glass, a pudgy computer geek, is transformed into a popular guy. All he has to do is go along and hack into the school computer, but in doing so he discovers a secret about Rob, a secret that will imperil Glass's life. (BBYA; Quick Picks)

Goobie, Beth. *The Lottery.* 2002. Sally Hansen "wins" the Shadow Council lottery, which makes her the victim of the hidden power structure in her high school and a pariah to whom no one will speak.

Griffin, Adele. *Amandine.* 2001. *MJ.* Fourteen-year-old Delia's parents have been trying to get her to make friends, so they are thrilled when she starts hanging out with Amandine—unaware that the girl is deeply disturbed and manipulative. (BBYA; Quick Picks)

Haddix, Margaret Peterson. *Leaving Fishers.* 1997. *MJS.* Wrenched away from her friend-filled small-town life, Dorry, lonely in the big city, is reeled into a cult by an apparently fun-loving, attractive group of kids at school. (BBYA)

Hartinger, Brent. *Geography Club.* 2003. *JS.* Five teens, all gay and lesbian, find that meeting to talk really helps. They form the Geography Club so that they can have a place and an excuse to meet at school.

Koertge, Ron. *The Brimstone Journals.* 2001. *MJS.* Annotated in Chapter 11, "Alternative Formats." (BBYA; Quick Picks)

Koss, Amy Goldman. *The Girls.* 2000. *M.* Middle school can be a minefield of problems. Suddenly, for no reason at all, Maya is cast out of the clique run by the popular and vicious Candace. (Quick Picks; IRAYAC; BBYA)

Oates, Joyce Carol. *Big Mouth & Ugly Girl.* 2002. *JS.* Matt Doneghy has a big mouth, but he never thinks that his juvenile antics will wind up getting him arrested as a psycho-terrorist. Ursula Riggs is a big girl, a strong girl, a girl who secretly refers to herself as Ugly Girl. She goes through life with a steely gaze and a disregard for what others think of her. She knows the truth about Matt and comes forward to clear him, but his ordeal has branded him an outcast. (BBYA)

Salinger, J. D. *Catcher in the Rye.* 1951. *S.* Alienated and cynical Holden Caulfield is a sixteen-year-old prep school dropout and the protagonist of this classic, and possibly best-known, coming-of-age novel.

Strasser, Todd. *Give a Boy a Gun.* 2000. *JS.* Armed and dangerous sophomores Gary Searle and Brendan Lawlor hold the attendees of a high school dance hostage. (VOYA)

Wallace, Rich. *Playing without a Ball.* 2000. *S.* Being cut from the school basketball team doesn't mean the end of the game for high school senior Jay McLeod, whose life revolves around pickup games and church league games along with school and job. (BBYA; Quick Picks)

Walter, Virginia. *Making Up Megaboy.* 1998. *MJS.* (Alternative format) On Robbie's thirteenth birthday, he shoots and kills an elderly man. This story is told in multiple voices, computer-generated graphics, and a comic book created by Robbie, a tragic loner. (BBYA)

Woodson, Jacqueline. *Hush.* 2002. *MJ.* When her police officer father witnesses a killing by other cops, Toswiah Green's family must go into the Witness Protection Program and give up everything—including their own names. Toswiah becomes Evie Green. (BBYA)

Homelessness and Foster Living

Many teens experience homelessness or foster care. Although there are no definitive statistics on homelessness, one can extrapolate from the National Coalition for the Homeless and the Urban Institute that homeless teens number in the hundreds of thousands in the United States. According to the Child Welfare League of America, in 2000, there were close to 250,000 people between the ages of eleven and eighteen in out-of-home placements. As with other serious issues, teens are interested in reading about what life is like for someone in a completely different situation from their own.

Ashley, Bernard. *Little Soldier.* 2002. *JS.* Kaninda, orphaned in tribal fighting, is taken from Africa to a foster home in London, where he finds gang warfare.

Bardi, Abby. *Book of Fred.* 2001. *S.* Fifteen-year-old Mary Fred is put in foster care when the second of her two brothers dies because of their parents' religious beliefs, which do not allow him to undergo medical treatment. Told from the viewpoints of Mary Fred (nicknamed M. F.), Alice (her librarian foster mom), Heather (her foster sister), and the secretly heroin-addicted Uncle Roy. (BBYA) **Adult**

Brooke, Peggy. *Jake's Orphan.* 2000. *M.* In the 1920s, twelve-year-old Tree and his younger brother Acorn see Tree's chance to work on a North Dakota farm as a way to escape the Minnesota orphanage where they live. (IRA 2001; VOYA)

Brooks, Martha. *Being with Henry.* 2000. *JS.* Laker is kicked out of his house by his pregnant mom after he attacks his stepfather. Homeless, he is befriended by an elderly widower who takes him in. (BBYA)

Burgess, Melvin. *Smack.* 1998. *S.* Gemma and Tar, two teen runaways, discover the truth about the drug culture while they live their fantasy life—and then try to escape from it. Titled *Junk* in the United Kingdom. (Carnegie; Popular Paperbacks; BBYA)

Cooney, Caroline B. *What Child Is This?* 1997. *MJS.* Eight-year-old Katie wants a family for Christmas, and her sixteen-year-old foster brother Matt, who isn't as closed off as he would like to be, tries to help her by hanging a paper bell on a giving tree at work with her wish on it. (BBYA)

Curtis, Christopher Paul. *Bud, Not Buddy.* 1999. *M.* Bud, a ten-year-old orphan in the 1930s, escapes from his foster home to search for the famous bandleader, Herman E. Calloway, who he thinks is his father. (IRA 2000; Newbery Award; BBYA)

Downing, Wick. *Leonardo's Hand.* 2001. *M.* One-handed Nard bounces around from foster home to foster home until he ends up at the Swedenborge farm, an old home-stead that has been surrounded by an upscale subdivision. In an attempt to win an in-ventor's contest, he connects with his foster mother Anna, her granddaughter Julie—and with a ghost who is more than half a century old. Although this title is also listed in the paranormal chapter, teens looking for characters living in foster living ar-rangements will want to know about it.

Flake, Sharon G. *Money Hungry.* 2001. *MJ.* Thirteen-year-old Raspberry is willing to work as hard as it takes to make money, even if it earns her the ridicule of her peers and gets her into trouble in school. She has a good reason for wanting to accumulate money, but that's her business. (Coretta Scott King Honor)

Frank, E. R. *America.* 2002. *S.* America, at age fifteen, is in a psychiatric facility after attempting suicide. It's no wonder. His life has been hell for the most part. When he was little, he had a great foster mom, but when he went on a home visit, his addict mother never returned him. At age five, America ended up living with his brothers af-ter his mother abandoned them. Later, as a runaway, America is found by the authori-ties and returned to his foster mom, but it turns out that she is now elderly and in poor health, and her stepbrother abuses the boy. Gritty and realistic. (BBYA; Quick Picks)

Grant, Cynthia D. *The White Horse.* 1998. *S.* Raina comes from a long line of addicted members of dysfunctional families. Now, pregnant and homeless at age sixteen, she comes to terms with the fact that her boyfriend is dead and her only friend is a teacher who takes her in. (Quick Picks)

Lawrence, Iain. *Ghost Boy.* 2000. *MJ.* Harold Kline lost his father and brother in the war; and his mother has metamorphosed into a stranger. An albino, he's always been an outcast, and Harold flees his tormenters to follow the circus, where he hopes to meet another albino, the famous Cannibal King. (BBYA)

Levine, Gail Carson. *Dave at Night.* 1999. *MJ.* Orphaned Dave sneaks out of the Hebrew Home for Boys to experience jazz and more in New York during the Harlem Renaissance of the 1920s. (BBYA)

Naidoo, Beverley. *No Turning Back.* 1997. *MJ.* Sipho flees his abusive stepfather and his pregnant mother to take to the streets of Johannesburg, South Africa. He joins up with a gang of *malunde,* kids who live on the streets, earning a few coins at a time by lugging groceries and begging.

Nolan, Han. *Born Blue.* 2001. *S.* Annotated in the Life Is Hard subsection of this chapter. (BBYA)

Rottman, S. L. *Hero. MJ.* 1997. Sean learns what it means to be a true hero after he is sentenced to Carbondale Ranch and is parented for the first time in his life.

Rottman, S. L. *Rough Waters.* 1998. *JS.* Two California brothers are left destitute and move to rural Colorado after their parents are killed in an accident. Taken in by an uncle they had not previously known, Scott (age fifteen) and Gregg (age seventeen) are recruited to help him with his rafting business on the Arkansas River. Exciting river rafting details make this a winning adventure story and a sympathetic coming-of-age tale. (Quick Picks)

Springer, Nancy. *Secret Star.* 1997. *M.* Tess Mathis is pretty happy taking care of her family's tiny home and disabled stepfather, but she begins to question why she has no memories before the age of ten and why she can't remember her real parents. Then Kamo, a disfigured boy, turns up claiming to be her brother.

Talbot, Bryan. *The Tale of One Bad Rat.* 1995. *MJS.* This not-to-be-missed tale is annotated in the Graphic Novel section of Chapter 11, "Alternative Formats." (Eisner Award)

Substance Abuse

The prevalence of drugs and drug abuse in our society elicits fears and morbid fascination, making this a popular theme in young adult literature. The harsh realities of addiction are usually portrayed as a trap, one difficult, if not impossible, to escape.

Burgess, Melvin. *Smack.* 1998. *S.* Annotated in the Homelessness and Foster Living section of this chapter. (Carnegie; Popular Paperbacks; BBYA)

Childress, Alice. *A Hero Ain't Nothin' but a Sandwich.* 1973. *MJS.* Thirteen-year-old Benjie is addicted to heroin. (BBYA; YALSA 100 Best Books) [Classic]

Glovach, Linda. *Beauty Queen.* 1998. *S.* Nineteen-year-old Samantha thinks that topless dancing is a good way to make a lot of money fast, but the heroin she needs to be able to do it takes her places she really doesn't want to go. (Quick Picks; IRAYAC)

Grant, Cynthia D. *The White Horse.* 1998. *S.* Annotated in the Homelessness and Foster Living section of this chapter. (Quick Picks)

Sparks, Beatrice, ed. *Go Ask Alice.* 1971. *JS.* This fictional diary, written in the voice of an anonymous teen, tells of how drugs ruin a young girl's life. (BBYA; YALSA 100 Best Books)

Stoehr, Shelley. *Wannabe.* 1997. *S.* Catherine, a native of New York's Little Italy, takes a job waiting tables at the private men's club frequented by local mobsters. She plans to go on to college and tries to keep her older brother from falling in with the gangsters but finds that she is falling in love with a gangster herself. She is also developing a real addiction to cocaine.

Williams, Lori Aurelia. *Shayla's Double Brown Baby Blues.* 2001. *JS.* In this sequel to *When Kambia Elaine Flew in from Neptune* (annotated in the Sexual Abuse section of this chapter) Shayla and Kambia become friends with Lemm, a sweet-talking thirteen-year-old alcoholic.

Missing Teens

An issue that hit its peak in the mid-1990s, the theme of missing teens, or of children who went missing and are now teens, is still with us, even though the faces have disappeared from the milk cartons and reappeared on the news and in flyers on supermarket bulletin boards. In light of teen-parent conflicts, teens may wonder if their parents are really theirs, if they were adopted, or just how they ended up in this strange family. More recent fiction about missing teens features protagonists who have been kidnapped by monstrous people and escape in one way or another to return to their families. Often these novels include strong elements of suspense and mystery.

Alphin, Elaine Marie. *Counterfeit Son.* 2000. *JS.* Cameron's father was a monster, the kind that kidnapped, tortured, and murdered young boys. After Pop is killed in a shootout with the police, fourteen-year-old Cameron assumes the identity of one of the victims. Neil Lacey's parents buy Cameron's claim that he is their missing son, but his siblings do not. When one of Pop's cronies reenters the picture, they are all in peril. (Edgar Award; Quick Picks)

Atkins, Catherine. *When Jeff Comes Home.* 1999. *S.* Annotated in the Sexual Abuse section of this chapter. (BBYA; Quick Picks; IRAYAC)

Cooney, Caroline. The Face on the Milk Carton series. *MJS.* Four titles of psychological suspense follow Janie's life and her coming to terms with her past, after she discovers, at age fifteen, that she was kidnapped when she was three years old.

The Face on the Milk Carton. 1990. (Film: *The Face on the Milk Carton*) When fifteen-year-old Janie Johnson recognizes her picture as a three-year-old on a milk carton, she starts a quest for her real identity. Film

Whatever Happened to Janie? 1993. (Film: *The Face on the Milk Carton*) Janie is reunited with the family that has spent years hoping and praying for her return. (BBYA) Film

The Voice on the Radio. 1996. Jenny/Janie's story continues. Annotated in Chapter 3, "Contemporary Life." (IRAYAC; BBYA)

What Janie Found. 2000. Janie discovers that her kidnapper is not really dead, so she sets off with her brother Brian and neighbor Reeve to find a conclusion to her tale.

Sykes, Shelley. *For Mike.* 1998. *JS.* The power of friendship and other worldly powers combine to help Jeff solve the mystery of his friend's strange disappearance. A gripping, suspenseful story.

Wynne-Jones, Tim. *Stephen Fair.* 1998. *JS.* Fifteen-year-old Stephen is worried that he has started to experience the same nightmares that led to his brother's disappearance when he was fifteen. Readers will realize early on that not all is as it should be in the quirky ark in which what remains of the Fair family live. (Canadian Library Association Book of the Year Award)

Chapter 3

Contemporary Life

Some teen readers enjoy books set in the here and now rather than in the shadowy past, a magical other world, or the distant future. They look for stories that feature protagonists like them—teens who live in their world and face the same challenges they face—teens with whom they can identify. For much of the history of young adult literature, issue-driven novels with contemporary settings have overshadowed other genres.

This chapter contains stories about common teen experiences—growing up, becoming an adult or young adult, playing sports, falling in love, having friends—all in a contemporary setting. The problems faced by teens in this chapter are generally the everyday problems involved in coming of age rather than the more intense problems faced in Chapter 2, "Issues." The tone of these novels is generally lighter than that found in issues fiction, and characters less troubled and intense, but realistic characters, settings, and stories are just as important to contemporary fiction as they are to issues novels. As with issues, teens generally look for protagonists their own age or older; male teens may specifically seek out books with male protagonists.

Series that portray slices of everyday teen life are common to this genre. These titles allow teens to follow specific characters through a series of challenges.

This chapter is organized by types that share a number of common characteristics—coming-of-age, romance, sports, humor, and series fiction.

Types

Coming of Age

One of the major challenges we face as human beings is going from child status, in which we are dependent on parents or guardians, to being an adult, responsible for our own lives. The *bildungsroman,* or coming-of-age novel, most often involves the teen years, the important period during which the transition from childhood to adulthood is made. These novels appeal to teens because they often portray characters and events with which it is easy for teen readers to identify. Classic literary tales, such as *Tom Jones, David Copperfield, Emma, Tom Sawyer,* and even Homer's *Ulysses,* fall into this category, as do many traditional folktales.

The following novels focus on a character seeking identity as he or she grows to adulthood. Contemporary fiction is all about characters, and the protagonist always undergoes a change—physical, emotional, or both. Invariably the change is for the better, even if tragedy is experienced along the way, and these books often have happy endings, or at least a sense of acceptance. Some coming-of-age novels feature serious and thoughtful growth, while at the other end of the spectrum, humor plays an important role in the process of emerging from childhood. Romance and relationships often factor in as well, but the focus is on the transformation of the main character.

Anderson, Laurie Halse. *Catalyst.* 2002. *S.* Motherless Kate, the eighteen-year-old daughter of a minister, only wants one thing—to get into the Massachusetts Institute of Technology (MIT). Her life is thrust into turmoil when Teri, a total outcast at school, is brought, with her little brother Mikey, into the parsonage to live while their home is repaired after a devastating fire. While Kate thinks in mathematical, scientific terms and the chemical elements, Teri is all about anger. Then the letter from MIT comes, and Kate's tightly controlled life begins to unravel. (BBYA)

Baskin, Nora Raleigh. *What Every Girl (Except Me) Knows.* 2001. *M.* At age twelve, motherless Gabby tries to figure out how to be a woman.

Bauer, Joan. *Backwater.* 1999. *MJ.* Unlike the rest of her lawyer-laden family, Ivy Breedlove, age sixteen, has a passion for history. She takes over writing her family's history when her Aunt Jo, "stuck in the backwater," has to give it up. This book features adventure, humor, and a dash of romance.

Bertrand, Diane Gonzales. *Trino's Time.* 2001. *J.* At age fifteen, Trino struggles to balance family, work, and school in this sequel to *Trino's Choice,* annotated in Chapter 10, "Multicultural Fiction."

Brooks, Martha. *Bone Dance.* 1996. *JS.* This reflective, thought-provoking, and eloquent tale is told from two viewpoints. Lonny's loving, widowed stepfather has sacrificed his inheritance, acreage with an Indian burial mound, so that Lonny can have a future. Alexandra, who never knew her drifting, alcoholic cowboy father, has inherited the piece of land from her dad. Both Lonny and Alexandra experience dreams—Lonny's filled with terrifying spirits that he unearthed digging in the mound as a child, and Alex's comforting visitations from her stepgrandfather, who is now in the spirit world. This spiritual trek, filled with loss and love set against the magnificent backdrop of the wide-open Manitoba landscape, touches the hearts of its readers. (BBYA; CLA YA Book Award)

Cabot, Meg. The Princess Diaries series. *MJS.* Annotated in the Contemporary section of Chapter 11, "Alternative Formats." (Quick Picks; BBYA; IRAYAC)

Chbosky, Stephen. *The Perks of Being a Wallflower.* 1999. *S.* High school freshman Charlie faces dating, drugs, and his own childhood sexual abuse in this poignant and sometimes amusing story. (Popular Paperbacks; BBYA; Quick Picks)

Cohn, Rachel. *Gingerbread.* 2002. *MJS.* Cyd Charisse has gotten into some trouble in her sixteen years, but right now she's pretty happy with her surfer boyfriend Shrimp, her job as a barista at Java's coffeehouse, a dear friend named Sugar Pie (who lives in a nursing home), and her telepathic doll Gingerbread. The only thing that isn't going well is her relationship with her mom, Nancy, and her stepdad, Sid. When Cyd spends the night at Shrimp's place, Sid and Nancy ship her off to her bio-dad's place in New York, whom she remembers meeting only once. Three weeks in New York are a real learning experience for this independent teen. (BBYA; Quick Picks)

Cooney, Caroline B. *The Voice on the Radio.* 1996. *MJS.* Janie discovers that sometimes even the best of friends and most admirable of young men can slip up—with devastating effects. Reeve Shields has finally gotten his chance to d-jay on the college radio station, but his mind goes blank. To fill in the time, he starts to tell the story of Janie, a story that has been cried out onto his shoulder, told to him by his beloved and vulnerable Janie. He knows it is wrong to betray her trust and to send out her most intimate feelings and fears over the airwaves to anyone listening, but he just can't help himself. The adulation of the listeners won't let him stop, but what if Janie finds out? What will it do to her? This is the third book in a series following *The Face on the Milk Carton* and *Whatever Happened to Janie?* Annotated in Chapter 2, "Issues." (BBYA; IRAYAC)

Creech, Sharon. *Bloomability.* 1998. *M.* Although she's only twelve, Dinnie has moved thirteen times, and now she's been sent to Switzerland to live with an aunt and uncle. A colorful cast of characters—from Dinnie's crazy Grandma Fiorelli to her oh-so-Southern aunts Grace and Tillie—populates this funny and touching tale. (IRAYAC)

Creech, Sharon. *Chasing Redbird.* 1997. *MJ.* The summer thirteen-year-old Zinny Taylor mourns her beloved Aunt Jessie's death, she also clears a historic trail. (BBYA; IRAYAC)

Creech, Sharon. *The Wanderer.* 2000. *M.* Annotated in the At Sea section in Chapter 4. (BBYA)

Crutcher, Chris. *Running Loose.* 1983. *JS.* Louie Banks's senior year is eventful. After spending his entire summer training so that he can make the football team, he takes a stand against the unprincipled coach. Then he finds the girl of his dreams, only to have tragedy intervene. (BBYA; YALSA 100 Best Books)

Davis, Terry. *If Rock and Roll Were a Machine.* 1992. *JS.* Seventeen-year-old Bert has been trying to regain a modicum of self-esteem years after a sadistic fifth-grade teacher destroyed his emotional well-being. Now he's ready to buy a motorcycle. Although Terry Davis does not publish often, both of his YA novels are powerful gems. His sports novel, *Vision Quest,* was recently reissued; it was made into a movie that was popular with many parents of today's teens. (BBYA)

Dessen, Sarah. *Keeping the Moon.* 1999. *JS.* Colie Sparks goes to a small town to stay with her eccentric Aunt Mira while her mother, aerobics queen and fitness guru Kiki Sparks, embarks on a European tour. The summer starts off as a great getaway for Colie because no one knows that she was formerly fat or that at her school in the city she has no friends and is called the "golf-course slut." After she starts a job and becomes friends with her co-waitresses and a unique young man, she begins to come out of her shell. But then her nemesis from school appears. (BBYA; Quick Picks; IRAYAC)

Dessen, Sarah. *That Summer.* 1996. *JS.* Haven is fifteen. She is too tall, her sister is planning a wedding, her father is getting married again, and nothing seems to be going right. (BBYA)

Dessen, Sarah. *This Lullaby.* 2002. *JS.* With a mom married numerous times and a musician dad who left her nothing but a well-known song he wrote for her without ever knowing her, high school grad Remy is cynical to the max. She won't go out with musicians, and she has a whole canon of laws relating to romantic relationships. But when an ever-so-persistent musician named Dexter shows up, Remy finds that the barriers she has so carefully erected are beginning to crumble. (BBYA)

Fletcher, Ralph. *Spider Boy.* 1997. *MJ.* After moving to a new town, Bobby finds a new friend and an enemy who kills his beloved tarantula. An affecting tale for the youngest end of the YA spectrum.

Frank, Hillary. *Better than Running at Night.* 2002. *S.* Ellie's freshman year at art school leads her right into the bed of the campus player while a fellow student yearns for her. (BBYA)

Friesen, Gayle. *Janey's Girl.* 1998. *MJ.* On a visit to her grandmother's, fourteen-year-old Claire discovers a half-brother and the father she had never met. (BBYA; CLA YA Book Award)

Hirsch, Karen, ed. *Mind Riot: Coming of Age in Comix.* 1997. *MJS.* Annotated in Chapter 11, "Alternative Formats," in the Graphic Novels section.

Hite, Sid. *A Hole in the World.* 2001. *MJ.* Sent to a farm for the summer after being caught lying, fifteen-year-old Paul comes to know, through Hennley's dog, a dead man, whom he resembles, and the people who knew the man.

Hobbs, Valerie. *Tender.* 2001. *MJS.* Liv, who dresses and wears her makeup like a Goth, was raised by her grandmother. Her father took off to be an abalone fisherman after her mother died giving birth to Liv. Now, with Gran suddenly gone, sixteen-year-old Liv is sent to California to live with her father.

Honeycutt, Natalie. *Twilight in Grace Falls.* 1997. *M.* A lumber town falls apart after a fire and the subsequent closing of the local mill. Told from the viewpoint of eleven-year-old Dasie Jensen.

Klass, David. *Screen Test.* 1997. *MJ.* Liz is gorgeous and talented, and she ends up in a Hollywood movie. But is the glitzy life for her, or should she return to New Jersey to finish high school? (IRAYAC)

Koertge, Ron. *Stoner & Spaz: A Love Story.* 2002. *JS.* Ben Bancroft is a sixteen-year-old orphaned film buff with CP (cerebral palsy), who lives with his over-protective grandmother. Colleen Minou is a major stoner who doesn't see Ben's CP as a handicap, only as a difference. As Colleen tries to fight her addictions, Ben tries to live like a teen. With the mentoring of a neighbor, he makes his own movie. (BBYA; Quick Picks)

Lawrence, Iain. *The Lightkeeper's Daughter.* 2002. *JS.* A literary tale of a seventeen-year-old who returns with her three-year-old daughter to the isolated island where she and her brother grew up with only each other and their parents for company. (BBYA)

Lynch, Chris. *Freewill.* 2001. *S.* Living with his grandparents, orphaned Will is a decidedly strange outcast. Claiming to be a pilot, he spends hours in wood shop at school. When kids start dying, perhaps committing suicide, he places wooden sculptures at the death sites. A complex, complicated story with many plot twists; not for readers who like a straightforward narrative. (BBYA; Booklist; Printz-Honor)

Mackler, Carolyn. *Love and Other Four-Letter Words.* 2000. *MJS.* "Absolutely, completely average" sixteen-year-old Sammie's life is thrown into chaos when her parents split up and she has to move to New York City with her broken-hearted mom. Taking her dog to a park, Sammie meets Phoebe, a girl who can see what kind of dog a person would be if he or she were a dog. A cute boy in the elevator and an old family friend may add up to romance as Sammie discovers that her old life back in Ithaca is over. (Quick Picks; IRAYAC)

Marchetta, Melina. *Looking for Alibrandi.* 1999. *JS.* Seventeen-year-old Josie Alibrandi is different from her schoolmates at the Catholic girl's school in Sydney. For one thing, she's illegitimate; for another, she's attending on scholarship; and then, too, she is torn between her "Australianess" and her Italian heritage. (BBYA; IRAYAC; Australian Book of the Year Award)

Meyer, Carolyn. *Jubilee Journey.* 1997. *MJ.* Annotated in the Mixed Heritage section of Chapter 10, "Multicultural Fiction." (BBYA)

Moore, Martha. *Angels on the Roof.* 1997. *M.* Shelby would like to stay put for once, but her flaky mom drags her off to a small Texas town to meet the elderly woman who raised her. Shelby discovers some things about her mother and learns the secret of the father she never met. Red Valley, peopled by likable but offbeat characters, provides an interesting backdrop for Shelby's quest to find her history and herself.

Moore, Martha. *Under the Mermaid Angel.* 1995. *MJ.* When thirty-year-old Roxanne, a free spirit, moves into the trailer next door in Ida, Texas, thirteen-year-old Jesse Cowan discovers much about life and comes to terms with her brother's death. Roxanne, who sports a tattoo and attracts men to the local diner, instigates a going-away party for Mr. Arthur, the eccentric owner of Ida's main attraction—a dilapidated wax museum. Jesse becomes involved with two other misfits when they start a school newspaper. (BBYA)

Myers, Walter Dean. *Handbook for Boys: A Novel.* 2002. *MJ.* Life lessons are learned when sixteen-year-old Jimmy Lynch is sentenced to community service in a barbershop. Through the conversations of a couple old men, Jimmy learns what it really means to be a man.

Nolan, Han. *Send Me Down a Miracle.* 1996. *MJ.* An artistic experiment in a small southern town throws a fourteen-year-old preacher's daughter and her town into a maelstrom of religious fervor.

Okimoto, Jean Davis. *The Eclipse of Moonbeam Dawson.* 1997. *MJ.* Fifteen-year-old Moonbeam has grown up on a commune, but the biracial (Haida and white) teen wants to be "normal."

Pennebaker, Ruth. *Conditions of Love.* 1999. *MJ.* Fourteen-year-old Sarah's life spirals out of control a year after losing her father, and she finds herself questioning everything she believed in.

Powell, Randy. *Tribute to Another Dead Rock Star.* 2003. *J.* Grady's grandma and her new hubby are off for a short vacation, while Grady goes to Seattle to attend a metal concert tribute to his mother and to visit his younger, developmentally disabled brother who has been living with his grandmother. While staying with his brother's family, who have gotten religion in a big way, Grady ponders his future. Should he move in with them or go to Europe for a year? At age fifteen, it's hard to make these decisions, but with a dad who died without even knowing Grady was on the way and a rock star mom who died of an overdose three years ago, Grady has to decide for himself. (BBYA).

Saldana, Rene, Jr. *The Jumping Tree.* 2001. *MJ.* As he goes from sixth to eighth grade, Rey learns who he is and where he fits into the world as a Mexican American.

Salisbury, Graham. *Shark Bait.* 1997. *MJS.* Mokes's dad, the chief of police, has told him to be in by six on the day that the navy puts into port on their Hawaiian island. Mokes's friend Booley is going to get into a fight with a sailor, and Mokes really wants to be there, but he's trying to do what's right. He knows he must defy his father when he discovers that the service revolver that his uncle gave him has been stolen and that the fight may turn into something far more deadly.

Savage, Deborah. *Kotuku.* 2002. *JS.* Seventeen-year-old Wim Thorpe has always seen a tattooed man who no one else believes is there. Her parents worry that, since the death from anorexia of her best friend, Wim does nothing but work. When great-aunt Kia moves in to wait for a nursing home space to become available, Wim discovers someone in her family who has her same looks and also sees the tattooed man. She also meets a Maori researcher named David, who has come from New Zealand to Provincetown to do historical research using their family's documents. (BBYA)

Shoup, Barbara. *Stranded in Harmony.* 1997. *JS.* Football captain and high school senior Lucas Cantrell is unhappy with his seemingly perfect life. To get away from it all, he starts spending time with an elderly, bedridden cousin. Then he meets Allie, an older woman with many secrets who has recently moved to quiet Harmony. (BBYA; IRAYAC)

Stanley, Diane. *A Time Apart.* 1999. *M.* Thirteen-year-old Ginny is shipped off to England to live with her archeologist father when her mother has to undergo cancer treatment. In England, Ginny lives in a re-created Iron Age village, giving this story a bit of a historical flavor. (BBYA; IRAYAC)

Thomas, Rob. *Rats Saw God.* 1996. *JS.* Steve York, an eighteen-year-old stoner and National Merit finalist, is both a likable and a believable character. To graduate and make up the credit for failing English, a school counselor, who happens to be pretty cool, requires Steve to turn in one hundred typewritten pages on any topic. Steve details his parents' divorce, life with his overachieving astronaut father, rebellion, first love, and heartbreak all with achingly true realism. The sometimes laugh-out-loud narrative alternates between Steve's senior year in San Diego and his first two years of high school in Houston. (Popular Paperbacks; BBYA; Quick Picks)

Van Draanen, Wendelin. *Flipped.* 2001. *MJS.* Told from Julianna's and Bryce's alternating points of view, this story details the lives of these next-door neighbors from second through eighth grade.

Wieler, Diana. *Drive.* 1999. *S.* After his dad has a heart attack, Jens, a high school senior, drops out of school to help support his family. When he is fired from the car dealership where he works, he takes a truck from work and hits the road with his brother, who tries to earn money with his musical talents.

Williams-Garcia, Rita. *Every Time a Rainbow Dies.* 2001. *JS.* This novel begins as sixteen-year-old Thulani tends his homing pigeons on the rooftop of the New York brownstone his mother left him and his brother before going back to Jamaica to die. While going about the task, he sees a girl being raped in the alley. Dashing to her rescue, Thulani drives off the attackers and covers the girl with his shirt. In the following weeks, he watches for her, trying to discover every little thing about this girl who wears brightly colored skirts, who is so secretive that she will not even tell him where she is from, though he guesses Haiti. Ysa's pride and determination are tempered by her inability to face up to the damage done by the rape. (BBYA)

Romance

Romance plays a major role in the life of most teens. Even teens who are not involved in romantic relationships wonder if they should be or may wish that they were. Romances written for teens are similar to those written for adults, focusing on the development of a relationship between boldly drawn characters. Emotional in tone, these books often contain highly descriptive passages, as well as lively dialogue. The major difference between YA romance and the romance genre in general is that romances for teens don't necessarily require the involved parties to live "happily ever after," as long as love and growth are involved. One other way that teen ro-mance fiction differs from adult romance is that several male YA authors write in the genre from a male point of view. Boys as well as girls experience the agony and ecstasy of young love.

YA literature does not avoid the controversial issues surrounding interpersonal rela-tionships. Judy Blume's classic *Forever* raised more than a few eyebrows when it was pub-lished in 1975 because of its frank discussions of sex, and, perhaps more important, because nothing bad happened to the young lovers as a result of having sex. Nancy Garden's *Annie on My Mind,* a love story involving two girls, has had numerous challenges since it first appeared in 1982.

Because romance plays such an enormous role in the lives of teens, it appears in almost every genre and every time period. Some teen readers will prefer romance with a historical setting, while others may prefer a science fiction setting or paranormal theme. Readers are encouraged to use the subject index to find titles with themes of love and romance com-bined with other genres. Some romances featured here are deadly serious, others are light-hearted romps, but all are set in the here and now. The full gamut of romance for teens is examined in the 2001 short story collection *Love and Sex,* edited by Michael Cart, annotated here.

Bernardo, Anilu. *Loves Me, Loves Me Not.* 1998. *JS.* Maggie has a crush on Zach. Justin has a crush on Maggie. Susie has a crush on Carlos. Is it possible for a Cuban Ameri-can girl and a bigot to get together, or is there a better match? (Popular Paperbacks)

Blume, Judy. *Forever.* 1975. *S.* High school seniors Katherine and Michael fall in love and decide to have sex responsibly. Nobody dies, and nobody gets pregnant. A classic in YA fiction.

Boock, Paula. *Dare Truth or Promise.* 1999. *JS.* New Zealand high school senior Louie Angelo has her life mapped out—continued high school achievement followed by law school. But she doesn't count on falling in love with Willa, who lives over a pub.

Cabot, Meg. *All American Girl.* 2002. *JS.* Fifteen-year-old Samantha has lots going on in her life—having a crush on her sister's boyfriend, dyeing all her clothes black, and saving the president's life.

Cart, Michael, ed. *Love & Sex.* 2001. *S.* (Short Stories) Leading YA authors contrib-uted stories that deal with teen sexuality in which romance can play a major role.

Clark, Catherine. *Truth or Dairy.* 2000. *JS.* Courtney's boyfriend has broken up with her and gone off to college, leaving her to her senior year and a job at Truth or Dairy, but now Grant has come into her life. (Popular Paperbacks)

Dessen, Sarah. *Keeping the Moon.* 1999. *JS.* Annotated in the Coming of Age section of this chapter. (IRAYAC; BBYA; Quick Picks)

Dessen, Sarah. *This Lullaby.* 2002. *JS.* Annotated in the Coming of Age section of this chapter.

Draper, Sharon M. *Romiette and Julio.* 1999. *MJS.* African American Romiette and Hispanic Julio, two sixteen-year-olds, have a relationship, despite the disapproval of others. (IRAYAC)

Ferris, Jean. *Of Sound Mind.* 2001. *MJS.* High school senior Theo is very interested in an exciting-looking girl he sees at a bus stop. But when she signs to him, he is dismayed because, as the only hearing person in his family, he is not interested in having another deaf person in his life. It turns out that Ivy, like Theo, is a hearing person who is also fluent in sign language, and she runs her own catering business. (BBYA)

Frank, Lucy. *Oy, Joy!* 1999. *MJ.* Great-Uncle Max moves in to Joy's crowded family apartment and sets out to find a boyfriend for the ninth-grader. (Popular Paperbacks; VOYA)

Garden, Nancy. *Annie on My Mind.* 1982. *S.* Annotated in the Sexual Identity section of Chapter 2, "Issues." (BBYA; Popular Paperbacks; YALSA 100 Best Books)

Garden, Nancy. *Good Moon Rising.* 1996. *JS.* When Jan is passed over for the role of Elizabeth in *The Crucible,* she never suspects that she will fall in love with Kerry, the girl who does get the role. (Lambda Award)

Johnson, Kathleen Jeffrie. *The Parallel Universe of Liars.* 2002. *S.* Fifteen-year-old Robin has a gorgeous mother and stepmother, and she lives next door to a gorgeous male model who has a gorgeous girlfriend. Although she is overweight and her only friend has moved away, a delicious-looking butterscotch boy has moved in and seems to really like her. The problem is, it seems that everyone who is in a relationship is cheating on his or her mate, which makes her feel like she's living in a totally different world.

Korman, Gordon. *Son of the Mob.* 2002. *JS.* The ultimate Romeo and Juliet tale. The son of a mob boss falls in love with the daughter of an FBI agent in this humorous tale. Even basic communications become problematic when your girlfriend's dad is the agent in charge of bugging your house. (BBYA; Quick Picks)

Lane, Dakota. *Johnny Voodoo.* 1996. *S.* Following her mother's death, fifteen-year-old Deirdre has moved from New York City to a small Louisiana bayou with her younger brother and their father. In her new environment, she finds herself drawn to a handsome and mysterious teen dropout called Johnny Voodoo. (Popular Paperbacks; BBYA; IRAYAC)

Mackler, Carolyn. *Love and Other Four-Letter Words.* 2000. *MJS.* Annotated in the Coming of Age section of this chapter. (Quick Picks; IRAYAC)

Mosier, Elizabeth. *My Life as a Girl.* 2000. *JS.* Jamie starts a new life as a freshman at Bryn Mawr, far away from her gambling dad and her former boyfriend. But then Buddy turns up.

Qualey, Marsha. *Revolutions of the Heart.* 1993. *JS.* Seventeen-year-old Cory is having an eventful spring in her strictly segregated Wisconsin hometown. First, her mother dies, and then she falls in love with Mac, a Native American. (BBYA; Quick Picks)

Randle, Kristen D. *Breaking Rank.* 1999. *JS.* When seventeen-year-old Casy starts tutoring Thomas Fairbairn, a member of a strange clique that eschews traditional education as well as drugs and violence, they find out that even for all their differences, they have enough common ground to fall in love. (BBYA)

Sanchez, Alex. *Rainbow Boys.* 2001. *JS.* Jason, Kyle, and Nelson are gay, but very different from one another. They attend the same high school, but Nelson is very much "out," and Jason, a jock, has a girlfriend. (BBYA)

Sones, Sonya. *What My Mother Doesn't Know.* 2001. *MJS.* Life and love in high school for fourteen-year-old Sophie. (BBYA; Quick Picks)

Spinelli, Jerry. *Stargirl.* 2000. *MJS.* Stargirl is odd, to say the least. When she starts a new school, theories fly as people try to understand her bizarre apparel, ukulele playing, and random acts of kindness. The story is told from the viewpoint of sixteen-year-old Leo, who is fascinated with her but tries to change her, only to discover that he liked her the way she was. (BBYA; IRAYAC)

Strasser, Todd. *Girl Gives Birth to Own Prom Date.* 1996. *MJS.* (Film: *Drive Me Crazy*) When Nicole's dream date for prom asks another girl, she decides to remake her neighbor, Chase, into the perfect prom date. This book was reissued under the title *How I Created My Perfect Prom Date,* and when the movie was released under the title *Drive Me Crazy,* the book was reissued under that title. Film

Thesman, Jean. *The Moonstones.* 1998. *JS.* Fifteen-year-old Jane meets local boy Carey when she travels to Royal Bay with her mother, who is working on settling her grandmother's estate. What would a girl do for a boyfriend who's this attractive? (IRAYAC)

Williams, Carol Lynch. *My Angelica.* 1999. *MJ.* Fifteen-year-old Sage enters a writing contest with a sexy historical romance—and real-life romance finds her as well.

Wilson, Jacqueline. *Girls in Love.* 2002. *MJ.* Starting the ninth grade, Ellie worries that she will be the only girl in her class without a boyfriend. In fact, her two best friends, Magda and Nadine, have already found boyfriends. Book 1 of the Girls Trilogy series.

Young, Karen Romano. *The Beetle and Me: A Love Story.* 1999. *MJS.* Daisy's first love is her purple 1957 Volkswagen Beetle, which she plans to restore to pristine condition before her sixteenth birthday. But then a couple of boys enter the equation. (BBYA)

Sports

Many teens participate or have participated in sports. Sports novels, embedded with the excitement and action of the game, can also provide a larger context for exploring other themes and subjects. The sports theme lends itself to greater analogies of competition, winning, authority, fair play, and doing one's best; it provides a rich area of meaning to which the reader can relate. Sports novels, usually set in contemporary times, also often address serious problems such as incest, loss of a loved one, or child abuse. Teens with an interest in sports enjoy reading sport novels, and these books can pull in some reluctant readers because of the subject matter, fast pace, and compelling underlying themes.

There is a great deal of diversity within this subgenre, and it behooves readers' advisors to familiarize themselves with specific authors and titles. For example, Thomas Dygard, a prolific writer of sports novels, produces novels that explore the sports themselves more intensely than most other sports novels, and he has written about several sports. Books by James W. Bennett and Chris Crutcher, on the other hand, use sports as settings for stories that feature teens dealing with serious social and personal issues. Some teen readers might prefer books about specific sports, but usually fans of this subgenre are equally interested in all sports.

Bennett, James W. *Blue Star Rapture.* 1998. *S.* College recruiters expect T. J. Nucci to help his learning-disabled friend Tyron circumvent the system so he can be eligible to play basketball for a college.

Bennett, James W. *Plunking Reggie Jackson.* 2001. *S.* High school senior Coley is a great baseball pitcher, but that doesn't seem to be enough to live up to his bad-boy big brother, who died in a drunken boating accident during spring training his first year in the pros. Coley's life is further complicated by Bree, a sexy sophomore who has problems of her own.

Bennett, James W. *Squared Circle.* 1995. *S.* High school All-American basketball player Sonny Youngblood enters Southern Illinois University on full scholarship and learns some harsh truths. (BBYA)

Bloor, Edward. *Tangerine.* 1997. *MJS.* Soccer. Annotated in the Physical Challenges section of Chapter 2, "Issues." (IRAYAC; YALSA 100 Best Books; BBYA; Popular Paperbacks)

Brooks, Bruce. *The Moves Make the Man.* 1984. *MJS.* Jerome, the only black student in an all-white school, has all the moves that make him a great basketball player. The only way that straightforward baseball player Bix will be allowed to visit his mom in the mental hospital is to win at basketball, and Jerome may be the only one who can show him the right moves. (Popular Paperbacks; Newbery Honor; YALSA 100 Best Books)

Carter, Alden R. *Bull Catcher.* 1996. *S.* Bull and Jeff experience high school as it relates to baseball in Wisconsin. (BBYA; Quick Picks)

Cochran, Thomas. *Roughnecks.* 1997. *JS.* Travis Cody made a crucial mistake the last time his team, the Oil Camp Roughnecks, played against the Pineview Pelicans. Now the Louisiana High School football championship and his hoped-for college scholarship hinge on a single game. (IRAYAC)

Coleman, Evelyn. *Born in Sin.* 2001. *MJS.* Denied her chance in an academically challenging summer program that will help her reach her goal of attending medical school, fourteen-year-old Keisha is sent to a day camp for at-risk teens. At camp she fights for swimming lessons as a safety issue and discovers that she has Olympic swimming potential. (IRAYAC)

Crutcher, Chris. *Athletic Shorts: Six Short Stories.* 1991. *MJS.* (Short Stories) Terrific stories, including "A Brief Moment in the Life of Angus Bethune," one of the funniest and most touching short stories of all time. The movie *Angus* claims to be based on the story, but it is virtually unrecognizable. (Popular Paperbacks; YALSA 100 Best Books; BBYA)

Crutcher, Chris. *Ironman.* 1995. *JS.* Seventeen-year-old triathlete Bo Brewster finds himself in Mr. Nak's anger management class. Gritty real-life situations and laugh-out-loud humor combine in one of Crutcher's finest works. (Popular Paperbacks; BBYA; YALSA 100 Best Books)

Crutcher, Chris. *Running Loose.* 1983. *JS.* Annotated in the Coming of Age section of this chapter. (YALSA 100 Best Books; BBYA)

Crutcher, Chris. *Staying Fat for Sarah Byrnes.* 1993. *JS.* Moby, an eighteen-year-old swimmer, works to keep on some of the weight that made him an outcast so he can continue to fit in with his best friend Sarah Byrnes, who was horribly disfigured by burns as a child. (Popular Paperbacks; BBYA; YALSA 100 Best Books)

Crutcher, Chris. *Whale Talk.* 2001. *MJS.* This book about a swim team made up of outsiders is annotated in the Outsiders section of Chapter 2, "Issues." (BBYA)

Davis, Terry. *Vision Quest: A Wrestling Story.* 1979. *JS.* Louden Swain makes weight and becomes a wrestling legend. Rereleased in 2002. (BBYA) [Film]

Deuker, Carl. *Night Hoops.* 2000. *JS.* Life is made up of choices, and as Nick enters high school, he chooses to win his father's attention and approval with basketball. (BBYA; Alex Award; IRAYAC)

Deuker, Carl. *On the Devil's Court.* 1988. *JS.* Joe Faust finds himself becoming a basketball success but keeps thinking back to that night in the deserted gym when, feeling lonely and inadequate, he just may have made a deal with the devil. (BBYA; YALSA 100 Best Books)

Deuker, Carl. *Painting the Black.* 1997. *JS.* Ryan Ward finds friendship and a weird fascination with his new neighbor Josh Daniels the summer before their senior year of high school. Josh is a talented baseball pitcher and talks Ryan into catching for him as he practices. Ryan, born too early, suffered many health problems as a child. He had only a brief period of wellness when he discovered he was a natural athlete before a tragic accident sidelined him. Now Ryan finds that he has talent as a catcher and decides to go out for baseball. Inspired by his wise grandfather, he develops into an excellent catcher, but along the way Ryan finds he must question the direction his life is taking, as well as the meaning of friendship and loyalty. (BBYA; IRAYAC)

Dygard, Thomas J. *Second Stringer.* 1998. *MJS.* Kevin Taylor may be on the high school football team, but his position is bench—that is, until Rob Montgomery, the star quarterback, is injured. Coached by Rob, Kevin ends up in a high-pressure position. (IRAYAC)

Glenn, Mel. *Jump Ball: A Basketball Season in Poems.* 1997. *JS.* (Poetry) Tower High's winning season is told in poems. (BBYA)

Jenkins, A. M. *Damage.* 2001. *JS.* Being a seventeen-year-old football star is not enough to make Austin want to go on living. (BBYA)

Klass, David. *Danger Zone.* 1996. *JS.* Basketball legend and high school junior Jimmy Doyle has been picked for a dream team and sent to Italy to play, but he never expected to run into international terrorists. (BBYA; Popular Paperbacks; IRAYAC)

Koss, Amy Goldman. *Strike Two.* 2001. *M.* Gwen and Jess—teammates, best friends, and cousins—find themselves on opposite sides when their fathers, twins who work for the same newspaper, end up on opposing sides in a strike that destroys the girls' softball season.

Macy, Sue, ed. *Girls Got Game: Sports Stories and Poems.* 2001. *MJ.* (Short Stories, Poetry) Stories and poems about girls involved in sports.

Myers, Walter Dean. *Slam!* 1996. *JS.* Slam's coach doesn't see basketball as the ticket that will get this seventeen-year-old out of the inner city. (BBYA; Quick Picks; Popular Paperbacks; Coretta Scott King Award; IRAYAC; YALSA 100 Best Books)

Powell, Randy. *Run If You Dare.* 2001. *JS.* Fourteen-year-old Gardner has a mom who works too much and a dad who has been laid off and is falling further away from ever going back to work again, but Gardner still manages to make the track team.

Powell, Randy. *Three Clams and an Oyster.* 2002. *JS.* After the death of their teammate and friend, a four-man flag football team loses another member to substance abuse and depression. Their quest for a new member takes them into the path of a very determined girl. (BBYA)

Ritter, John. *Over the Wall.* 2000. *MJ.* Annotated in Chapter 2, "Issues."

Rottman, S. L. *Head above Water.* 1999. *JS.* High school junior Skye swims, hoping to get a scholarship, takes care of her Down's syndrome brother, and tries to fend off the sexual advances of her boyfriend. (BBYA).

Sweeney, Joyce. *Players.* 2000. *MJS.* High school senior Corey is captain of the St. Philip's basketball team. He has the talent to make all-city, but when Noah joins the team, everything falls apart. Could Noah really be so evil as to attempt to ruin lives in return for a place on the team? (Quick Picks)

Wallace, Rich. *Playing without a Ball.* 2000. *JS.* This basketball tale is annotated in the Outsiders section of Chapter 2, "Issues." (BBYA; Quick Picks)

Wallace, Rich. *Shots on Goal.* 1997. *MJS.* It looks as if fifteen-year-old Bones's underdog soccer team is going to make it all the way to the district playoffs.

Wallace, Rich. *Wrestling Sturbridge.* 1996. *JS.* Ben needs to escape his small Pennsylvania town, and he needs to prove to himself that he doesn't have to be the second-best wrestler. (BBYA)

Humor

With the tremendous changes brought on by the transition to adulthood, teens certainly have their share of stress, and humor can help to relieve it. Teens usually have a sense of humor. Most enjoy humorous writing, either as a predominant theme or a subtext in a book, although what hits the funny bone varies wildly from reader to reader. Humor books move at a fast clip, often spiked with snappy dialogue. A great deal of emphasis is put on the protagonist's character, and humor serves almost as a heroic attribute in facing life's challenges. The titles listed in this section are ones in which humor dominates the characters, dialogue, and story. Other titles with elements of humor can be found in other chapters and are listed in the subject index.

Bauer, Joan. *Hope Was Here.* 2000. *JS.* Sixteen-year-old Hope travels around from diner to diner with her Aunt Addie, a great but itinerant cook. After landing in Mulhoney, Wisconsin, Hope becomes involved in the mayoral campaign that the diner's owner is waging—along with his battle against leukemia. (BBYA; IRAYAC; Newbery Honor)

Bauer, Joan. *Rules of the Road.* 1998. *MJS.* Sixteen years old and nearly six feet tall, Jenna Boller sells shoes. She is also extremely good at it, which does not go unnoticed by Mrs. Gladstone, the elderly president of the shoe-store chain for which she works. When Mrs. Gladstone decides to go to the shareholders' meeting in Texas and check out the stores along the way, she asks that Jenna drive her and act as a shoe-store spy. A plot to take over the company teams them up with Harry Bender, the greatest shoe salesman of all time. (Popular Paperbacks; BBYA; Quick Picks; YALSA 100 Best Books)

Cabot, Meg. *All American Girl.* 2002. *JS.* Annotated in the Romance section of this chapter.

Cabot, Meg. *The Princess Diaries. MJS.* Annotated in Chapter 11, "Alternative Formats."

Conford, Ellen. *The Frog Princess of Pelham.* 1997. *M.* Annotated in the Humorous Fantasy section of Chapter 6.

Creech, Sharon. *Absolutely Normal Chaos.* 1996. *MJ.* Mary Lou's summer diary reveals romance, intrigue, and plenty to laugh about the summer she is thirteen. (Popular Paperbacks)

Eberhardt, Thom. *Rat Boys: A Dating Experiment.* 2001. *MJS.* When the obnoxious beauty queen Jennifer Martin asks Marci and Summer to baby-sit her neighbor's dog for the Spring Fling, Marci puts her foot in it by claiming that both she and Summer have dates. Coincidentally, on the same day, their boss Weird Doris, who owns a junk shop, buys a locked box. Inside is a ring with the magical power to transmute things—in the same way that Cinderella's Fairy Godmother transmutes a pumpkin into a coach. Things can't help but go outrageously awry when Doris transmutes herself into a glamorous soap star and her two pet rats into really cute dates for Marci and Summer. (Quick Picks)

Ferris, Jean. *Love among the Walnuts.* 1998. *JS.* Sandy's entire wealthy family, including the servant and the family pet, Attila the hen, go into comas after Sandy's uncles serve up a poisoned birthday cake. Those stricken are moved next door to Walnut Manor, a "looney bin" for the wealthy. (BBYA)

Grant, Cynthia D. *The Cannibals: Starring Tiffany Spratt.* 2002. *MJS.* Tiffany, head yell leader at Hiram Johnson High, faces adventure and romance in her senior year. After her boyfriend is exiled by his parents, she meets a gorgeous new boy named Campbell, but mishears his name as Cannibal and has T-shirts and sweatshirts emblazoned with the word "Cannibals" made up for the entire yell squad. Things really heat up for her when a movie company wants to film a teenage slasher movie at the high school, and she campaigns for it because it may be her big chance to become a model and an actress. Meanwhile, Campbell hangs in there as a friend, even though Tiffany thinks they are a couple.

Hayes, Daniel. *Flyers.* 1996. *JS.* Gabe Riley lives in a small town with his gentle, decent, but taken-to-drink lawyer dad and his brilliant but quiet younger brother. He and his friends make off-the-wall movies, including a current effort that involves a family of swamp monsters in family therapy. (Popular Paperbacks; BBYA)

Hiaasen, Carl. *Hoot.* 2002. *M.* Roy Eberhardt, the target of a middle school bully, sees a boy running barefoot, and his imagination is captured. Bonking the bully in the nose, Roy gives chase, and his life becomes entangled with that of a young police officer. Meanwhile, back at the ranch—oops!—at the building site of the new Mother Paula's pancake house, Curley the foreman is experiencing a series of construction setbacks, ranging from alligators in the Travlin' Johnnys to pulled survey stakes to cottonmouth moccasin snakes with glittered tails. When Roy does catch up to the running boy, who is called Mullet Fingers, he becomes friends with Beatrice, Mullet Finger's stepsister who is a big, tough middle school soccer player. Together, they fight the company that wants to bulldoze the building site and bury several families of burrowing owls. Over-the-top Hiaasen humor with a strong environmental flavor. (BBYA; Newbery Honor)

Howe, Norma. *The Adventures of Blue Avenger.* 1999. *J.* On his sixteenth birthday, Dave decides to take on the persona of the comic book character he has been drawing. He saves the school principal from killer bees and creates a recipe for weepless lemon meringue pie. (Popular Paperbacks; BBYA)

Koertge, Ron. *Confess-O-Rama.* 1996. *MJS.* After his mother's fourth husband dies, Tony starts in at a new high school. His plan to keep a low profile is foiled when his angst-filled calls to the Confess-O-Rama hotline go public. (Popular Paperbacks)

Korman, Gordon. *Losing Joe's Place.* 1990. *JS.* When Jason and his two best friends sublease his older brother's Toronto apartment for a summer, disaster ensues. (Popular Paperbacks; BBYA)

Korman, Gordon. *Son of the Mob.* 2002. *JS.* Annotated in the Romance section of this chapter.

Lynch, Chris. The Elvin series. *JS.*

> *Slot Machine.* 1995. Overweight Elvin just cannot find a sport that works for him at the camp where he and all incoming students at his all-male high school are required to attend. (BBYA; Quick Picks)

Extreme Elvin. 1999. Elvin is now in high school and has some major problems—including hemorrhoids!

McCafferty, Megan. Jessica Darling series. *S.*

Sloppy Firsts. 2001. Honest, realistic coming-of-age tale of sixteen-year-old honor student Jessica Darling in the year after her best friend moves away. Crushes, friendships (or lack thereof), cliques, and attractive bad boys fill the pages.

Second Helpings. 2003. Are Jessica and Marcus going to finally get together?

McCants, William D. *Much Ado about Prom Night.* 1995. *MJS.* Peer advisor Becca has some good advice, but some people think that she is advocating promiscuity. (Popular Paperbacks; BBYA; Quick Picks).

Moore, Christopher. *Lamb, the Gospel According to Biff, Christ's Childhood Pal.* 2002. This wildly crazily humorous take on the hidden years of Jesus Christ starts when Josh, as He is called, and Biff meet up at age six. The two team up with Maggie, the new girl in town, and have typical kid and adolescent adventures. How exactly would a six-year-old or a fourteen-year-old learn how to be the Messiah? This BBYA Top Ten selection was written for adults, but is enjoyed by mature teen readers. (BBYA) **Adult**

Moriarty, Jaclyn. *Feeling Sorry for Celia.* 2001. *MJS.* (Alternative format) Hilarious letters and notes portray fifteen-year-old Elizabeth's life. (BBYA)

Nodelman, Perry. *Behaving Bradley.* 1998. *MJS.* Bradley, an eleventh-grader, attempts to change the high school Code of Conduct and faces opposition from all directions. (Popular Paperbacks)

Paulsen, Gary. *The Schernoff Discoveries.* 1998. *MJ.* In this slapstick comedy, Harold, the narrator's best friend, has theories about everything from fishing to bullies to how to get a girlfriend. (Popular Paperbacks; BBYA)

Rennison, Louise. Georgia Nicholson series. *MJ.* Annotated in Chapter 11, "Alternative Formats." (BBYA; Quick Picks; Printz Honor; IRAYAC)

Sacher, Louis. *Holes.* 1998. *MJS.* Annotated in Chapter 4, "Adventure." (Quick Picks; BBYA; Newbery Award; IRAYAC; YALSA 100 Best Books)

Strasser, Todd. *How I Spent My Last Night on Earth.* 1998. *MJS.* When rumor has it that a giant asteroid is going to destroy life on Earth, or at least southern California, Legs sets out to spend the last night of her life with hunky surfer Andros. (Popular Paperbacks)

Tolan, Stephanie S. *Surviving the Applewhites.* 2002. *M.* Jake Semple, a smartass troublemaker, is taken into the Applewhites' Creative Academy when he is kicked out of middle school. The very creative Applewhites always have something interesting going on, but E. D. (the practical one) is none too glad to have a boy near her own age around all the time. (BBYA; Newbery Honor)

Welter, John. *I Want to Buy a Vowel: A Novel of Illegal Alienation.* 1996. *MJS.* Clever puns and social satire combine in a southern small-town story featuring an illegal immigrant who learned English from television commercials and game shows, a minister's two daughters, and a teenage satanist who sacrifices Vienna sausages. (Popular Paperbacks; BBYA)

Williams, Carol Lynch. *My Angelica.* 1999. *MJ.* Fifteen-year-old Sage enters a writing contest with a sexy historical romance.

Series

Books in series give the reader a chance to stay with characters they like beyond the pages of a single book. Contemporary series novels often follow a group of friends as they deal with school issues, friendship problems, new romances, and painful breakups. These books offer readers a sense of belonging, as they get to know the characters intimately. In the 1980s, the Sweet Valley High series ruled, and some teens who read Sweet Valley Twins as children continue to read the various Sweet Valley series.

Readers who like contemporary series with a touch of the paranormal will also enjoy many of the series in the Chapter 8, "Paranormal." The paranormal series have a contemporary setting and also deal with many of the concerns involved in the series in this chapter—but with ghosts, vampires, or paranormal abilities playing a part in the action.

Baer, Judy. The Cedar River Daydreams series. *J.* This series features characters who experience a range of teen concerns and are influenced by their Christian beliefs. Listed and annotated in Chapter 12, "Christian Fiction."

Black, Jonah. Black Book: Diary of a Teenage Stud. *S.* With a title like this, it's no surprise that teen boys are snapping this up.

The Black Book: Diary of a Teenage Stud. Volume I. Girls, Girls, Girls. 2001. Jonah Black is back in Pompano Beach after being expelled from a private prep school in Pennsylvania, which involved a mysterious and undisclosed scandal. Jonah is glad to be reunited with old friends, but the rumor mill has been rife with outrageous tales of his exploits. He constantly daydreams and fantasizes about Sophie, but leaves the reader with the feeling that something awful has happened to her. (Quick Picks)

The Black Book: Diary of a Teenage Stud. Volume II. Stop, Don't Stop. 2001. The reason Jonah was expelled from his last school is revealed. (Quick Picks)

The Black Book: Diary of a Teenage Stud. Volume III. Run, Jonah, Run. 2001. Jonah may be unlucky at love, but he keeps trying.

The Black Book: Diary of a Teenage Stud. Volume IV. Faster, Faster, Faster. 2002. The conclusion of Jonah's story.

Cabot, Meg. The Princess Diaries. *MJS.* Annotated in Chapter 11, "Alternative Formats."

Cann, Kate. Love Trilogy. *S.*

> *Ready?* 2001. Collette and Art meet at the pool, but will what they have together turn out to be true love?
>
> *Sex.* 2001. Collette and Art consummate their relationship, but Collette is not thrilled with the changes it causes.
>
> *Go!* 2001. After backing off from a sexual relationship with Art, Collette tries to stay friends with him.

Lewis, Beverly. Holly's Heart series. *M.* Starting at age thirteen, Holly uses her Christian values to get through middle school and into high school. Originally published by Zondervan in the 1990s, the series is being reissued by Bethany House. Listed and annotated Chapter 12, "Christian Fiction."

MacDougal, Scarlett. Have a Nice Life series. *J.* Zola, Min, Olivia, and Sally band together to prove that their lives don't have to be disasters, even if prom was.

> *Start Here.* 2001. Clarence Terence, a male fairy godmother, shows the girls what their lives may be like in ten years. (Quick Picks)
>
> *Play.* 2001. Min plots to replace Ozzy in Tobias's affections, but a Yorkie is tough competition. (Quick Picks)
>
> *Popover.* 2001. Zola really wants to get her ex-boyfriend back. (Quick Picks)
>
> *Score.* 2001. A rival fairy godmother comes onto the scene and tells the girls what they want to hear, but is he really acting in their best interests? (Quick Picks)

Naylor, Phyllis Reynolds. Alice series. *MJ.* Many teen readers have grown up with the motherless Alice, and now she is going from the realm of children to that of young adults, dealing with all kinds of adolescent issues. They are written in a humorous style, but pull no punches.

> *Outrageously Alice.* 1998. At thirteen, Alice has a lot to think about, including sexy lingerie. (BBYA)
>
> *Achingly Alice.* 1998. As an eighth-grader, Alice faces sexual feelings and learns about pelvic exams.
>
> *Alice on the Outside.* 2000. The second half of eighth grade is not necessarily smooth sailing for Alice.
>
> *The Grooming of Alice.* 2001. The summer before high school requires a lot of preparation.
>
> *Alice Alone.* 2001. Alice starts high school and breaks up with Patrick.
>
> *Simply Alice.* 2002. Will ninth-grader Alice find romance?

Parker, Daniel. The Wessex Papers. *S.* A soap opera series set in an exclusive boarding school.

> *Trust Falls.* 2002. The cast of characters at the ultra-snobbish Wessex Academy is introduced, all of whom seemingly have more dollars than sense.

Fallout. 2002. Noah is busted in a compromising position.

Outsmart. 2002. Sunday and Fred expose the blackmailers.

Tiernan, Cate. Sweep Series. *JS.* Another series featuring the paranormal, this time involving a high school witch. Annotated in Chapter 8, "Paranormal."

Turning Seventeen. *JS.* Four girlfriends in their senior year of high school share joy and troubles.

Any Guy You Want. Rosalind Noonan. 2000. Kerri can get any guy she wants—except for one. (Quick Picks)

More than This. Wendy Corsi Staub. 2000. Even though Jessica loves Alex, Scott is rather enticing. (Quick Picks)

For Real. Christa Roberts. 2000. Motherless Maya's father is sometimes overprotective. (Quick Picks)

Show Me Love. Elizabeth Craft. 2000. Erin's story. (Quick Picks)

Can't Let Go. Rosalind Noonan. 2000. Kerri is not going to let one guy ruin her life.

This Boy Is Mine. Wendy Corsi Staub. 2001. What is Jessica up to?

Secrets and Lies. Christa Roberts. 2001. Maya's dad is making her spend the week with Ms. Perfect and her daughter.

We Have to Talk. Violette Smith. 2001. Erin catches her mom and Aunt Joyce arguing about her.

Just Trust Me. Rosalind Noonan. 2001. The senior class trip will change Kerri's and Jessica's lives forever.

Von Ziegesar, Cecily. Gossip Girl. *S.* The kind of spoiled rich kids the kids from the *Nanny Diaries* would probably grow up to be.

Gossip Girl. 2002. Gossip Girl dishes all the news about Blair Waldorf, her stoned hottie of a boyfriend, Nate, and her former best friend Serena van der Woodsen.

You Know You Love Me. 2002. Who exactly was it that went off to visit Brown together?

All I Want Is Everything. 2003. Christmas in Manhattan for the rich and beautiful.

Wilson, Jacqueline. Girls Trilogy. *MJ.* Humorous British import looks at teen angst from boyfriends to body image.

Girls in Love. 2002. Starting ninth grade, Ellie is worried that she will be the only one without a boyfriend since her two best friends, Magda and Nadine, have already found boyfriends.

Girls under Pressure. 2002. While Ellie flirts with an eating disorder, Magda's flirting gets her into hot water, and Nadine realizes that models aren't sought for their dazzling intellect.

Girls out Late. 2002. When Ellie finally finds a boyfriend, she talks her friends into staying out past curfew with her.

Chapter 4

Adventure

The thrill of beating the odds and surviving adversity is part of the attraction of adventure. Adventure stories generally have plenty of action, and the story moves at a fast pace, keeping teen readers interested. The characters in these stories are often easy to identify with, sharing many traits with teens, but the situations of the story bring out the best in them—courage, intelligence, skill—and these are qualities to which many teens aspire. Because of its strong appeal to the teen audience, adventure is an important feature in many genres popular with teens. Elements of adventure appear in science fiction, fantasy, mystery, and historical fiction.

Recently, some popular scenarios in books with adventure as a main theme include teens in hiding as part of the Witness Protection Program and teens with parents who are members of extremist militias or cults. Espionage á la James Bond is also showing up; survival in adverse conditions remains strong. Wilderness survival, including titles such as *Hatchet* by Gary Paulsen and the numerous titles by Will Hobbs, is one of the most popular subgenres with middle school boys.

Some of the books in this genre fall into distinct types—survival stories, tales of espionage and terrorism, sea adventures, and war stories—that share many qualities that readers seek. These subgenres are presented first; books that share popular themes of militias and cults or heroism are featured at the end of the chapter.

Types

Survival

Survival stories feature teen protagonists testing the limits, possibly making life-threatening mistakes, but triumphing over adversity in the end. This is a plot with great appeal to teen readers. Many teens have not tested their survival skills in the world (without family support), and thus the issue is a charged one for this audience. Also, the action is physical, which appeals to many readers, and suspense can run high. Readers who enjoy fictional survival stories may also enjoy true adventure, such as the plethora of books written about polar expeditions. Although nonfiction titles are not covered in this guide, true stories of adventure are easy to find in library and bookstore collections.

Fama, Elizabeth. *Overboard.* 2002. *MJS.* Fourteen-year-old Emily, is an American living in Sumatra, where her family is running a children's clinic. She's so angry at her parents that she decides to take the ferry away from Sumatra to another island, where she plans to meet her uncle. But when the ferry sinks, she is on her own in the water without a life jacket. (BBYA)

George, Jean Craighead. Julie series. *M.*

> *Julie of the Wolves.* 1972. A thirteen-year-old Inuit girl runs away from an unhappy marriage only to become lost on Alaska's Northern Slope. The friendship of a wolf pack is all that allows her to survive. (Newbery Award; Popular Paperbacks)

> *Julie.* 1994. Julie, now fourteen and living in a village with her father, tries to keep safe the musk oxen she attends and the wolves she loves.

> *Julie's Wolf Pack.* 1997. Julie is now grown and ready to be married, but the real story is that of Kapu, the wolf pup she nursed back to life in *Julie of the Wolves,* who has been captured for research. (IRAYAC)

Hill, David. *Take It Easy.* 1997. *JS.* Rob, an experienced camper, is unable to keep his companions safe after their guide on a New Zealand wilderness trek dies on the trip.

Hobbs, Valerie. *Charlie's Run.* 2000. *M.* Eleven-year-old Charlie, a good kid, runs away when his parents announce they are planning to divorce. He meets up with a girl named Dooans and some rough characters. (VOYA)

Hobbs, Will. Downriver Duo. *MJ.*

> *Downriver.* 1991. A group of teens take their own trip on the unpredictable waters of the Colorado River. (BBYA; Popular Paperbacks; YALSA 100 Best Books)

> *River Thunder.* 1997. Hobbs reunites the disparate group of teens from *Downriver* to run the Colorado River through the Grand Canyon once again, this time at flood stage. Adventure readers and whitewater rafters will love the detailed descriptions of challenging nature at its wildest.

Hobbs, Will. *Far North.* 1996. *MJ.* Fifteen-year-old Gabe and his roommate Raymond, a Dene Indian, must survive alone in the Canadian wilderness after a plane crash and the death of a wise elder. (BBYA; Quick Picks; Spur Award; YALSA 100 Best Books)

Hobbs, Will. *The Maze.* 1998. *MJ.* Annotated in Chapter 2, "Issues." (BBYA)

Hobbs, Will. *Wild Man Island.* 2002. *J.* Andy Galloway, age fourteen, sneaks away from an Alaskan tour to try to find the spot where his father died so he can place a memento there. Thus starts the adventure of his life. Swept away by a storm to Admiralty Island, Andy struggles to survive and meets a Newfie named Bear, companion to a hermit. In the hermit's cave Andy makes some amazing discoveries.

Lawrence, Iain. *The Wreckers.* 1998. *MJS.* Shipwrecked after a storm, fourteen-year-old John attempts to save himself and his father while dealing with the evil secret of the English coastal town where they are stranded. His story is continued in *The Smugglers* and *The Buccaneers,* annotated in the At Sea section of this chapter. (BBYA; Quick Picks; Geoffrey Bilson Award for Historical Fiction for Young People)

Marsden, John. Tomorrow Series. *JS.* When Ellie and her friends return to their rural homes after a camping trip in an isolated canyon, they discover that Australia has been invaded and that they may be the only ones left to wage guerrilla warfare on the aggressors. As the teens face loss and find themselves forced into horrific situations, they fight to free their country. Exciting suspense.

> *Tomorrow, When the War Began.* 1995. After returning from a camping trip, Ellie and her friends find life has changed—their families are gone and their country, Australia, has been invaded. (YALSA 100 Best Books)

> *The Dead of Night.* 1997. Australian teens take to the wilderness and struggle to survive in a valley called Hell after their country is invaded.

> *A Killing Frost.* 1998. (Australian title: *Third Day, the Frost*) Ellie and her friends continue their fight for survival and launch guerilla attacks on the invaders of their country.

> *Darkness Be My Friend.* 1999. They thought they were safe. After being rescued and transported to New Zealand, Ellie and her friends find themselves on another dangerous mission.

> *Burning for Revenge.* 2000. As their numbers dwindle and their spirits flag, Ellie and her friends continue their fight to free their country.

> *The Night Is for Hunting.* 2001. Ellie and friends take on a group of wild orphans and continue their guerilla warfare campaign.

> *The Other Side of Dawn.* 2002. High action as the war comes to a climax and a group of Australian teens fights tooth and nail to survive.

Matcheck, Diane. *The Sacrifice.* 1998. *JS.* A fifteen-year-old Native American orphan, Weak-one-who-does-not-last, arrogantly sets out to avenge her father's death and fulfill the destiny she believes is hers in this historical novel set on the Great Plains in the eighteenth century. (BBYA)

Mikaelsen, Ben. *Red Midnight.* 2002. *MJ.* A harrowing journey of two siblings battling the sea, fleeing soldiers and pirates, nearly starving, and fighting valiantly for survival makes for a page-turning adventure. More in the Politics section of Chapter 2, "Issues."

Paulsen, Gary. Brian series. *MJ.* These thrilling, classic teen survival stories follow the adventures of Brian, sole survivor of a plane crash, who must learn to survive in the wilderness and who then faces other equally daunting challenges.

> *Hatchet.* 1987. After a plane crash, thirteen-year-old Brian spends fifty-four days in the Canadian wilderness—his only survival tool a hatchet. (Newbery Honor; Popular Paperbacks)

> *The River.* 1991. Brian, now fifteen, returns to the Canadian wilderness to demonstrate his survival skills for military scientists. However, not everything goes as planned.

> *Brian's Winter.* 1996. What if Brian hadn't been rescued? In a twist on the ending of *Hatchet,* Brian survives the winter before being rescued. (Quick Picks; IRAYAC)

> *Brian's Return.* 1999. Brian, now sixteen, finds "civilization" more of a challenge than the harsh wilderness he survived. (Quick Picks)

Philbrick, Rodman. *The Journal of Douglas Allen Deeds: The Donner Party Expedition, 1846.* 2001. *M.* In hope of finding a better life, a recently orphaned boy joins a wagon train from Missouri heading to California. But fate brings heavy snow to the mountains, when the group is only sixty miles from its goal.

Thomas, Rob. *Green Thumb.* 1999. *M.* Thirteen-year-old science whiz Grady is invited to the Brazilian Amazon to join a study project where he uncovers some diabolical doings and must take to the jungle to survive.

White, Robb. *Deathwatch.* 1972. *JS.* Ben, a college student, took a temporary job as a guide for a hunting party. But now he has become the prey and must survive being hunted in the desert. A thrilling teen classic. (BBYA; YALSA 100 Best Books; Edgar Award) [Classic]

Espionage and Terrorism

In the current political climate, spies and terrorism are hot topics, and as in adult fiction, political intrigue and espionage make for popular teen reading. In addition to the action and suspense of adventure, this subgenre features exotic locales, heroic protagonists, despicable antagonists, and fascinating technological effects—all of great appeal to teens. Readers who enjoy these books may also enjoy the nonfiction title *Hidden Secrets* by David Owen (Firefly Books, 2002) to get the real scoop on how accurate the novels are.

Cooney, Caroline B. *The Terrorist.* 1997. *MJ.* A year in England turns into a disaster for the Williams family when a terrorist bomb kills eleven-year-old Billy. Billy's sister, sixteen-year-old Laura, who has never been interested in much beyond the next school dance, decides to learn all she can about politics and world affairs so that she can find and punish the terrorist who has robbed the world of her exceptional younger brother. (Quick Picks)

Horowitz, Anthony. Alex Rider series. *MJ.* Alex Rider is a fourteen-year-old who works for MI6, Britain's top intelligence agency. Heart-thumping action and technological wizardry make these books thrilling reads.

Stormbreaker: An Alex Rider Adventure. 2001. Britain's top intelligence agency, MI6, enlists Alex to work on the case that killed his uncle Ian. He is sent into the home of an Egyptian millionaire who is giving every school in England a free Stormbreaker computer. Hidden inside each computer lurks a biological bomb that will annihilate the country with smallpox. This is an over-the-top spy adventure. (Quick Picks)

Point Blank: An Alex Rider Adventure. 2002. Alex continues his intelligence work for MI6 and investigates a fancy boarding school in the French Alps, where teens are acting uncommonly well behaved.

Skeleton Key. 2003. Alex must stop a man who has a nuclear bomb and wants to make Russia the dominant world power.

Klass, David. *Danger Zone*. 1996. *JS*. International terrorists and basketball! (BBYA; Popular Paperbacks; IRAYAC)

Tolan, Stephanie S. *Flight of the Raven*. 2001. *MJ*. Annotated in the Militias and Cults section of this chapter.

Turner, Megan Whalen. *The Queen of Attolia*. 2000. *MJ*. In this sequel to *The Thief,* annotated in the Epic Fantasy section of Chapter 6, "Fantasy," Eugenides (Gen) is captured and his hand amputated. Espionage, excitement, and war set in a fantasy land.

At Sea

Pirates and storms are just two of the elements that can fill a journey at sea with adventure. Life at sea is isolated and distant, and the powers of nature are immense. Fans of sea adventures have a particular interest in the ocean setting and the human dramas set within the context of natural dramas. Some sea adventures are set in contemporary times, but many are set in the past.

Creech, Sharon. *The Wanderer*. 2000. *M*. Thirteen-year-old Sophie goes on an ocean voyage with her uncles and male cousins. Her talent is telling stories of their grandpa, who the others know she has never met. As everyone gets to know each other, it comes out that Sophie is adopted, and the story of how she lost her parents is revealed. (BBYA)

Hesse, Karen. *Stowaway*. 2000. *MJ*. When eleven-year-old Nicholas Young stowed away on Captain Cook's ship in 1768, he had no idea of the adventures he would face in the South Seas.

Hoh, Diane. *Titanic: The Long Night*. 1998. *MJ*. Everyone thinks the *Titanic* is unsinkable. Beautiful, rich, and petulant Elizabeth Farr couldn't care less. She's concerned with her future. She wants to go to college, but her parents want her to marry wealthy and dull Adam and lead a boring life. (Quick Picks)

Lawrence, Iain. *High Seas Trilogy*. *MJ*. Set in the early nineteenth century, this series features sixteen-year-old John Spencer, an English boy with a yen for the sea. Mad captains, hardened sailors, pirates, ghosts, and high jinks make for suspenseful reading. (Note: *The Wreckers,* the first volume in the series does not take place at sea and is annotated in the Survival section of this chapter.)

The Smugglers. 1999. John Spencer's father has bought the trading vessel *The Dragon* and now, as sixteen-year-old John takes a cargo of wool to London, he discovers that the mad captain of the ship may be involved in numerous nefarious activities. (Quick Picks; BBYA)

The Buccaneers. 2001. *The Dragon* sails to the Caribbean, and John Spencer, now seventeen, encounters pirates and other deadly dangers. When the ship's captain falls ill, John must steer the crew to safety.

Smith, Sherri L. *Lucy the Giant*. 2002. *JS.* Lucy may be only fifteen, but with her towering height and large build, people are willing to believe that she's older. When a stray dog she loves dies, she runs away from her home in Sitka, Alaska, and her drunken father. She ends up working on a fishing boat in life-threatening arctic conditions. (BBYA)

Zindel, Paul. *Reef of Death*. 1998. *MJ.* Seventeen-year-old PC McPhee goes to Australia to help his uncle and becomes immersed in a mystery surrounding aboriginal treasures and a strange ship. (Quick Picks; IRAYAC)

War

War stories appeal to patriotic sentiments and generally espouse more of a team approach to facing conflict. High on action, these stories often contain prevailing themes of justice and place a strong emphasis on relationships. Many, like tales of espionage, are set in far-off locales. Readers who enjoy adventure centered on military conflicts may also find titles of interest in the historical fiction chapter.

Elliott, L. M. *Under a War-Torn Sky*. 2001. *M.* When nineteen-year-old Henry Forester is shot down by the Luftwaffe in occupied France during WWII, ordinary French citizens offer aid during his trek.

Ellis, Deborah. *Parvana's Journey*. 2002. *MJ.* As war rages across Afghanistan, thirteen-year-old Parvana searches for her family and creates a new one made up of other displaced children. This is a sequel to *The Breadwinner,* annotated in the Chapter 10, "Multicultural Fiction." (BBYA)

Marsden, John. Tomorrow series. *JS.* A group of teens battle for survival and launch guerilla attacks after their country, Australia, is invaded. This series is annotated in the Survival section of this chapter.

Mead, Alice. *Girl of Kosovo*. 2001. *MJ.* An eleven-year-old Albanian girl, Zana, faces the horrors of ethnic war.

Wulffson, Don *Soldier X*. 2000. *JS.* Sixteen-year-old Erik dons the uniform of a downed enemy soldier to avoid being captured as a Nazi soldier. He then must fake amnesia to survive as a German soldier on the Russian front. (IRAYAC)

Themes

Militias and Cults

The extremists who join militias and cults create great possibilities for adventurous stories. These stories often have a psychological element of suspense, and many readers are intrigued by the nefarious characters found in these books.

Bardi, Abby. *Book of Fred.* 2001. *S.* Fifteen-year-old Mary Fred has ended up in foster care because of her family's involvement in a cult, but this novel (annotated in the Homelessness and Foster Living section of Chapter 2, "Issues") becomes an adventure when Mary is reunited with her mother, who has joined a different, more dangerous cult.

Gilbert, Barbara Snow. *Paper Trail.* 2000. *MJS.* High. A fifteen-year-old whose family has spent the last ten years with the Soldiers of God runs for his life after members of the group murder his mother. (VOYA)

Miklowitz, Gloria D. *Camouflage.* 1998. *MJ.* Kyle discovers surprising secrets about his dad's "gun club" when he goes to visit him in rural Michigan for the summer and finds himself in the middle of a militia conspiracy. His budding romance with the daughter of an ATF agent adds to the story's appeal.

Naylor, Phyllis Reynolds. *Walker's Crossing.* 1999. *MJ.* Ryan Walker doesn't know what to think about the beliefs espoused by his older brother, who has joined the white-supremacist Mountain Patriots Association.

Thompson, Julian F. *Brothers.* 1998. *JS.* Seventeen-year-old Chris finds his older brother, who is suffering from mental illness, at a camp belonging to the Sons of Liberty Two, a heavily armed antigovernment, racist militia.

Tolan, Stephanie S. *Flight of the Raven.* 2001. *MJ.* Twelve-year-old Amber's father is a terrorist and the leader of the Free Mountain Militia in this thriller with science fiction overtones.

Yolen, Jane, and Bruce Coville. *Armageddon Summer.* 1998. *MJ.* (Alternative format) Teenagers Marina and Jeff are 2 of the 144 people that Reverend Beelson has gathered at a mountaintop camp to await the end of the world. The events leading up to this are told through excerpts from sermons, FBI files, camp schedules, and e-mails. (BBYA; Quick Picks)

Heroism

The heroic qualities that can be found in fictional characters appeal to many teen readers. The following titles all feature protagonists who find strengths within themselves that help them triumph over adversity. The character of the protagonist becomes the focus of the book, overriding other themes and topics. Other books with strong heroes can be found in various chapters, and users are encouraged to consult the subject index for additional title suggestions.

Bell, William. *Death Wind.* 2002. *MJS.* (High-Low). Allie, thinking she is pregnant, runs away from home to join her friend Razz, a Canadian skateboarding champion who is on tour. Returning to her hometown, the two teens encounter tornadoes, death, and devastation. The old-school descriptions make sense when it turns out that it is set in 1985.

Bodett, Tom. *Williwaw!* 1999. *M.* Thirteen-year-old September and her younger brother Ivan have already made some bad decisions while staying alone, but when they take the boat out on their Alaskan bay, they are caught in a terrifying storm called a *williwaw*.

Branford, Henrietta. *White Wolf.* 1999. *MJ.* A white wolf, captured by humans and nursed by a dog, escapes to the wild and must learn how to live like a wolf.

Hobbs, Will. *Ghost Canoe.* 1997. *MJ.* Fourteen-year-old Nathan MacAllister tries to find clues to answer the puzzle of mysterious footprints that were seen on the beach after a shipwreck, the victims of which were all reported dead.

Hobbs, Will. Jason series. Annotated in Chapter 9, "Historical Novels."

> *Jason's Gold.* 1999. *MJ.*
>
> *Down The Yukon.* 2001. *MJS.*

Philbrick, Rodman. The Mighty series.

> *Freak the Mighty.* 1993. *MJS.* (Film: *The Mighty*) Max and Freak, two outcasts, are great together, especially after Max is kidnapped by Killer Kane and the two prove they are more than the sum of their parts. (BBYA; Popular Paperbacks) Film
>
> *Max the Mighty.* 1998. *MJ.* Max rescues an eleven-year-old girl called Worm from a tormenting gang-banger and later witnesses her being abused by her evangelizing stepfather. Max steps in to rescue her again, only to find himself on the run and accused of kidnapping. Worm has always tried to escape her problems by keeping her nose in a book, but now she and Max are headed across the country, hitching rides with old hippies and hopping freights to try to find her real father.

Sacher, Louis. *Holes.* 1998. *MJ.* (Film: *Holes*) This book entwines fairy-tale-like family legend and the story of a boy who is sentenced to a juvenile correctional facility where he has to dig holes all day. (Quick Picks; BBYA; Newbery Award; IRAYAC; YALSA 100 Best Books) Film

Smith, Roland. *Sasquatch.* 1998. *MJ.* Thirteen-year-old Dylan Hickok's adventures begin when he discovers his dad's involvement in a Sasquatch hunt. Could there be such a thing as Bigfoot? (Quick Picks)

Stevenson, James. Pete Duet. *MJ.* Eleven-year-old Pete is on the run because of his father's criminal activities.

> *The Bones in the Cliff.* 1995. Pete's criminal dad is on the run, so Pete, age eleven, is supposed to keep watch for any gunmen arriving on Cutlass Island by ferry who may be after his father.
>
> *Unprotected Witness.* 1997. Pete now lives with his friend Rootie and her wealthy grandmother in New York, his dad having disappeared into the safety of the Federal Witness Protection Program. Pete's sense of safety proves false when his father is murdered. When the bad guys come after Pete, he must determine why and find a way to elude them forever.

Chapter 5

Mystery and Suspense

Mystery and suspense are closely related and tightly linked, but as times change, trends veer from one to the other. Suspense novels often let the reader know something terrible has happened, and the reader feels a sense of foreboding. Mysteries are more puzzlelike, involving detection—an attempt to find out who and why.

Although the suspense boom of a decade ago is seemingly over and the huge demand for books like those written by R. L. Stine, Christopher Pike, and Richie Tankersley Cusick has fallen off, there seems to have been an upsurge in mysteries, especially in mystery series involving the paranormal. The number of mysteries written specifically for teens does not compare with the vast number produced for adults every month, but it is a growing area of interest for teen readers and YA fiction publishing. The Mystery Writers of America even offer an annual Edgar Allan Poe Award, referred to as an Edgar, in the area of Best Young Adult Mystery.

Teen mysteries differ from adult mysteries in that the sleuth is always an amateur—because he or she is always a teen. (This may also partially account for the fewer number of teen mysteries.)

What do teen readers enjoy in mystery and suspense stories? Like adults, teens enjoy the mental challenge of trying to figure out a solution to a problem. Like adults, although perhaps somewhat less, teens are drawn to protagonists whom they admire, or with whom they are fascinated, or whom they wish to emulate. Older teens often enjoy reading adult suspense and mystery. Adult authors popular with this group include John Grisham, Lillian Jackson Braun, Jeffrey Deaver, and James Patterson.

In addition, many of the mysteries written for teens are combined with other genres, such as historical fiction, romance, and paranormal. For readers who enjoy these other genres, the element of mystery offers an additional twist to the story—and additional appeal.

The YA mystery and suspense genre falls into distinct types—suspense, contemporary mystery, historical mystery, and paranormal mystery—which is reflected in this chapter's organization. These subgenres each have distinctive characteristics that earn loyal followings among specific groups of teen readers. In addition, there are a number of mystery series, which have their own appeal and are covered at the end of the chapter.

Types

Suspense

Although not as popular as it was a decade ago, suspense is still a vital subgenre among many teen fans. In the suspense story, the appeal of suspense is nail-biting tension and uncertainty, which is relieved at the story's end. The suspense can be psychological, physical, or both. What draws readers to this type of story are the dark and moody atmosphere, fast pacing, and strong resolution. Heroic protagonists, whom the reader often comes to know intimately through thoughts and emotions expressed in the narrative, and contemporary, realistic settings also contribute to the genre's popularity.

Cormier, Robert. *Tenderness*. 1997. *S.* Annotated in the Crime and Criminals section of Chapter 2, "Issues."

McColley, Kevin. *Switch*. 1997. *S.* In this creepy tale, seventeen-year-old Ken, an epileptic, doesn't have any friends, but he strikes up an acquaintance with a homeless man who seemingly disappears and is replaced by someone else.

McDonald, Joyce. *The Shadow People*. 2000. *S.* Four alienated teens band together, and the crimes they commit rapidly escalate in severity.

Napoli, Donna Jo. *Three Days*. 2001. *M.* When her father dies of a sudden heart attack, eleven-year-old Jackie is left alone on an Italian roadside. Two men pick her up, but instead of taking her to the police, they take her to a remote home in the countryside—and they won't tell her why.

Plum-Ucci, Carol. *What Happened to Lani Garver*. 2002. *S.* Claire remembers that the last time she saw Lani, he was struggling in a freezing sea. The story flashes back through their time together. Claire is a cancer survivor and happy to be part of the in crowd at her island high school. Her best friend is cruel, but Claire finds much in her that she likes—until a mysterious new kid, Lani Garver, starts school. At first glance, nobody can tell whether Lani is a boy or a girl, and this doesn't go over well on the macho island where the Fish Frat rules. (BBYA)

Qualey, Marsha. *Thin Ice*. 1997. *JS.* When the brother who has raised Arden for most of her life is presumed dead, the seventeen-year-old girl doesn't believe it. Convinced that in truth he has run away, she begins a search to find him. (Quick Picks)

Roberts, Willo Davis. *Hostage*. 2000. *M.* After surprising burglars in her home, eleven-year-old Kaci, along with an elderly neighbor, is taken captive and held hostage.

Sleator, William. *House of Stairs.* 1974. *JS.* Someone has put five fifteen-year-old orphans in a house of endless stairs and performed strange psychological experiments on them. Why? (YALSA 100 Best Books)

Smith, Roland. *Zach's Lie.* 2001. *MJ.* Thirteen-year-old Zach is uneasy with the new identity he has had to assume as his family entered the Witness Protection Program. (Quick Picks)

Springer, Nancy. *Blood Trail.* 2003. *J.* When Booger is heading home after a visit to the local swimming hole, his best friend, Aaron, tells the seventeen-year-old football player that he is scared and asks him to telephone him in ten minutes. When police cars go past, Booger knows that something has happened at Aaron's house. Arriving on the scene, he discovers that Aaron has been brutally slain with more than seventy stab wounds.

Werlin, Nancy. *The Killer's Cousin.* 1998. *JS.* Acquitted of murder, high school senior David tries to start a new life in Boston, but the ghost of his dead cousin and the presence of her spooky sister lead to new troubles in this tense psychological thriller. (Quick Picks)

Contemporary Mysteries

Mystery readers who seek characters, settings, and stories they can relate to will find them in contemporary mysteries. The realism of a story set in the present intensifies the mystery, intellectually and emotionally drawing in readers. It's as if these stories present the tacit premise, "imagine something like this happening to you." Joan Lowery Nixon dominated this subgenre in the 1990s, but recently more authors, such as Caroline Cooney, Gillian Cross, and Marsha Qualey, seem to be stepping in with compelling stories.

Cooney, Caroline B. *Hush Little Baby.* 1999. *MJS.* Kit, a teen who divides her time between the houses of her two parents, is shocked when her ditzy former stepmother thrusts a baby into her arms and then takes off. Car chases, kidnappings, and loads of bad guys populate this fast-paced mystery. (Quick Picks)

Cooney, Caroline B. *Wanted.* 1997. *MJ.* Alice's dad calls her and tells her to take two computer disks and his beloved Corvette to their favorite ice cream place to meet him. Before she can leave, an intruder breaks in, and Alice hides until he is gone. She then flees to carry out her assignment—but her father never shows up. Listening to the radio, she hears that he has been murdered, and that she has e-mailed a confession to the crime! Unable to turn to her mother, who seems to believe she did it, Alice goes underground to find the real murderer. (Quick Picks)

Cross, Gillian. *Phoning a Dead Man.* 2002. *MJS.* Haley travels with her brother's fiancée, Annie, to Siberia, where they are trying to find out what happened to Haley's brother, a demolition expert who supposedly blew himself up.

Gilstrap, John. *Nathan's Run.* 1996. *S.* Twelve-year-old Nathan is on the run from both the authorities and a hit man. (Popular Paperbacks; BBYA) **Adult**

Glenn, Mel. *Foreign Exchange: A Mystery in Poems.* 1999. *MJS.* (Alternative format) A small-town high school is hosting an exchange program with an urban high school. A beautiful blonde girl from the small-town school was last seen in the company of an African American boy. Now she's been found dead in the lake. Glenn again delivers a compelling read in the form of poems that tell the story of a murder from several viewpoints. (Popular Paperbacks; Quick Picks)

Glenn, Mel. *Who Killed Mr. Chippendale?* 1996. *MJS.* A Tower High School English teacher is murdered while running on the track one morning before school. In single- page poems, everyone touched by the murder tells their view of the events and of those involved. (Popular Paperbacks; Quick Picks)

Green, Timothy. *Twilight Boy.* 1998. *MJS.* Is it a "skinwalker" that is terrorizing Jesse Begay's grandfather? And who or what is responsible for the death of his father, an officer of the Navajo Tribal Police? Jesse, whose respect for tradition and strong moral character is much like a young Jim Chee, is wrongly accused of stealing a horse from Carolyn Manchester, who has just arrived at the Standing Rock Trading Post. As the two teens are drawn together, they find deadly evil linked to some ancient Spanish gold coins.

Guy, Rosa. *The Disappearance: A Novel.* 1979. *JS.* No sooner is Imamu Jones acquitted of a murder than the daughter of the people with whom he is staying disappears. Of course, the African American teen becomes the prime suspect. (YALSA 100 Best Books) [Classic]

Harrison, Michael. *It's My Life.* 1998. *MJ.* Martin has been kidnapped and is being held for ransom. But why? And what does his mother and her boyfriend have to with it? (IRAYAC)

Holmes, Barbara Ware. *Following Fake Man.* 2001. *M.* When Homer Winthrop was only three years old, his father died. Now twelve, Homer doesn't remember his dad, but he wants to find out why his wealthy mom will never talk about him.

Levitin, Sonia. *Yesterday's Child.* 1998. *JS.* When sixteen-year-old Laura is going through some of her recently deceased mother's belongings, she uncovers some things that don't add up. To put things together, she travels on a school trip to the town where her mother grew up.

Nixon, Joan Lowery. *Murdered, My Sweet.* 1997. *MJ.* Jenny Jake's mom Madeline is a famous mystery writer who sometimes gets caught up in other people's fantasies that make her out to be a sleuth herself—á la *Murder She Wrote.* Jenny and Carlos, a gorgeous bellhop, find themselves keeping Madeline's image afloat as they try to solve a mystery at a San Antonio hotel.

Nixon, Joan Lowery. *Nobody's There.* 2000. *MJS.* After throwing a rock through her father's girlfriend's window, seventeen-year-old Abbie is sentenced to spending time as a companion to Edna Merkel, an elderly woman. When Mrs. Merkel is attacked and hospitalized, Abbie searches for the perpetrator.

Nixon, Joan Lowery. *Playing for Keeps.* 2001. *MJS.* While on a Caribbean cruise with her grandmother, Rose Ann meets a young Cuban baseball player who is seeking political asylum in the United States and needs her help.

Nixon, Joan Lowery. *Who Are You?* 1999. *MJS.* When an art collector is shot, a file on sixteen-year-old artist Kristi Evans is found in his house. Kristi wants to know why. (Quick Picks)

Plum-Ucci, Carol. *The Body of Christopher Creed.* 2000. *JS.* After class geek Chris Creed disappears, leaving behind a cryptic note, popular sixteen-year-old Torey Adams finds himself drawn into the search. (BBYA; Printz-Honor)

Qualey, Marsha. *Close to a Killer.* 1999. *JS.* Seventeen-year-old Barrie has quirky reading tastes that she fulfills by hanging out at a used bookstore when she doesn't have to work in her mother's beauty salon. The salon, called Killer Looks because it's run by ex-cons, falls on hard times after a news show links it to the murders of two prominent citizens. (BBYA; Quick Picks)

Roberts, Willo Davis. *Twisted Summer.* 1996. *MJ.* Fourteen-year-old Cici finds a year-old murder to solve during the summer at her family's cabin at the lake. (IRAYAC; Edgar Award)

Wynne-Jones, Tim. *The Boy in the Burning House.* 2001. *MJS.* Fourteen-year-old Jim teams up with Ruth Rose, the pastor's stepdaughter, after she tells him that she thinks Father Fisher was involved in his father's disappearance two years earlier. As they delve into the mystery, they find a photo that shows a link between the missing Hub, Father Fisher, and a boy who was killed decades ago. (Edgar Award)

Yep, Laurence. *The Case of the Goblin Pearls.* 1997. *M.* Twelve-year-old Lily's great-aunt, the famous actress Tiger Lil, is coming to Chinatown to promote Lion Salve in the New Year's parade. While Tiger Lil is in town, Lily embarks on an adventure after witnessing the theft of the famous Goblin Pearls.

Historical Mysteries

Historical mysteries add the intrigue of far-off places and times to the usual appeal of mystery. Detailed descriptions of the setting lend a tone of realism to the stories. These books are often well researched to portray characters and their milieu in an authentic and accurate manner, and a strong sense of place and the times permeates the stories. Other genre elements, such as romance or suspense, blend well with this subgenre, providing readers with a rich and multifaceted reading experience.

Avi. *Midnight Magic.* 1999. *MJ.* Twelve-year-old Fabrizio goes to the castle with his master, a magician, to find out whether the princess is really seeing a ghost, or if something else is going on. A story with elements of fantasy and adventure. (Quick Picks)

Coles, William E., Jr. *Compass in the Blood.* 2001. *S.* College freshman Dee Armstrong becomes so fascinated by the century-old case of Katherine Soffel, the wife of a prison warden who helped two murderers escape, that she tries to solve the mystery here and now.

Dowell, Frances O'Roark. *Dovey Coe.* 2000. *MJS.* Dovey Coe, a strong-willed twelve-year-old girl, is accused of murder in 1928 North Carolina. (Edgar)

Hawke, Simon. Smythe and Shakespeare series. *S.* Symington Smythe, a theater apprentice, and aspiring playwright Will Shakespeare keep stumbling into mysteries.

> *A Mystery of Errors.* 2000. A young theater apprentice, Symington Smythe, and would-be playwright Will Shakespeare become embroiled in a mystery.

> *The Slaying of the Shrew.* 2001. Young Symington Smythe and Will Shakespeare go with their company to provide entertainment for a wedding. Unfortunately, the bride turns up dead.

Hoobler, Dorothy, and Thomas Hoober. Samurai series. *MJS.* Seikei, a fourteen-year-old in eighteenth-century Japan becomes a crime solver.

> *Ghost in the Tokaido Inn.* 1999. In eighteenth-century Japan, Seikei, a fourteen-year-old boy, witnesses a crime. His bravery in stepping forth to clear someone who was falsely accused brings him the respect of Judge Ooka, who then hires Seikei to investigate the crime and solve the mystery. (BBYA; IRAYAC)

> *The Demon in the Teahouse.* 2001. Fourteen-year-old Seikei, the adopted son of a Samurai judge, goes undercover in a tea house to try to find a serial killer who is targeting Geishas in eighteenth-century Japan.

Horowitz, Anthony. *The Devil and His Boy.* 2000. *M.* Tom Falconer is on his own in the mean streets of Elizabethan London after his employer is murdered. (VOYA; IRAYAC)

Lasky, Kathryn. *Alice Rose and Sam.* 1998. *M.* Alice Rose, a motherless twelve-year-old in Nevada during the Civil War, teams up with her father's new employee at the newspaper, Samuel Clemens (aka Mark Twain), to solve a murder that is connected to the war. (Popular Paperbacks)

Pullman, Philip. Sally Lockhart series. *JS.* Set in Victorian England, Sally Lockhart, an independent young woman, becomes embroiled in mysteries.

> *The Ruby in the Smoke.* 1987. Sixteen-year-old Sally encounters all types as she tries to solve a mystery she learned of from a cryptic message that puts her on the trail of a legendary ruby. (Popular Paperbacks; YALSA 100 Best Books)

> *The Shadow in the North.* 1988. At age twenty-two, Sally, now established in business, teams up with Frederick and Jim to find a lethal weapon developed by a wealthy man.

> *The Tiger in the Well.* 1990. Twenty-four-year-old Sally is now a single mom, and someone is out to destroy her as Jewish immigrants are preyed upon by an unknown foe.

Paranormal Mysteries

The mysteries in this section contain a generous helping of the paranormal, which adds another dimension to the suspense. Readers can expect dark and sinister atmospheres and a more emotional or psychological tone and response to these books, although the cerebral aspect of solving a mystery is very much present.

Buffie, Margaret. *Angels Turn Their Backs.* 1998. *MJ.* An agoraphobic fifteen-year-old named Addy is drawn into a mystery surrounding the death of someone who once lived in the apartment she can't leave. (IRAYAC)

Carroll, Jenny. 1-800-WHERE-R-YOU series. *MJS.* Titles are listed in the Mystery Series section of this chapter.

Duncan, Lois. *Gallows Hill.* 1997. *MJ.* Sarah Zoltanne is miserable in her new high school after her mother undergoes a strange midlife crisis and moves them to a small town, forgoing former friends and career. Sarah begrudgingly accepts the task of acting as a fortuneteller in the school carnival. Much to her surprise, she actually sees events in the crystal ball that she found in her late father's stuff. The class president and the daughter of her mother's boyfriend manipulate her into a partnership with them to make money by telling fortunes. As events escalate, Sarah has troubling dreams and visions linking her and the townspeople to the Salem witchcraft trials. (Quick Picks; IRAYAC)

Naylor, Phyllis Reynolds. *Jade Green.* 2000. *MJS.* The ghost of Jade Green haunts the house where Judith Sparrow lives. Annotated in Chapter 8, "Paranormal."

Nixon, Joan Lowery. *The Haunting.* 1998. *MJ.* A ghostly mystery is contained within the walls of Graymoss plantation, and Lia intends to solve it. (Quick Picks; IRAYAC)

Wieler, Diana. *RanVan: The Magic Nation.* 1998. *JS.* Rhan is off to study cinema, television, stage, and radio at Southern Alberta Institute of Technology. He finds he has a true gift for one-camera video that is enhanced by flashes of precognition. Meeting new people and running into someone from his past as a video knight, Rhan becomes enmeshed in a skinhead murder conspiracy.

Mystery Series

Like other series fiction, series mysteries allow readers to follow a character or characters through a series of events over time. Thus, the characters of these stories—sometimes a single protagonist and sometimes a group of friends—are often the major appeal. Series titles tend to be shorter in length and are often lighter in tone than nonseries mysteries. Unlike romance series, in which different authors often pen the various titles, mystery series are usually published under one author's name, a tradition that may be linked to the many mystery series titles attributed to Carolyn Keene but actually written by a stable of writers.

Carroll, Jenny. 1-800-WHERE-R-YOU series. *MJS.* Sixteen-year-old Jessica (Jess) Mastriani uses psychic powers to solve crimes.

> *When Lightning Strikes.* 2001. A bolt of lightning gives Jess Mastriani the psychic ability to find missing children.
>
> *Code Name Cassandra.* 2001. Both police and kidnappers stalk Jess Mastriani after she vows to not use her special abilities again.
>
> *Safe House.* 2002. Jess uses her abilities to solve a cheerleader's murder.

Chandler, Elizabeth. Dark Secrets series. *JS.* Three teen girls are haunted by the past.

> *Legacy of Lies.* 2000. Living with her cold grandmother, Megan begins having strange dreams. Then objects begin to move around the house. This book features suspense, romance, and the supernatural. (Quick Picks)
>
> *Don't Tell.* 2001. After her mother's drowning, Laurel goes to live with her Aunt Jule. But someone's watching her. (Quick Picks)
>
> *No Time to Die.* 2001. At a theater camp, Jenny's murdered sister Liza begins speaking to her. And who is it that keeps following her? (Quick Picks)

Cray, Jordan. Danger.Com series. *MJ.* Mystery, suspense, and the Internet.

> *Gemini7.* 1997. Jonah and Jen are quite a couple until Jonah starts picking up girlfriends on an Internet chat line. It's not too much of a problem until one of his cyberpals, the gorgeous Nicole Gemini, comes to town. That's when strange events start happening. (Quick Picks)
>
> *Firestorm.* 1997. Who might have imagined that the information superhighway would pose a threat to Randy Kincaid's life?
>
> *Shadow Man.* 1997. Annie only wanted to scare Pepper Oneida, but when she sends the e-mail to the wrong person, she finds herself in serious trouble.
>
> *Hot Pursuit.* 1997. The Internet can be hazardous to your health.
>
> *Stalker.* 1998. Mina's friend Camille has disappeared, leaving a trail of mysterious e-mails behind.
>
> *Bad Intent.* 1998. Only Brian can stop LoneLobo's mean tirades.
>
> *Most Wanted.* 1998. When sixteen-year-old Andy finds out he was adopted, he searches the Internet to find his real parents. What he finds is danger.
>
> *Dead Man's Hand.* 1998. Nick and Annie are thrown into a deadly murder investigation in Key West after Nick's e-mail draws attention from the wrong people.

Dahl, Michael. Finnegan Zwake Mysteries. *MJ.* Thirteen-year-old Finnegan travels the world with his Uncle Stoppard, solving mysteries.

> *The Horizontal Man.* 1999. Finnegan and his mystery-writing uncle are plunged into a real-life mystery when a rodent-chewed body is found in a basement storage room.

Ruby Raven. 1999. A trip to North Africa for Uncle Stoppard to accept a mystery award plunges Finnegan into another mystery.

The Worm Tunnel. 1999. An archaeological dig in Central America brings up more murders.

The Viking Claw. 2001. When visiting Iceland, Finnegan encounters a case involving missing mountain climbers.

The Coral Coffin. 2002. Washed overboard in the South Seas, Finnegan and Uncle Stoppard are picked up by ruthless pirates.

Delaney, Mark. Misfits series. *MJ.* Four high school students have a knack for stumbling upon and solving mysteries.

The Vanishing Chip. 1998. Peter, Byte, Jake, and Mattie, four high school students, try to find a missing computer chip and clear Mattie's grandfather of the crime.

Of Heroes and Villains. 1999. The four Misfits stumble into a mystery at a comic book convention.

Growler's Horn. 2000. A missing jazz musician is the focus of this Misfits case.

The Kingfisher's Tale. 2000. The four Misfits find their next mystery in a national forest.

The Protester's Song. 2001. The Misfits delve into a mystery that ties into the 1970 Kent State shootings.

Golden, Christopher. Body of Evidence. *S.* After Jenna Blake starts college at Somerset University near Boston, she lands a job helping in the medical examiner's office. There, she encounters all kinds of bizarre murders and works to solve them.

Soul Survivor. 1999. Bizarre ritual murders and a budding romance for Jenna.

Head Games. 2000. Returning home on Christmas break, Jenna discovers that three of her high school classmates have been brutally murdered.

Meets the Eye. 2000. Are the living dead behind a Boston crime wave? Jenna Blake is going to piece together the clues to tell her who or what is behind these "zombie" crimes. (Quick Picks)

Skin Deep. 2000. College student Jenna looks into the murder of an African American couple on campus, but her own interracial relationship may be putting her and her boyfriend in peril.

Brain Trust (Rick Hautala, coauthor). 2001. Jenna and her roommate Yoshiko travel to Florida on spring break—and stumble into a nest of murders.

Burning Bones (Rick Hautala, coauthor). 2001. When two people burst into flames, is it spontaneous human combustion—or is it murder?

Golden, Christopher. Prowlers series. *JS.* Annotated in Chapter 8, "Paranormal."

Rushford, Patricia H. Jennie McGrady Mystery series. *MJ.* As Jenny McGrady tries to solve the mystery of her father's disappearance, she finds herself involved in various mysteries connected to her family, to her school, and to her Christian church. Titles are listed and annotated in Chapter 12, "Christian Fiction."

Van Draanen, Wendelin. Sammy Keyes series. *M.* Thirteen-year-old Sammy Keyes, who lives—illegally—in a senior-citizens-only apartment building, is a sassy sleuth with a nose for trouble in this humorous series.

> *Sammy Keyes and the Hotel Thief.* 1998. Sammy starts sleuthing when she sees a crime but doesn't want to call 911 and jeopardize her living arrangement. (Edgar Award)

> *Sammy Keyes and the Skeleton Man.* 1998. Sammy interrupts a mugging by a skeleton-clad burglar.

> *Sammy Keyes and the Sisters of Mercy.* 1999. Sammy is doing time—community service time, that is—at St. Mary's Church when an ivory cross is stolen.

> *Sammy Keyes and the Runaway Elf.* 1999. Sammy faces a dog-napping, a kid who keeps running away, and a missing neighbor.

> *Sammy Keyes and the Curse of Moustache Mary.* 2001. When Sammy spends New Year's Eve at a friend's house, she meets the elderly Lucinda Huntley and her two-hundred-pound pet pig and ends up involved in a mystery involving the burning of a historic cabin.

> *Sammy Keyes and the Hollywood Mummy.* 2001. Sammy worries that her mother, an actress, may be in deadly danger.

> *Sammy Keyes and the Search for Snake Eyes.* 2002. A bag containing a baby is thrust into Sammy's hands at the mall.

Zindel, Paul. P. C. Hawke Mysteries. *M.* Teenagers P. C. Hawke and Mackenzie team up to solve mysteries.

> *The Scream Museum.* 2001. When Tom, a custodian at the Museum of Natural History, is accused of murder, high school juniors P. C. Hawke and Mackenzie Riggs dig into the crime and discover a stolen world-famous necklace.

> *The Surfing Corpse.* 2001. Nearly the whole junior class witnesses the waterfall plunge of Timmy Warner, which makes it all the stranger when he is sighted several months later.

> *The E-Mail Murders.* 2001. P. C. and Mac accompany Mac's dad on a business trip to Monaco, where a woman at the conference is murdered, apparently by a vicious serial killer known as Cyrano.

> *The Lethal Gorilla.* 2001. An unpopular celebrity scientist is murdered at the Bronx Zoo.

The Square Root of Murder. 2002. Fifteen-year-olds P. C. Hawke and Mackenzie Riggs try to solve the mystery of a teacher found pinned to a chalkboard with the bolt from a crossbow.

Death on the Amazon. 2002. P. C. and Mac end up escorting a mummy on an Amazon voyage.

The Gourmet Zombie. 2002. P. C. and Mac are on the case of Manhattan chefs dropping dead after eating their own signature dishes.

The Phantom of 86th Street. 2002. Can a bus really be haunted?

Chapter 6

Fantasy

Fantasy literature leads readers into realms of imagination and magic, of inexplicable occurrences that don't have a solid foundation in reality as we know it. Here readers find worlds inhabited by faerie, dragons, unicorns, and sorcerers. With fantasy, readers can travel through time and dimensions to alternate realities that do not necessarily share the same physical laws of our world. Of course, in the world of fantasy we do not have to worry whether the devices we use are logically, scientifically, or even remotely possible, as long as they are consistent within the fantasy realm.

Recently, fantasy fiction, led by the Harry Potter books, has enchanted millions and rekindled the interest of readers of all ages, from elementary school age children to adults, and certainly teens. Indeed, J. K. Rowling's Harry Potter series has made fantasy the hottest genre in the early twenty-first century. The popularity of the movie versions of the Lord of the Rings trilogy has also played its part in enticing teens to read fantasy. Because of this, publishers are releasing many new fantasy titles, as well as reissuing out-of-print titles such as Diana Wynne Jones's wonderful *Howl's Moving Castle* and Patricia C. Wrede's *Mairelon the Magician*. For fantasy fans, this is definitely a good time to be reading. This trend has even given rise to two new imprints—TorTeen, and Firebird from Penguin Putnam—both created specifically to reprint fantasy and science fiction for teen readers.

The near impossibility of distinguishing between fantasy and science fiction with respect to certain titles is discussed in greater detail at the beginning of "Science Fiction," Chapter 7. Classification of some titles is difficult, and a certain amount of subjectivity is inevitable. There will, no doubt, be disagreement on the placement of specific titles and authors. The division between the paranormal and fantasy is also a fine one, leaving even more room for personal opinion. That said, this guide defines fantasy as literature that embraces imagination and magic, with the presence of nonrational phenomena as the principal criterion for distinguishing fantasy from other types of literature. This quality of magic, more than any other, attracts fans of the genre.

Fantasy generally has a strong story line with well-defined forces of good and evil, which appeals to many readers, especially teens. In addition, setting plays an important role, with some of the most detailed and exotic worlds (e.g., Tolkien's Middle Earth, Anne McCaffrey's Pern, and L. Frank Baum's Land of Oz) born of fantasy literature. Whether the setting evokes a distant past, a distant future, or an alternate present reality, fantasy is, in a sense, timeless. The characters and creatures inhabiting these worlds are generally drawn in mythical proportions—fantastically good or fantastically evil.

Age and gender are not as crucial in fantasy as they are in other literary forms because protagonists are archetypal figures, but their character is important because it defines the story and its outcome. Because of the archetypal quality that many fantasy characters possess, fans of the genre are generally not too picky about which age group a book was written for. Adults read YA and even children's fantasies, and teens often read fantasies written for adults.

The pacing of a fantasy tale may be slow, particularly in the beginning of the story, when the author takes time to define, construct, and evoke the fantasy realm and its inhabitants. Yet against the larger-than-life backdrop of the fantasy world, great dramas unfold.

Coming of age is probably the most common theme in fantasy literature. Is it any wonder, then, that teen readers are drawn to this genre? Within this body of literature, there is also great diversity, however—from high-action adventure stories and spiritual quests to the more literary forms of magical realism, romantic tales, and moody, dark fantasies. Each of these subgenres holds special attractions that appeal to different readers.

This chapter is organized in two broad sections—the first based on distinct subgenres common to YA fiction, and the second based on popular themes that teen readers seek. A list of adult epic fantasy titles—written for adults but often enjoyed by teens—can be found in Appendix II at the end of this guide. Those interested in a more detailed treatment of the genre, with an orientation to adult readers, are encouraged to consult *Fluent in Fantasy* (Herald 1999).

Subgenres

There are many fantasy subgenres, but the ones listed here are those most commonly published for or read by young adults. Such subgenres as urban fantasy and dark fantasy can be found in teen literature, but not in great enough numbers to warrant their own sections. For subgenres that are not defined here, readers are encouraged to consult the subject index.

Epic Fantasy

Swashbuckling action and daring swordplay in worlds of magic are what you'll discover in this popular and predominant subgenre of fantasy. For many readers, epic fantasy *is* fantasy. The essence of these stories is the conflict between good and evil, along with the intervention or involvement of magic. The focus may be on a quest by a party of diverse personalities or on a singular heroic figure. These stories can run to many volumes and often have several subseries.

The group quest is one of the most successful motifs of fantasy. Tolkien's Lord of the Rings trilogy falls into this category and, often imitated, has also served as an inspiration for a plethora of fantasy novels. Trilogies are common, but if the series sells well, the publisher can add more volumes, almost always written by a single author.

Teens love epic fantasy published for adults, so a list of those titles is included in Appendix II. The popularity of the movie *Lord of the Rings* has brought Tolkien's trilogy to an entire new generation of readers who have begun to look for other books like these.

Nicholson, William. The Wind on Fire Trilogy. *MJS*. This series follows a twin sister and brother, Kestrel and Bowman Hath, in the dark and oppressive world of Aramanth as they search for freedom.

> *The Wind Singer.* 2000. A twin brother and sister, Bowman and Kestrel Hath, go on a quest for a silver whistle that will give a voice to a statue that signifies their people.

> *Slaves of the Mastery.* 2001. When the Mastery swoops in to take all their people as slaves, twins Kestrel and Bowman are separated. Bowman is taken on the long trek into slavery, and Kestrel follows and becomes the friend and servant of a beautiful princess, who is traveling to the Mastery to wed the Master's son.

> *Firesong.* 2002. Freed from the Mastery, Kestrel and Bowman, along with their family, head for the promised land.

Pattou, Edith. The Songs of Eirren. *JS*. In a Celtic world, brimming with wizards, warriors, and sorcerers, three heroes find adventure.

> *Hero's Song: The First Song of Eirren.* 1991. In a quest with several stalwart companions, Collun finds his missing sister Nessa and his own mysterious past, while saving the land from evil invaders.

> *Fire Arrow: The Second Song of Eirren.* 1998. While on her quest to revenge her father's murderer, Breo-Saight, "Brie," finds a magical arrow.

Pierce, Tamora. Circle of Magic. *MJ*. Four young people, all outcasts among their own people, are taken by Niklaren Goldeye to Winding Circle, a monastery-like isolated community. All four, not fitting in well at the dorms, are sent to live in a cottage called Discipline. Each has an unusual skill, a magical talent uncommon enough to be unrecognized until Nik found them. As the four housemates learn to tolerate each other, they also begin to learn to deal with their magic. While each title focuses on a different character's talent, each follows the events in the lives of all four.

> *Sandry's Book.* 1997. Four outcast youths—Daja, Briar, Tris, and Sandry—are brought to the Winding Circle Temple to learn magic and crafts.

> *Daja's Book.* 1998. Daja uses her powers to protect the land of the Traders, the people who turned her away.

> *Briar's Book.* 1998. Briar knows plant magic, but the skills of all four youths are needed to heal Briar's beloved friend.

> *Tris's Book.* 1999. Tris summons her powers with weather, and the skills of her fellow mages, to defeat the forces of the Pirate Queen Pahua. (Quick Picks)

Pierce, Tamora. The Circle Opens. *MJ.* The characters from the Circle of Magic Quartet—Sandry, Tris, Daja, and Briar—are now four years older and out on their own.

Magic Steps. 2000. Sandry, now fourteen, and her reluctant apprentice Pasco work together to stop the brutal killings in Emelan.

Street Magic. 2001. Briar begins to mentor a street urchin named Evvy, who has stone magic, and ends up fighting gang violence in the City of Chammur.

Cold Fire. 2002. Daja, accompanied by her teacher Frostpine, travels to Kugisko for a rest, but ends up tutoring twin girls in magic and fighting the fires set by arsonists.

Shatterglass. 2003. Tris must help glassblower Kethlun Warder control his magic and his temper.

Roberts, Katherine. The Echorium Sequence. *M.* The Singers maintain peace in their world by using their most extraordinary weapons—songs of power.

Song Quest. 2000. In the Isle of Echoes, only the Singers can keep the peace.

Crystal Mask. 2002. A wild girl, a Singer boy, and a horselord prince join to face the evil Khiz priest and his forces.

Turner, Megan Whalen. Eugenides series. *MJ.* Long ago, in a mysterious and faraway land, a talented young thief, Eugenides (Gen), finds adventure and intrigue.

The Thief. 1996. Eugenides, sentenced to life in prison, may be able to win his freedom if he can retrieve a legendary gemstone. (Newbery Honor; BBYA)

The Queen of Attolia. 2000. Caught between two warring queens, Eugenides is captured and his hand amputated.

Faerie

The world of Faerie should not be confused with the world of fairy tales. It is inhabited by elven creatures who have powers that to us seem magic. It can be dark, sinister, and dangerous. Time moves at a different pace in a world that coexists, side by side, with ours. Sometimes a rift between the worlds allows someone of Faerie into our world or someone of ours into theirs. Often, the interaction of humans and residents of Faerie sets up the conflict. There also seems a great proclivity for humans and those of Faerie blood to fall in love. Derived from Celtic folklore, Faerie folk are often referred to as Sidhe.

Barron, T. A. *Tree Girl.* 2001. *M.* When she was a baby, Rowanna was rescued by the ancient Mellwyn from beneath the High Willow tree in a forest that is haunted by tree ghouls. Now nine years old, she wants to find out who her parents are. So she ventures into the forest, where she discovers that there are no tree ghouls, but that she isn't exactly human.

Black, Holly. *Tithe, a Modern Faerie Tale.* 2002. *S.* When Kaye moves to New Jersey with her dysfunctional mother, she hopes she will see her childhood faerie friends again. One night, walking home after being attacked, Kaye hears a noise in the woods and meets Roiben, a silver-haired elven knight who has been wounded. A trip to the Seelie court under a hill and Kaye finds herself designated as a sacrifice to keep the unaffiliated fey free for seven years. This is a gruesome take on the world of faerie, along with a little romance and a generous helping of teen angst. (BBYA)

Colfer, Eoin. Artemis Fowl series. *MJ.* Twelve-year-old Artemis Fowl is rich, intelligent, and greedy. His criminal mind takes him into a fantastic realm of adventure.

> *Artemis Fowl.* 2001. An evil boy genius schemes to take a member of LEP-recon hostage to further fill the family's bulging coffers.

> *The Arctic Incident.* 2002. Enemies Captain Holly Short and Artemis team up to thwart a goblin plot and rescue Artemis's kidnapped father.

> *The Eternity Code.* 2003. After five years as a prisoner, Artemis Fowl's father returns home an honest man who makes Artemis promise to forego his life of crime. But Artemis has one last scheme to run. It involves the C Cube, which will make all human technology obsolete.

de Lint, Charles. *Seven Wild Sisters.* 2002. *MJS.* Sarah Jane, the middle sister of seven, befriends Aunt Lillian, who lives in a remote patch of the woods. The teen learns a great deal about the natural world from the old woman but also hears stories of sangmen and bee fairies. Just knowing about them doesn't protect her or her sisters when she finds a wounded sangman and interferes in the affairs of a different world. Vess's charming pen-and-ink illustrations work well with the text. (BBYA)

Mythic Reality

Stories in this section feature artfully re-created reality, focusing on life's mysteries; where a recognizable reality veers into the fantastic. Often beings from myth and legend are present. The stories in this subgenre often appeal to readers who enjoy literary fiction.

Allende, Isabel. *City of the Beasts.* 2002. *JS.* Fifteen-year-olds Alexander Cold and Nadia Santos venture deep into the heart of the Amazon on a quest for a Yeti-like beast. What they find is much more.

Almond, David. *Heaven Eyes.* 2001. *MJ.* Three troubled orphans escape from an orphanage on a makeshift raft and meet up with Heaven Eyes, a strange web-fingered girl.

Almond, David. *Skellig.* 1998. *MJ.* Michael finds a strange creature in the dilapidated garage of the house into which his family has just moved. (Printz-Honor; Carnegie Award; Whitbread Award)

Berry, Liz. *The China Garden.* 1996. *JS.* Having just finished her final exams and ready to go to university, Clare Meredith finds out that her mother is going to Ravensmere, where the legends of the Guardians go deep into the past. Clare insists on accompanying her mother to Ravensmere, where she meets the handsome, leather-clad biker Mark. Together they must find the mysterious treasure of legend, the Benison, and restore the tradition of Guardians to ensure the well-being of the community. (Popular Paperbacks; BBYA)

Block, Francesca Lia. *Dangerous Angels: The Weetzie Bat Books.* 1998. *JS.* This collection includes all of Block's Weetzie Bat novels (listed following this entry) that tell the surrealistic tales of Weetzie Bat, Dirk, Duck, My Secret Agent Lover Man, and their offspring in a magical L.A.

> *Weetzie Bat.* 1989. Weetzie Bat has a bleached-blonde flat top, pink sunglasses, and she's all punk. She and her equally crazed friend are just trying to survive in modern L.A. A teen classic. (BBYA)

> *Witch Baby.* 1991. The story of Witch Baby, the spirited and purple-eyed daughter of Weetzie Bat's lover.

> *Cherokee Bat and the Goat Guys.* 1992. Weetzie's teenage daughter Cherokee starts a rock band, the Goat Guys, and comes of age in L.A.

> *Missing Angel Juan.* 1993. When Angel Juan leaves for New York City, it breaks Witch Baby's heart.

> *Baby Be-Bop.* 1995. The story of Weetzie Bat's friend Dirk, growing up gay.

Cohn, Rachel. *Gingerbread.* 2002. *MJS.* Cyd Charisse has gotten into some trouble in her sixteen years, but she has her telepathic doll, Gingerbread. Annotated in the Coming of Age section of Chapter 3, "Contemporary Life."

Goobie, Beth. *Before Wings.* 2001. *JS.* After surviving a brain aneurysm, fifteen-year-old Arden goes to work for her aunt at a summer camp in Canada, where five spirits haunt her and she uncovers a mystery tied to the past. (Young Adult Canadian Book Award)

Hoffman, Alice. *Aquamarine.* 2001. *M.* Two twelve-year-olds, Hailey and Claire, discover a mysterious and beautiful mermaid in the swimming pool of a neglected beach club.

Kindl, Patrice. *The Woman in the Wall.* 1997. *MJS.* Anna, who is extremely handy but shy, fades into the woodwork to the extent that people, including her family forget she exists. (BBYA; Popular Paperbacks; IRAYAC)

Shetterly, Will. *Dogland.* 1997. *JS.* Fantasy elements are subtly woven into this tale of young Chris Nix, whose parents have opened a Florida theme attraction that features every dog breed. Magic and human relationships are set against a frightening backdrop of the battle for integration in the South.

Shusterman, Neal. *Downsiders.* 1999. *MJ.* When fourteen-year-old Lindsay meets Talon, who lives in the secret Downsider community that evolved in the subterranean passages of the subway built in New York in 1867, she and her new friend try to bridge the differences between their two cultures. (Popular Paperbacks; BBYA; Quick Picks)

Myth and Legend

Tales anchored in traditional myths and legends remain popular with today's teen readers. Myths and legends are related to quest in that traditional stories generally involve adventure and quest, and they contain the larger truths common to fantasy quests, as well as heroic characters. Likewise, coming of age is a frequent theme in this subgenre, as it is in the quest story.

Most of the recent publications in this area are not retellings of the ancient stories, however, but extrapolations or entire reworkings of the tales. Sometimes the focus of the story shifts to another character—possibly a minor character or the antagonist, or even a character never mentioned in the original tale—and thus an alternative or opposite perspective is explored, which can be enlightening or humorous. Sometimes the story is extended with further exploits and events of the heroes, building upon the original story and filling in fascinating details.

Teens are generally in a stage of questioning old truths and stories, and readers familiar with the original versions of these myths delight in digging deeper into the milieu, considering both the extensions of and the challenges posited against the original stories, and discovering the possibilities of "what if?"

Fans of myths and legends may also respond to the particular settings and characters of these works. For example, Robin Hood and King Arthur are frequent subjects of current releases in this subgenre, because many readers are attracted to Robin Hood's rebellious reform or to Arthur's romantic heroism.

Coville's anthology *Half-Human,* annotated in the Short Stories section of this chapter, features many of the different "creatures" of myth and legend, including a gorgon.

General

Cadnum, Michael. Robin Hood series. *JS.*

> *In a Dark Wood.* 1998. In a fascinating turnaround, the Sheriff of Nottingham is depicted in a sympathetic light. Forced by his office to seek Robin Hood, the sheriff really doesn't want to hurt anyone—he just wants to keep his position as a king's man.

> *Forbidden Forest.* 2002. Little John is the focus of this gritty portrayal of medieval life.

Cooney, Caroline B. *Goddess of Yesterday*. 2002. *M.* At age thirteen, Anaxander is sent from her island home to Troy, offering readers new perspective on the Iliad.

Geras, Adele. *Troy*. 2001. *MJS.* Marpessa, nursemaid to Hector's baby son, and her sister, maid to Helen, sees the events of the Trojan War unfolding before their eyes as gods and goddesses make brief appearances but erase any memories of them left behind. Both girls fall in love—but with the same young soldier because of the interference of the gods. (BBYA)

McKinley, Robin. *Outlaws of Sherwood*. 1988. *JS.* A fresh iteration of the Robin Hood story. (BBYA)

Napoli, Donna Jo. *Sirena*. 1998. *JS.* Sirena, a mermaid, falls in love and becomes involved in the Trojan War. (BBYA; IRAYAC)

Springer, Nancy. Rowan Hood series. *MJ.*

> *Rowan Hood: Outlaw Girl of Sherwood Forest.* 2001. Thirteen-year-old Rowan goes into the forest to find her father, Robin Hood, after her mother is murdered.

Lionclaw. 2002. After being disowned, Lionel, Lord Lionclaw's extremely shy, seven-foot son, joins Rowan in Sherwood Forest.

Arthurian Legend

Stories about King Arthur and the characters around him are rampant in the fantasy genre, and the books on this theme form a distinct group that certain readers seek out. The Arthurian milieu is one of romantic idealism, which appeals to many readers, as do the various characters within it. Many of the titles listed here are older ones that have proved their appeal for teens over several years. It seems that several titles are published each year featuring Arthur, Merlin, Guinevere, Mordred, Morgan le Fay, and others associated with the era.

Cochran, Molly, and Warren Murphy. Arthur Blessing series. *JS.* Arthur Blessing may look like an ordinary child, but he holds the Holy Grail by right of birth.

> *The Forever King.* 1992. Who would guess that ten-year-old Arthur Blessing is destined to be king?

> *The Broken Sword.* 1997. Further exploits of Arthur, Beatrice, and Hal (Sir Galahad).

Crossley-Holland, Kevin. Arthur Trilogy. *MJ.* Living in twelfth-century England, thirteen-year-old Arthur is given an obsidian "seeing stone" by Merlin that lets him look in on the parallel life of another Arthur who lived long before him.

> *The Seeing Stone.* 2001. Looking into an obsidian stone given to him by Merlin, Arthur, the thirteen-year-old son of Sir John de Caldicot, finds strange parallels between his life and that of Arthur, son of Uther, who lived centuries before him.

> *At the Crossing Places.* 2002. The twelfth-century Arthur, now fourteen, goes to serve as squire to Lord Stephen and continues to follow the story of the other Arthur in his seeing stone.

Morris, Gerald. Arthurian series. *MJ.* Various characters from Arthurian legend are thrown together with young protagonists and a touch of humor to make the tales come alive for younger readers.

> *The Squire's Tale.* 1997. Fourteen-year-old Terence becomes squire to Sir Gawain and discovers the secret of his parentage.

> *The Squire, His Knight, and His Lady.* 1999. When Gawain is imprisoned, young Terence must rescue him. (BBYA)

> *The Savage Damsel and the Dwarf.* 2000. Sixteen-year-old Lady Lynet escapes her besieged castle to request help from King Arthur. (BBYA; VOYA)

> *Parsifal's Page.* 2001. Eleven-year-old Piers goes to Arthur's court, where he discovers that Parsifal is in dire need of a page who knows the rules of chivalry. (IRAYAC)

> *The Ballad of Sir Dinaden.* 2003. Raised to be a knight, young Dinaden would prefer to be a minstrel.

Springer, Nancy. I Am series. *MJ.* Stories told from the perspectives of other characters in the King Arthur legend.

> *I Am Morgan le Fay.* 2001. Morgan le Fay's own story of how she went from a young girl to a being despised as a villain.
>
> *I Am Mordred: A Tale from Camelot.* 1998. Fifteen-year-old Mordred attempts to avoid the fate that will destroy both Arthur and himself.

Stewart, Mary. The Merlin series. A romantic retelling of the Arthurian tale, this one featuring Merlin, from a master of romantic suspense. **Adult** Classic

> *Crystal Cave.* 1970. The early life of Merlin in fifth-century Britain. (YALSA 100 Best Books)
>
> *The Hollow Hills.* 1973. Merlin places Arthur in hiding. (Mythopoeic Award)
>
> *The Last Enchantment.* 1979. Merlin can do nothing to keep Arthur safe from Morgause, but he can help with the fight against the Saxons.
>
> *Wicked Day.* 1983. Mordred returns to his father's court to destroy him, and Merlin can do nothing to stop him.

Thomson, Sarah L. *The Dragon's Son.* 2001. *JS.* The Arthurian legend with a Welsh slant.

Yolen, Jane. *Sword of the Rightful King: A Novel of King Arthur.* 2003. *MJ.* A different twist on the Arthurian legend and the sword in the stone.

Fairy Tales

Retelling and reworking traditional fairy tales and folktales is a growing trend in publishing and in teen and adult reading. These stories combine familiar characters or story lines with new twists and fresh perspectives. Readers will be well acquainted with some of the stories told in the following novels, and other stories are seemingly brand new, but with a tone that elicits the underlying feeling that the story has been told before.

Humor is often used in retellings and reworkings. Ed the Troll with his malapropisms in Ferris's *Once upon a Marigold* is an example of the sometimes laugh-out-loud humor to be found in this subgenre. Other reworkings can be deadly serious, like McKinley's *Deerskin,* the tale of a princess who must fear the advances of her father.

Readers interested in exploring the permutations of fairy tale derivatives are encouraged to consult *New Tales for Old* (Altmann and de Vos, 1999) and *Tales, Then and Now* (Altmann and de Vos 2001), both resources for exploring reworkings of fairy tales and folktales for teens.

Block, Francesca Lia. *I Was a Teenage Fairy.* 1998. *JS.* Annotated in the Sexual Abuse section of Chapter 2, "Issues." (Quick Picks)

Card, Orson Scott. *Enchantment.* 1999. *JS.* On the edge of the Carpathian mountains, young Ivan sees a wondrous sight. It appears to be a beautiful woman sleeping on a hidden pedestal in the middle of a perfectly circular chasm guarded by an unseen monster rustling under a fill of leaves. As an adult, Ivan returns to what is now Ukraine and uses the skills he perfected by participating in track to defeat—temporarily—the bear under the leaves so he can leap to the pedestal and kiss Sleeping Beauty awake. But this is only the beginning.

Ferris, Jean. *Once upon a Marigold.* 2002. *MJ.* Christian, raised in a cave by Ed the Troll, falls for the Princess Marigold and leaves to take up a position at the castle so he can be near her. A witty and humorous original fairy tale. (BBYA)

Haddix, Margaret Peterson. *Just Ella.* 1999. *MJS.* After Ella Brown discovers that happily ever after isn't all it's cracked up to be, she takes destiny into her own hands and escapes from the castle. (BBYA; Quick Picks; IRAYAC)

Kindl, Patrice. *Goose Chase.* 2001. *MJS.* No good deed goes unpunished, and to Goose Girl's chagrin her kindness to an old crone results in beauty and riches that are now ruining her life. Hair that sheds gold dust and tears that are diamonds make her incredibly attractive, not only to the silly local prince, but also to the evil king of a neighboring kingdom. Goose Girl locks herself in a tower to avoid marriage but is eventually rescued by her gaggle of geese, only to end up in the lair of a trio of ogresses. As more adventures ensue, Goose Girl proves her mettle.

Levine, Gail Carson. *Ella Enchanted.* 1997. *MJS.* In this enchanting take on the Cinderella story, resourceful Ella makes the best of things, considering that she is under an extremely unfortunate curse, and has an uncaring father, unlikeable stepsisters, and an almost evil stepmom. A delightful read. (Popular Paperbacks; BBYA; Quick Picks; IRAYAC; Newbery Honor)

Levine, Gail Carson. *The Two Princesses of Bamarre.* 2001. *MJ.* Princess Addie is afraid of nearly everything, while her sister, Princess Meryl, craves adventure. But when Meryl is struck down by the Gray Death, Addie is willing to battle dragons and slay ogres to save her sister.

Marillier, Juliet. *Daughter of the Forest.* 2000. *JS.* Sorcha would have been the seventh son of a seventh son had she been born male. With her mother dead soon after her birth, Sorcha's six older brothers have pretty much raised her in the family's Irish keep, while their father has tried to keep the shores free of raiding Britons and others. Seemingly ensorcelled, their father remarries, and Sorcha's brothers are put under a curse. They must live as swans until Sorcha can spin and weave the poisonous and prickly starwort into shirts for them. (Alex Award; BBYA; IRAYAC)

McKinley, Robin. *Beauty.* 1978. *MJS.* The story of "Beauty and the Beast" is recast with an intelligent and talented Beauty whose two sisters are kind and lovely. (BBYA; YALSA 100 Best Books)

McKinley, Robin. *Rose Daughter.* 1997. *MJS.* A reworking of "Beauty and the Beast" with fully realized characters in the three sisters and their failed merchant father. Unlike the traditional versions, Beauty's sisters are decent and likable characters. Roses and their cultivation play a large role in this tale, as does the magical castle of the beast. (BBYA)

Napoli, Donna Jo. *Beast.* 2000. *JS.* Set in Persia and France, this reworking of "Beauty and the Beast" is told from the viewpoint of the beast.

Napoli, Donna Jo. *Crazy Jack.* 1999. *MJ.* Everyone thinks Jack is crazy because he frequently throws himself against the unscalable cliff where he saw his ne'er-do-well father disappear several years earlier. Will greed win out, or will he emerge triumphant in time to claim the hand of his childhood sweetheart?

Napoli, Donna Jo. *Zel.* 1996. *MJS.* In this reworking of "Rapunzel," Zel catches the eye of a young nobleman while helping the smith with a horse on one of her rare visits to town. Then Mother takes Zel to a tower where she tells her she will be safe from bad people who are trying to find and kill her. Zel, isolated and suffering from the horrendous headaches that her magically long hair causes, descends into madness. Mother struggles with her decisions and the issues of eternal damnation. Konrad relentlessly searches for the young woman who is inextricably linked to him on a level that no one else can understand. (Popular Paperbacks)

Napoli, Donna Jo, and Richard Tchen. *Spinners.* 1999. *MJ.* Rumplestiltskin is recast in a more sympathetic light.

Pierce, Meredith Ann. *Treasure at the Heart of the Tanglewood.* 2001. *JS.* Hannah, a young healer without memories, lives at the edge of the mysterious and deadly tanglewood with her talking animal companions. She heals the local cotters with herbal remedies that she plucks from her hair to infuse as medicines. Once a month she must pluck all the plant life from her tresses to brew a tea she takes to the wizard in the tanglewood. When she begins to rebel by secretly allowing some of the plants and flowers in her hair to grow unplucked, Spring begins to touch the land, and her gauzy dress takes on a new color. (BBYA)

6

Pullman, Philip. *Clockwork.* 1998. *MJS.* A quick-to-read parable-like fairy tale, this circular story ties together divergent stories in a magical way. (Quick Picks)

Schmidt, Gary D. *Straw into Gold.* 2001. *MJ.* What would have happened if the miller's daughter failed to guess Rumplestiltskin's name? On Tousle's first foray into town, he is the only one to step forward to protest the execution of a band of the poor who have been accused of treason. To save them and help them avoid their fate, he sets out, accompanied by the blinded Innes, on a quest to find the answer to a riddle asked by the king.

Yolen, Jane. *Briar Rose.* 1992. *S.* "Sleeping Beauty" is infused with horrors of the holocaust. (YALSA 100 Best Books)

Humorous Fantasy

Fantasy frequently has a humorous element, but in humorous fantasy, the humor figures more prominently. Language devices, especially word play and puns, are heavily employed in some humorous fantasy, while satire, parody, and even slapstick are among the other techniques used. Teens generally enjoy humor—it's a great equalizer and stress reliever—and although every person's sense of humor is unique, the titles that follow are proven favorites among teen readers.

Alexander, Lloyd. *Gypsy Rizka.* 1999. *M.* Orphaned Rizka, a trickster extraordinaire, finds a place in the hearts of Greater Dunitsa's residents.

Conford, Ellen. *The Frog Princess of Pelham.* 1996. *M.* At age fifteen, poor little rich orphan Chandler has never been kissed, her shyness mistaken for aloofness. Her odious guardian plans to send her off to survival camp during a school break while he vacations in Switzerland, but Chandler wants to find some way—any way—out of it. On the last day of school, Danny asks if he can kiss her, with the hilarious result of her being transformed into a frog. Luckily, the travel arrangements allow her to go un-missed as she and Danny try to find a way to return her to human form.

Jones, Diana Wynne. *Howl's Moving Castle.* 1985. *MJS.* When seventeen-year-old Sophie is transformed into a seventy-year-old crone, she seeks relief by decamping in mobile castle belonging to a mysterious wizard. Reissued in 2001. (BBYA) Classic

Pratchett, Terry. Discworld series. *MJS.* Pratchett's lengthy series is set on a world that rests on the backs of four elephants, riding on a turtle. It started in 1983 with *The Color of Magic* and is still going strong with *Night Watch,* published in 2002. The following titles were published specifically for younger readers. **Adult**

> *The Amazing Maurice and His Educated Rodents.* 2001. A talking cat, a stupid-looking boy, and several highly intelligent rats are running a Pied Piper scam on the villages they travel through. As Pratchett's first Discworld novel written for teens and older children, this title holds appeal for adults as well.

> *The Wee Free Men.* 2003. A nine-year-old witch named Tiffany teams up with the wee free men, blue tattooed pictsies in kilts, to rescue her kidnapped little brother from the Queen of the Elves.

Snicket, Lemony. A Series of Unfortunate Events. *MJS.* The hideously hilarious happenings in the lives of the family Baudelaire are detailed in the events that ensnare Violet, Klaus, and Sunny (who bites) after they are orphaned and entrusted to Mr. Poe, a guardian who keeps placing them in situations that just go from bad to worse. No matter what happens, the villainous Count Olaf—who will go to any lengths to obtain their money—always shows up.

> *The Bad Beginning.* 1999. The Baudelaire children are informed that their parents perished in a fire that destroyed their home and are sent off to live with evil Count Olaf, who hatches a plot to marry Violet.

> *The Reptile Room.* 1999. The Baudelaire orphans go to live with Dr. Montgomery, who travels, studies snakes, and cooks up coconut cream cakes, but of course nothing is going to end happily.

> *The Wide Window.* 2000. Violet, Klaus, and Sunny are taken to live with Aunt Josephine, who is afraid of everything.

> *The Miserable Mill.* 2000. Things, as always, have gone from bad to worse for the Baudelaire orphans, who are now sent to labor in the Lucky Smells Sawmill.

> *The Austere Academy.* 2000. The pitiable trio is sent off to Prufrock Preparatory School where they think life will get better because they love books, but, alas, they are shuffled off to live in the horrible Orphan's Shack made of tin.

The Ersatz Elevator. 2001. Because orphans are "in," trendy Esmé Gigi Geniveve Squalor takes the three Baudelaires in to live in her seventy-one-bedroom penthouse apartment , but because elevators are "out" they must climb the sixty-seven flights to get there.

The Vile Village. 2001. Because "it takes a village to raise a child," the Baudelaires are sent to an unfortunately crow-infested village.

The Hostile Hospital. 2001. Falsely accused of murder, the three Baudelaires seek refuge in a hospital disguised as volunteers.

The Carnivorous Carnival. 2002. The unfortunate siblings go into hiding as freaks in a carnival side show.

Wrede, Patricia C. Enchanted Forest Chronicles. *MJS.* A series featuring tongue-in-cheek humor and an assortment of characters who lurk on the edge of familiarity.

Dealing with Dragons. 1990. Princess Cimorene searches for happiness and fulfillment by moving in with a dragon. (YALSA 100 Best Books)

Searching for Dragons. 1991. The king of the enchanted forest meets a most unusual princess, and together they are able to save the kingdom.

Calling on Dragons. 1993. Troublesome wizards have found their way back into the enchanted forest, and Queen Cimorene must call on her friends for help.

Talking to Dragons. 1993. Sixteen-year-old Prince Daystar, the son of Queen Cimorene and King Mendanbar, is sent out on a mysterious quest.

Short Stories

Some tales just work best in a shorter form, and some readers enjoy the shorter length that this format offers. Short story collections also offer readers a way to become familiar with a wide range of authors. Because the stories in a collection do not fall into the same subgenres or even the same themes, readers can experience a broad sampling of story types. The short story is not a subgenre, but a format; nonetheless, the titles here share multiple characteristics, the way a subgenre does. Thus, short stories have been grouped with other fantasy subgenres.

Coville, Bruce, ed. *Half-Human.* 2001. *MJS.* Stories featuring teens who are not all human, including Dusie who is a gorgon, Icarus who has wings but cannot fly, a selkie, a mermaid, a princess with dragon blood, and other partially human teens.

Datlow, Ellen, and Terri Windling, eds. *The Green Man: Tales from the Mythic Forest.* 2002. *JS.* (Alternative formats) Short stories and poems by leading fantasy authors featuring the mythic Green Man in one form or another. (BBYA)

de Lint, Charles. *Waifs and Strays*. 2002. *S*. A collection of urban fantasy stories featuring teenage protagonists, vampires, Native American myth, magic, and more.

McKinley, Robin, and Peter Dickinson. *Water: Tales of Elemental Spirits*. 2002. *JS*. Each of these stories has some connection to water. The concluding story is connected to McKinley's Damar series, annotated in the Heroes and Heroines section of this chapter.

Van Pelt, James. *Strangers and Beggars*. 2002. *S*. A giant spider that encapsulates a student and a teacher in its web, a kid who has always felt he is an alien (and really is), and an endless trip in awful traffic that even death can't end are just a few of the story lines in this collection that spans fantasy, science fiction, and the paranormal. (BBYA)

Wrede, Patricia C. *Book of Enchantments*. 1996. *MJ*. Ten enchanting stories and a recipe by a master of humorous fantasy showcase a variety of settings and types. "Utensile Strength," set in the same world as the Enchanted Forest Chronicles (annotated in the Humorous Fantasy section of this chapter), features a stranger who turns up with a mysterious magical weapon called the Frying Pan of Doom. "Roses by Moonlight" is a sensitive story with a contemporary setting and a powerful, although not preachy, message.

Yolen, Jane. *Twelve Impossible Things before Breakfast*. 1997. *MJS*. From the troll's bridge retelling the story of the three billy goats to "Wendy" meeting Peter Pan again, these twelve stories mix fantasy, horror, and plenty of imagination.

Themes

Some readers look for specific themes in the fantasy fiction they read. There are those who want only tales of heroic girls, or dragons, or psionic abilities. The themes that follow are especially popular with teen readers. For titles with other themes, readers are encouraged to consult the subject index of this guide.

Heroes and Heroines

People who accomplish deeds that make them larger than life are the protagonists in the following novels. They often start out as seemingly ordinary individuals who, through sacrifice, hard work, and courage, accomplish heroic deeds.

Aiken, Joan. *The Cockatrice Boys*. 1996. *MJS*. Humans have been forced underground since England has been overrun by monsters. A small band of heroes tries to find the source of the infestation and save humanity.

Bell, Hilari. *The Goblin Wood*. 2003. *MJS*. Makenna, the child of a hedgewitch, goes on the run after new laws result in the execution of her kindly and gentle mother. Unable to see anything held captive in a snare, Makenna frees a goblin, making him indebted to her. In this world, goblins have always been left offerings of milk and bread, but the new laws that killed Makenna's mother have also wreaked havoc on the goblins.

Dickinson, Peter. *The Ropemaker.* 2001. *JS.* The valley has lived in peace and prosperity for twenty generations, guarded by impregnable glaciers at one end and an enchanted forest that sickens men at the other. The women in Tilja's family have kept the forest defenses strong by singing to the cedars, while the men of Tahl's family have listened to the streams running from the mountains. But now the protections are wearing off, and to renew them, Tilja and Tahl, along with her grandmother and his grandfather, must venture into the empire in search of the powerful magician who granted the valley its safety so long ago. (Printz-Honor)

Jordan, Sherryl. *The Hunting of the Last Dragon.* 2002. *MJ.* When Jude's family falls victim to a terrifying dragon, he despairs. Then he meets a remarkable girl from a distant land who has the knowledge that might help him find and slay the dragon. (BBYA)

McKinley, Robin. Damar series. *MJS.* Aerin, daughter of a king and a witchwoman, seeks her destiny in the ancient kingdom of Dama. Fans of the series will enjoy the Damar story that appears in McKinley and Dickinson's short story collection *Water: Tales of Elemental Spirits* (2002), annotated in the Short Stories section of this chapter.

> *The Hero and the Crown.* 1984. Aerin, a dragon-slaying princess, wins the approval of her father's people. (BBYA; Newbery) Classic

> *The Blue Sword.* 1982. Orphaned Harry Crewe is kidnapped by a Hillfolk king, which leads her to the realization that she has mysterious powers. This is set in the Damar world long after *The Hero and the Crown.* (BBYA; YALSA 100 Best Books; Newbery Honor)

Pierce, Tamora. Protector of the Small series. *MJS.* Follows the exploits of a young girl, Kelandry, from age ten to eighteen, and from page to knight.

> *First Test.* 1999. At age ten, all Kelandry wants to do is prove herself as a page—and as the first known girl to be admitted to the training.

> *Page.* 2000. Kelandry finds support from friends, as well as adversity from other pages, as she spends three years undergoing the required training to become a squire—the first girl ever to do so.

> *Squire.* 2001. Following a difficult path, Kelandry, in the kingdom of Tortall, becomes a squire at age fourteen for Raoul, the Knight Commander of the King's Own, until she is eligible for knighthood four years later. Along the way, she slays a centaur, rescues a gryphon, and falls in love. (BBYA)

> *Lady Knight.* 2002. Kelandry achieves her goal of becoming a knight, but in the midst of a war, she must face a deadly enemy.

Smith, Sherwood. Crown and the Court Duet. *MJ.* A brother and sister, Bran and Meliara, risk all to save the people from a tyrannical king.

> *Crown Duel.* 1997. Countess Meliara and her brother Bran fight the evil King Galdran to save the people of Remalna.

Court Duel. 1998. Countess Meliara finds life at the castle more treacherous than that on the battlefront.

Magic

Magic is an important element of fantasy. The ability to bend the world according to one's will is powerfully attractive. Magic in literature is akin to special effects in movies. Among a certain group of readers, it is the most important aspect of the book. The tales in this section feature youth with supernatural abilities. The popularity of the Harry Potter books has made this one of the hottest topics in fantasy publishing today.

Jones, Diana Wynne. Derkholm series. *MJS.* Derk, an unconventional wizard, resides in a world of magic with his fantastic family.

> *Dark Lord of Derkholm*. 1998. Plagues of tourists are ruining a magical world and making life miserable for Derk's family. Derk is a wizard who is chosen to be the Dark Lord for the annual Pilgrim Parties led by the onerous Mr. Chesney. (Mythopoeic Award)

> *Year of the Griffin*. 2000. The scions of several families (including Derk's griffin daughter) apply to Wizard's University, where they are welcomed in the hopes that they will help fill the depleted coffers, but none of them are there with their family's blessings or funds. The "school" setting will charm Harry Potter fans, and the fascinatingly diverse students will be a hit with fantasy afficionados. (BBYA)

Leavitt, Martine. *The Dollmage*. 2002. *MJS.* The Dollmage of Seekvalley decrees that her successor will be born on a certain day. When that day comes, two boys and two girls are born whose lives will be linked. There can be only one Dollmage at a time, but both girls show that they have the required magical skills, which eventually leads to death and loss. (BBYA)

Nix, Garth. Old Kingdom Trilogy. *MJS.*

> *Sabriel*. 1995. After Sabriel receives her father's necromancy tools, she ventures into the land of Death to find him. (BBYA; YALSA 100 Best Books)

> *Lirael*. 2001. By age fourteen, Lirael has still not come into the precognitive powers that show up in all the other Clayr. So, she becomes a librarian in the vast warren of a library that houses not only books but also monstrous dangers and arcane magic. As Lirael's adolescence passes, she continues her explorations in the library, learning how to assume an animal shape. She even discovers a remote hidden room that has her name on it. Lirael also discovers that she can see into the past and has a vision that shows her an image of her father, whose identity is unknown to any of the Clayr. (BBYA; Ditmar; IRAYAC)

> *Abhorsen*. 2003. Lirael, now the Abhorsen-in-Waiting, and her companions must fight the Destroyer.

Rowling, J. K. Harry Potter series. *MJS.* This tale of an underdog orphan who is summoned to a secret boarding school where magic is practiced was published for children, but teens and adults are among its biggest fans. Starting when Harry is ten years old, each book covers another year in his life, evolving from a children's series to a young adult series as Harry hits his teens. For many teens, "Harry" has made reading fashionable again, and the success of this series triggered the tremendous renaissance in fantasy publishing.

Harry Potter and the Sorcerer's Stone. 1998. (Film: *Harry Potter and the Sorcerer's Stone*) Originally published in England under the title *Harry Potter and the Philosopher's Stone,* the first volume introduces ten-year-old Harry, his odious relatives, and the wonderful Hogwarts School of Witchcraft and Wizardry. (BBYA; IRAYAC; YALSA 100 Best Books) Film

Harry Potter and the Chamber of Secrets. 1999. (Film: *Harry Potter and the Chamber of Secrets*) Harry is having a perfectly terrible summer vacation away from Hogwarts when his friends rescue him in a flying car. In his second year at Hogwarts, surrounded by a close-knit group of friends, he attempts to find the mysterious chamber of secrets and faces a terrifying, time-traveling foe. (BBYA; IRAYAC) Film

Harry Potter and the Prisoner of Azkaban. 1999. Harry's third year at Hogwarts reveals more secrets about his dead parents. (BBYA; IRAYAC; Whitbread Award; Locus)

Harry Potter and the Goblet of Fire. 2000. In this installment, Harry is entered in the Triwizard Tournament, which thrusts him into deep danger as Voldemort takes action against him. Because of the tournament, there is no Quidditch at Hogwarts this year, but Harry does get to attend the Quidditch World Cup with his friends the Weasleys. (Hugo; IRAYAC)

Harry Potter and the Order of the Phoenix. 2003. What will happen to teenage wizard Harry in his fifth year at Hogwarts?

Vande Velde, Vivian. *Magic Can Be Murder.* 2000. *MJS.* A young witch can use a hair in a container of water to view what someone is doing elsewhere.

Wrede, Patricia C. Mairelon and Kim Duet. *JS.* The English Regency–era setting, complete with Jane Austen–style manners, makes this a captivating series.

Mairelon the Magician. 1991. Kim, a street urchin, is convinced that there is more to Mairelon the Magician than meets the eye. Could he be practicing real magic? Long out of print, this title has recently been reissued under Tor's Starscape imprint.

Magician's Ward. 1997. Kim, the ward of Lord Merrill (aka Mairelon the Magician), is appalled when Mairelon's mother decides she must take her place in London society. After all, they are in the midst of an investigation, trying to find out why their library was the target of a bungled burglary. The ordinary magic workers from the backstreets have disappeared, allegedly hired by a mysterious individual, and someone is flinging around bizarre magic that has unpredictable results.

A Bestiary

Just as some kids love dinosaurs, dogs, or teddy bears, some teen fantasy readers feel a special affinity for magical creatures and will read any book that features them. Mythological creatures function as characters in these tales, and oftentimes they have a symbolic significance. Although the plots of the following tales are widely divergent, they exert an appeal to readers who have a connection with the unicorns, dragons, or other creatures featured.

Mythical Creatures

Coville, Bruce. The Unicorn Chronicles. *M.*

> *Into the Land of the Unicorns.* 1994. Eleven-year-old Cara falls into Luster, the land of the Unicorns, where she teams up with Lightfoot, a unicorn teenager. Together, they attempt to take a message to the Queen of the Unicorns. (Quick Picks)

> *Song of the Wanderer.* 1999. Cara struggles to find the gateway to Earth so that she can bring her Grandmother, "the Wanderer," back to Luster. (IRAYAC)

Gray, Luli. Falcon and Egg series. *MJ.* Although this series is written for children, it does have proven appeal for teens.

> *Falcon's Egg.* 1995. Eleven-year-old Falcon finds a remarkable red egg in Central Park—and it hatches into a most amazing creature.

> *Falcon and the Charles Street Witch.* 2002. When Falcon and Toody are swept out of an airplane, Falcon is magically wafted down to the New York garden of Blinda Cholmondely, certified witch. Egg has saved her and her brother, but now Egg must be rescued. The dragons speak in verse and in fractured quotes from Shakespeare, T. S. Eliot, and Euripides.

Norton, Andre, and Mercedes Lackey. Halfblood Chronicles. *JS.* A world where elves rule, dragons fly, and humans are slaves.

> *Elvenbane.* 1991. A human slave, impregnated by one of the Elven rulers, flees to the desert to have her baby, who as a half-breed would be sentenced to death. A kindly dragon finds her, and then fosters baby Shana when the mother dies. Shana grows up to be the Elvenbane, the prophesied doom of the elven kind.

> *Elvenblood.* 1995. As Shana and her band of outcasts fight for freedom, she seeks to uncover the secret that has kept the Iron People free from the ruling wizard's tyranny.

> *Elvenborn.* 2002. Elven lord Kyrtian, a victim himself of some underhanded elven dealings, begins to see his people in a different light.

Uncommon Common Animals

The animals in this section exist in our world, but in these stories they do not act as we expect mere animals to behave.

Adams, Richard. *Watership Down.* 1972. *S.* A warren of rabbits flees the destruction of their home in search of a safe haven. (BBYA; YALSA 100 Best Books) **Adult** *Classic*

Clement-Davies, David. *Fire Bringer.* 2000. *MJS.* Rannoch, a young buck, must face his destiny and lead the herd to freedom. (BBYA)

Clement-Davies, David. *The Sight.* 2002. *JS.* Two Transylvanian wolf cubs are at the heart of a prophecy that may allow them to save the pack from evil.

Jacques, Brian. The Redwall series. *MJS.* In this popular series, woodland animals battle evil.

> *Redwall.* 1986. Cluny the Scourge, an evil one-eyed rat warlord, plans a bloody takeover of Redwall Abbey, a tranquil haven for many small animals. (BBYA)

> *Mossflower.* 1988. In this prequel to *Redwall*, Tsarmina, the self-proclaimed Queen of the Thousand Eyes and ruler of Mossflower Woods, finds a worthy foe in Martin the Warrior, who fights for the woodland residents.

> *Mattimeo.* 1990. Slager, an evil fox, plans to kidnap young Mattimeo, the son of Redwall Abbey's guardian.

> *Mariel of Redwall.* 1991. Mariel, a fierce young mousemaid, and her bellmaker father were thrown overboard by Gabool, a pirate rat. Now Mariel sets forth with a band of stalwart companions to recover the bell Gabool stole.

> *Salamandastron.* 1992. Ferhago the Assassin, an evil weasel, attacks Salamandastron.

> *Martin the Warrior.* 1993. An evil stoat holds a quiet young mouse captive.

> *The Bellmaker.* 1994. When Mariel disappears, her father, Joseph the Bellmaker, together with Martin the Warrior, goes to find and rescue her and her companions from an evil fox who wears the skin of a wolf.

> *Outcast of Redwall.* 1996. Veil, a foundling ferret, was being raised at Redwall until he committed a crime that caused the community to cast him out. On his own, Veil is torn by loyalty to his foster family and ties to his birth father, an evil warlord. (IRAYAC)

> *Pearls of Lutra.* 1996. Mad Eyes, a pine marten, threatens disaster upon Redwall if its inhabitants cannot find and return to him the missing pearls.

> *The Long Patrol.* 1998. Tammo longs to join Long Patrol, the legendary army of fighting hares in service to the ruler of Salamandastron. (IRAYAC)

Marlfox. 1998. The Marlfoxes steal Redwall's most treasured tapestry, which depicts Martin the Warrior, so the young warrior squirrels of Redwall set out to retrieve it.

The Legend of Luke. 1999. After hearing a ballad about his long lost father Luke, Martin the Warrior sets out to sea in search of answers.

Lord Brocktree. 2000. Heroic Lord Brocktree was the greatest badger lord of all, especially after he saved Salamandastron.

Taggerung. 2001. Members of the evil Sawney Rath clan think that Deyna, an otter born in Redwall, is destined to be their Taggerung. (IRAYAC)

Triss. 2002. Triss, Shogg, and Welfo, a squirrel, otter, and hedgehog, escape from slavery to Redwall.

Jarvis, Robin. The Deptford Mice Trilogy. *MJS.*

The Dark Portal. 2000. Audrey and other mice venture through the grille and into the terrifying depths of the sewer, where they face heart-thumping adventure and the evil rat ruler, Jupiter.

The Crystal Prison. 2001. A journey to the country proves not to be a bucolic getaway for Audrey and the other mice.

The Final Reckoning. 2002. The evil Jupiter returns from the dead.

Oppel, Kenneth. *Silverwing.* 1997. *M.* Shade, an inquisitive Silverwing bat, is separated from his colony during their migration and experiences many adventures—including a brush with giant carnivorous bats—as he tries to find them. (Canadian Library Association Book of the Year for Children Award)

Pratchett, Terry. *The Amazing Maurice and His Educated Rodents.* 2001. *MJS.* Annotated in the Humorous section of this chapter.

Shapeshifters

Are they human, animal, or both? The protagonists of the following titles shift from human to animal form, and back again.

Kindl, Patrice. *Owl in Love.* 1993. *MJS.* When Owl Tycho was born fourteen years ago, her parents recognized that she had inherited a rare family ability to shift into owl form, as long as she ate like one. Now she is in love—with her teacher—and a strange, seemingly deranged young male owl has moved into the neighborhood. (BBYA; Popular Paperbacks; YALSA 100 Best Books)

Thompson, Kate. Switchers series. *MJ.*

Switchers. 1998. Tess and Kevin, who secretly have the ability to change into the form of any animal, are called upon to help save the world.

Midnight's Choice. 1999. Kevin, in the shape of a phoenix, is being held in the zoo, and it's up to Tess to free him.

Wild Blood. 2000. As Tess nears her fifteenth birthday, she must decide which shape to keep when she can no longer switch between the forms of different animals.

Alternate and Parallel Worlds

Some stories postulate that parallel worlds exist alongside ours. Differences between real and parallel worlds may be subtle, with parallel worlds that look, smell, and feel almost exactly like ours. At the other end of the spectrum, the differences may be so vast that the parallel world is almost completely alien. Many of these stories operate on the premise that there is a continuum of worlds, with those closest the most similar and those farther away the most different, but all are reached through a rent in the fabric of reality. Many of the tales dealing with parallel worlds involve travel between worlds. Usually alternate worlds are fully realized in a different reality, where our world does not even exist. Obviously, setting is an important element of these stories, and whether the parallel world is similar or vastly different, these books provide escapist appeal.

Applegate, K. A. Everworld. *MJS.*

Search for Senna. 1999. When Senna is dragged under the lake waters by a strange beast, David, Jalil, April, and Christopher set out on a quest to find her through a world filled with gods, trolls, and all manner of bizarre beings and mythological creatures. (Quick Picks)

Land of Loss. 1999. The four teens who are searching for Senna find themselves in a world that is beyond belief with huge wolves, immortals, and mythological gods. (Quick Picks)

Enter the Enchanted. 1999. The four teens still have not found Senna, but at least they're still alive and have met Merlin, who may know where she is. (Quick Picks)

Realm of the Reaper. 1999. David, Jalil, April, and Christopher see a live dragon, fight Aztecs, and are hunted by trolls. (Quick Picks)

Discover the Destroyer. 2000. If the four cannot outwit a dragon, they won't live to make it home even if they do find Senna.

Fear the Fantastic. 2000. The four become involved in an Olympic conflict involving the Greek gods.

Gateway to the Gods. 2000. The dangers of Everworld continue, and survival seems to be increasingly difficult.

Brave the Betrayal. 2000. When Jalil, David, Christopher, and April trade a chemistry book for an unbelievably sharp knife, they don't realize that aliens are planning to use the textbook information with their own technology to create horrific new weapons.

Inside the Illusion. 2000. Senna explains all.

Understand the Unknown. 2000. A journey to Atlantis may be the end of David, Christopher, April, and Jalil.

Mystify the Magician. 2001. When Senna, Jalil, April, Christopher, and David escape from Neptune, they end up in Eire, or ancient Ireland.

Entertain the End. 2001. With Senna gone, it looks like April, David, Christopher, and Jalil may never make it back and that they need to try to solve some of the problems that Senna created.

Barker, Clive. *Abarat.* 2002. *S.* Candy Quackenbush walks into a Minnesota field and finds a sea. Suddenly, her life is not the same old boring one she had while living in Chickentown, USA. In the archipelago of Abarat, each island has its own time. An illustrated tale. (BBYA)

Brennan, Herbie. *Faerie Wars.* 2003. *MJS.* In a world parallel to ours, the crown prince, who has been living as a commoner, is targeted for assassination after rescuing a basket of kittens from a glue factory. Sent to our world, he first appears as a tiny, winged fairy, but he soon resumes his normal size and shape. Henry Atherton, a teen who is helping an elderly neighbor with yard work, is drawn into the middle of the magical conflict.

Brooks, Terry. *Magic Kingdom for Sale. Sold!* 1986. *JS.* Ben cashes out of his life to buy a kingdom. The first volume of the lighthearted Magic Kingdom of Landover series. (YALSA 100 Best Books; BBYA) **Adult**

Buffie, Margaret. *The Watcher.* 2000. *MJS.* Having never dreamed before, fifteen-year-old Emma finds herself exploring two other worlds that seem very real, but in which the people and dogs cannot see her.

Calhoun, Dia. *Aria of the Sea.* 2000. *MJ.* Following her mother's death, Cerinthe turns away from her interest in healing and focuses everything on the dancing that was so important to her mother. (BBYA)

Calhoun, Dia. *Firegold.* 1999. *MJS.* Jonathon is sent to live with his grandmother in the land of the Dalriada, feared and hated by those in the valley. All Dalriada must go on a quest their fourteenth year, returning with their own magical steed or dying in the process. Jonathon's journey brings his dual heritage together in a satisfying and hope-filled climax. (BBYA; IRAYAC)

Chabon, Michael. *Summerland.* 2002. *M.* Eleven-year-old Ethan Feld, an unsuccessful baseball player, is recruited to travel between worlds to save his own.

Dalkey, Kara. Water series. *MJS.*

Ascension. 2002. Nia of the Atlantis Bluefin Clan is sure she will become an avatar, a king of her people who achieves a psychic link with the squidlike alien Farworlders. But her cousin is selected to represent their family in the trials. Meanwhile, she falls in love with Cephan, who is from a lower-caste clan. She also discovers a pair of kings locked in a prison in the lowest levels of Atlantis. During the trials, Nia senses that someone is tampering with the contests.

Reunion. 2002. Corwin finds Nia, the girl of his dreams, who happens to be a mermaid, and together they search for a missing seashell.

Transformation; The Quest Is Fulfilled at Last. 2002. Nia returns to Atlantis to find a magical sword but finds her city enslaved.

Duane, Diane. Wizardry series. *MJ.*

So You Want to Be a Wizard. 1983. A library book takes thirteen- year-old Nita into another dimension as she tries to escape a gang of bullies. This is a lighter version of travel to an alternate universe.

Deep Wizardry. 1985. Nita, along with her friends Kit and S'ree, team up to combat an evil power.

High Wizardry. 1990. Dairine, Nita's eleven-year-old sister, figures out how to transport herself across the universe when she finds a software wizard's manual on the family's new computer.

A Wizard Abroad. 1997. Now fourteen, Nita becomes involved in a magical battle when she visits her aunt in Ireland.

The Wizard's Dilemma. 2001. Nita searches the universes in an attempt to find a cure for her mother's brain cancer.

Gurney, James. *Dinotopia: A Land apart from Time.* 1998. *MJS.* Lavishly illustrated fictional journal where dinosaurs have an advanced culture. (BBYA; YALSA 100 Best Books)

Jones, Diana Wynne. *The Merlin Conspiracy.* 2003. *MJS.* As the children of court magicians, Arianrhod Hyde, known most commonly as Roddy, and her best friend Grundo have spent their lives on the king's progress. The islands of Blest maintain their magic and safety because the king constantly travels from town to town accompanied by his court and the Merlin. Nick, from our world, has always wanted to travel between worlds and has suddenly and inexplicably ended up in another world, where he is mistaken for a novice magician.

Jordan, Sherryl. *Secret Sacrament.* 2001. *MJS.* Everyone is shocked when Gabriel is selected to take holy vows and go to the citadel to train as a priest-healer. There, he comes to the attention of the empress, for whom he interprets dreams. As a powerful enemy of one of the empress's advisors, Gabriel is accused of treason and joins up with the small band of indigenous people who live on the plain, where he finds true love and fulfills a prophecy. (BBYA)

Lewis, C. S. The Chronicles of Narnia. *MJS.* This classic series for all ages is often considered to be a Christian allegory, but the magical land of Narnia is the setting of a wonder-filled fantasy adventure for all, where time moves at a pace different from that of our world. The series is listed here in order of its internal chronology. *The Lion, the Witch, and the Wardrobe* was the first released.

The Magician's Nephew. 1955. Polly and Digory fall into the wood between the worlds.

The Lion, the Witch, and the Wardrobe. 1950. Lucy looks into the wardrobe and discovers the world of Narnia.

The Horse and His Boy. 1954. Riding a talking horse, a prince journeys to freedom.

Prince Caspian. 1951. Peter, Susan, Edmund, and Lucy return to Narnia, which has fallen into the evil grip of King Mirax.

The Voyage of the Dawn Treader. 1952. Lucy, Edmund, and cousin Eustace set sail with King Caspian to the end of the world on the *Dawn Treader.*

The Silver Chair. 1953. A mission to Underland brings the children into the haunts of an evil witch.

The Last Battle. 1956. An imposter in Narnia.

Lubar, David. *Wizards of the Game*. 2003. *M*. Eighth-grader Mercer loves playing Wizards of the Warrior World, so he comes up with the idea of staging a gaming convention for the school fundraiser to benefit the local soup kitchen and shelter. When fellow student Ed writes an editorial calling the game satanic and demonic and the letter is printed in the local paper as well as the school's, a church group starts demonstrating against gaming at Oscar Wilde Middle School. In the midst of all this, Mercer meets a quartet of wizards at the shelter who call him a magus and try to enlist his assistance in returning to their home world. They had been stranded in ours, thanks to a crooked (and devoured) tour guide. A stunning climax when a portal is opened and the statues of evil beings from the game come to life and attack reveals a real wizard.

Pullman, Philip. His Dark Materials. *MJS.*

The Golden Compass. 1995. Lyra Belacqua, a child, has been pretty much on her own living in one of the colleges of Oxford. Like all humans in her world, she has a daemon. Hers, named Pantalaimon, will continue to change shape until Lyra reaches adulthood. With a cohort of stalwart companions—including Iorek Byrnison, an armored bear whom Lyra rescues from a life of slavery and degradation—Lyra heads for the North where strange occurrences have been happening and where a mystery of missing children may be solved. (YALSA 100 Best Books; Carnegie Medal under the British title *Northern Lights*)

The Subtle Knife. 1997. Lyra hooks up with Will, a boy from our world. In a recently deserted city in a parallel world, they try to recoup—he, from killing an invader in his home; she, from the cataclysmic events in *The Golden Compass.*

The Amber Spyglass. 2000. Lyra and Will conclude their adventures as they grow into adulthood. (BBYA; Whitbread)

Time Travel

These tales of time travel, in which characters are snatched away from their own time and deposited in another, will intrigue anyone who has ever wondered what it would be like to live in another time. The discrepancies and problems that evolve for characters in other time settings also provide a rich source for storytelling, romance, and adventure. Some teens who enjoy the milieu of another time that they find in historical fiction may also enjoy this time travel fantasy. Likewise, teens who enjoy these titles may find titles of interest in the historical fiction genre.

Bennett, Cherie, and Jeff Gottesfeld. *Anne Frank and Me*. 2001. *MJ*. The sound of gunshots mars a school field trip to a traveling Anne Frank exhibition, and Nicole, who is more interested in Jack than in school and her Anne Frank assignment, is flung back in time to the Holocaust. Living as a Jew in Paris during the Holocaust, Nicole experiences persecution, starvation, and fear. (IRAYAC)

Cooney, Caroline B. Time series. *MJ*. After time traveling to the late nineteenth century, Annie Lockwood finds romance and adventure.

> *Both Sides of Time*. 1995. After graduating from high school, Annie falls in love and through time to 1895. (Popular Paperbacks)

> *Out of Time*. 1996. Annie returns to the 1890s to free her beloved Strat, who is being held captive in an insane asylum.

> *Prisoner of Time*. 1998. Strat's sister, Devonny, is transported to modern times from Victorian England.

> *For All Time*. 2001. Annie tries to reach across time for Strat—and ends up in Ancient Egypt.

Cooper, Susan. *King of Shadows*. 1999. *M*. Orphaned Nat Field is preparing to perform in *A Midsummer Night's Dream* at the restored Globe Theatre in London when he is transported back to Shakespeare's time to perform in the same play with the bard himself. (BBYA)

Curry, Jane Louise. *Dark Shade*. 1998. *J*. Kip is recovering from being badly burned in the same fire that killed his parents. Maggie follows him into the western Pennsylvania woods, up a mountain, and back in time to 1758, when Kip is about to be adopted by the Lenape Indians.

Garfield, Henry. *Tartabull's Throw*. 2001. *JS*. Annotated in Chapter 8, "Paranormal."

Heneghan, James. *The Grave*. 2000. *MJS*. When he was a baby, Tommy was abandoned in a Liverpool department store and then raised in foster care. In 1974, when his school attempts to build an addition, a mass grave is discovered. One night while exploring, Tommy falls into the grave and is transported back to Ireland during the great famine of 1847, where he uses cardiopulmonary resuscitation to save the life of Tully, a boy who looks exactly like him. He soon falls in love with Hannah, Tully's sister, and connects with the entire Monaghan family. A blow to the head returns him to his own time, but he travels back again, having discovered a sense of family and belonging that changes his life in his own time. (BBYA)

Psionic Abilities

The possession of paranormal powers is an enticing subject. Psionic powers can include telepathy, the power to communicate mind to mind; teleportation, the ability for the mind to transport the body from place to place; telekinesis, the ability to move objects with the mind; and precognition, the ability to see the future. Whether some of these titles are science fiction or fantasy is not always clear. Stories of psionic powers can be found in both sections.

Hill, Pamela Smith. *The Last Grail Keeper.* 2001. *M.* While on an archaeological dig, Felicity's mother reveals that they are members of a long line of Grail Keepers and that it is their responsibility to protect an artifact that they've just found.

Vance, Susanna. *Sights.* 2001. *MJS.* Baby Girl and her mother flee her abusive father and settle in a small town, where for the first time in her life Baby Girl is not admired. After using her psychic skills to learn to play the accordion, she becomes friends with two others in her high school, and they start a band. Set in the 1950s. (BBYA)

References

Altmann, Anna, and Gail de Vos. *New Tales for Old.* Englewood, Colo.: Libraries Unlimited, 1999.

Altmann, Anna, and Gail de Vos. *Tales, Then and Now.* Englewood, Colo.: Libraries Unlimited, 2001.

Herald, Diana Tixier. *Fluent in Fantasy.* Englewood, Colo.: Libraries Unlimited, 1999.

Chapter 7

Science Fiction

Science fiction is a literature of ideas. These tales can also be described as "what if" stories. What if . . . there were life on other planets? What if . . . one could travel through time? What if . . . the world as we know it were to end? Often a "what if" premise is combined with adventure in unknown locales, or a time after huge changes in the world, to make for fast-paced and exciting action fiction. For the purposes of this guide, science fiction is defined as tales set in a future time or on another planet where science plays a role.

How to differentiate between fantasy and science fiction is frequently debated. Many readers adamantly argue that stories about dragons belong in fantasy, yet best-selling author Anne McCaffrey vehemently claims that her books belong in science fiction rather than fantasy, asserting that her dragons are rooted in scientific theory. The publishing industry doesn't always offer much help either. Publishers often label paperbacks as either science fiction or fantasy, but this is not always the case with hardcover books.

Author Orson Scott Card, winner of both Hugo and Nebula awards, once stated that if rivets are pictured on the cover, a book is science fiction; if foliage is present, it belongs in fantasy. Others say SF (the accepted acronym of the genre) is left-brained, whereas fantasy is right-brained. When it comes to advising readers, none of these explanations is sufficient.

Because the readers, writers, and publishers of SF and fantasy all tend to have differing (and usually strong) opinions on where a particular work fits, there will probably never be a foolproof and undisputed way to make the distinction. Most libraries and bookstores shelve science fiction and fantasy together. Unless the collection is extremely large, this is probably the best way to serve readers' needs.

What draws readers to this genre? Science fiction offers readers the chance to speculate about the way things are and the way they might be. These stories often lead their protagonists into a moral or philosophical dilemma—one with long-ranging consequences. Popular assumptions are revoked and universal truths questioned. Teens can relate to this skeptical stance, and those who enjoy philosophical challenge and find satisfaction in flexing their intellectual muscle discover much to appreciate in these stories. In addition, the science and technology in SF titles intrigue fans, who often debate the scientific credibility of specific titles. As teens develop their mental capabilities, what could be more intriguing than a story that tests them? Then, too, most science fiction features a strong story line, with plenty of action and adventure, a feature that pleases many readers.

Science fiction and fantasy readers do not stick to "age-appropriate" books. Adult readers of those genres can often be found reading science fiction and fantasy published for teen readers; teen readers feel no compunction whatsoever about reading from the adult collection. The books listed in this chapter have been particularly popular with teens, but teen fans of science fiction will also find many adult titles appealing, as listed in *Strictly Science Fiction* (Herald and Kunzel 2002).

For an interesting overview of science fiction written for teens, *Tomorrowland: Ten Stories about the Future* (Cart 1999), a Best Book for Young Adults, features stories by Jon Scieszka, Rodman Philbrick, Tor Seidler, Gloria Skurzynski, Ron Koertge, Lois Lowry, Katherine Paterson, Jacqueline Woodson, James Cross Giblin, and Michael Cart.

Some science fiction stories fall into subgenres, the largest and most popular being the adventure story. Many SF fans are attracted to books with particular themes, however, such as time travel, aliens, and genetic engineering.

Subgenres

Adventure

Exploration, battles, and other heart-pounding occurrences make adventure a popular science fiction subgenre. The story line is the most important feature of an adventure, and pacing runs from brisk to break-neck speed, as conflicts are resolved in the physical plane. Books in this category usually feature strong and heroic characters—either individual protagonists or teams. Many of the earliest science fiction novels, such as those written by H. G. Wells and Jules Verne, fall into this category.

Card, Orson Scott. Ender series. *JS.* Can six-year-old Andrew "Ender" Wiggin be the military genius needed to save the planet against invading Buggers? The saga of Ender Wiggin started out as a short story that was later expanded into an award-winning novel. Card followed it up with a series of philosophical novels that are read by his most serious fans, but on the whole are not popular with teens. In 1999, *Ender's Shadow,* the first of a series of companion novels having broad appeal for teens, was published.

> *Ender's Game.* 1985. Ender Wiggin, a brilliant young boy, is taken away from his family at an early age and sent to battle school. There he and other bright children are taught how to fight against the attack of the alien Buggers. (Hugo; Nebula; Locus; YALSA 100 Best Books)

Ender's Shadow. 1999. Having lived his entire young life on the streets, Bean is an impressive strategist, even at age four, which brings him to the attention of the powers that be and takes him to battle school, where he becomes Ender's lieutenant. (BBYA)

Shadow of the Hegemon. 2001. The battle school kids are still struggling to fit in with families they left behind years ago when they were all abducted—except for Bean and his brother, who become the target of assassins. Bean knows that as long as he is in protective custody, he is at risk. Petra, who is being held captive, knows that if she is clever enough, she can get necessary information out to Bean and to Ender's brother, Peter Wiggin. (BBYA)

Shadow Puppets. 2002. Bean and Petra team up when Peter brings Achille into the heart of the Hegemon's compound. They marry and try to make babies that won't suffer from Bean's unlimited growth and early demise.

Gerrold, David. Starsiders Trilogy. *S.* A dysfunctional family, a giant space elevator called the beanstalk, and a trip to the moon make for thrilling reading in this series.

Jumping off the Planet. 2000. Thirteen-year-old Charlie Dingillian and his two brothers are kidnapped by their father and taken off Earth on the Beanstalk, an elevator that goes to the moon.

Bouncing off the Moon. 2000. The three brothers Dingillian have left their parents behind and gone to the moon, where dangers abound.

Leaping to the Stars. 2002. Charlie divorces his parents and heads out into space, as far as humans can go.

Golden, Christopher, and Thomas E. Sniegoski. *Force Majeure.* 2002. *JS.* Shane Monroe, a twenty-year-old genius, figures out how to artificially replicate a tornado. When his process is used for nefarious ends, he must run for his life.

Hogan, James P. *Outward Bound.* 1999. *JS.* Juvenile delinquent Linc Marani takes the option to go to a special program rather than a labor camp to serve his time. The program turns out to be a boot camp–like experience, in which he learns that he has inner strength and is prepared for a destiny in space.

Jeapes, Ben. *The Xenocide Mission.* 2002. *JS.* A secret base the Commonwealth has been using to observe the murderous Xenocides is attacked, and Lieutenant Joel Gilmore and a Rustie stay behind to make sure that vital information is destroyed. They discover that all is not as it appears.

Sheffield, Charles. *Billion Dollar Boy.* 1997. *JS.* The spoiled and petulant scion of one of Earth's wealthiest families goes on a drunken spree that lands him in the middle of a space mining operation.

Sheffield, Charles. *The Cyborg from Earth.* 1998. *JS.* Jefferson Kopal is sent out to the flourishing settlements in the Messina Dust Cloud, where he becomes a pawn in a conspiracy that just might result in a solar-system-wide civil war.

Sheffield, Charles, and Jerry Pournelle. *Higher Education.* 1996. *JS.* Sixteen-year-old Rick Luban is kicked out of school after a prank played on a new teacher goes awry. A kindly teacher, who actually taught him something, talks to him after his expulsion and gives him a card to take to Vanguard Mining in quest of a job. Surprisingly, Rick is hired, whisked off to New Mexico for strenuous testing, and then sent into space for a trip to an asteroid mining station and more training. Along the way he makes friends and enemies, finds a lover, and discovers that he does have the ability to solve problems—even those in math and reading.

Skurzynski, Gloria. *The Clones.* 2002. *JS.* Corgan's reward for winning the Virtual War is an island of his own, but when Sharla brings a young clone of Brig's to the island, Corgan's peaceful existence evaporates. A sequel to *The Virtual War,* annotated in the Hard Science Fiction section of this chapter.

Hard Science Fiction

Technology and science, often described in great detail, take center stage in this subgenre. Space exploration and scientific discovery, clones, virtual reality, cyborgs, robots, nanotechnology, and black holes are among the themes, gimmicks, and gadgetry that captivate the imaginations of hard SF fans. Like special effects in films, they must be believable. This is the subgenre that stretches the mental muscle. It is also the one that is sometimes thought of as defining science fiction. The category includes stories set on other planets where humans have settled, space travel, and other scientifically conceivable situations—usually in the not-too-distant future. Virtual reality has been a popular theme in recent publications. It is usually depicted as a computer-generated alternate reality, in which people are sucked into situations within a computer-created world that makes them wonder what is real and what is virtual. Teens who have an appetite for science are likely to enjoy hard science fiction. Readers who enjoy hard science fiction should also check the Genetic Engineering section in this chapter. Titles that are compared with Robert A. Heinlein's "juveniles" are often considered hard SF.

Dickinson, Peter. *Eva.* 1988. *JS.* After a terrible car accident, fourteen-year-old Eva finds that she—her consciousness, what it is that makes her herself—is now residing in the body of a chimpanzee. (YALSA 100 Best Books; BBYA)

Gresh, Lois, and Danny Gresh. *Chuck Farris and the Tower of Darkness.* 2001. *M.* When Chuck plays some new electronic games, he becomes the hero.

Hogan, James P. *Bug Park.* 1997. *JS.* Eric Heber has created a neural interface for controlling tiny robots that his teenage son Kevin and pal Taki play around with to create a new type of entertainment. This revolutionary technology may just be enough to kill for, and who knows which side the various players are on? When the boys inadvertently overhear Kevin's stepmother plotting with the head of a rival firm, they start some sleuthing on their own, which leads them and their tiny alter-ego mechs into deadly peril. (BBYA; Quick Picks)

Skurzynski, Gloria. *Virtual War.* 1997. *MJS.* Corgan who has spent his life training for this war, will compete in a virtual reality "game" that simulates the blood, gore, and violent trauma of a real war, although no one is actually injured. A sequel, *The Clones,* is annotated in the Adventure section of this chapter. (BBYA)

Sleator, William. *Boltzmon!* 1999. *M.* Eleven-year-old Chris is ostracized at school, mainly because his popular older sister really has it in for him. When he goes upstairs to break up a party on the instructions of his mom, he sees a darting, glowing blob, which he quickly pockets. The blob can take on any form that it wants. It's the "Boltzmon"—the remnant of a black hole from the future that, when perturbed, moves into other places. The blob takes Chris to Arteria, a parallel world that is forty years further down the time continuum. In Arteria, Chris encounters an odious woman, who he comes to believe is his older sister. (Quick Picks)

Humorous Science Fiction

Science fiction with a strong dose of humor makes for a delightful, mind-stretching read. Many teens enjoy humor, including those who read science fiction. These titles can be extremely entertaining—with wacky characters and situations, word play, and biting satire. Humorous science fiction will take a potshot at anything—including science fiction. The late Douglas Adams was possibly the most well-known writer of humorous science fiction. His "increasingly misnamed trilogy," which stood at five volumes at the time of his death, is simply good fun. The Hitchhiker's Trilogy has been a television series and also a successful audio production. Humor is the major feature of the titles in this section. Other titles with elements of humor can be found by consulting the subject index. Readers who are drawn to this subgenre may also appreciate humorous fantasy.

Adams, Douglas. Hitchhiker's Trilogy. *JS.* The continuing adventures of Arthur Dent and Ford Prefect through space and time. A hilarious romp, and a classic series for science fiction readers. ⟦*Classic*⟧

> *The Hitchhiker's Guide to the Galaxy.* 1979. Poor Arthur Dent. One minute he's lying in front of a bulldozer, trying to keep his house from being torn down to make way for an expressway. The next, he's hitchhiking through space with his friend Ford Prefect, a native of Betelgeuse who has been stranded on the Earth for the past fifteen years. Ford is a writer for *The Hitchhiker's Guide to the Galaxy* and so has the connections to get a ride for himself and his friend when he discovers that the Earth is to be destroyed to make room for an expressway in space. (BBYA; YALSA 100 Best Books; Popular Paperbacks)

> *The Restaurant at the End of the Universe.* 1980. Arthur Dent and a strange assortment of friendly characters are desperate for a place to eat.

> *Life, the Universe and Everything.* 1982. Arthur and Ford travel all the way to prehistoric time—to save Earth.

So Long and Thanks for All the Fish. 1984. Arthur's back on Earth, but why have all the dolphins disappeared? And what does the cryptic message in the fishbowl mean?

Mostly Harmless. 1992. Arthur has a daughter he never knew about, someone is trying to take over the offices of the *Hitchhiker's Guide,* and it looks like the Vogon want to destroy Earth after all.

Dodd, Quentin. *Beatnik Rutabagas from Beyond the Stars*. 2001. *MJ.* Teenage science fiction fans are recruited to serve as commanders by feuding aliens—the Lirgonians and the Wotwots, who have no common sense.

Murphy, Pat. *There and Back Again*. 1999. *S.* This joyful romp through time and space takes norbit Bailey Beldon from the comforts of his hollowed-out asteroid to the ends of the universe after the Farr clone commandeers him to be part of their expedition to find wormhole maps. Murphy has written a rollicking, entertaining space opera version of *The Hobbit* that stands as a tribute to Tolkein, the master of fantasy. Mobius strips, pirates, clones, powerful drink, and adventure abound, as the tone-deaf but courageous little miner proves to be a hero. `Adult`

Peck, Richard. Cyberspace series. *M.*

Lost in Cyberspace. 1996. Sixth-grader Josh and his pal Aaron build a time machine.

The Great Interactive Dream Machine. 1996. The humorous time-traveling adventures of Josh and Aaron continue, but now the time machine can grant wishes.

Willis, Connie. *To Say Nothing of the Dog*. 1998. *S.* Lady Shrapnel, a filthy-rich American, is funding time travel so that she can rebuild Coventry Cathedral to the way it was when her great grandmother experienced an epiphany there in front of the Bishop's Bird Stump. When a time-lagged historian from the future is sent to the Victorian era to escape Lady Shrapnel, he finds love—and a problem that could rend the fabric of time. (BBYA; Hugo; Locus) `Adult`

Themes

The themes covered in this chapter are those that are most popular with teen readers. Titles with other SF themes can be located by consulting the subject index.

Alternate Worlds

The premise that alternate worlds exist on some dimension parallel to our own is used in both science fiction and fantasy. Stories about scientifically explainable, nonmagical means of moving from one world to another are included here. You'll also find stories about worlds that may have been similar to ours before a time-line divergence. In addition, some of these tales are set so far in the future that the setting takes on the qualities of an alternate world. Other types of worlds, which are more magical, can be found in the Chapter 6, "Fantasy."

Gould, Steven. *Wildside*. 1996. *S.* Eighteen-year-old Charlie has inherited a pristine, untouched world on the other side of a door in a barn. To explore it, he needs the money he obtains by importing an extinct species from the other side, where saber-toothed tigers and immense herds of bison still roam. He needs stalwart companions with survival and flight skills—and he needs legal protection. The creatures that he and his assembled partners face are armed and dangerous, but lethal teeth and claws may not be the biggest challenge. (BBYA)

Howarth, Lesley. MapHead series. *MJ.* Twelve-year-old MapHead lives in a parallel world, but now it's time to move.

> *MapHead.* 1994. Twelve-year-old MapHead is a strange kid—small, bald, and able to depict geographic maps on his head. He lives with his father, Powers, in the Subtle World, a parallel universe. Now he must travel to this world to find his mother, who has no memory of him.
>
> *MapHead: The Return.* 1997. MapHead ends up on his own and must learn how to control his supernatural powers.

L'Engle, Madeleine. *A Wrinkle in Time.* 1962. *MJ.* In this classic tale, Meg and Charles Wallace Murray, along with their friend Kevin, go on an adventure—through space and time, as well as into alternate worlds—as they embark on a quest to find their father. (Newbery Award) Classic

Lerangis, Peter. Watchers series. *MJ.* Eerie things happen in worlds that are like ours, but curiously different.

> *Last Stop.* 1998. David sees ghostly people on a subway platform.
>
> *Rewind.* 1999. Adam uses a camera to determine what really happened in the past.

> *I. D.* 1999. Is Eve the result of a scientific experiment?
>
> *War.* 1999. Will Jake's passion for the Civil War suck him into real danger?

> *Island.* 1999. Rachel finds that the people never seem to age on the island where Collin has taken her.
>
> *Lab 6.* 1999. Sam finds that the source of the voice he hears in his head may be related to his dead twin—and to the artificial intelligence experiments his parents are working on.

Paulsen, Gary. *The Transall Saga.* 1998. *MJS.* On a solo camping trip, Mark sees a strange light that sucks him in and then disgorges him into a world with red foliage, yellow skies, and a plethora of strange critters. While spending many months learning alien survival skills, he discovers his own strengths and his inner resourcefulness. After joining a band of humanoids, Mark is captured by another race and becomes a slave. But even in captivity Mark's bravery, strength, and intelligence lead to greatness. (Quick Picks)

Sleator, William. The Boxes series. *MJ.* Annie has two mysterious boxes and instructions not to open them—can she resist?

The Boxes. 1998. When her mysterious uncle leaves Annie with two boxes and instructions not to open them—and to keep them apart—Annie can't stand the suspense for long. She opens the box in the basement, and a strange buglike creature escapes. A few days later, it has grown, reproduced, and started talking to her through telepathy. Compelled to see what's in the other box hidden in her closet, Annie opens it to find a being, both clock- and plantlike, that can slow down time while allowing Annie and the creature in the basement to move at what seems like incredible speed. (Popular Paperbacks; Quick Picks)

Marco's Millions. 2001. This prequel to *The Boxes* is full of adventure, as well as scientific concepts that illuminate what happens in *The Boxes*. Marco goes through a portal in the basement into another world, where he captures a box that affects time. In this other world, time and gravity are different from how they seem in our world, so a journey of a few days keeps him away from home for several years. This is Sleator at his finest, making scientific concepts real and personal, while creating unforgettable characters.

Time Travel

Traveling through time is a popular story device that takes characters to exotic or remote settings in the past or future. Sometimes it is merely a segue for a historical novel. In science fiction, the travel usually reveals a technological problem with far-reaching effects. Contemporary teens are sometimes better able to envision the past through the eyes of a contemporary who is traveling there. The stories found here use some scientific or pseudo-scientific ploy to explain the mechanics of time travel. Novels that do not give a "scientific" or mechanical explanation of time travel appear in Chapter 6, "Fantasy."

Card, Orson Scott. *Pastwatch: The Redemption of Christopher Columbus*. 1996. *S.* Researchers studying the past in the Earth's heavily polluted future discover that they are no longer limited to mere observation. They can interact with the past and even change it. But if they do, they'll also change the future. Can anything be worth sacrificing the future? After much deliberation and soul searching, they decide that ridding the United States of its history of slavery is worth such a sacrifice. Their analysis of the development of slavery in the world shows that all time lines intersect with one individual, Christopher Columbus, and one point in time, his arrival in the New World. Someone from the future is going to have to make the trip back in time and be there to stop him. (BBYA) **Adult**

Crichton, Michael. *Timeline*. 1999. *S.* (Film: *Timeline*) Could quantum teleportation work as a type of time travel to take people to parallel universes? (BBYA) **Adult** **Film**

Hautman, Pete. *Mr. Was*. 1996. *JS.* Jack travels back in time and falls in love with his own grandmother. (Popular Paperbacks; BBYA)

Levitin, Sonia. *The Cure*. 1999. *MJS.* In the year 2407 conformity is everything, so after sixteen-year-old Gemm is found creating music, which is forbidden, he must choose either execution or "The Cure," which will send him back to the Middle Ages and the Black Plague.

Price, Susan. *The Sterkarm Handshake.* 2000. *JS.* Twenty-first-century linguist Andrea travels through the Time Tube to land in the middle of the sixteenth-century Scottish-English border wars, where she falls in love with one of the members of the violent Sterkarm clan.

Sleator, William. *Rewind.* 1999. *MJ.* After being killed by running out in front of a car, eleven-year-old Peter gets the chance to go back to some point in time prior to his death to try to do things differently. He tries to change his adoptive parents' view of him by presenting a puppet show and helping his pregnant mom. (Quick Picks)

Psionic Powers

The possession of paranormal powers is an intriguing subject. Psionic powers can include telepathy, the power to communicate mind to mind; teleportation, the ability for the mind to transport the body from place to place; telekinesis, the ability to move objects with the mind; and precognition, the ability to see the future.

Clements, Andrew. *Things Not Seen.* 2002. *JS.* A teenager wakes up one morning to discover that he is invisible. He sets out to find out why and if the same thing ever had happened to anyone else. (BBYA)

Cormier, Robert. *Fade.* 1988. *S.* Paul has inherited the ability to disappear at will—but is it a gift or a curse? (YALSA 100 Best Books)

Farmer, Nancy. *The Ear, the Eye and the Arm.* 1994. *MJS.* In Zimbabwe of 2194, three detectives with unusual abilities search for the three missing children of General Matasika. (YALSA 100 Best Books; Newbery Honor; Popular Paperbacks; BBYA)

Gould, Steven C. *Jumper.* 1992. *S.* After blinking out of two threatening situations, Davy discovers he has the ability to teleport. (BBYA; Popular Paperbacks)

Lubar, David. *Hidden Talents.* 1999. *MJS.* Edgeview Alternative School is the end of the line for kids with behavioral problems who can't cut it in regular schools. Martin Anderson has an uncanny knack for irritating everyone with whom he comes in contact—until he hooks up with the kids who are misfits in a boarding school full of misfits, including his roommate Torchie and other kids named Trash, Lucky, Cheater, and Flinch. (BBYA; Quick Picks)

McCaffrey, Anne. Harper Hall Trilogy. *MJS.* On the planet Pern, genetically engineered dragons and little fire lizards can bond with individuals and establish telepathic links. McCaffrey, a Margaret A. Edwards award winner, has written numerous books for adults set on Pern, and most fans of this subseries will be eager to find the others.

> *Dragonsong.* 1976. Fifteen-year-old Menolly has musical talent, but her parents, the holders of Half Circle Hold, have other plans for her, so she runs away and makes a major discovery.

Dragonsinger. 1977. Menolly has finally become a Harper, but finds that musical ability and a way with words are not all that's needed. (YALSA 100 Best Books)

Dragondrums. 1979. When Piemur hits puberty and loses his soprano voice, Master Robinton makes him his special assistant.

Shusterman, Neal. Star Shards Trilogy. *S.*

Scorpion Shards. 1995. Six outcast teenagers are drawn together and then across the country, to a place where they must face the power that has given each of them an affliction that could destroy their lives. (BBYA; Quick Picks)

Thief of Souls. 1999. The five surviving Star Shards use their powers for good.

Shattered Sky. 2002. Dillon, Winston, and Lourdes must bring the other Star Shards back from death to defeat the soul-eating Vectors, who want to conquer the Earth.

Tolan, Stephanie S. *Welcome to the Ark*. 1996. *MJS.* Four kids, ranging in age from eight to seventeen, are put in an experimental group home, where they use psionic abilities to become even more powerful. A sequel, *Flight of the Raven,* is annotated in the Militias and Cults section of Chapter 4, "Adventure," because it does not focus on the science fiction aspects of the story. (Popular Paperbacks)

Aliens

Aliens, lovable or loathsome, are creatures from other worlds. What they might be like and how they might interact with humans offer countless possibilities in the world of science fiction. In the titles that follow, readers will find every type of alien imaginable—and then some.

Bell, Hilari. *A Matter of Profit*. 2001. *MJS.* Sickened by war, Ahvren, a young Vivitare, joins his family on T'Chin, the capital of a four-planet confederation that the Vivitare Empire has recently conquered. Ahvren accepts his father's challenge of trying to find out who is planning to assassinate the emperor, hoping it will free him from going off to war again. He also hopes it will offer him the chance to free his foster sister, who is being forced into marrying the crown prince. His investigation takes him to a bibliogoth (librarian) who, even though he looks like a giant ant, becomes his mentor as Ahvren learns the real meaning of honor, courage, and victory. (BBYA)

Blacker, Terence. *The Angel Factory*. 2002. *M.* Twelve-year-old Thomas Wisdom discovers that his perfect family really isn't his—in fact, they aren't even human. They were created by the people of a distant planet to serve as Angels, to try to help humans save themselves from their violent and destructive tendencies. Should Thomas join them, or should he fight to keep humanity human?

Gilmore, Kate. *The Exchange Student*. 1999. *MJS.* Sixteen-year-old Daria lives in a zoo. Well, actually, her family breeds endangered species. When a group of young people come from Chela to the Earth, Daria's mother volunteers the family to play host to Fen, a seven-foot-tall alien. (BBYA; Quick Picks)

Goodman, Alison. *Singing the Dogstar Blues*. 2003. *JS.* Seventeen-year-old Joss, who started life in vitro, is paired up with MavKel, an alien, to train to travel in time and ends up enmeshed in a mystery. (Australian Aurealis Award)

Logue, Mary. *Dancing with an Alien*. 2000. *JS.* Branko is looking for a female for breeding purposes. Will he find true love? (BBYA; Quick Picks)

Lowenstein, Sallie. *Focus*. 2001. *JS*. Sixteen-year-old Andrew refuses to focus on his future and choose an augmentation that will allow him to learn a career. So, his father, a diplomat, accepts a job on Miner's Planet, where the uncommunicative natives occasionally drop valuable information. On Miner's Planet with his bodyguard-augmented mother and his two younger sisters, Andrew writes stories and wonders about the Natives and the Water People, as well as about the hunched, white-haired clerk at "the club," where all the Miners except for Andrew's family live.

Shusterman, Neal. *The Dark Side of Nowhere*. 1997. *MJS*. After one of Jason Miller's friends dies mysteriously, a school janitor gives him a glove with strange powers. It leads Jason to discover that there is an alien conspiracy to conquer Earth—and that he is part of it. (BBYA; Quick Picks)

Silverberg, Robert. *The Longest Way Home*. 2002. *S*. Fifteen-year-old Joseph Master Keilloran is the only survivor at his cousin's estate after the Folk rise up against the Masters and massacre all members of the ruling race. On his 10,000-mile journey home, Joseph encounters all the various types of sentient life on the planet—from a Noctumbos, who has two personalities sharing one body, to the Indigenes, who think in a way totally alien to Masters. And then there's the Folk, the first humanlike inhabitants of the planet, who were conquered by the feudal Masters.

Sleator, William. Piggy series. *JS*.

> *Interstellar Pig*. 1984. Barney's boring vacation at the beach becomes more interesting when he starts playing a game with the three neighbors. Then he discovers that there is more to the game than meets the eye.
>
> *Parasite Pig*. 2002. Sixteen-year-old Barney is kidnapped by a parasitic alien and thrust into a horrifying situation.

Thompson, Kate. *The Beguilers*. 2001. *MJ*. Rilka, who never really fit in, expresses her grand intention to find out about the beguilers, the mysterious beings that entice people who go out after dark and meet their deaths. Unlike everyone else in her world, Rilka is allergic to the cuddly, furry creatures that take away humans' grief and anxiety. Her quest estranges her from her family and friends, but leads her to important knowledge.

Utopia/Dystopia

Would the world be a better place if everyone knew that the best career would be chosen for them, if anyone who was not born perfect was not allowed to live, if all families were limited to only two children? Or would it be a nightmare? These are the types of questions posited in utopian/dystopian novels. Focusing on the way society functions, these books rebuild the world in ways we never imagined. The backdrop of these worlds is an ever-present feature of the story, and setting may be elaborately described.

Anderson, M. T. *Feed*. 2002. *S*. In this dystopian future, parents select the features they want in their children and then implant them as babies with a computer link directly to their brains. By adolescence, Titus and his friends are inarticulate and obsessed with whatever the Feed wants them to buy. He does begin to question the Feed when a girl he falls in love with is infected with a computer virus that endangers her life. (BBYA)

Haddix, Margaret Peterson. Hidden series. *MJ*. Luke, a third child in a world where only two children are allowed per family, has lived his life in hiding.

> *Among the Hidden*. 1998. Twelve-year-old Luke, a third child in a society where being a third child is an executable offense, discovers he is not alone after a new house is built next door and he sees a girl in the window. (BBYA)

> *Among the Imposters*. 2001. Luke has been taken to an isolated private school, assuming the identity of Lee, a wealthy boy, who was legal but has died. Tormented by another boy in his eight-bed dorm room, Luke/Lee discovers that others are sneaking out of the building. They are also thirds hiding behind false identities. (Quick Picks; IRAYAC)

> *Among the Betrayed*. 2002. Nina, a third child, escapes the Population Police and tries to survive along with the three children she was supposed to betray.

Lowry, Lois. *Gathering Blue*. 2000. *MJ*. According to custom, Kira should have been exposed to the elements and left to die in the place of the dead when she was born lame, but her mother fought for her life. After her mother dies, Kira is given the job of restoring the cloak that is embroidered with the history of the people. (IRAYAC)

Lowry, Lois. *The Giver*. 1993. *MJ*. A society where everything is the same, everyone is equal, and everyone receives the same treatment may not be as great as it seems. (Newbery Award; YALSA 100 Best Books; BBYA)

Thompson, Kate. *The Beguilers*. 2001. *MJ*. Annotated in the Aliens section of this chapter.

Post-Apocalypse

The end of the world as we know it is the theme in postapocalyptic science fiction. The reasons for the destruction vary from war to plague and even civic uprisings, but the end result is a world where survival is the first priority. Most of the books using this theme have a high degree of adventure.

Armstrong, Jennifer, and Nancy Butcher. Fire-Us Trilogy. *MJS*. After a virus wipes out all adults and takes the memories of those left, teens and kids struggle to survive.

> *The Kindling*. 2002. In a Florida town, teenage Mommy, Teacher, and Hunter form a family to take care of younger kids Action Figure, Teddy Bear, Baby, and Doll after a virus wipes out all their memories, as well as the lives of all adults.

> *Keepers of the Flame*. 2002. On their way to Washington, the Fire-Us survivors from Florida meet some adult survivors who have formed a cult.

The Kiln. 2003. The family made up of surviving kids discovers the cause of the virus that decimated the world.

Bell, Hilari. *Songs of Power.* 2000. *MJ.* The world's food supply has been decimated by a terrorist crop virus. Imani, a shaman-in-training and the daughter of a scientist, lives in an undersea habitat where scientists are trying to develop an alternative food source. When the habitat is threatened, Imani is the only one who can uncover the true culprits.

Butler, Susan. *The Hermit Thrush Sings.* 1999. *M.* More than a century after a giant meteor strike has devastated the Earth, Leora, a young girl with psychic abilities flees her village.

Hautman, Pete. *Hole in the Sky.* 2001. *MJS.* In a not-so-distant future in which the human population has been decimated by a deadly flu, Ceej and Harryette, a teen brother and sister, live with their uncle at the Grand Canyon. When a trader comes to the settlement, he tells them that while the floodgates of the Glen Canyon Dam were closed, the town of Page was hit by the flu. If the gates aren't opened, the dam will eventually give way, and the resulting flood will sweep everything before it into the Gulf.

Hoffman, Alice. *Green Angel.* 2003. *JS.* Green was resentful when her parents and sister went off to the city to sell their produce, but when the city went up in flames, she was so devastated that she cut off her beautiful hair, sewed thorns to her clothing, covered herself with black tattoos, and changed her name to Ash. This story is her journey back to recovery. It contains a veiled reference to terrorism and the backlash that ethnic hate engenders.

Kaye, Marilyn. *The Vanishing.* 1998. *MJ.* Twenty-five New York high school seniors leave their old bomb-shelter classroom in the bowels of the overcrowded building to find that everyone else has vanished. No dead bodies, no obvious signs of people leaving, just abandoned cars and bikes tell them that they are the sole inhabitants of New York—and possibly of the world. (Quick Picks)

Nix, Garth. *Shade's Children.* 1997. *JS.* In a horrifying world where everyone over the age of thirteen is turned into a hunting machine or food, a band of teens under the direction of a computer program tries to sabotage the Overlords. (BBYA)

O'Brien, Robert C. *Z for Zachariah.* 1975. *JS.* After a nuclear war, Ann thinks she is the sole survivor, but when a man makes his way to her isolated valley, she discovers that being alone may not have been the worst thing. (Popular Paperbacks; BBYA; YALSA 100 Best Books) Classic

Philbrick, Rodman. *The Last Book in the Universe.* 2000. *MJ.* Spaz, an epileptic, is one of the few people in a postapocalyptic world who cannot use the brain-rotting mindprobe, which might allow him to learn to read and write—skills he discovers while on a quest to find his dying sister. (BBYA)

Rapp, Adam. *Copper Elephant.* 1999. *S.* Eleven-year-old Whensday lives in The Shelf, a postapocalyptic world where acid rain raises blisters and kids are worked to death.

Weaver, Will. *Memory Boy.* 2001. *MJS.* Miles Newell, a teen inventor, creates a vessel that will take his family away from the dangers and shortages in Minneapolis after volcanic activity has devastated "life-as-we-know-it."

Genetic Engineering

Tampering with the genetic makeup of people, animals, and plants is a popular theme in science fiction. Whether the intentions are good or evil, when humans try to control creation, the result is usually disastrous. Cloning is a popular topic.

Farmer, Nancy. *The House of the Scorpion.* 2002. *MJS.* When the sheltered Matteo is injured jumping through the window of his isolated home to try to save a girl, he is taken to the mansion of El Patron, where it is discovered that he is a clone and not human. In fact, he is El Patron's clone, created to provide spare parts for the ruler. However, he has also inherited many of the gifts that allowed El Patron to carve a country between Azatlan (Mexico) and the United States—a country using mindless drones to grow, harvest, and process the fields of poppies that yield the drugs that make him wealthy. (BBYA; Printz-Honor; Newbery Honor)

Haddix, Margaret Peterson. *Turnabout.* 2000. *MJ.* Two orphaned teenage girls are facing the reality that soon they will not be able to take care of themselves as they continue aging backward toward infancy from the nonagenarians they once were.

Halam, Ann. *Dr. Franklin's Island.* 2002. Semi, Miranda, and Arnie are stranded on an almost-deserted island after surviving a horrifying plane crash. Unfortunately, mad scientist Dr. Franklin is already there—and he needs specimens for his experiments in genetic engineering. (BBYA)

Kaye, Marilyn. Replica series. *M.* Amy, a seventh-grader, discovers that she is a clone with some very special abilities. Through her adventures, she uncovers conspiracies, other clones, and additional talents.

> *Amy, Number Seven.* 1998. An autobiographical writing assignment in seventh grade and stonewalling by her scientist mother sends Amy on a quest to solve the mystery of her birth, just as she discovers that she is stronger and faster than other girls her age. (Quick Picks)

> *Pursuing Amy: Who Can You Trust?* 1998. Amy's mom has started dating a man who makes Amy very uneasy as she faces the changes puberty is triggering that make her superhuman.

> *Another Amy.* 1998. When Amy meets someone who looks just like her, she discovers that they are very different inside.

> *Perfect Girls.* 1999. Amy wakes up in a hospital in the midst of other clones.

> *Secret Clique.* 1999. Why would Amy want to forego her friends and join the popular clique at her school?

And the Two Shall Meet. 1998. A week of Wilderness Adventure camp should have been fun for Amy, Tasha, and Eric, but it turns into a struggle for survival.

The Best of the Best. 1999. Eric is chosen to mentor a new student at Parkside Middle School, a nine-year-old prodigy.

Mystery Mother. 1999. A woman turns up who claims that she is Amy's birth mother and that Amy is not a clone but rather the original from which the other Project Crescent clones were created.

The Fever. 1999. Up to this point, Amy's superior genes have guaranteed her perfect health, but now she doesn't feel so well. Will she survive with her talents intact?

Ice Cold. 2000. Amy's worst enemy, Jeanine, knows that Amy is a clone—and she may even try to sell Amy's story to a sleazy tabloid.

Lucky Thirteen. 2000. Amy starts running with Amy, Number Thirteen, also known as Aly, who lives on the wild side.

In Search of Andy. 2000. When Amy goes to Paris, Andy, a clone who she met the previous summer, is the last person she would expect to see.

The Substitute. 2000. Ms. Heartshorn, the new substitute teacher, seems to have it in for Amy.

The Beginning. 2000. A class trip takes Amy to Washington, D.C., the place where she was cloned.

Transformation. 2000. Everyone around Amy seems to be changing—it's almost as if they were possessed.

Happy Birthday, Dear Amy. 2001. Amy wakes up on her thirteenth birthday to discover that she has experienced some drastic physical changes overnight.

Missing Pieces. 2001. All the people at Parkside Middle School seem to be losing their talents.

Return of the Perfect Girls. 2001. All the Amy and Andy clones are gathered on an island.

Dreamcrusher. 2001. When Amy is struck by lightning, she acquires extrasensory powers.

Like Father, Like Son. 2001. When Amy's boyfriend Chris is tapped to make a bone marrow donation for his dad, Amy realizes there are many reasons that clones could have been created.

Virtual Amy. 2001. Amy downloads into her consciousness a game that may mean life or death.

The Plague Trilogy: Rewind. 2002. Amy travels back in time to try to find a cure for a plague that is decimating the world.

The Plague Trilogy: Play. 2002. In her quest to stop a deadly plague, Amy agrees to be injected into the body of someone with the plague and sees up close the interior battle.

The Plague Trilogy: Fast Forward. 2002. Amy enters a world where everyone is as perfect as she is.

All about Andy. 2002. Amy and Andy learn shocking truths about Project Crescent.

War of the Clones. 2002. A tabloid reports that human clones exist and are trying to create a master race.

Amy, on Her Own. 2002. In the finale of the Replica series Amy's crescent moon mark starts fading, and so do her extraordinary powers. Will she become normal?

Lasky, Kathryn. *Star Split*. 1999. *J*. In a time when the Bio Union regulates all cloning, thirteen-year-old Darci begins to worry that she may be an illegal clone.

Luiken, Nicole. *Silver Eyes*. 2001. *MJ*. A teenager working as a security agent discovers that she has been mentally manipulated to forget the past.

Singleton, L. J. Regeneration series. *JS*. Five teens discover that they are clones and that the scientist who created them also injected them with a formula that gave them super powers; but then the mastermind of the experiment decides they should be terminated, and their adventures really begin.

Regeneration. 2000. Varina's normal life comes to an end when a stranger named Chase tells her she is one of five clones. (Quick Picks)

The Search. 2000. When Eric's sister is kidnapped by Dr. Victor, he joins up with the other clones. (Quick Picks)

The Truth. 2000. Allison meets the gorgeous model from whom she was cloned. (Quick Picks)

The Imposter. 2000. Sandee, the last of the clones, has been found.

The Killer. 2000. Chase, finding out he was cloned from a serial killer, has left the group and is working on a remote ranch, but a tabloid reporter is on his trail, hoping to expose him as a killer.

Skurzynski, Gloria. *The Clones*. 2002. *JS*. Annotated in the Adventure section of this chapter.

References

Cart, Michael. *Tomorrowland: Ten Stories about the Future.* New York: Scholastic, 1999.

Herald, Diana Tixier, and Bonnie Kunzel. *Strictly Science Fiction.* Westport, Conn.: Libraries Unlimited, 2002.

Chapter 8

Paranormal

In the last decade of the twentieth century, horror fiction was the favorite genre of many teens, as well as many adults—and with both groups, King was king. In fact, Stephen King's work was so popular, it was said that he had not just one but several spots permanently reserved on the best-seller lists. This wasn't the first time horror fiction had achieved popularity. Two previous surges in interest occurred—one in the 1930s, when H. P. Lovecraft reigned, and the other in the 1960s, manifesting mainly in films and television shows (e.g., *Twilight Zone, Rosemary's Baby*).

A decade ago, vampires, ghosts, werewolves, zombies, and other menacing supernatural monsters recaptured the American imagination in new iterations that particularly intrigued teens. However, readers in the new millennium, perhaps because of the dark events of current times, are generally less interested in the extremes and absolutes of the genre—the relentless graphic violence of slasher stories or the macabre blood and gore of splatterpunk. Readers, especially teens, are instead drawn to new horror hybrids tempered with the lighter features of other genres—humor, for example, or romance. But if the pure horror novels of the nineties are behind us, many of the elements that made them appealing continue to hold broad appeal. Teens are still captivated by the idea of having supernatural powers; paranormal beings, such as ghosts, vampires, or werewolves, continue to fascinate as well. Today's young adult horror fiction is more aptly called "paranormal," because it is in its paranormal aspects that the genre lives on. It has more of the haunting atmosphere of *Twilight Zone* than the macabre spirit of Michael Jackson's "Thriller."

What draws readers to this type of literature? Above all, current paranormal fiction retains the ambiance of horror. The tone and atmosphere are moody, dark, and often psychological and suspenseful. Characters in these novels are usually troubled, haunted, or downright unstable. Paranormal tales are intellectually provocative, but they also stir the emotions, generally eliciting some level or type of fear, from haunted uneasiness and spine-tingling dread to unmitigated terror. They give readers a bit of an adrenaline rush, a little like a carnival ride. Many teens, who are questioning the status quo and fascinated with the rough edges of experience, enjoy stories of the supernatural.

Anthony Fonseca and June Pulliam (2003), in their guide *Hooked on Horror,* now in its second edition, posit the theory that the most compelling feature of horror literature is the character of the "monster." Fans of the horror genre gravitate toward titles about a certain type of monster—vampires, ghosts, witches, and so forth. Each type is embedded in deep symbolic or psychological implications. Furthermore, to a great extent the kind of monster dictates the atmosphere, mood, and other qualities of the novel. Thus, this chapter is organized accordingly, with the exception of a section of short story collections at the end.

Themes

Ghosts

Ghosts are standard fare in horror or paranormal literature. They have been around for a long time, being strongly rooted in the oral tradition. Stories about spirits beings bound to this world instead of moving on after death can be poignant, sad, or frightening. They often touch on unresolved issues from the past, and ghosts can sometimes be viewed as signals of guilt or fear. The atmosphere of traditional ghost stories is haunting or spooky, even spine-tingling, but ghost tales can also be downright terrifying.

Alphin, Elaine Marie. *Ghost Soldier.* 2001. *M.* Alexander, who often sees ghosts, becomes enmeshed in a mystery when he goes to North Carolina and meets a Civil War ghost.

Bennett, Cherie. *The Haunted Heart.* 1999. *J.* Gina has moved into a haunted mansion with her family, where she meets Thomas, a sensitive ghost. First book in the Enchanted Hearts series that combines romance with a different paranormal theme in each book. (Quick Picks)

Buffie, Margaret. *Angels Turn Their Backs.* 1998. *MJ.* Annotated in Chapter 5, "Mystery and Suspense." (IRAYAC)

Buffie, Margaret. *The Dark Garden.* 1997. *JS.* After a bicycling accident, Thea, age sixteen, starts having memories of a different family and different time.

Downing, Wick. *Leonardo's Hand.* 2001. *M.* A ghost figures into this tale that is annotated in Chapter 2, "Issues."

Hawes, Louise. *Rosey in the Present Tense.* 1999. *S.* Rosey may be dead, but romantic Franklin still loves her. (Popular Paperbacks)

Johnson, Angela. *Looking for Red.* 2002. *MJS.* (Alternative format) A heart-wrenching tale in verse format about a middle school girl who is trying to get over the loss of her brother.

Kimmel, Elizabeth Cody. *In the Stone Circle.* 1998. *J.* Crystin's summer in Wales with her professor father, his friend, and the friend's two children turns out to be anything but boring as ghosts drift in and out of the picture—especially since one of the ghosts may be Crystin's mother.

Nixon, Joan Lowery. *The Haunting.* 1998. *MJ.* A ghostly mystery is contained within the walls of Graymoss plantation, and Lia intends to solve it. (Quick Picks; IRAYAC)

Roberts, Laura Peyton. *Ghost of a Chance.* 1997. *MJ.* What do you do when you discover that you're in love with the same guy as your best friend—and that the object of this affection has been dead for decades? Melissa's best friend Chloe has just moved into an old mansion and discovered that the ghost of James, a gorgeous eighteen-year-old boy, inhabits the place. When Chloe and her family go out of town and ask Melissa to take care of the house, she finds herself spending a lot of time getting to know James.

Singer, Marilyn. *Deal with a Ghost.* 1997. *MJ.* Annotated in the Psionic Powers section of this chapter.

Vande Velde, Vivian. *Ghost of a Hanged Man.* 1998. *M.* A ghostly tale set in the American West of the 1870s. (Quick Picks)

Vande Velde, Vivian. *Never Trust a Dead Man.* 1999. *JS.* Seventeen-year-old Selwyn has been accused of murder. A witch resurrects Farold's spirit and gives the two young men a week to find the real murderer. (BBYA; Quick Picks)

Vande Velde, Vivian. *There's a Dead Person Following My Sister Around.* 1999. *MJ.* Eleven-year-old Ted searches through old journals and learns about the Underground Railroad in his attempt to solve the mystery of the ghosts who are haunting his little sister and their 150-year-old house. (IRAYAC)

Yolen, Jane. *Here There Be Ghosts.* 1998. *MJ.* (Short Stories) (Alternative format) An illustrated collection of ghost stories and poems from master storyteller Yolen.

Wallace, Rich. *Restless.* 2003. *S.* A strange encounter with a ghost in a cemetery leaves seventeen-year-old Herbie with the ability to see auras—and maybe finally to hear what his brother, ten years dead, is trying to tell him.

Monsters, Werefolk, and Other Beasties

Zombies, werewolves, and other strange creatures elicit some of our darkest fears. Whether humans turn into wolves, or the undead, or a monster is made by human masters, themes of creation and transformation are at work here. Teens, undergoing their own changes, can often relate to this theme. The sensuality of becoming an animal also holds appeal. Monsters have captivated the teen imagination at least since *Franken-stein,* which was written by a teenager, Mary Shelley, and published in 1818.

Garfield, Henry. *Tartabull's Throw.* 2001. *JS.* Baseball, werewolves, time travel, and young love are entwined in a tale that takes place in several alternate realities.

Golden, Christopher. *Meets the Eye.* 2000. *S.* Are the living dead behind a Boston crime wave? Jenna Blake starts to piece together the clues to tell her who or what is behind these "zombie" crimes. (Quick Picks)

Golden, Christopher. Prowlers series. *MJS.* Packs of savage beasts are roaming the countryside, preying on human flesh.

> *Prowlers.* 2001. After his murdered friend Artie returns from the Ghostlands to warn him of the danger, nineteen-year-old Jack Dwyer battles the prowlers, savage werewolf-like predators.

> *Laws of Nature.* 2001. Jack and Molly go to rural Vermont on the trail of the prowlers and end up being murder suspects themselves.

> *Predator and Prey.* 2001. The spirits in the Ghostlands who have been helping Jack are now endangered by a vicious beast called the Ravenous.

> *Wild Things.* 2002. Because prowler strength seems to be building on many fronts, Jack and friends must work harder and smarter than ever.

Klause, Annette Curtis. *Blood and Chocolate.* 1997. *JS.* Beautiful Vivian Gandillon is lonely at her new high school in Maryland. She and her mother moved there with the rest of her pack after her father was killed. Without a leader, the pack is undirected and at loose ends, a disaster waiting to happen. When humans start turning up dead, savaged by strong teeth, the pack is in peril. The description of a human changing into a wolf is conveyed so vividly you'll want to howl. (BBYA; Quick Picks; IRAYAC)

Sleator, William. *The Beasties.* 1997. *M.* Fifteen-year-old Doug and his little sister Colette discover strange subterranean beings, who take needed limbs and organs from humans. (Quick Picks; IRAYAC)

Windsor, Patricia. *The Blooding.* 1996. *JS.* A young American, Maris, takes a job as an au pair for the Forrest family in England. The reader sees the unfamiliar English landscape through Maris's eyes and observes the strange behavior of Derek Forrest and the mysterious illness of Barb Forrest. Mundane details make the wolf transformation all the more believable. (Quick Picks; Popular Paperbacks)

Zindel, Paul. *Night of the Bat.* 2001. *MJS.* A gigantic bat terrorizes a research team. (Quick Picks)

Zindel, Paul. *Rats.* 1999. *MJ.* When their home is paved over with asphalt, mutant rats from a garbage landfill invade New York and begin devouring humans. (Popular Paperbacks; Quick Picks)

Psionic Powers

Telekinesis, telepathy, teleportation, and precognition are just a few of the extraordinary psionic powers that appear in paranormal fiction for teens. The idea of having powers beyond the normal appeals to readers. Readers who enjoy stories about psionic powers will find sections on this theme in the fantasy and science fiction chapters as well.

Chandler, Elizabeth. Dark Secrets series. *S.* Three teen girls haunted by the past.

> *Legacy of Lies.* 2000. When she visits the old plantation where her grandmother lives, sixteen-year-old Megan has dreams that reveal dangers. (Quick Picks)

> *Don't Tell.* 2001. Seven years after her mother's drowning, Lauren returns home—only to find that someone wants her dead. (Quick Picks)

> *No Time to Die.* 2001. Jenny goes to the campus where her dead sister Liza spent the previous summer to find her murderer, but Jenny experiences visions that send her reeling right into the arms of the killer. (Quick Picks)

Duncan, Lois. *Gallows Hill.* 1997. *MJ.* Sarah Zoltanne seems to have developed clairvoyant powers. Is she a witch? (Quick Picks; IRAYAC)

Ewing, Lynne. Daughters of the Moon series. *MJ.* Teen girls with supernatural powers.

> *Goddess of the Night.* 2000. Vanessa is a pretty typical teenager, except that when she gets excited, her molecules start to fly apart and she disappears. This can make kissing a disaster. Fortunately, her best friend also has a strange power, so she is not alone. (Quick Picks)

> *Into the Cold Fire.* 2000. The daughters of the Moon goddess go up against the followers of the evil Atrox. (Quick Picks)

> *Night Shade.* 2001. Jimena is shocked when Veto, who was killed a year ago, reappears.

> *The Secret Scroll.* 2001. Catty's ability to go back in time may help her find her birth mother.

> *The Sacrifice.* 2001. Can Serena win Stanton away from Atrox's dark forces?

> *The Lost One.* 2001. How can there be a fifth daughter of the moon?

> *Moon Demon.* 2002. Vanessa has been feeling cut off and out of control.

> *Possession.* 2002. Serena is spiraling out of control.

> *The Choice.* 2003. Jimena has been sent back to her gang past.

Hill, Pamela Smith. *The Last Grail Keeper.* 2001. *M.* Annotated in the Psionic Abilities section of Chapter 6, "Fantasy."

Karr, Kathleen. *Playing with Fire.* 2001. *M.* Greer's mother is a popular medium during the 1920s spiritualism fad, but it is Greer who can actually see auras—and he knows that Drake Morley is dangerous.

Lubar, David. *Hidden Talents.* 1999. *MJS.* Annotated in Chapter 7, "Science Fiction."

Metz, Melinda. Fingerprints. *MJ.* Rae's mind is being invaded by thoughts—thoughts that aren't hers, thoughts that make her think that she may be going crazy. Her mother went crazy, and now she, too, has done time in a mental hospital. Could the thoughts she's hearing be real thoughts from other people?

Gifted Touch. 2001. When Rae begins to hear voices, she thinks she's going crazy. Then weird things begin to happen, things the voices warned her about. (Quick Picks)

Haunted. 2001. Someone Rae loves is in trouble—and she has to help him. (Quick Picks)

Trust Me. 2001. Mysterious pictures, a box of ashes, and a desperate search for Anthony's father. (Quick Picks)

Secrets. 2001. Rae discovers the truth about her dead mother. (Quick Picks)

Betrayed. 2001. Is Anthony friend or foe?

Revelations. 2001. Rae discovers who's trying to kill her. Now she must act.

Payback. 2002. Rae thought Yana was her best friend.

Singer, Marilyn. *Deal with a Ghost.* 1997. *MJ.* Deal has a knack for making boys like her, even if they already have girlfriends. Her mom has the knack too, and she's dumped Deal with her grandmother while she goes to make a new life with a new boyfriend. Deal decides to be different, and not to steal a boyfriend just because another girl makes her mad. But an encounter with a mysterious ghost really lets her know the possible consequences of her actions.

Wieler, Diana. *RanVan: The Magic Nation.* 1998. *JS.* Annotated in Chapter 5, "Mystery and Suspense."

Unexplained Phenomena

There are certain things beyond our control, and feeling out of control is both scary and thrilling. While the books in the previous section deal with unexplainable powers, those in this section deal with inexplicable occurrences.

Almond, David. *Kit's Wilderness.* 2000. *MJ.* Thirteen-year-old Kit goes to the mining village and meets a kid who shows him that both of them, named for long-gone relatives, are listed in a memorial at the cemetery. As the kids play a game called death, Kit sees something very strange. (Printz Award; BBYA)

Bennett, Cherie. *Love Him Forever.* 1999. *J.* High school senior Colleen has fallen in love with Luke—in more than one incarnation. Sixth in the Enchanted Hearts series. (Quick Picks)

Bradbury, Ray. *From the Dust Returned.* 2001. *JS.* The strange immortal Elliot family, who Bradbury introduced in the 1940s in his classic short story collection, has a reunion at the house high on an Indiana hill.

Bruchac, Joseph. *Skeleton Man.* 2001. *MJ.* After her parents fail to come home one night, sixth-grader Molly is sent to live with an uncle she has never even heard of before, who locks her up at night. Molly's dreams lead her to find her parents, who have also been kidnapped by the "uncle." A spooky tale, based on Mohawk folklore.

Gaiman, Neil. *American Gods.* 2001. *S.* Just before his long-anticipated release from prison, Shadow discovers that his wife has been killed in an automobile accident, along with a friend who was to have been his employer. On his release, Shadow meets the mysterious, charismatic Wednesday, who introduces him to the old gods who are on the verge of war with the new gods. Only for the most mature teen readers. (Bram Stoker Award; Hugo Award; Nebula Award) **Adult**

Gaiman, Neil. *Coraline.* 2002. *MJS.* While exploring their new flat, Coraline discovers a passage into a strange place that looks like her home and is inhabited by people who look like her own parents, but with black buttons where their eyes should be. Returning home, Coraline discovers that her real parents are missing, so she makes another foray down the scary passage to the other flat. She strikes a deal with the other mother that she and her parents can go free if she can find the souls of the three dead children imprisoned in the basement. Gaiman at his terrifying best. (BBYA; Hugo Award)

Littke, Lael. *Lake of Secrets.* 2002. *JS.* Carlene's brother disappeared three years before she was born. Now at fifteen Carlene has returned, along with her mother, to the lake where he was lost, and she begins to experience memories that are not hers.

McDonald, Joyce. *Shades of Simon Gray.* 2001. *MJS.* Strange things begin to happen in the small town of Bellehaven when Simon Gray, brilliant student and all-around good guy, wraps his car around the town's ancient hanging tree. While in a coma, Simon finds himself in different places, most notably at the tree, where he meets a mysterious young man who says he was hanged there in the early history of the town. Meanwhile, Simon is being investigated for hacking into the school's computers, and one of his friends finds evidence in her historical research that the town's past was not always as honorable as it presented itself. (BBYA)

Moench, Doug. *The Big Book of the Unexplained.* 1997. *S.* (Alternative format) The paranormal presented in visual form, using the talents of several graphic-novel artists. (Popular Paperbacks) **Adult**

Murphy, Rita. *Night Flying.* 2000. *MJS.* The Hansen women can fly, but they have to follow some very strict rules, enforced by Grandmother. On the eve of Georgia's sixteenth birthday, her rebellious Aunt Carmen turns up, and Georgia flies solo in the daylight. (BBYA)

Naylor, Phyllis Reynolds. *Jade Green.* 2000. *MJS.* Orphaned, Judith Sparrow is taken in by her uncle and his housekeeper under the condition that she never bring anything green into the house. Happy, but wary of her middle-aged cousin, Judith begins working as an assistant in a millinery shop, where she hears about Jade Green, an orphaned girl who committed suicide in the house. Is Jade Green trying to haunt her because she brought in a green picture frame, or is something else going on? Delicious gothic ambiance and a charming romance, as well as heart-thumping suspense. (Quick Picks; IRAYAC)

Rylant, Cynthia. *The Islander.* 1998. *M.* On a remote island, ten-year-old Daniel meets a mermaid, and it changes his life forever.

Sebold, Alice. *The Lovely Bones*. 2002. *S.* A fourteen-year-old who is raped, murdered, and dismembered by a neighbor goes to a heaven that looks like a high school and watches those left behind. This is an adult novel that has a senior high school following. (BBYA) **Adult**

Vampires

The undead, who suck bloody sustenance from their victims and cannot be exposed to the light of day, have been popular with teen readers since Bram Stoker's *Dracula* was published in 1897. Vampire stories often have an erotic or romantic subtext—sometimes subtle, sometimes overt—which appeals to readers of all ages. (Although many teens love Anne Rice's vampire series, Rice's erotic take on the legendary beings are not for the faint of heart.) Other times, the vampire's parasitic dependency suggests the parent-child relationship or other power structures. Darkly atmospheric, these stories also explore themes of mortality and immortality. Titles listed in this section were published specifically for teen readers.

Anderson, M. T. *Thirsty.* 1997. *JS.* Chris is shocked and appalled to discover that he is turning into a vampire on the eve of the Sad Festival, his community's yearly ritual to keep the Evil Vampire Lord Tch'muchgar locked away on another plane. If he does not kill and feed his bloodlust, he will die; but if he does attack, he will surely be caught and executed. The surreal setting of everyday suburbia is a creepy counterpoint to this tale of teen angst. (Quick Picks)

Atwater-Rhodes, Amelia. *Demon in My View.* 2000. *JS.* A teenage witch tries to save seventeen-year-old Jessica from Aubrey, an alluring vampire. (Quick Picks; IRAYAC)

Atwater-Rhodes, Amelia. *In the Forests of the Night.* 1999. *JS.* Risika (aka Rachel), a three-hundred-year-old vampire, takes her revenge on the evil Aubrey who made her what she is. (Popular Paperbacks; Quick Picks)

Atwater-Rhodes, Amelia. *Midnight Predator.* 2002. *JS.* Turquoise Draka has gone undercover in the mythical city of Midnight to try to assassinate the evil vampire Jeshikah.

Atwater-Rhodes, Amelia. *Shattered Mirror.* 2001. *JS.* Seventeen-year-old witch Sarah pursues the vampire Nikolas. (Quick Picks, IRAYAC)

Klause, Annette Curtis. *The Silver Kiss.* 1990. *MJS.* As Zoe's mother lies dying, Zoe and Simon become involved in a vampire romance. The quintessential teen vampire novel. (BBYA; YALSA 100 Best Books) [Classic]

Pierce, Meredith Ann. *The Darkangel.* 1982. *MJS.* When Aeriel sees the tiny glowing spark of humanity in her vampire master, it affects her decision to kill him. (BBYA; IRA 1983) [Classic]

Shan, Darren. Cirque Du Freak series. *M.* When Darren Shan attends a freak show with his best friend, he is turned into a half-vampire.

> *A Living Nightmare.* 2001. Darren Shan will do anything for his friend Steve—he'll even become a vampire.

> *The Vampire's Assistant.* 2001. Darren, a lonely half-vampire, tries his best to hone his vampire skills.

> *Tunnels of Blood.* 2002. On an outing to the city with Mr. Crepsley and Evva the snake boy, Darren discovers dead bodies, the handiwork of a dangerous fiend.

> *Vampire Mountain.* 2002. Darren and Mr. Crepsley travel to the Halls of Vampire Mountain.

> *Trials of Death.* 2003. Five fearsome trials must be passed if Darren Shan is to prove himself to the vampire clan.

Smith, L. J. *Soulmate.* 1997. *MJ.* Sixteen-year-old Hannah Snow goes to a shrink when she starts receiving terrifying warnings that are written in her own handwriting. The messages warn her away from a vampire named Thierry, but then she begins to doubt herself. Opening with a thrilling were-wolf attack, this supernatural romance is a real page-turner and a great example of genreblending of paranormal, romance, and suspense.

Somtow, S. P. *The Vampire's Beautiful Daughter.* 1997. *MJS.* Johnny Raitt—one-quarter Lakota, one-quarter Polish, and one-half Jewish—has been told he'll fit in at Claudette Colbert High School just between Beverly Hills and Encino; but he never expected to find his soul mate and the girl of his dreams, who happens to be half human, half vampire.

Vande Velde, Vivian. *Companions of the Night.* 1995. *JS.* Kerry helps Ethan escape from some men who seem to be trying to kill him, only to discover that he has some unique qualities. (Popular Paperbacks; BBYA; Quick Picks)

Witches

Witchcraft, which suggests female power, fascinates some and threatens others. Tales of dangerous girls who have supernatural powers are on the rise today—in the media and in books. Recent television series, for example, include *Charmed* and *Sabrina the Teenage Witch,* and many new books that feature witches have been published in series format.

Bird, Isobel. Circle of Three series. *MJS.* Three diverse high school girls discover the nature-based religion of Wicca.

> *So Mote It Be.* 2001. As Kate Morgan works on a school assignment about the Salem witchcraft trials, she discovers a book she didn't remember

checking out from the library. Using a spell from it, she creates trouble for herself and, in an attempt to undo it, looks for others who have checked it out in the past, which introduces her to Annie and Cooper. (Quick Picks)

Merry Meet. 2001. Kate learns more about the Craft after taking a class at a bookstore and the three decide to participate in Ostara, the sabbat celebration of the equinox. (Quick Picks)

Second Sight. 2001. A kidnapped girl appeals to Cooper for help through dreams and visions. (Quick Picks)

What the Cards Said. 2001. Annie discovers that she has a knack for reading Tarot cards. (Quick Picks)

In the Dreaming. 2001. The three decide to join in with all the area covens in celebrating Midsummer's Eve. (Quick Picks)

Ring of Light. 2001. Cooper leaves the circle of three. (Quick Picks)

Blue Moon. 2001. Annie's experimental channeling goes awry when she attempts to use it during the second full moon of the month. (Quick Picks)

The Five Paths. 2001. The Wiccan symbol Cooper wears is mistaken by others for a satanic symbol, and the three find themselves in the middle of controversy.

Through the Veil. 2001. The veil between the worlds thins on Samhain, so Annie hopes to contact those in her family who have passed over into the spirit world.

Making the Saint. 2001. Kate steps outside the bounds of Wicca when the three are introduced to Santeria by a mysterious stranger.

The House of Winter. 2001. Cooper, Annie, and Kate go to a remote haunted house to celebrate the winter solstice.

Written in the Stars. 2001. Cooper, Kate, and Annie find what astrology tells them to be alarmingly true.

And It Harm None. 2002. Annie, Kate, and Cooper face a dilemma when they uncover what looks like a crime but isn't.

The Challenge Box. 2002. Kate must succeed in her final challenge to be initiated in Wicca along with Annie and Cooper.

Initiation. 2002. After a year and a day, Kate, Annie, and Cooper have made it to their Wiccan initiation ritual and a new beginning.

Ravenwolf, Silver. Witches' Chillers series. *JS.* This series features Bethany Salem, a sixteen-year-old witch and member of the Witches' Night Out coven.

Witches' Night Out. 2000. Bethany Salem is angry—so angry that she summons the hounds of Hel to help her find the person responsible for the death of her boyfriend. Afraid that it was someone in her teen coven, Bethany feels isolated—especially when her father shows up with an odious individual who claims to be her future stepmom.

Witches' Night of Fear. 2001. Bethany and her friends try to solve the murder of another teenager's mother.

Witches' Key to Terror. 2001. Bethany, Nam, and Tillie find jobs at an orchard and are drawn into another mystery when they discover that someone is practicing an evil form of magick.

Rees, Celia. Mary Newbury series. *MJS.* What would it be like to be a teen witch in colonial America?

Witch Child. 2001. When Mary Newbury's guardian is burned as a witch, Mary is saved and sent off to the American colonies for safety—ending up near Salem in 1659. (BBYA; IRAYAC)

Sorceress. 2002. When Agnes, a contemporary Native American, reads a portion of the diary of Mary Newbury, things begin to click.

Tiernan, Cate. Sweep series. *JS.* Seventeen-year-old Morgan is drawn to Cal, a new senior at her high school who turns out to practice Wicca and belong to a coven. Cal senses a power in her and concludes that she must be a blood witch. A combination of paranormal and teen romance.

Book of Shadows. 2001. When Morgan's friend Bree drags her to a meeting of the Cirrus Coven, everything begins to look different and Morgan begins to think that witchcraft may be choosing her. It doesn't hurt that Cal, on whom she's had a crush forever, is leading the ceremony. (Quick Picks)

The Coven. 2001. What is it about her past that Morgan's parents are keeping secret from her? (Quick Picks)

Blood Witch. 2001. Cal claims that he and Morgan are witches who are meant to be together, but when Hunter turns up and claims that Cal is practicing dark magick, Morgan begins to have doubts. (Quick Picks)

Dark Magick. 2001. Cal seems a little too anxious to get his hands on the Wiccan tools that belonged to Morgan's birth mother. (Quick Picks)

Awakening. 2001. Morgan has begun studying the Craft with Hunter after Cal's betrayal, but dark magick still seems to be at work. (Quick Picks)

Spellbound. 2001. Morgan can sense that Hunter is in danger.

The Calling. 2001. Hunter's quest to learn all he can to end the Woodbane conspiracy takes him and Morgan to New York City, where she tries to find out more about her birth parents and ends up in terrible danger. (Quick Picks)

Changeling. 2001. Morgan discovers something about her birth family that she didn't want to know. Could she be evil herself? (Quick Picks)

Strife. 2002. Discord grows all around Morgan as her parents get on her case for neglecting her schoolwork and the members of her coven are persecuted. (Quick Picks)

Seeker. 2002. Hunter is reunited with his long-lost dad, who Morgan senses is hiding a dark secret. (Quick Picks)

Origins. 2002. Hunter and Morgan find a chronicle written by one of Morgan's own ancestors that tells the history of the Woodbane conspiracy.

Eclipse. 2002. Everyone that Morgan loves is in jeopardy in the struggle between bright magick and dark magick, and Hunter and Morgan have found a new ally in Alisa.

Reckoning. 2002. Alisa must make a choice that could change her future.

Full Circle. 2002. Hunter, Morgan, and Alisa face a new danger.

Short Stories

Short stories are plentiful in the horror or paranormal genre. Some readers enjoy the shorter length, and the brevity seems to give more of a surprise to whatever twist is involved.

Cowley, Joy. *The Hitchhikers.* 1997. *JS.* The title story is about a couple of storytellers who have the ability to warp reality with their tales. "Totara Hill" sounds and feels like a familiar fairy tale, but it isn't. The contemporary ghost story "The Cottage by the Sea" makes the landscape of a girl's dream all too real. These are just three of the dozen tales in this collection.

Etchemendy, Nancy. *Cat in Glass and Other Tales of the Unnatural.* 2002. *S.* The title story is particularly haunting: a cat sculpture, made of glass, destroys four generations of a family. (BBYA)

Vande Velde, Vivian. *Being Dead.* 2001. *MJ.* Seven stories of the paranormal. (BBYA; IRAYAC)

Vande Velde, Vivian. *Curses, Inc. and Other Stories.* 1997. *MJS.* From sad to hilarious, this collection of ten stories of witches and a few ghosts features spells, hexes, jinxes, and more. (Quick Picks; IRAYAC)

References

Fonseca, Anthony, and June Pulliam. *Hooked on Horror.* 2d ed. Englewood, Colo.: Libraries Unlimited, 2003.

Chapter 9

Historical Novels

     The lure of historical fiction calls out to readers on many levels, not the least of which is the evocative historical setting, complete with characters that fit the times and loads of historically accurate details. Accuracy and authenticity are almost always important issues for fans of this genre. Reading a good historical is like time travel—the story takes you to a different time and place and allows you to experience that milieu vicariously. Many teens enjoy historical novels, with the adventure and romance of dashing heroes and heroines set against the backdrop of other times. They enjoy gaining new insights about history or seeing historical events from a new perspective.

     Teens often have an added incentive for reading historical fiction: it has been assigned in history class. When written to authentically reflect the past, historical fiction can be both entertaining and extremely informative, giving readers new perceptions and perspectives on historical events and milieus and expanding their overall worldviews.

     Teens consider anything that happened before they were born to be history, so this guide defines historical fiction as fiction set prior to the mid-eighties and in which the time period plays a prominent role.

     Historical fiction is a diverse genre, ranging from regency romances to Native American survival stories. It blends effortlessly with other genres, and there are numerous historical novels that could also be classified as mysteries, fantasy, romance, adventure, and so on—and some combine more than one of these genres. The subjects of historical fiction range over all of the continents and through all times past, from prehistory and the distant past to more recent times that many adult readers remember well, such as the civil rights movement and the Vietnam War in the 1960s. Because historical novels are often assigned for school, educators may wish to use the following listings for that purpose. Keep in mind, however, that this selection is primarily provided to assist teens in finding the stories they want to read. Other sources of listings for historical fiction are included in the Appendix I.

Teen readers who enjoy historical fiction can become knowledgeable about history, for this is a genre in which fiction often leads to expository reading. Without prodding, teen readers often research further the time periods that they have discovered in historical fiction. This link between fiction and nonfiction is a good thing to keep in mind when advising readers. Many teens know that reading authentic historical fiction has the beneficial side effect of providing them with a good background understanding for history class.

Interestingly, and purely from anecdotal evidence, it seems that many historical fiction writers read historical fiction as teens. For example, Steven Saylor, author of a popular adult series of mystery novels set in the Roman Empire, has mentioned reading the We Were There books as a youth and described the influence they had on him.

The level of historical authenticity varies, as does the amount of historical information included in historical fiction. These novels can give the reader a glimpse of life in another time or fully invoke in the reader the feeling that he or she is actually there. Whereas some novels merely use the historical setting as a rich backdrop, others focus on major historical events of the time.

Tastes in historical fiction vary widely. Readers frequently explore specific eras and events (e.g., the American Civil War, the Age of Exploration), reading multiple titles on a given topic. When advising readers, however, subgenre and overriding themes should also be considered. Whereas one teen may enjoy the gentle Christian prairie romances published by Bethany House, another may be looking for an action-packed Western; yet another might reach for a novel about this era written from a Native American perspective. The prairie romance reader is interested not only in the era of westward expansion, but also in the themes of romance and Christian salvation. The teen looking for books from a Native American perspective may also be interested in contemporary titles about the Native American experience or may enjoy books with a western setting. Although setting is generally a primary appeal of historical fiction, readers' advisory in this genre involves more than simply finding novels set in the right time and place.

There has been a recent rise in historical fiction publishing, with numerous titles being published in 2001 and 2002, addressing topics from ancient Troy to the civil rights movement. In 2002, the Avon True Romance series, featuring historical novels by well-known romance writers, was initiated.

A recent trend in historical novels published for teens is the use of a diary format, as exemplified in the My Name Is America series, the Dear America series, the Royal Diaries series, and many others. This format lends a more intimate air to the writing and more completely immerses readers in experiencing the past, while the structure of the series provides teens with continuity between titles.

Because the most common way that teen readers approach historical fiction is through time frame, whether for pleasure reading or a class assignment, this guide organizes titles thematically, by broad historical eras, arranged in two sections—for U.S. and world history, with some strictly thematic subsections, such as First Peoples (Native Americans), Civil War and Slavery, and Westward Expansion.

Themes

American History

This section contains historical fiction set in what is now the United States, from the precolonial times of first peoples to the mid-1980s. The themes and topics in this section may be familiar to readers, but often they offer an alternative or inside perspective on events. Many of these novels complement studies in U.S. history.

First Peoples (Native Americans)

Native Americans make up a significant proportion of the characters in historical fiction for teens. The titles in this section are set in various historical periods throughout American history, but all focus on the culture and ways of North America's first peoples, which is a theme that appeals to many teen readers. They also feature Native American protagonists. Additional titles with Native American themes, such as those about captives, appear in other parts of this chapter and throughout the book and can be accessed through the subject index. Readers interested in contemporary Native American stories can find then in Chapter 10, "Multicultural Fiction."

Although the titles that follow offer authentic portrayals, many novels published in this area promote stereotypical or romanticized images of Native Americans, so educators are strongly encouraged to review titles before assigning them.

Adler, Elizabeth. *Crossing the Panther's Path*. 2002. *M*. Irish and Mohawk by birth, Jesuit-trained fifteen-year-old Billy Calder becomes an interpreter for Tecumseh in the early 1800s.

Bruchac, Joseph. *The Journal of Jesse Smoke: A Cherokee Boy, Trail of Tears, 1838*. 2001. *M*. My Name Is America series. Sixteen-year-old Jesse and his family must leave behind all they know and travel west, on the Trail of Tears with the other Cherokee people.

Bruchac, Joseph. *Winter People*. 2002. *MJ*. Fourteen-year-old Saxso, of the Abenaki people, feels responsible for his widowed mother and the two younger sisters with whom he lives in the Indian village of St. Thomas. The villagers are practicing Catholics who speak French and live in homes much the same as their European North American counterparts. Fortunately, they also have a strong traditional background, which helps Saxso when Rogers' Rangers attack the village in 1759 and kidnap his mother and sisters. After a long and arduous trek, Saxso uses his skills and determination to single-handedly rescue his family.

Burks, Brian. *Walks Alone*. 1998. *MJ*. Walks Alone, a fifteen-year-old Apache girl, struggles to survive as she looks for the remnants of her band following a massacre in 1879.

Erdrich, Louise. *The Birchbark House*. 1999. *M*. Omakayas (Little Frog), a seven-year-old Objibwa girl, introduces readers to Native American life on an island in Lake Superior in the nineteenth century. Although written for a younger audience, middle school readers who like historical fiction dealing with Native Americans will enjoy this book. It has been called a Native American rebuttal to the Little House on the Prairie books.

Matcheck, Diane. *The Sacrifice.* 1998. *MJ.* In the 1700s, on the Great Plains, a young Native American girl proves her mettle. Annotated further in the Survival section of Chapter 4, "Adventure." (BBYA)

Seventeenth and Eighteenth Centuries: Colonial and Revolutionary Days

The early days of American history provide an exciting and sometimes thought-provoking setting. The birth of a country is, indeed, thrilling, and many of these stories contain strong elements of adventure. The American Revolution, the settling of the colonies, and the Salem witchcraft trials are some of the most popular themes in historical fiction set in this era. Although it has received less attention, the Spanish colonial influence was strong in the American Southwest and in Florida during the early days of the European settlement of North America; this part of history has also become popular in recent historical fiction.

Anderson, Laurie Halse. *Fever, 1793.* 2000. *JS.* A sixteen-year-old Philadelphian, Melinda Cook, copes with a yellow fever epidemic. (BBYA)

Blackwood, Gary. *Year of the Hangman.* 2002. *JS.* Although this is an alternate history in which the American Revolution failed, it features such historical characters as Ben Franklin, as well as an exciting story about an English teen who is sent to the colonies as a disciplinary action and discovers a cause worth fighting for. (BBYA)

Cooney, Caroline B. *The Ransom of Mercy Carter.* 2001. *M.* In the dead of winter of 1704, the village of Deerfield, Massachusetts, is attacked by a huge band of Indians, who take those not killed captive on a long march to various villages in Canada. Eleven-year-old Mercy Carter is adopted by an Indian family.

Curry, Jane Louise. *Dark Shade.* 1998. *J.* Sixteen-year-old Maggie Gilmore time travels to 1758 and is thrown into the midst of the French and Indian War. Annotated further in the Time Travel section of Chapter 6, "Fantasy."

Goodman, Joan Elizabeth. *Hope's Crossing.* 1998. *MJ.* In a raid on her father's farm during the Revolutionary War, Hope is kidnapped by a Tory, who hopes to garner a significant ransom.

Jacobs, Paul Samuel. *James Printer: A Novel of Rebellion.* 1997. *MJS.* Bartholomew Green, the son of a Cambridge, Massachusetts, printer, relates this tale of King Philip's war (1675–1676) and how events forced his Nipmuck Indian friend James Printer to flee for his life.

Kirkpatrick, Katherine. *Trouble's Daughter: The Story of Susanna Hutchinson, Indian Captive.* 1998. *M.* The Lenape Indians massacred Susanna's family in 1643 and then adopted her. Based on the true story of a real person.

Rees, Celia. *Witch Child.* 2001. *MJS.* Mary Newbury's guardian was burned as a witch, but Mary was saved. She is sent off to the American colonies for safety—and ends up near Salem in 1659. (BBYA)

Rinaldi, Ann. *Hang a Thousand Trees with Ribbons: The Story of Phillis Wheatley.* 1996. *MJ.* Phillis was brought to America via the Middle Passage, the horrifying transatlantic journey that Africans made before being sold into slavery. She was sold to an affluent and kind family, who chose to educate her. Phillis Wheatley became the first female African American poet, while yearning to be free.

Rinaldi, Ann. *The Second Bend in the River.* 1997. *MJ.* Set around the turn of the eighteenth century, Rebecca Galloway, a teenage member of an Ohio pioneer family, falls in love with the great chief Tecumseh. But is love enough to leave her world for his? (Popular Paperbacks)

Nineteenth Century

The nineteenth century was a time of enormous change in the United States—including westward expansion, industrialization, the abolition movement, the Civil War, the abolition of slavery, Reconstruction, and increasingly diverse immigration. There are so many titles dealing with themes of slavery and the Civil War that they are covered in their own section, which follows this one. Westerns and novels of the West are also plentiful and covered in a separate section.

General Themes

Armstrong, Jennifer. Mairhe Mehan series. *MJ.* Mairhe Mehan and her family immigrate to the United States from Ireland during the Civil War.

> *The Dreams of Mairhe Mehan.* 1996. Life is not easy for Mairhe or for the rest of the Mehan family, who have come from Ireland and are living in Washington, D.C., during the Civil War. As an Irish immigrant, sixteen-year-old Mairhe faces hostility and discrimination, as well as the horrors of working as a nurse during a extraordinarily violent war.

> *Mary Mehan Awake.* 1997. Following the Civil War, Mairhe, now called Mary, finds peace, regains hope, and discovers love while working as a domestic in the home of a naturalist in upstate New York.

Carbone, Elisa. *Storm Warriors.* 2001. *M.* Twelve-year-old Nathan hopes to join the all-black crew at the Pea Island lifesaving station where he moves following his mother's death in 1895.

Fletcher, Susan. *Walk across the Sea.* 2001. *MJ.* In the late 1880s, fifteen-year-old Eliza Jane McCully, a California lighthouse keeper's daughter, defies her neighbors to help a Chinese boy who has shown her kindness.

Heuston, Kimberley. *The Shakeress.* 2002. *JS.* In the early 1800s, after her parents and younger brother die in a fire, Naomi keeps her siblings together by moving them into a Shaker commune. Years later, wanting to start her own family, she leaves to ply her craft as a healer and ends up becoming a Mormon.

Hobbs, Will. *Ghost Canoe.* 1997. *MJ.* Fourteen-year-old Nathan MacAllister works hard helping his father run the lighthouse at Cape Flattery off the Washington coast. He also spends a lot of time exploring and trying to find clues to answer the puzzle of the mysterious footprints seen on the beach after a shipwreck, when all aboard had been reported dead.

Hobbs, Will. *Jason series.* *MJ.* In the late 1800s, fifteen-year-old Jason Hawthorne travels west in search of his fortune.

> *Jason's Gold.* 1999. In 1897, Jason travels 10,000 miles to reach the gold fields of the Yukon. (BBYA; Quick Picks)

> *Down the Yukon.* 2001. Just when Jason's life looks close to perfect, he and his brothers lose their lumber mill to a devious fight promoter. When Jamie, the love of Jason's life, returns to Dawson with news of a race down the Yukon, the two set out on the adventure of a lifetime.

Holm, Jennifer L. *Boston Jane: An Adventure.* 2001. *MJ.* In the mid-nineteenth century, Jane Peck, a tomboy-turned-lady, travels to Oregon to meet her fiancé, only to find that he has taken off. Now she must learn to rely on the skills she had abandoned when her fiancé suggested finishing school. (BBYA)

Karr, Kathleen. *The Boxer.* 2000. *MJ.* Fifteen-year-old Johnny learned to box while he was in prison. Now he hopes to make a living of it in 1885 New York.

Paterson, Katherine. *Lyddie.* 1991. *MJS.* Lyddie follows the path of many young women of the early nineteenth century and becomes a "factory girl." She goes to work in a Lowell, Massachusetts, mill, where she endures horrible conditions in an attempt to save the family farm. (YALSA 100 Best Books)

Rinaldi, Ann. *An Acquaintance with Darkness.* 1997. *MJ.* Fourteen-year-old Emily Pigbush knows her life is going to change drastically. The Civil War will soon end and her mother is dying, so Emily will be taken in by her neighbors and lifelong friends, the Surratts. But greater changes happen than she expected when President Lincoln is assassinated and Mary Surratt is implicated. Against her will, Emily must move in with her uncle, a doctor who may be involved with grave robbing for scientific research purposes.

Rinaldi, Ann. *The Coffin Quilt: The Feud between the Hatfields and the McCoys.* 1999. *JS.* An 1880s Appalachian-style Romeo and Juliet story set in West Virginia and Kentucky, told by young Fanny McCoy. (Popular Paperbacks)

Taylor, Theodore. *Walking up a Rainbow*. 1986. *MJ*. Susan's inheritance is nearly two thousand sheep—and a huge debt. She sets out to drive the sheep to California from Iowa in the 1880s.

Warner, Sally. *Finding Hattie*. 2001. *M*. Orphaned, fourteen-year-old Hattie is sent off to her cousin's very proper boarding school in Tarrytown, New York, in the 1880s.

Slavery

The strength and determination of those who were victims of slavery and those who fought to abolish it make for compelling stories. These books allow readers to explore one of the darker chapters of our history, a time when people had to take a stand for their convictions and struggle for their own freedom or the freedom of their fellow human beings. Themes of abuse and heroic deeds are common to these titles. The struggle for freedom and moral imperative to oppose injustice and abuse speak loudly to teen readers.

Ayres, Katherine. *North by Night: A Story of the Underground Railroad*. 1998. *JS*. When Lucinda goes into seclusion to ostensibly nurse an ailing local widow, she discovers a great deal about herself and her heart, not to mention her strengths, as she helps a party of women and children escape slavery on the Underground Railroad.

Ayres, Katherine. *Stealing South: A Story of the Underground Railroad*. 2001. *JS*. Sixteen-year-old Will Spencer, with his family, has worked for the Underground Railroad for years. But now, as he heads out to start a new life as a peddler, he travels South to rescue two more slaves. (IRAYAC)

Paulsen, Gary. Sarny series. The brutality of slavery and the freedom of reading and writing told through the stories of two courageous individuals who defied the status quo.

> *Nightjohn*. 1993. *MJS*. A brutal tale of slavery featuring a twelve-year-old girl, Sarny, who learns to read from a man who has willingly returned to slavery so he can secretly teach the slaves to read and write.

> *Sarny*. 1997. *MJ*. Sarny's husband dies from overwork. Then, just six days before freedom arrives with the Union Army, Sarny's beloved children are sold South. She and Lucy subsequently set out to find young Delie and Tyler. On the way to New Orleans, she meets the beautiful, rich, and powerful Miss Laura, who holds a secret. A story about Reconstruction and the terror inflicted by the Klan and other racists. (Quick Picks; IRAYAC)

Schwartz, Virginia. *Send One Angel Down*. 2000. *MJ*. Told from the viewpoint of her orphaned male cousin, this is the story of Eliza, a beautiful, light-skinned slave who grows up on the plantation owned by her father, playing with her sisters without knowing her relationship to them. When one of her sisters becomes angry with her, Eliza is sent to auction. A good read for those who liked Paulsen's *Nightjohn*. (BBYA)

Taylor, Mildred D. *The Land*. 2001. *JS*. Paul-Edward Logan, the ancestor of the characters from Taylor's award-winning *Roll of Thunder Hear My Cry,* is the protagonist in this sometimes graphic fictional retelling of the author's own ancestor—the son of a plantation owner and a slave who had to make his way between two worlds when he belonged to both and neither at the same time. (BBYA; Coretta Scott King Award; IRAYAC)

Civil War

The difficult issues surrounding a country torn in two, with brother fighting against brother, and the tremendous upheaval that was the American Civil War interest readers of all ages. Stories of the Civil War may convey the exciting heroics or the grim horror of combat, the glamour of the Antebellum South, or other themes. Recent publications in this area have focused on heroic girls and on the harshness of war.

Armstrong, Jennifer. *The Dreams of Mairhe Mehan*. 1996. *MJS*. Annotated in the General Themes section of this chapter. (IRAYAC)

Brenaman, Miriam. *Evvy's Civil War*. 2002. *JS*. In 1860s Virginia, fourteen-year-old Evvy doesn't really want to be a Southern lady. After changes in her family and the advent of the Civil War, she must take charge.

Fleischman, Paul. *Bull Run*. 1993. *M*. Annotated in Chapter 11, "Alternative Formats." (YALSA 100 Best Books)

Matas, Carol. *The War Within: A Novel of the Civil War*. 2001. *MJ*. When the Union forces take Holly Springs, Mississippi, Hannah's family is forced to leave because they are Jewish.

Paulsen, Gary. *Soldier's Heart*. 1998. *MJ*. At age fifteen, Charley thinks going off to fight in the Civil War will be a grand adventure, but by age twenty, after all he has seen and experienced, he is an old man. (Popular Paperbacks; Quick Picks; BBYA; IRAYAC; YALSA 100 Best Books)

Rinaldi, Ann. *Girl in Blue*. 2001. *MJ*. When Sarah's father wants her to marry a man she despises, the sixteen-year-old poses as a boy and runs away to join the Union Army to fight in the Civil War. After Bull Run, it is discovered that she is really a girl, and Sarah goes undercover as a spy for the Pinkerton agency to determine how a rebel spy is getting word out.

Westward Expansion

The lure of the American West still calls to teen readers. Many male reluctant readers have found the joys of reading after picking up Louis L'Amour novels. Traditional westerns are compelling adventure stories set in the historical American West of the nineteenth and, sometimes, the early twentieth centuries. In addition to the appeal of their dramatic settings, Westerns feature a strong delineation between right and wrong, fast-paced action, and a strong, heroic character protagonist (the cowboy), who follows a strict moral code.

Stories following include traditional westerns as well as stories based on other themes of westward expansion. Stories of the West share the setting of time and place with the traditional western and usually contain a fair amount of action and adventure, but characters may not be cowboys or as heroic, and the definition between right and wrong is not always clear.

Burks, Brian. *Soldier Boy*. 1997. *JS.* A homeless teen, pursued by a criminal fight promoter, flees Chicago, only to find himself under Custer's command in the Army of the West, helping steal land promised to the Indians and going to war against them. (IRAYAC)

Burks, Brian. *Wrango*. 1999. *J.* George McJunkin, a slave freed by the Civil War, goes West to become a cowboy. Based on a real character.

Durham, David Anthony. *Gabriel's Story*. 2001. *S.* During the tough years of Reconstruction, Gabriel, an African American teenager, unhappily accompanies his mother to Kansas, where they will homestead with his new stepfather. (Alex Award)

Garland, Sherry. *The Last Rainmaker*. 1997. *M.* When her beloved grandmother dies, thirteen-year-old Caroline is betrayed by her father and her cousin. She runs away and joins a Wild West show, where she learns of her true heritage at the turn of the century.

Laxalt, Robert. *Dust Devils*. 1997. *JS.* When Ira Hamilton falls in love with his best friend's sister, he is not prepared for the disapproval of his white father—or of her Indian father. (Popular Paperbacks)

Myers, Walter Dean. *The Journal of Joshua Loper: A Black Cowboy*. 1999. *M.* My Name Is America series. Annotated in the Diaries section of Chapter 11, "Alternative Formats."

Patrick, Denise Lewis. *The Adventures of Midnight Son*. 1997. *MJ.* Becoming a cowboy is more than learning to ride, herd cows, and toss a lariat when all you've known is slavery.

Paulsen, Gary. Tucket series. *M.* Starting at age fourteen, Francis Tucket experiences all the Wild West has to offer. These books feature survival adventures in the American West.

Mr. Tucket. 1969; reissued in 1994. After escaping from his kidnappers, the Pawnee, on the Oregon Trail, fourteen-year-old Francis Tucket must learn how to survive.

Call Me Francis Tucket. 1995. Now fifteen, Francis joins a wagon train, only to be caught up in a buffalo stampede.

Tucket's Ride. 1997. Francis continues his travels west with Lottie and Billy and meets up with a hostile U.S. Cavalry officer and a band of Comancheros.

Tucket's Gold. 1999. Francis, Billy, and Lottie are on the run when two ruthless thieves appear.

Tucket's Home. 2000. Still journeying to Oregon, Francis, Lottie, and Billy run into outlaws, wagon trains, and an eccentric English adventurer.

Peck, Robert Newton. *Cowboy Ghost.* 1999. *JS.* Sixteen-year-old Titus, with his brother Micah, suffers hardships and ultimately proves himself when he goes on a cattle drive across Florida in the early 1900s. (Popular Paperbacks)

Spooner, Michael. *Daniel's Walk.* 2001. *JS.* In 1856, fourteen-year-old Daniel LeBlanc joins a westward bound wagon train, walks more than a thousand miles, and suffers intense hardships on the Oregon Trail in a quest to find his father.

Humorous Westerns

Encompassing both picaresque and parody, the following stories do not necessarily present the "good guys" as strong heroes. Sometimes they are bumbling, if well-meaning, fools. They can also be misguided outlaws, showing hearts of gold by their actions. These stories appeal to some western fans, and also to those who enjoy humorous fiction.

Hahn, Mary Downing. *Gentleman Outlaw and Me—Eli: A Story of the Old West.* 1996. *M.* Twelve-year-old Eliza Yates cuts her hair and, masquerading as a boy, heads west to find her missing father. (Popular Paperbacks)

Hardman, Ric Lynden. *Sunshine Rider: The First Vegetarian Western.* 1998. *MJ.* Seventeen-year-old Wylie is thrilled at the opportunity to go on a cattle drive, but hilarity prevails when he becomes a vegetarian. His pet "cattalo" is a hoot.

Hite, Sid. *Stick and Whittle.* 2000. *MJ.* Two Melvins, one age sixteen, the other a twenty-seven-year-old Civil War veteran, meet up and find adventure as they travel together from Texas to Kansas.

Karr, Kathleen. *The Great Turkey Walk.* 1998. *MJ.* Fifteen-year-old Simon Green comes up with the brilliant idea of driving a thousand head of turkeys from Missouri to Denver to make his fortune. (Popular Paperbacks)

Twentieth Century

Contemporary fiction, if it stays around long enough, can eventually be considered historical fiction, especially if there is sufficient background information on the setting and times. For example, Jane Austen's books were contemporary novels when she wrote them in the early nineteenth century, yet in this century we enjoy them as delightful historical fiction. To today's teens, the civil rights movement and the Vietnam War—even events from the seventies and eighties—are history, because these events happened before they were born.

The twentieth century is more immediate, less foreign than previous times, and teen readers who may be interested in events from their parents' or grandparents' time will naturally explore these eras. Such topics as immigration, the Great Depression, the World Wars, and the civil rights movement provide fascinating backdrops to the human drama.

The Early Years (1900–1920)

Our nation experienced huge waves of immigration, industrialization, World War I, and such dramatic disasters as the San Francisco earthquake of 1906, the Great Burn, and the sinking of the *Titanic* in the first decades of the twentieth century.

Auch, Mary Jane. *Ashes of Roses*. 2002. *JS.* When the Nolan family arrives at Ellis Island from Ireland, their baby is diagnosed with trachoma and denied entry to the United States. Sixteen-year-old Rose and her younger sister, Maureen, decide to stay in America and move in with an uncle. Both find jobs at the Triangle Shirtwaist Company. (BBYA)

Crew, Linda. *Brides of Eden*. 2001. *JS.* A charismatic preacher seduces women and girls into accompanying him to an island off the Oregon coast in the early twentieth century. Eva Mae wants to break free. Based on the true story of an actual cult.

Day, Dianne. *Fire and Fog*. 1996. *S.* Fremont, an independent young woman in turn-of-the-century San Francisco, is awakened by the Great Quake of 1906. Amid mysterious disappearances and bloody murder, Fremont finds adventure on many fronts. `Adult`

Ingold, Jeanette. *The Big Burn*. 2002. *MJS.* The flames of the 1910 Big Burn, the massive wildfire that devastated millions of acres in Idaho and Montana, come to life through the tales of several fictional characters. Sixteen-year-old Jarrett Logan, fired after his first day of work on the railroad, heads out to be a firefighter and meets up with his brother Samuel, a forest ranger. Lizbeth and her Aunt Celia are trying to eke out a living while waiting to claim their 160-acre homestead so they can sell lumber from the property. Seth, an African American soldier, discovers his strength when he must forgo friendship to maintain his own standards.

Joinson, Carla. *A Diamond in the Dust*. 2001. *J.* At age sixteen, Katy Sollis dreams of a new life in St. Louis. She knows there must be more to life than the dangers faced by miners in turn-of-the-century Buckey City, Illinois.

Peck, Richard. *Amanda/Miranda*. 1999. *MJ.* Miranda, a servant, assumes the identity of Amanda, her employer, after the sinking of the *Titanic*.

Roaring Twenties, Depression and Dust Bowl Years (1920–1940)

Brockett, D. A. *Stained Glass Rose*. 2002. *JS.* The summer of 1937 is an eventful one for Rose, a seventeen-year-old good Italian girl in a western Colorado town. She meets a nice young man, even though her abusive widowed father doesn't allow her much freedom, and she finds a best friend in Mari, a young woman who works as a housekeeper and chauffeur for a notorious madam from the Shantytown area. Then a murder makes Rose look at everyone around her differently.

Brooke, Peggy. *Jake's Orphan*. 2000. *M.* In 1926, twelve-year-old Tree and his younger brother, Acorn, see Tree's chance to work on a North Dakota farm as a way to escape the Minnesota orphanage where they live. But not everything turns out as well as they had hoped. (VOYA; IRA)

Curtis, Christopher Paul. *Bud, Not Buddy*. 1999. *M.* In Depression-era Michigan, Bud escapes from his foster home to search for Herman E. Calloway, the standup-bass player for the Dusky Devastators of the Depression, who he thinks is his father. (BBYA; IRA; Newbery Medal Winner)

DeFelice, Cynthia. *Nowhere to Call Home*. 1999. *M*. After her father kills himself in the aftermath of the stock market crash of 1929, twelve-year-old Francesca becomes a hobo.

Hesse, Karen. *Out of the Dust*. 1997. *MJS*. (Alternative format) After her mother is accidentally killed, Billie Jo struggles to forgive herself and her father and tries to survive farm life in the Oklahoma dust bowl of the 1930s. This novel is told in verse. (Newbery Award; Scott O'Dell Award)

Hesse, Karen. *Witness*. 2001. *MJS*. (Alternative format) Told in verse from several viewpoints; a small Vermont town is infiltrated by the Ku Klux Klan in the 1920s. Only when a shooting occurs do the citizens decide to act.

Levine, Gail Carson. *Dave at Night*. 1999. *MJ*. Orphaned, Dave sneaks out of the Hebrew Home for Boys to experience jazz and more in New York during the Harlem Renaissance. (BBYA)

Peck, Richard. *A Year Down Yonder*. 2000. *MJ*. Fifteen-year-old Mary Alice is trying to weather out the Depression in 1937 by living with her fearsome grandmother in rural Illinois. (Newbery Award)

Ritter, John. *Choosing Up Sides*. 1998. *MJ*. Fourteen-year-old Luke struggles with baseball, romance, and his strict preacher father in 1920s Ohio. (BBYA; IRA 1999; IRAYAC)

Thesman, Jean. *The Storyteller's Daughter*. 1997. *MJ*. One night when Beau John is home from the only job he can find in Prohibition-era Seattle, his fifteen-year-old daughter, Quinn, overhears a conversation that makes her think he may have become involved in illegal rum-running. When he doesn't return home the following weekend and the family doesn't hear from him, Quinn decides to find him—even if it means venturing out among the frightening men living in the Hooverville under the bridge. (IRAYAC)

WWII and Its Aftermath (1940–1960)

After struggling through the end of the Depression and the dust bowl years, the United States entered another global conflict, which culminated in the dropping of the atomic bomb. Postwar prosperity, rock and roll, and Chevrolet brought us to the brink of the 1960s, when everything changed again. This section contains titles that focus on what was happening in the States during the decades before, during, and after WWII.

Bat-Ami, Miriam. *Two Suns in the Sky*. 1999. *JS*. At a Jewish refugee camp in New York during World War II, Catholic Chris, who has snuck in with her friends, falls for a Jewish boy, Adam. When her father finds out, he banishes her from the family home. (BBYA; Scott O'Dell Award)

Cormier, Robert. *Heroes: A Novel*. 1998. *JS*. Francis has returned home to Frenchtown after World War II, his face destroyed in battle. He has come home to kill his former idol and try to discover what happened to his first love. (BBYA; Quick Picks)

Crowe, Chris. *Mississippi Trial, 1955.* 2002. *MJS.* A white fourteen-year-old boy goes to Money, Mississippi, to visit his grandfather and meets all the players in the infamous Emmet Till lynching case. (BBYA)

Kerr, M. E. *Slap Your Sides.* 2001. *MJ.* The brother of a conscientious objector during WWII falls in love with a girl whose brothers are both serving overseas.

Lisle, Janet Taylor. *The Art of Keeping Cool.* 2000. *M.* During WWII, Robert and his mother go to Rhode Island to live in a cottage near his paternal grandparents. His cousin, Elliot, is a phenomenal artist. Elliot has befriended a famous German painter, who fled the Nazis but is now persecuted by the townspeople, who say he is a Nazi spy. (Scott O'Dell Award)

Paterson, Katherine. *Jacob Have I Loved.* 1980. *MJ.* Set on a Chesapeake island during the 1940s, Louise is envious of her sister Caroline, who she believes is prettier, more talented, and more loved. (BBYA; Newbery Award; YALSA 100 Best Books) ⌐Classic¬

Ryan, Pam Munoz. *Esperanza Rising.* 2000. *MJ.* On the eve of her thirteenth birthday, Esperanza, the spoiled only child of a wealthy Mexican family, loses everything. After her father is killed in an accident, Esperanza's avaricious uncles burn her and her mother out of their home. Traveling with their former servants, Esperanza and her mother go to California, where they become fieldworkers, but hardship doesn't keep Esperanza down. (BBYA; Pura Belpre Award; IRAYAC)

Sheppard, Mary C. *Seven for a Secret.* 2001. *JS.* Three cousins spend the summer of 1960 together in an isolated Newfoundland village where two of the fifteen-year-old girls live. It is a pivotal summer for them—each girl comes to decisions about her future as they uncover secrets from the past. (BBYA)

Wolff, Virginia Euwer. *Bat 6.* 1998. *M.* The fiftieth anniversary softball game between two nearby towns in 1949 has all the sixth-grade girls working hard at honing their batting skills. Each team has a new girl. Eleven-year-old Aki has finally returned with her family to the community after years in exile at a relocation camp. Angry Shazam has come to live with her grandmother at the gravel pit, because her mother is unable to care for her and her father is dead at the bottom of Pearl Harbor.

Zindel, Paul. *The Gadget.* 2001. *MJ.* Stephen is sent to Los Alamos to live with his physicist father after the bombs start falling on London, but instead of heading into safety, he finds he is heading for more danger.

The Sixties and Beyond

The Vietnam War, hippies and psychedelics, the civil rights movement, the women's movement, and into the 1980s and AIDS—today's adults may have difficulty seeing the historical aspects of the books included in this section. How can something we lived through be history? Yet to younger generations, that is exactly what it is. Several of the titles here do not deal with big social issues of the time; the setting does convey a sense of what life was like back then.

Easton, Kelly. *The Life History of a Star.* 2001. *MJ.* Set in the post-Vietnam milieu of 1973, this diary tells of Kristen's life as she enters puberty as a late bloomer and grieves for her brother, who has returned from combat with broken and missing body parts, including his mind.

Kidd, Sue Monk. *The Secret Life of Bees.* 2002. *MJS.* Running away from an abusive father while trying to save the housekeeper who raised her from a lynching in 1964 South Carolina, a young girl finds belonging with an eccentric trio of African American sisters. (BBYA; VOYA) `Adult`

Krisher, Trudy. Kinship series. *JS.*

> *Spite Fences.* 1994. The civil rights struggle in 1960s Georgia. Annotated in the Racism section of Chapter 2, "Issues." (BBYA; IRA 1995)

> *Kinship.* 1997. Further developments in the small town community of 1960s Kinship, Georgia. This novel is a companion to *Spite Fences.*

Lynch, Chris. *Gold Dust.* 2000. *M.* Racism and baseball in 1975 Boston.

Myers, Walter Dean. *Fallen Angels.* 1988. *JS.* Perry, a Harlem teen, didn't plan to join the army, but he ends up in the middle of the Vietnam War. (BBYA; Coretta Scott King Award; YALSA 100 Best Books)

Shetterly, Will. *Dogland.* 1997. *JS.* Chris Nix lives in Dogland, a 1960s Florida theme attraction park that features every dog breed. This is a rich, multilayered tale of magic and human relationships against the frightening backdrop of the battle for integration in the South.

Weaver, Beth Nixon. *Rooster.* 2001. *J.* Kady seems to always be doing housework and taking care of her next-door neighbor, the motherless and mentally handicapped Rooster. But then in 1969, a rich boy takes notice of her, and things begin to change in this tale set in Florida. (BBYA)

White, Ellen Emerson. *The Road Home.* 1995. *JS.* Rebecca returns from serving as a nurse in the Vietnam War, but she can't get Michael out of her mind. (BBYA; Popular Paperbacks)

World History

Prehistory

Tales of prehistory filled with adventure and discovery offer readers the most fantastic settings. What would it be like to be one of the first peoples on Earth? Humans face monolithic and otherworldly creatures and the tremendous forces of nature, usually resulting in gripping adventure stories in which a survival theme often figures prominently.

Baxter, Stephen. *Longtusk.* 1999. *MJ.* The legendary Longtusk, a mammoth, starts his adventures as a young adolescent when he is separated from his herd. He becomes involved with humans, first befriending a child of the Dreamers, then becoming a slave of the Fire Hands after they destroy the Dreamers community. Learning from the mastodons held in captivity by the Fire Hands, Longtusk eventually finds his family again and leads them to safety.

Brooke, William J. *A Is for AARRGH!* 1999. *M.* In this Stone Age satire, Mog invents language.

Dickinson, Peter. The Kin series. *M.* This prehistoric survival story features a band of children from the Moonhawk Kin tribe. It was revised in a 2003 omnibus edition.

> *Suth's Story.* 1998. Four orphans have been left to die, but Suth and Noli decide to survive.

> *Noli's Story.* 1998. Guided by her dreams, Noli has managed to stay alive, but can she survive earthquakes, floods, and a demon lion?

> *Po's Story.* 1998. A test of courage for Po.

> *Mana's Story.* 1999. Searching for a new home, Mana and her tribe confront a dangerous enemy.

Ancient Civilizations

The ancient civilizations of Egypt, Greece, Rome, the Vikings, and others are explored in this section. The appeal of these books is that of distant, sometimes almost mythological, times. Teens who enjoy mythology may enjoy these, and vice versa. Chapter 6, "Fantasy," has a section of titles on myths and legends.

Barrett, Tracy. *Anna of Byzantium.* 2000. *M.* Anna Comnena was raised to rule the Byzantine Empire, but certain relatives have their own agendas that send her into exile. Based on the story of an actual historical figure. (BBYA)

Blacklock, Dyan. *Pankration: The Ultimate Game.* 1999. *MJ.* Nic attempts to escape his kidnappers in time to meet his friends at the Olympics for the bloody sport of pankration. Set in Ancient Greece—430 B.C.E.

Cadnum, Michael. *Raven of the Waves.* 2001. *JS.* At age seventeen, Lidsmod, a Viking, is off to England on his first raiding mission when he encounters Wiglaf, a young Anglo-Saxon who has been captured.

Fletcher, Susan. *Shadow Spinner.* 1998. *MJ.* In ancient Persia, thirteen-year-old Marjan finds stories for Shahrazad to tell to the Sultan so that she can keep her life. (BBYA)

Galloway, Priscilla. *The Courtesan's Daughter.* 2002. *MJS.* Fourteen-year-old Phano has always wanted to grow up to be a proper and respectable Athenian wife. After she marries politically prominent Theo, she must find a way to save not only herself and her husband from her enemy Phyrion, but also to save Athens.

Geras, Adele. *Troy.* 2001. *MJS.* Annotated in the Myth and Legend section of the Chapter 6, "Fantasy." (BBYA)

Lester, Julius. *Pharaoh's Daughter.* 2000. *M.* Teenaged Moses has been raised as the adopted son of the Pharaoh's daughter, but now he is caught between two worlds—that of his Hebrew blood and of his adoptive Egyptian family.

McLaren, Clemence. *Inside the Walls of Troy.* 1996. *JS.* In Part One, told from Helen's viewpoint, we meet a girl handicapped by her extraordinary beauty and mythological characters who vividly spring to life. Part Two, told in Cassandra's voice, gives an insider's view of the fall of Troy and of Cassandra's acquaintance with the fair Helen.

Western Europe

The romance of historical European settings conjures up visions of turreted castles, ladies fair, and knights in gleaming armor. The legends of King Arthur and Robin Hood are popular motifs of European history, but because of the legendary nature of those characters in early eras, they are covered in Chapter 6, "Fantasy." For teen readers who enjoy books with these themes, please consult that chapter.

Middle Ages (900–1500)

Alder, Elizabeth. *King's Shadow.* 1995. *JS.* In eleventh-century Wales, Evyn's dreams of becoming a storyteller are dashed when his tongue is cut out. After he learns to read and write, he is adopted as the foster son of Harold, who becomes king. (BBYA; Popular Paperbacks)

Avi. *Midnight Magic.* 1999. *M.* Twelve-year-old Fabrizio goes with his master, a magician, to the castle to find out if the princess is really seeing a ghost, or if something else is going on. Set in fifteenth-century Italy. (Quick Picks)

Branford, Henrietta. *Fire, Bed & Bone.* 1998. *MJ.* In the 1300s, the time of King Richard, serfs are taxed unmercifully, but when they turn to rebellion, horrible things happen. This captivating tale is told from the viewpoint of a dog, who loves her family and saves the children, having lost two of her own pups, when her humans are captured and imprisoned.

Brooks, Geraldine. *Year of Wonders.* 2001. *S.* Anna Frith is an eighteen-year-old widow with two small children when the bubonic plague hits her English village. (Alex Award)

Cushman, Karen. *Catherine, Called Birdy.* 1994. *MJ.* The humorous diary of a young noblewoman in the year 1290, featuring everyday life in Medieval England as well as bizarre information about saints. (BBYA; YALSA 100 Best Books; Popular Paperbacks)

Cushman, Karen. *Matilda Bone.* 2000. *MJ.* Orphaned Matilda has been raised by a priest in a wealthy household and has learned the lives of the saints, Latin, and prayers. After she is sent to live in London's Blood and Bone alley with a bonesetter, she learns important lessons about human nature.

Cushman, Karen. *The Midwife's Apprentice.* 1995. *MJ.* An orphan found in a dung heap is apprenticed to a midwife in fourteenth-century England. (Newbery Award; BBYA; YALSA 100 Best Books)

Hunter, Mollie. *The King's Swift Rider: A Novel on Robert the Bruce.* 1998. *MJ.* Thirteen-year-old Martin spies for Scotland in its war against England in the late 1200s. (Popular Paperbacks)

Yolen, Jane, and Robert J. Harris. *Girl in a Cage*. 2002. *MJ*. Marjorie, the daughter of Robert the Bruce, king of Scotland, goes from princess to prisoner when she is captured by Edward Longshanks. (BBYA)

Sixteenth to Eighteenth Centuries

Blackwood, Gary. Shakespeare series. *MJ*.

> *The Shakespeare Stealer*. 1998. *M*. Fourteen-year-old Widge is compelled by his master to infiltrate Shakespeare's company and use his shorthand skills to steal a play. (BBYA)

> *Shakespeare's Scribe*. 2000. Widge, now fifteen, joins Shakespeare's theatrical troupe on the road.

> *Shakespeare's Spy*. 2003. Widge is back in London and trying to keep the Bard's scripts safe.

Chevalier, Tracy. *Girl with a Pearl Earring*. 2001. *S*. In seventeenth-century Delft, Holland, sixteen-year-old Griet is a maid and assistant to the famous Dutch painter, Johannes Vermeer. (BBYA) **Adult**

Horowitz, Anthony. *The Devil and His Boy*. 2000. *M*. Adventurous tale involving Tom, on his own in Elizabethan London after his employer is murdered. (VOYA; IRAYAC)

Meyer, Carolyn. The Royals. *MJS*.

> *Mary, Bloody Mary*. 1999. This book details Mary Tudor's troubled childhood as the daughter of Henry VIII. (BBYA; IRAYAC)

> *Beware, Princess Elizabeth*. 2001. Elizabeth Tudor's turbulent life as a princess before becoming a powerful monarch.

Sturtevant, Katherine. *At the Sign of the Star*. 2000. *M*. In this vividly depicted view of publishing in Elizabethan England, a girl's life plan is sidetracked after her stationer father remarries, which means she may no longer be his heir.

Nineteenth Century

Anderson, K. J. *Captain Nemo: The Fantastic History of a Dark Genius*. 2002. *S*. Jules Verne and his two best friends, Andre Nemo, the inventive son of a poor shipbuilder, and Caroline Aronnax, the daughter of a wealthy merchant, come of age in the late nineteenth century. While Jules stays in France, Andre's adventures take him all over the world. **Adult**

Avi. Beyond the Western Sea series. *M*.

> *The Escape from Home*. 1996. Twelve-year-old Patrick and fifteen-year-old Maura O'Conner, Irish peasants, team up with an eleven-year-old English lord, Sir Laurence Kirkle—all wanting to sail to America in the mid–nineteenth century. (BBYA; IRAYAC)

Lord Kirkle's Money. 1996. The lives of Maura, Patrick, and Laurence continue as they journey toward their new lives.

Giff, Patricia Reilly. *Nory Ryan's Song.* 2000. *M.* In the 1800s, twelve-year-old Nory Ryan's family and village are torn asunder by the Irish potato famine. She learns herbal lore from an elderly neighbor and fights to keep her loved ones alive.

Holeman, Linda. *Search of the Moon King's Daughter.* 2002. *JS.* Emmaline's ventures into London in an attempt to find her deaf younger brother, who was sold by their mother to be a chimney sweep in the 1830s. (BBYA)

Newth, Mette. *The Dark Light.* 1998. *M.* Thirteen-year-old Tora is banished to a hospital for lepers in early-nineteenth-century Norway. She discovers an escape of sorts when she finds a friend who can teach her to read. (BBYA; IRAYAC)

Twentieth Century (WWII and the Holocaust)

Looking at teen historical novels set in Western Europe in the twentieth century, one would conclude that this was a century of war. World War II and the Holocaust predominate, with new titles coming out every year, but a couple of World War I novels also have been published in recent years. The required reading in school of Anne Frank's *The Diary of a Young Girl* is often the catalyst that sparks interest in teen readers. Adventure and romance both play a role in the popularity of books of this type. Battle scenes and survival stories are common fare for this era. Some titles also have the characteristic of something horrific happening to characters of the readers' same age.

Breslin, Theresa. *Remembrance.* 2002. *JS.* A haunting tale of World War I, featuring British teens from different classes. (BBYA)

Booth, Martin. *War Dog.* 1997. *M.* Jet, a well-trained Labrador retriever, joins the British armed services in WWII and faces danger and death while saving lives.

Hughes, Dean. *Soldier Boys.* 2001. *J.* Sixteen-year-old Spencer and fifteen-year-old Dieter have a lot in common, even though they are on opposite sides of a war. Now they have been brought together on a snowy Belgian hillside.

Huth, Angela. *Land Girls.* 1996. *S.* Agatha, Stella, and Pru leave the city to work on a farm as their part of the British war effort. (Popular Paperbacks) **Adult**

Isaacs, Anne. *Torn Thread.* 2000. *JM.* Twelve-year-old Eva and her older sister Rachel cling to life and each other as they struggle to survive the Holocaust in a labor camp.

Lawrence, Iain. *Lord of the Nutcracker Men.* 2001. *MJ.* A ten-year-old English boy's father goes off to fight in World War I.

Magorian, Michelle. *Good Night, Mr. Tom.* 1981. *M.* After the war, Mr. Tom takes nine-year-old Willie Beech in to live with him in the English countryside. (YALSA 100 Best Books)

Matas, Carol. *Greater than Angels.* 1998. *JS.* Caring French people risk their own lives to help Anna and others as they struggle to survive the Nazi Holocaust.

Unique Settings

The historical novels in this section are set in times and places not often encountered in the historical fiction published today in the United States. They give teens insights into countries, cultures, and pieces of history with which they may not be familiar.

Bagdasarian, Adam. *Forgotten Fire*. 2000. *MJS*. Twelve-year-old Vahan Kenderian is the comfortable youngest son of a prosperous Armenian family when the Turks begin their genocide in the early twentieth century. After losing his entire family, seeing most of them killed before his eyes, Vahan faces incredible hardship and heartache as he strives for survival. Based on the life of the author's uncle. (BBYA)

Berry, James. *Ajeemah and His Son*. 1991. *JS*. The eponymous characters are snatched from Africa in 1807 and sold into slavery in Jamaica. (Popular Paperbacks)

Disher, Garry. *The Divine Wind, a Love Story*. 2002. *J*. A white boy and his sister's best friend, who happens to be Japanese, are torn apart as the war affects their small coastal Australian town.

Hesse, Karen. *Stowaway*. 2000. *M*. When eleven-year-old Nicholas Young stowed away on Captain Cook's ship in 1768, he had no idea of the adventures he would face in the South Seas.

Matas, Carol. Ruth series. *MJ*. Ruth survives the Holocaust and starts a new life in Palestine.

> *After the War*. 1996. Buchenwald survivor Ruth is only fifteen, but that is old enough to lead a group of children to Palestine.

> *The Garden*. 1997. In this sequel to *After the War,* Ruth and other young Jews who survived the Holocaust find themselves fighting a war in Palestine around the creation of the modern state of Israel.

McCaughrean, Geraldine. *The Kite Rider*. 2002 . *MJ*. After seeing his father killed testing the winds before going out to sea in thirteenth-century China, Haoyou, a young boy, supports his mother by making kites and then uses them to fly. (BBYA)

Namioka, Lensey. *An Ocean Apart, a World Away*. 2002. *JS*. A companion volume to *Ties That Bind, Ties That Break* that follows the life of Yanyan, a young Chinese girl who wants to become a doctor and leaves her homeland to go to America in the 1920s.

Namioka, Lensey. *Ties That Bind, Ties That Break*. 1999. *JS*. Ailin, an upper-class Chinese girl living in the early 1900s, bucks tradition and refuses to have her feet bound. (BBYA; IRAYAC)

Park, Linda Sue. *A Single Shard*. 2001. *MJ*. In a twelfth-century Korean seaside village, Tree Ear is a homeless orphan who lives under the bridge with Crane Man, who has lost everything but his honor. They scavenge for food, but then Tree Ear becomes fascinated by the crafting of the locally made Celadon pottery—especially that of Min, a master potter. (BBYA; Newbery Award)

Park, Linda Sue. *When My Name Was Keoko: A Novel of Korea in World War II*. 2002. *M*. During the Japanese occupation of Korea, Sun-hee and Tae-yul were forced to give up not only their beloved Rose of Sharon trees, an emblem of Korea, but their names and language, too. (BBYA)

Walters, Eric. Eagles series. *MJ*.

> *War of the Eagles*. 1998. Jed, the son of a British fighter pilot and a Tsimshian Indian, has just begun to question his feelings about war and his Canadian homeland when he learns that his best friend Tadashi is going to be sent away to an internment camp—just because his family is Japanese.

> *Caged Eagles*. 2001. Although his family is interned in a camp in Vancouver far from their fishing village, Tadashi Fukushima still finds adventure and excitement.

Whelan, Gloria. *Angel on the Square*. 2001. *MJ*. The Russian Revolution from the viewpoint of the daughter of one of the empress's ladies-in-waiting.

Chapter 10

Multicultural Fiction

We live in an increasingly diverse society and in a shrinking world where many cultures coexist side by side, a trend reflected in the publishing industry and in reading tastes. Titles written by and about minority ethnicities and cultural groups are popular not only with members of those groups, but with readers in general, who enjoy getting an inside view of what it might be like to live within another milieu.

Multicultural fiction is not a formal genre, but a broad underlying theme, which often has stylistic ramifications. In fact, titles within this category can be classified in almost any other genre, but some readers seek out and enjoy reading books that feature multicultural characters, settings, and themes. Microsoft Bookshelf 98 defines multicultural as

> *1. Of, relating to, or including several cultures. 2. Of or relating to a social or educational theory or program that encourages interest in many cultures within a society rather than in only a mainstream culture.*

The Center for Adolescent Reading (http://www.teensread.com) is one of many organizations that has recognized the importance of fiction that creates an identity bond with the reader in instilling a love of reading as well as reading competency. Many libraries publish multicultural book lists, including Franklin Middle School in Chantilly, Virginia; Fairfax County Public Library, Virginia; Millard Central Middle School in Omaha, Nebraska; and the Los Angeles Public Library. It is obvious from perusing the lists that no general consensus exists as to what constitutes multicultural fiction. Whereas one list titled "multicultural" may feature only books depicting the African American experience, another may define it so widely that tales of Irish immigrants are included.

The common thread in the books listed here is protagonists who are profoundly influenced by their culture, whether in their ancestral homeland or within a world dominated by another culture. "Other cultures" can mean minority groups within this country or groups in other nations. Books about specific groups may often share a vernacular or even a tone or atmosphere. In addition, these books are written by "insiders"—members of the culture. Most of the titles in this section are set in contemporary times or in the recent past. Fans of multicultural fiction share an affinity for the "real" with readers of issues fiction, but there is also a similarity with historical fiction, another genre that offers readers fresh perspectives on reality.

One way of looking at this body of literature is to consider two main types that appear on bookshelves. The first includes the novels that explore the lives of ethnic or multicultural characters inside their culture, giving readers a vicarious journey to another place or insight into another's perspective. These novels have some of the same appeal as historical fiction. The other category contains books that focus on the clash of cultures or cultural encounters, when an individual or group must interact with those who are not of the same cultural group. In YA literature, these titles often share the same appeal as issues or coming-of-age novels.

One of the biggest challenges that teens face is finding out who they are and where they fit in the general scheme of life. Reading about characters who share one's background, ancestry, or culture can be an affirming experience. Other teens read multicultural fiction because they are curious about a specific group or because they enjoy seeing things from a different perspective, or simply because they like the escapism of traveling to another place or experiencing another culture.

This chapter is organized thematically by American ethnic or cultural group, with additional sections for books about multiple cultures and individuals of mixed heritage. The final section, Cultures around the World, includes titles about cultural groups in other countries.

Themes

Multiple Cultures and Culture Clash

The titles in this section include works that feature characters of different cultural backgrounds interacting with each other, sometimes in a romantic scenario or friendship, but usually involving a conflict. Themes of healing and unity are common to these stories.

Draper, Sharon M. *Romiette and Julio.* 1999. *MJS.* The story of the relationship between African American Romiette and Hispanic Julio is annotated in the Romance section of Chapter 3, "Contemporary Life." (IRAYAC)

Fleischman, Paul. *SeedFolks.* 1997. *MJ.* A nine-year-old Vietnamese girl plants a few seeds in a vacant lot to honor her dead father and brings an inner-city community together to create a community garden on a dumping site. (Popular Paperbacks)

Hewett, Lorri. *Lives of Our Own.* 1998. *MJ.* When she moves from Denver, Colorado, to the South, African American Shawna uses the school newspaper to fight the mores that prohibit interracial dating and segregate community functions. (IRAYAC)

Lynch, Chris. *Gold Dust.* 2000. *M.* In 1975 Boston, the love of baseball brings white working-class Richard and black Napoleon together in one tragic summer.

Mosher, Richard. *Zazoo.* 2001. *MJS.* Fourteen-year-old Zazoo lost her parents to a landmine in Vietnam and has lived in France with her adoptive grandfather for as long as she can remember. Operating the locks on a canal gives her an opportunity to meet many people, and she enjoys rowing her punt on the water. Then one day she meets a strange boy on a bicycle, and they start up a secret art postcard correspondence, which leads Zazoo to a mystery involving her grandfather. (BBYA)

Nye, Naomi Shihab. *Habibi.* 1999. Liyana, a fourteen-year-old Arab American girl, moves with her family to Jerusalem, where she falls in love with a Jewish boy. (Popular Paperbacks)

Qualey, Marsha. *Revolutions of the Heart.* 1993. *JS.* Some people in a small, strictly segregated Wisconsin town are willing to go to great lengths to keep apart seventeen-year-old Cory, a white girl, and Mac, who is Cree. (Quick Picks; BBYA)

Walters, Eric. *War of the Eagles.* 1998. *MJ.* Jed, the son of a British fighter pilot and a Tsimshian Indian, begins to question his feelings about war and his Canadian homeland when he learns that his best friend Tadashi is going to be sent away to an internment camp—because he is Japanese.

Williams-Garcia, Rita. *Every Time a Rainbow Dies.* 2001. *JS.* This story of a Jamaican boy and a Haitian girl living in Brooklyn is annotated in the Coming of Age section of the Chapter 3, "Contemporary Life." (BBYA)

Mixed Heritage

Sometimes the relationship or conflict between two cultures is contained within a single character. With increasing numbers of biracial marriages, the face of America is changing. Often portrayed as caught in the middle, these characters must deal with stereotypes and prejudice from both sides.

Adler, Elizabeth. *Crossing the Panther's Path.* 2002. *M.* Irish and Mohawk Bill Calder's story is annotated in Chapter 9, "Historical Novels."

Meyer, Carolyn. *Jubilee Journey.* 1997. *JM.* In this stunning sequel to *White Lilacs,* Rose's biracial great-granddaughter returns to Texas to find her identity, just as the seventy-fifth anniversary of Freedomtown's demise is commemorated with a Juneteenth celebration. (BBYA)

Werlin, Nancy. *Black Mirror.* 2001. *MJS.* High-schooler Frances not only must come to terms with her brother's apparent suicide, she also must reconcile the mixed heritage that has left her unhappy with her combination of Jewish and Japanese features. Having remained a stranger to the other students at the private prep school she attends on scholarship, Frances now believes she must start interacting with others if she is ever to discover the truth behind Daniel's death. Daniel had been her best and only friend, as well as her brother, until he became involved with Unity, a campus-based philanthropic organization that Frances now suspects was responsible for his death. As Frances ventures out, the school's reputed drug dealer seems to be the only one who is not standing against her. (BBYA)

Woodson, Jacqueline. *The House You Pass on the Way.* 1997. *MJ.* Being half-white, fourteen-year-old Staggerlee has always felt like an outsider in her African American community, but she finds a sense of belonging the summer that her adopted cousin Trout comes to visit, and they fall in love, wondering if they are lesbians. (Lambda Award)

Multicultural Americans

As minority populations swell, books about the experiences of teens who are members of minority groups in the United States are being published in increasing numbers. Stories about American ethnic subcultures appeal to members of those cultures, as well as to "outsiders." Many of the authors in these sections have published other titles, annotated in other chapters of this book and accessible through the author/title index.

African Americans

The African American literary tradition is well established in this country, and the range of authors and styles covers the entire genre and literary spectrum. Only in the past decades, however, has the YA African American novel come into its own, with such vibrant voices as Sharon Draper, Walter Dean Myers, Rita Williams-Garcia, and many others sharing their stories. The following subsection offers a sampling of some of the newest titles in this area. Many other titles by and about African Americans are included in this guide, and readers are encouraged to consult the indexes for complete listings.

Coleman, Evelyn. *Born in Sin.* 2001. *MJS.* Just because she lives in a housing project, does that mean fourteen-year-old Keisha must attend a camp for at-risk kids? Keisha's tale is further annotated in the Sports section of Chapter 3, "Contemporary Life." (IRAYAC)

Draper, Sharon M. *Forged by Fire.* 1997. *JS.* Gerald Nickleby, age nine, is crushed when his mother returns from prison to reclaim him. Annotated further in the Life Is Hard section of Chapter 2, "Issues." (Coretta Scott King Award; Popular Paperbacks; BBYA)

Flake, Sharon G. *Money Hungry.* 2001. *MJ.* Thirteen-year-old Raspberry is willing to work as hard as necessary to make money—even if it earns her the ridicule of her peers and gets her into trouble in school. Raspberry has a good reason for wanting to accumulate money, but that's her business. (Coretta Scott King Honor)

Flake, Sharon G. *The Skin I'm In.* 1998. *MJ.* Seventh-grader Maleeka, who is self-conscious about her dark skin, discovers that she is more than just the color of her skin. (Quick Picks; BBYA; IRAYAC; Coretta Scott King Award)

Johnson, Angela. *Toning the Sweep.* 1993. *MJ.* Fourteen-year-old Emily helps her dying grandmother pack up a lifetime of memories. (Popular Paperbacks; Coretta Scott King Award)

Myers, Walter Dean. *Fallen Angels.* 1988. *MJS.* Richie Perry "accidentally" enlists in the army at age seventeen, just after graduating from a Harlem high school. Now he will spend the next year of his life—1967—facing the horrors of the war in Vietnam. (BBYA; Coretta Scott King Award; YALSA 100 Best Books)

Myers, Walter Dean. *Somewhere in the Darkness.* 1992. *JS.* Jimmy, age fourteen, and his father, Crab, who has escaped from prison, leave Harlem to go back to Arkansas. Annotated further in the Life Is Hard section Chapter 2, "Issues." (Popular Paperbacks; Coretta Scott King Honor; YALSA 100 Best Books)

Patrick, Denise Lewis. *The Adventures of Midnight Son.* 1997. *MJ.* When all you've known is slavery, becoming a cowboy means more than learning to ride, herd cows, and toss a lariat.

Williams, Lori Aurelia. *When Kambia Elaine Flew in from Neptune.* 2000. *JS.* Annotated further in the Life Is Hard section of Chapter 2, "Issues." (VOYA; BBYA)

Williams-Garcia, Rita. *Like Sisters on the Homefront.* 1995. *JS.* When fourteen-year-old Gayle gets pregnant for the second time, her mother sends her to Georgia to live with her uncle, a pastor, and his family. Fortunately, Gayle also meets her great-grandmother. (BBYA; Quick Picks; Popular Paperbacks; Coretta Scott King Honor)

Woodson, Jacqueline. *Miracle's Boys.* 2000. *MJS.* Three brothers, Ty'ree, Charlie, and Lafayette, struggle to survive after their father dies. Annotated further in the Social Concerns section of Chapter 2, "Issues." (BBYA; Coretta Scott King Award; VOYA)

Asian Americans

Asians began immigrating to the United States in the nineteenth century, but it was only at the end of the twentieth century that many Asian American voices began to be heard in our literature. The category itself contains a great deal of diversity—Chinese, Japanese, Korean, Indian, Pakistani, and many other cultures contribute to this rich area of fiction. As this population grows and prospers in the Untied States, we will likely see many more titles from Asian American authors.

Desai Hidier,Tanuja. *Born Confused.* 2002. *JS.* As Dimple, a talented photographer, stumbles through a New Jersey summer, she discovers friendship with her cousin, who has left India to attend New York University. She also begins to explore her own Indian identity, a new closeness to her parents, an estrangement from lifelong best friend Gwen, and a serious attraction to Karsh, the boy the marriage mafia has picked out for her. Desai Hidier's luminous prose shines a bright light on what it means to be seventeen and caught between cultures. Heartfelt and also laugh-out-loud funny in places, this novel is not to be missed. (BBYA)

Na, An. *A Step from Heaven.* 2001. *MJS.* Korean immigrant Young Ju's story is annotated in the Physical and Emotional Abuse section of Chapter 2, "Issues." (BBYA; Printz Award)

Vijayaraghavan, Vineeta. *Motherland.* 2002. *JS.* This is the compelling coming-of-age story of fifteen-year-old Maya, born in India, but raised in the United States. Maya is sent to live with relatives in India for the summer after being in a car accident with her boyfriend, who had been drinking. Maya arrives to live with her aunt and uncle, grandmother, and ten-year-old cousin just after an assassination that has the government looking closely at anyone who may be a Tamil Tiger. The thoroughly American girl finds herself on an isolated tea plantation, where it looks as if a marriage may be arranged for her. (BBYA; Alex Award) **Adult**

Yamanaka, Lois-Ann. *Name Me Nobody.* 1999. *JS.* Fourteen-year-old Emi-Lou Kaya, a lonely and overweight Japanese American girl, struggles to be accepted at her school on Hawaii's Big Island. Annotated further in the Sexual Identity section of Chapter 2, "Issues."

Yep, Laurence. *The Case of the Goblin Pearls.* 1997. *M.* Annotated in the Contemporary Mysteries section of Chapter 5, "Mystery and Suspense."

Hispanic Americans

Latinos are today's fastest-growing minority in the United States, and Hispanic fiction, rich in both traditions and current developments of diverse Latino cultures here and abroad, radiates a fresh and irresistible vitality.

Alvarez, Julia. *Before We Were Free.* 2002. *M.* Anita de la Torre, a twelve-year-old in the Dominican Republic, stays behind with her parents when other family members flee the Trujillo dictatorship to go to the United States. (BBYA)

Bernardo, Anilu. *Loves Me, Loves Me Not.* 1998. *JS.* In the Cuban American milieu of Miami, Florida, love takes a few twists and turns. Maggie has a crush on Zach. Justin has a crush on Maggie. Susie has a crush on Carlos. Is it possible for a Cuban American girl and a bigot to get together, or is there a better match? (Popular Paperbacks)

Bertrand, Diane Gonzales. **Trino series.** Trino, a Latino seventh-grader who lives in a Texas trailer, struggles with issues of identity and belonging.

> *Trino's Choice.* 1999. *J.* Trino, living in a Texas trailer park, thinks his life is far different than that of other seventh-graders—like Lisana, whom he meets when he runs into a bookstore to escape the eighth-grade bully who wants to lead him into a life of crime.

> *Trino's Time.* 2001. *J.* Trino, now fifteen, struggles to balance family, work, and school.

Cofer, Judith Ortiz. *An Island Like You.* 1995. *JS.* (Short Stories) A dozen connected short stories of Puerto Rican teens in Patterson, New Jersey. (Popular Paperbacks; BBYA; Quick Picks; Pura Belpre Author Award)

Gonzales, Albino. *No Lack of Lonesome.* 2001. *MJS.* On a walk in New Mexico, a young boy receives important life lessons from his grandmother in this lyrically poetic tale.

Hernandez, Jo Ann Yolanda. *White Bread Competition.* 1997. *M.* When high school freshman Luz wins a school spelling bee, three generations of women in her family are affected—especially after she is accused of cheating, simply because of her Hispanic ethnicity.

Herrera, Juan Felipe. *Crashboomlove: A Novel in Verse.* 1999. *S.* (Alternative format) Sixteen-year-old Mexican American Cesar Garcia attempts to survive his Los Angeles high school. (Quick Picks; Americas Award 1999; Best Poetry Book [English] by the Latino Literary Hall of Fame)

Jimenez, Francisco. *Breaking Through.* 2001. *MJS.* When fourteen-year-old Francisco returns to California after being deported to Mexico, his hard work and inner strength take him to success. (BBYA; Americas Award 2001)

Jimenez, Francisco. *The Circuit: Stories from the Life of a Migrant Child.* 1997. *M.* (Short Stories) A dozen autobiographical stories tell of life as a Mexican migrant child in the United States. (Popular Paperbacks; Americas Award 1997)

Martínez, Victor. *Parrot in the Oven.* 1996. *JS.* Fourteen-year-old Manuel Hernandez, nicknamed "Manny," is surviving life in the projects, an alcoholic father, and pressure to join a gang. (National Book Award; Americas Award 1996; NYPL Books for the Teen Age; Pura Belpre Author Award)

Osa, Nancy. *Cuba 15.* 2003. *MJS.* Violet Paz finds her crazy Cuban family great material for her speech team competitions in the year she prepares for her *quinceanera,* even though she is already fifteen.

Rice, David. *Crazy Loco.* 2001. *MJS.* (Short Stories) Nine tales of Chicano life in small-town Texas. An authentic voice and stories that resonate with truth, pain, and humor. (BBYA)

Saldana, Rene, Jr. *The Jumping Tree.* 2001. *MJ.* As he progresses from sixth to eighth grade, Rey learns who he is and where he fits into the world as a Mexican American.

Santana, Patricia. *Motorcycle Ride on the Sea of Tranquility.* 2002. *S.* Fourteen-year-old Yolanda, "Yoli," is overjoyed that her favorite brother Chuy is coming home to San Diego from Vietnam. But the Chuy who returns is not the same one who left. As he heads across the country on a new Harley-Davidson chopper, Yoli and her remaining seven siblings experience life in 1969. This book offers an authentic feel for the period and the ambiance of a Mexican American family of the time. (BBYA) **Adult**

Soto, Gary. *Buried Onions.* 1997. *S.* Eddie, a nineteen-year-old Mexican American teen, tries to break out of the poverty and gang violence of the Fresno streets. Annotated further in the Life Is Hard section of Chapter 2, "Issues." (BBYA; Popular Paperbacks; Quick Picks)

Soto, Gary. *Petty Crimes.* 1998. *MJ.* (Short Stories) Ten stories about growing up Latino in California. (Quick Picks)

Native Americans

In the past, Native Americans, the first people to inhabit the Americas, were both demonized and romanticized in our literature. Even today, books about Native Americans often focus on the way Indians looked, dressed, and lived in the past. We also have some strong voices emerging from First Nations to show us the diverse contemporary realities of Native American life, but most are written for adults or children, with very few well suited to teen readers. Many would like to see more new titles and authors emerging in this area in the coming years.

Brooks, Martha. *Bone Dance.* 1996. *JS.* This story about Alexandra Marie Sinclair, half Scottish, half Indian, set in Manitoba, is annotated in the Coming of Age section of the Chapter 3, "Contemporary Life." (BBYA; CLA YA Book Award)

Carvell, Marlene. *Who Will Tell My Brother?* 2002. *MJS.* (Alternative format) High school senior Evan Hill, whose Indian heritage does not show in his face, decides to carry on the battle his older brother started—to change his school's offensive mascot. Deserted by people he once thought friends, Evan comes up against a brick wall in the form of the school board. A visit to elder relatives reassures him that he is part of his family, even though he doesn't look like his father or brother. Then his brother's loyal and beloved dog is killed. A novel in verse.

Smith, Cynthia Leitich. *Rain Is Not My Indian Name.* 2001. *M.* When her fourteenth birthday dawns, Cassidy Rain Berghoff, one of the few Native Americans in a small Kansas town, discovers that her boyfriend, who is also her lifelong best friend, has died. Aunt Georgina, a retired science teacher, has organized an Indian camp that Rain's brother wants her to attend, but the dead boy's mother, a politician, is dead-set against the town paying any of the expenses. Rain's brother's fiancée, who runs the local paper, gives Rain the perfect "out" when she asks her to photograph the camp for the newspaper, making it a conflict of interest for Rain to be one of the campers. Teamed up with reporter "Flash," Rain comes to recognize who she is in this powerful and moving first novel.

Cultures around the World

Poverty, upheaval, oppression, corruption, and war are some of the issues that have had an impact on cultures in other parts of the world, which puts teen protagonists in dramatic situations. Teen readers enjoy learning about other countries, reading about the experiences of "kids like them" in distant locales, and gaining insights into the world sociopolitical situation.

Abelove, Joan. *Go and Come Back.* 1998. *JS.* In a Peruvian jungle village, "two old white ladies," who are actually young anthropologists, come to study childrearing and farming, much to the amusement of the primitive villagers and adolescent Alicia, who has just adopted a baby. (BBYA)

Ellis, Deborah. *The Breadwinner.* 2000. *M.* Parvana, a young Afghani girl, must masquerade as a boy to earn money for the necessities that keep the females in her family alive under the Taliban's rigid rule. Her story is continued in *Parvana's Journey* annotated in the War section of Chapter 4, "Adventure."

Kessler, Cristina. *No Condition Is Permanent.* 2000. *JS.* Reluctantly accompanying her anthropologist mother to Sierra Leone, fourteen-year-old Jodie meets Khadi, who becomes her best friend. But the friendship is imperiled when Khadi joins a secret society that practices female circumcision, and Jodie decides she must try to stop her.

Kurtz, Jane. *Storyteller's Beads.* 1998. *MJS.* Orphaned Sahay flees the only home she has known, as famine grips Ethiopia and the army approaches. On the treacherous trail toward hope, she meets Rahel, a girl who is a member of a group even more reviled than her own ethnic group—the blind. Together they help each other survive, even after they reach a refugee camp.

Laird, Elizabeth. *Kiss the Dust.* 1991. *MJS.* Annotated in the Politics section of Chapter 2, "Issues." (BBYA; YALSA 100 Best Books)

Mead, Alice. *Girl of Kosovo.* 2001. *MJ.* Annotated in the War section of Chapter 4, "Adventure."

Min, Anchee. *Wild Ginger.* 2001. *S.* Coming of age during the 1960s Chinese Cultural Revolution. **Adult**

Naidoo, Beverley. *No Turning Back.* 1997. *MJ.* On the eve of Mandela's election, twelve-year-old Sipho flees his abusive stepfather and his pregnant mother to take to the streets of Johannesburg, where he joins a gang of street kids (*mulande*) and tries to survive on his own.

Naidoo, Beverley. *The Other Side of Truth: A Novel of South Africa.* 2001. *MJ.* In a family that has always valued truth above all, Sade's life is dramatically changed by it. After her journalist father refuses to back down from telling the truth about the corrupt Nigerian government, his wife is murdered. Sade and her brother must lie about their identities to be smuggled to London. When their professor uncle fails to meet them, they end up in foster care, afraid to tell the truth because they fear for their father's safety. (BBYA; Carnegie Award)

Park, Linda Sue. *When My Name Was Keoko: A Novel of Korea in World War II.* 2002. *MJ.* A Korean brother and sister during the Japanese occupation tell their story. Annotated further in Chapter 9, "Historical Novels." (BBYA)

Placide, Jaira. *Fresh Girl.* 2002. *MJ.* Haitian-born Mardi, age fourteen, is chastised for being a fresh-mouthed girl because she has come to the States, but she is hiding a horrific event that happened before her family fled. Mardi takes out her anger on her favorite uncle, who has been in a refugee camp in Cuba, and on her aunt, who is a little strange. (BBYA)

Snell, Gordon, ed. *Thicker than Water: Coming of Age Stories by Irish and Irish-American Writers.* 2001. *S.* (Short Stories) This collection includes stories set here and abroad—by Gordon Snell, Shane Connaughton, Jenny Roche, Maeve Binchy, Vincent Banville, Tony Hickey, Peter Cunningham, Ita Daly, June Considine, Marita Conlon-McKenna, Helena Mulkerns, and Emma Donoghue. **Adult**

Staples, Suzanne Fischer. Shabanu series. *JS.*

> *Shabanu: Daughter of the Wind.* 1989. A nomadic girl is given to an older man to become his fourth wife in contemporary Pakistan. (BBYA; YALSA 100 Best Books; Popular Paperbacks)

> *Haveli.* 1993. A widowed teen mom struggles to survive in contemporary Pakistan. (BBYA)

Staples, Suzanne Fischer. *Shiva's Fire.* 2000. Pavarti has the strange ability to remember everything that has happened since she was born. She becomes a classical dancer in India, giving up much to dedicate herself to the religious and philosophical responsibilities of her art. Then she finds that her destiny is entwined with that of a maharaja's son. (VOYA)

Whelan, Gloria. *Homeless Bird.* 2000. *MJ.* Thirteen-year-old Koly enters into an ill-fated arranged marriage and finds she must either fight Indian tradition or suffer for a lifetime. (Popular Paperbacks; BBYA)

Yumoto, Kazumi. *The Letters.* 2001. *S.* After her father dies, a young Japanese girl and her mother move into an apartment owned by a landlady who promises that when she dies she will take letters to the girl's father.

Chapter 11

Alternative Formats

One of the biggest developments and hottest new trends in fiction for teens has been that of using nontraditional formats to present stories. These new formats range from novels written in verse, or written as connected short stories, to fictional diaries, to graphic novels and picture books for teens, and many variations and combinations thereof. The appeals of these formats to young readers are as diverse as the formats themselves, but in general, alternative formats are suited to today's visual learners. Teens who have grown up with the sound bites and splash of the media don't have as much patience for lengthy stretches of narrative. This is not to say that the books included in this chapter are "easy reads." In fact, the vocabulary and sentence length may challenge some readers. But the added graphics, compressed story lines, and rap rhythms of these novels intrigue today's teen readers.

Walter Dean Myers's *Monster,* the first winner of the prestigious Printz award in 2001, was written as a screenplay interspersed with journal entries. When describing the qualities that made *Monster* the winner, Frances Bradburn commented on its distinctive format, noting that Myers "creates narrative and moral suspense that will leave readers with questions that have no real answers" (YALSA News Release announcing winners: http://www.ala/ Content/NavigationMenu/YALSA/Booklists_and_Book_Awards/Michael_L_Printz_ Award/Previous_Winners/2000_Michael_L_Printz_Award.htm).

Graphic novels, which tell a story through illustrated comic book panels, have also gained tremendous popularity in recent years. The 2002 YALSA preconference at the American Library Association's annual conference focused on graphic novels, and the theme for National Teen Read Week in 2002 was "Get Graphic @ your library," featuring a manga-style illustration. In addition, graphic novels have even been the focus of Popular Paperbacks lists—not once, but twice.

Another format that has recently risen in popularity is the story told in diary or journal entries. Modern teens like the sense of immediacy and intimacy achieved by delving into someone's most personal thoughts. More than thirty years after it was first published, teens still know and love *Go Ask Alice,* a fictional diary of drug abuse that made YALSA's list of the 100 Best Books. Numerous other titles with diary and journal formats were released in the years that followed. Other alternative formats are epistolary novels, verse novels, and connected short stories, in which elements of one short story appear in the other stories.

Because teens often seek specific formats when looking for reading material, this chapter is organized by format type. Although technically formats are not genres, books that share a format also share other qualities. For example, graphic novels often share a "look" and a certain pacing and rhythm dictated by the frames, as well as the use of techniques such as sound effects. Diaries, written in first person, generally feature short chapters and share the sense of intimacy and confidentiality that some readers enjoy. Thus, for purposes of this guide, formats are considered as subgenres. Because this chapter deals with formats, many of the titles included here are also included in the chapters on various genres.

Subgenres

Mixed Formats

The books in this section tell stories, but they are told in unusual or mixed formats. For example, the text of a radio play may be combined with traditional narrative, or the text may blend diary entries, letters, and news clippings. The lively combinations move the story along and keep readers interested.

Fleischman, Paul. *Seek***.** 2001. *JS.* Robert, a high school senior in search of the DJ father he never knew, writes his autobiography as a radio play, rich with sound bites. (BBYA)

Gray, Dianne E. *Holding Up the Earth***.** 2000. *MJ.* Letters, diary entries, and an oral history help fourteen-year-old Hope come to terms with her mother's death as she learns about the women and girls who have lived on her foster mother's farm through its history.

Myers, Walter Dean. *Monster***.** 1999. *S.* Sixteen-year-old Steve, on trial for murder, presents the trial proceedings as a screenplay, interspersed with entries from his journal. Annotated further in the Crime and Criminals section of Chapter 2, "Issues." (Printz Award; BBYA; Quick Picks; Coretta Scott King Honor)

Strasser, Todd. *Give a Boy a Gun***.** 2000. *JS.* Armed and dangerous, two sophomores, Gary Searle and Brendan Lawlor, hold hostage the attendees of a high school dance. Told through interviews and quotes interspersed with facts and statistics about school violence. (VOYA; IRAYAC)

Walter, Virginia. *Making Up Megaboy***.** 1998. *MJS.* Told in multiple voices, computer-generated graphics, and a comic book created by thirteen-year-old Robbie, aka Megaboy. Annotated in the Outsiders section of Chapter 2, "Issues." (BBYA)

Connected Stories

Connected stories are novels made up of several short stories, most often featuring different protagonists whose lives intersect. Each chapter stands on its own as a story, while the collection presents another story. This format allows readers to see a situation from many perspectives or from various time points. The short, self-contained stories allow readers to get through the book in a series of brief sittings.

Appelt, Kathi. *Kissing Tennessee and Other Stories from the Stardust Dance.* 2000. *MJ.* The Stardust Dance, the last event at Dogwood Junior High for the graduating eighth-graders, brings issues such as sexual identity and abuse to light through nine connected stories. (BBYA; VOYA; Quick Picks)

Cofer, Judith Ortiz. *An Island Like You: Stories from the Barrio.* 1995. *JS.* Connected tales of Puerto Rican teens and their immigrant families in Patterson, New Jersey. (Popular Paperbacks; BBYA; Quick Picks; Pura Belpre Author Award)

Conford, Ellen. *Crush: Stories.* 1998. *MJ.* In these delightful, interrelated stories, a high school class prepares for a Valentine's Day dance—and romances pop up in the most unlikely places. (Popular Paperbacks; Quick Picks)

Fleischman, Paul. *Bull Run.* 1993. *M.* A series of twelve vignettes told in the voices of people who were affected by the Battle of Bull Run—soldiers, mothers, sisters, witnesses, and so on. (YALSA 100 Best Books)

Frank E. R. *Life Is Funny: A Novel.* 2000. *JS.* Eleven tough Brooklyn teens tell their stories.

Myers, Walter Dean. *145th Street: Short Stories.* 2000. *MJ.* Life in Harlem through the eyes of teens in the 'hood. (BBYA; Quick Picks; Popular Paperbacks)

Peck, Richard. *A Long Way from Chicago: A Novel in Stories.* 1998. *MJ.* Eight humorous encounters involving a brother, a sister, and a feisty, rule-breaking grandmother in small-town Illinois during 1929–1942. (BBYA; Newbery Honor; Popular Paperbacks; IRAYAC)

Stolz, Karen. *World of Pies: A Novel.* 2000. *S.* Ten connected nostalgic stories tell the tale of Roxanne growing up in Annette, Texas, from girlhood to motherhood, along the way introducing Roxanne's dad, proprietor of Carl's Corsets; her cousin, Tommy, through whom readers experience the vicissitudes of the Vietnam War and its aftermath; and an assortment of other eccentric relatives, friends, and lovers. **Adult**

Thomas, Rob. *Doing Time: Notes from the Undergrad.* 1997. *JS.* Ten connected stories that revolve around teen volunteering. (BBYA; Quick Picks; Popular Paperbacks)

Thomas, Rob. *Slave Day*. 1997. *JS*. Told from multiple viewpoints, the events happen in a brief fourteen hours, fifty-two minutes, at a high school in Texas. Annotated in the Racism section of Chapter 2, "Issues."

Diaries and Journals

A format with many fans, diaries and journals let the reader vicariously experience the life of the protagonist. The format is given two distinct applications. First, it is often used with historical fiction, which lends greater immediacy to past events and allows readers a "firsthand" experience of history.

The approach has been so well received that several publishers have come out with series in this format. Scholastic publishes a number of historical novels for younger teen and middle-grade readers in a diary format, including the Royal Diaries series, the Dear America series, the My Name Is America series, and the Dear Canada series.

Stories from smart, sassy contemporary characters are also found in diary format. Jonah Black's Black Book: Diary of a Teenage Stud series draws male readers, and girls flock to Rennison's Georgia Nicholson series and Meg Cabot's Princess Diaries series. In these books, the voice is more informal, even chummy, and the contents reveal the deepest and innermost thoughts of teens. The tone can range from serious and sincere to hopelessly tragic to hilariously funny.

This section is subdivided into two categories that reflect the two types—historical and contemporary. Fans of one type may or may not be interested in reading books of the other.

Historical

Ayres, Katherine. *North by Night: A Story of the Underground Railroad*. 1998. *JS*. In the mid-1800s, fifteen-year-old Lucinda works for the Underground Railroad in Ohio. Annotated in the Slavery section of Chapter 9, "Historical Novels."

Cushman, Karen. *Catherine, Called Birdy*. 1994. *MJ*. Annotated in the Middle Ages section in Chapter 9, "Historical Novels." (BBYA; YALSA 100 Best Books; Popular Paperbacks)

Denenberg, Barry. *The Journal of William Thomas Emerson: A Revolutionary War Patriot*. 1998. *MJ*. My Name Is America series. The Boston tavern where twelve-year-old Will Emerson works is a meeting place of Revolutionary War patriots. (IRAYAC)

Hunt, Caroline Rose. *Primrose Past: The 1848 Journal of Young Lady Primrose*. 2000. *S*. The manners, lifestyle, and worldview of Victorian England are conveyed through the diary of Cygnet, a fictional fifteen-year-old girl.

Kirwan, Anna. *Victoria May Blossom of Britannia*. 2001. *M*. Royal Diaries series. Fictionalized account of Queen Victoria's girlhood.

Myers, Walter Dean. *The Journal of Joshua Loper: A Black Cowboy*. 1999. *M*. My Name Is America series. Sixteen-year-old Joshua, son of a former slave, hits the Chisholm trail in 1871, herding cattle from Texas to Abilene, Kansas.

White, Ellen Emerson. *Kaiulani: The People's Princess: Hawaii, 1889.* 2001. *M.* Royal Diaries series. The tragic story of Hawaii's beloved princess, educated in England, who campaigned for her country's independence when American business interests took over.

Contemporary

Black, Jonah. The Black Book: Diary of a Teenage Stud series. S. Jonah Black looks for love and tries to get through high school in Pompano Beach, Florida. Annotated further in the Series section of Chapter 3, "Contemporary Life."

Cabot, Meg. The Princess Diaries. *MJS.* The hilarious trials and tribulations of Mia Thermopolis, an eccentric teen from Greenwich Village who discovers she is royalty of sorts.

> *The Princess Diaries.* 2000. (Film: *The Princess Diaries*) Ninth-grader Mia Thermopolis, who lives in Greenwich Village with her artist mother, is shocked to discover that her father, a European businessman, is actually the reigning prince of a tiny country and, due to testicular cancer, is unable to have any more children. After Mia is named as heir to the kingdom, her terrifying Grandmere attempts to teach her how to be a princess while she fights with her best friend and befriends the only other girl in her school who has a bodyguard. Mia gets her first kiss from the most popular boy at school only to discover who her true friends really are. (Quick Picks; BBYA; IRAYAC) [Film]

> *Princess in the Spotlight.* 2001. Mia's adventures continue, but now she has a secret admirer and a possible date that may be totally messed up when her grandmother decides to stage a wedding for Mia's mother and her Algebra teacher after Mia announces their pregnancy on national TV. (Quick Picks)

> *Princess in Love.* 2002. Mia finally, after a few embarrassing events, has become comfortable with her self and her situation.

> *Princess in Waiting.* 2003. Mia spends Christmas in Genovia then returns to life in New York, with hilarious situations all the way.

Cole, Sheila. *What Kind of Love? The Diary of a Pregnant Teenager.* 1995. *JS.* It only took once for fifteen-year-old Valerie Larch to get pregnant. Now she must decide what to do. (Quick Picks)

Creech, Sharon. *Absolutely Normal Chaos.* 1996. *M.* Mary Lou's summer diary reveals romance and intrigue the summer she is thirteen. (Popular Paperbacks)

Haddix, Margaret Peterson. *Don't You Dare Read This, Mrs. Dunphrey.* 1996. *JS.* Annotated in the Multiple and Unique Issues section of Chapter 2, "Issues." (BBYA; Quick Picks; IRA 1997; IRAYAC)

Martin, Ann M. California Diaries series. *M.* Amalia, Sunny, Ducky, and Maggie all have stories to tell. Each book in the series is titled with the character's name and the number of his or her diary.

Rennison, Louise. Georgina Nicolson series. *MJ.*

> *Angus, Thongs, and Full-Frontal Snogging: Confessions of Georgia Nicolson.* 2000. *MJ.* Fourteen-year-old Georgia Nicholson tries to decrease the size of her nose, prevent her mad cat from terrorizing the other animals in the neighborhood, and win the love of sex-god Robbie. (BBYA; Quick Picks; Printz Honor; IRAYAC)
>
> *On the Bright Side, I'm Now the Girlfriend of a Sex God: Further Confessions of Georgia Nicolson.* 2001. Now that Georgia is Robbie's girlfriend, her parents want to take her off to the other side of the world. (Quick Picks)
>
> *Knocked Out by My Nunga-Nungas: Further, Further Confessions of Georgia Nicolson.* 2002. More sassy angst from the obnoxious Georgia.
>
> *Dancing in My Nuddypants: Even Further Confessions of Georgia Nicolson.* 2003. Georgia has picked Robbie the Sex God over Dave the Laugh, and life continues for her as obnoxiously as ever.

Sparks, Beatrice. *Kim: Empty Inside: The Diary of an Anonymous Teenager.* 2001. *JS.* Annotated in Chapter 2, "Issues."

Sparks, Beatrice. *Treacherous Love: The Diary of an Anonymous Teenager.* 2000. *JS.* Annotated in the Sexual Abuse section of Chapter 2, "Issues." (Quick Picks)

Sparks, Beatrice, ed. *Go Ask Alice.* 1971. *JS.* Annotated in the Substance Abuse section of Chapter 2, "Issues." (BBYA; YALSA 100 Best Books)

Epistolary Novels

Almost as intimate as journals and diaries, correspondence between characters in epistolary novels—through letters, notes, or e-mail—also creates a relationship between the reader and the purported writers. Reading an epistolary novel also has a delicious element of voyeurism.

Brashares, Ann. *The Sisterhood of the Traveling Pants.* 2001. *MJS.* A seemingly magical pair of pants keeps four lifelong friends united when they decide to mail the pants and updates on their activities throughout their first summer apart. Lena goes to Greece for a summer with her grandparents, where she meets a remarkable young man; Bridget goes to soccer camp in Mexico; Carmen goes to spend the summer with her father and discovers that he has a new family; and Tibby stays home, working in a discount store and wearing a hideous smock, but finding a young friend who transforms her life. (BBYA)

Chbosky, Stephen. *The Perks of Being a Wallflower.* 1999. *S.* A high school freshman confronts dating, drugs, and memories of the sexual abuse he experienced as a child. (Popular Paperbacks; BBYA; Quick Picks)

Danziger, Paula, and Ann M. Martin. Tara and Star series. *M.*

P.S. Longer Letter Later. 1998. Junior high students and forever friends, Tara*Star and Elizabeth, know that moving will put stress on their friendship, but when things begin to change, neither is prepared for it. (Quick Picks)

Snail Mail No More. 2000. In this sequel to *Longer Letter Later*, Tara*Star and Elizabeth, now in eighth grade, can communicate much faster because they both have e-mail. (Quick Picks)

Moriarty, Jaclyn. *Feeling Sorry for Celia.* **2001.** *MJS.* Hilarious letters and notes portray fifteen-year-old Elizabeth's life as she worries about her friend Celia, who is a bit of a drama queen. (BBYA)

Poetry and Verse Novels

In these books, the story is told in a series of poems. With the resurgence of popularity in poetry among teens, this format is achieving more popularity. Passionate and intense, poetry packs an emotional wallop. Those who read for the beauty of language often like this format. It is also a hit with teens who need a quick read for a book report!

Cormier, Robert. *Frenchtown Summer.* **1999.** *MJS.* The melancholy story of Eugene's twelfth summer is told in a series of poems. The setting is the French Canadian district of Monument, called Frenchtown.

Creech, Sharon. *Love That Dog.* **2001.** *M.* Middle-schooler Jack learns to love poetry and is inspired by meeting author Walter Dean Myers.

Glenn, Mel. Tower High series. *JS.*

Who Killed Mr. Chippendale? 1996. A mystery told in verse from several different viewpoints. Annotated in the Contemporary Mysteries section of Chapter 5, "Mystery and Suspense." (Popular Paperbacks; Quick Picks; BBYA)

The Taking of Room 114. 1997. This is a continuation of the saga of bizarre events happening at Tower High that started with the murder of a teacher in *Who Killed Mr. Chippendale?* This small volume introduces the reader to several individuals in a classroom full of teens, who are held hostage by a teacher who has reached the end of his rope. (BBYA)

Foreign Exchange: A Mystery in Poems. 1999. Annotated in the Contemporary Mysteries section of Chapter 5, "Mystery and Suspense." (Popular Paperbacks; Quick Picks)

Split Image. 2000. Everyone at Tower High sees Laura Li, a Chinese American high school student, differently. Each chapter is written from a different character's perspective. (BBYA; IRAYAC)

Grimes, Nikki. *Bronx Masquerade*. 2002. *MJS*. Open-mike poetry sessions for a culturally diverse group of students in a Bronx high school. (BBYA; Quick Picks; VOYA; Coretta Scott King Award)

Herrera, Juan Felipe. *Crashboomlove: A Novel of Verse*. 1999. *JS*. Annotated in the Hispanic Americans section of Chapter 10, "Multicultural Fiction." (Quick Picks; Americas Award 1999; Best Poetry Book [English] by the Latino Literary Hall of Fame)

Hesse, Karen. *Out of the Dust*. 1997. *MJS*. After her mother is accidentally killed, Billie Jo struggles to forgive herself and her father and to survive farm life in the Oklahoma dust bowl of the 1930s. (Newbery Award; Scott O'Dell Award; BBYA)

Hesse, Karen. *Witness*. 2001. *MJS*. Residents of a small Vermont town are affected by the Ku Klux Klan in the 1920s.

Janeczko, Paul. *Stardust Hotel*. 1993. *MJ*. Fourteen-year-old Leary, whose parents were hippies of the Woodstock generation, experiences life and love. (BBYA)

Koertge, Ron. *The Brimstone Journals*. 2001. *MJS*. Koertge's tale of troubled kids is told by different voices and viewpoints. Readers may be reminded of the events at Columbine High School. (BBYA; Quick Picks)

Sones, Sonya. *Stop Pretending: What Happened When My Big Sister Went Crazy*. 1999. *MJS*. Annotated in the Mental, Emotional, and Behavioral Problems section of Chapter 2, "Issues." (Popular Paperbacks; BBYA; Quick Picks; IRAYAC)

Wolff, Virginia Euwer. Make Lemonade series.

> *Make Lemonade*. 1993. *JS*. Fourteen-year-old LaVaughn knows she wants to go to college, so she accepts a baby-sitting job, caring for Jolly's two small children. Jolly, a teen mom, is LaVaughn's neighbor in the projects. (Popular Paperbacks; YALSA 100 Best Books; BBYA)

> *True Believer*. 2001. *MJS*. Fifteen-year-old LaVaughn continues toward her goal of going to college and develops a crush on a boy from her past. (BBYA; Printz-Honor; National Book Award)

Graphic Novels

Some people call them overgrown comic books, but graphic novels are an art form unto themselves. Through the use of comic book–type frames, the combination of graphics and brief text tells a story in a distinctive way, imposing more of the artists' vision on the reader.

Because the stories in graphic novels move frame to frame, rather than in the linear narrative of traditional novels, they have a certain rhythm and pacing. Although some may justifiably argue that they are a format, not a genre, graphic novels function like a genre in that they comprise a recognizable subset of fiction with specific conventions and appeals that link them in a reader's mind. The conventions include such things as dialogue balloons and thought bubbles. Sound effects are included, giving many graphic novels a cinematic touch. The use of visual clues, including the contrast of light and dark, impart information that is not present in the text but is essential to the meaning of that section of the story. Certainly, many readers (especially teens) specifically seek books in this format.

To some degree, subgenres within this body of literature parallel standard genres—mystery, horror, science fiction, and so on. However, the most popular subgenres include real-life themes, superheroes, manga, and fantasy and science fiction. There are now several resources for finding and selecting graphic novels for libraries. Weiner's (2001) *The 101 Best Graphic Novels* and Rothschild's (1995) *Graphic Novels: A Bibliographic Guide to Book-Length Comics* are informative guides. There are also several useful resources online. D. Aviva Rothchild's the Comics Get Serious Web Site (http://www.rationalmagic.com/Comics/.html) and Graphic Novels for Library Discussion List (http://www.topica.com/lists/GNLIB-L) are two of the best.

The rising popularity and acceptance of graphic novels in young adult library collections is well illustrated by the fact that graphic novels were the focus of the 2002 YALSA preconference, the theme of the 2002 Teen Read Week, and that they are receiving more coverage in library journals. The August 1, 2002, *School Library Journal* featured "What Teens Want," an article by Michele Gorman that featured "Thirty Graphic Novels You Can't Live Without," and VOYA, always on the forefront in reviewing graphic novels for teens, announced that Kat Kan's long-running graphic novel column would be appearing in every issue. Most graphic novels are published for adults, although teens read them in great numbers

Assorted Graphic Novels

The following titles, along with the featured subgenres, do not fit into the larger categories that follow and demonstrate some of the diversity in graphic novels.

Aragonés, Sergio. *Groo and Rufferto.* 2000. *JS.* Long ago and far away, Groo, a barbarian wanderer, and his loyal hound Rufferto wander the world with the best of intentions, but leave a trail of destruction behind them.

Golden, Christopher. *Buffy the Vampire Slayer: The Origin.* 1999. *JS.* The beginning of the Buffy mythos told in graphic novel format.

Robinson, James, and Paul Smith. *Leave It to Chance: Shaman's Rain.* 1997. *S.* A blend of mystery and the paranormal, featuring a fourteen-year-old female protagonist.

Thompson, Craig. *Good-bye Chunky Rice.* 1999. *MJS.* Chunky Rice, a turtle, sets off on a sea voyage in a very shaky craft, while back on land Dandele, the mouse who loves him, sends him messages in bottles. (Popular Paperbacks)

Winick, Judd. *The Adventures of Barry Ween, Boy Genius.* 2000. *S.* Off-color tales of a boy genius's hilarious misadventures. (Popular Paperbacks)

Real-Life Themes

The same factors that make contemporary and issue novels popular with teens make real-life themes popular in graphic novels. Even though many of the following titles could be cataloged as nonfiction if they were presented in a traditional format, the graphic format novel leads to more extrapolation of what something looked like or what someone was thinking and turns them into a unique combination of fact and fiction.

9-11: Artists Respond. 2002. *S.* Graphic novelists tell how the September 11 terrorist attacks affected them in a book that benefits the American Red Cross.

Arnoldi, Katherine. ***The Amazing True Story of a Teenage Single Mom.*** 1998. *JS.* The depth of emotion that can be conveyed through a combination of cartoon drawings and text balloons is amazing. Arnoldi's story is real and touching, bringing the difficulties endured by too many teenagers to life. Skillfully crafted, the story invites the reader in and then gradually builds up the back story, so that by the end one is really pulling for this young mother, empathizing with what she has gone through and sharing her feelings. (BBYA; Quick Picks)

Clowes, Daniel. *Ghostworld.* 1997. *S.* (Film: *Ghostworld*) Best friends and outsiders Enid and Becky grow apart when they choose diverging paths after high school. (Popular Paperbacks) Film

Geary, Rick. Treasury of Victorian Murder. JS. Carefully researched depictions of real-life murders and the mysteries surrounding them.

> *The Borden Tragedy.* 1997. Discover the circumstances that put Lizzie Borden on trial for the murder of her parents back in 1892.
>
> *Jack the Ripper: A Journal of the Whitechapel Murders 1888–1889.* 1995. The murder mystery that has haunted generations.
>
> *The Mystery of Mary Rogers.* 2001. In the mid–nineteenth century, the brutalized body of Mary Rogers, an attractive woman who worked at a cigar store, was found floating in the Hudson River.

Gonick, Larry. Cartoon History of the Universe. *MJS.* A humorous—and surprisingly accurate— crash course in history.

> *Larry Gonick's The Cartoon History of the Universe.* 1990. Everything you ever wanted to know about history, starting with the Big Bang.
>
> *The Cartoon History of the Universe II: From the Springtime of China to the Fall of Rome.* 1994.
>
> *Gonick's The Cartoon History of the Universe III: From the Rise of Arabia to the Renaissance.* 2002.

Hirsch, Karen, ed. *Mind Riot.* 1997. *MJS.* This wonderful collection of short stories includes contributions by Ida Marx Blue Spruce, Ann Decker, Phoebe Gloeckner, David Greenberger, Roberta Gregory, Glenn Head, Peter Kuper, Caryn Leschen, Diane Noomin, Kevin Quigley, Vicky Rabinowicz, Dean Rohrer, Carol Swain, Carol Tyler, Colin Upton, and Maurice Vellekoop. The stories depict a wide range of adolescent angst, and the varied drawing styles are a delight to the eye.

Hosler, Jay. *Clan Apis.* 2000. *M.* The story of Nyuki, a honey bee, whose colony migrates to a new hive, offers readers a sweet serving of natural science. (Popular Paperbacks)

Moore, Terry. *Strangers in Paradise High School!* 1999. *JS.* Francine, a sheltered suburbanite, and Katchoo, a "bad girl," become best friends as high school outcasts. (Popular Paperbacks)

Spiegelman, Art. *Maus.* 1986. *S.* The true story of Spiegelman's father during the Holocaust is depicted in graphic novel format, with Jews as mice, Germans as cats, Poles as pigs, and so on. (YALSA 100 Best Books; Pulitzer; BBYA)

Spiegelman, Art. Maus II: A Survivor's Tale: And Here My Troubles Began. 1991. *S.* Speigelman continues to ferret out the story of his father's survival in Auschwitz and Dachau in relation to his own life. (BBYA)

Talbot, Bryan. *The Tale of One Bad Rat.* 1995. *JS.* The artwork evolves with the story of Helen, a young woman who finds homelessness is preferable to life with a sexually abusive father. Set in England, Helen's story begins in a Tube station, where she becomes prey to weirdos and criminals. Other homeless teens befriend her, and Helen moves into a squat with them. Her one true friend is her pet rat. After tragedy strikes, Helen ends up in the area where Beatrix Potter wrote and illustrated her beloved children's stories. She finds new friends, a new life, a job, and faces her problems. (Eisner Award)

Winick, Judd. *Pedro and Me: Friendship, Loss and What I Learned.* 2000. *JS.* Aspiring cartoonist Winick was selected to be on MTV's *Real World* San Francisco, where he forged a close friendship with Pedro Zamora, an exceptional young AIDS educator. In graphic novel format, Winnick tells of Pedro's life, death, and legacy. (Quick Picks; BBYA; Popular Paperbacks)

Superheroes

Superman, Spider-Man, Wonder Woman, and countless others are the mythic heroes of our times. Rather than being touched by the gods like the heroes of ancient myth, these heroes have other reasons for the powers they bear. Superheroes blend the heroics of adventure and crime fighting with a touch of the fantastic. Long a standard in the world of comics, superheroes appear regularly in graphic novels and have also become a staple of television and film.

Bendis, Brian-Michael. 2001. *S.* ***Ultimate Spider-Man Power and Responsibility.*** Orphaned high school student Peter Parker gains extraordinary powers after being bitten by a spider in a lab, but he discovers that responsibility is essential for wielding such power. (Popular Paperbacks; Quick Picks)

Brennan, Michael. *Electric Girl.* 2000. *JS.* Virginia, the Electric Girl, can discharge electricity at will, but with an invisible gremlin for a companion, she can't stop things from going wrong. (Popular Paperbacks)

Busiek, Kurt. *Kurt Busiek's Astro City: Life in the Big City. What It's Like to Live in the City of Superheroes.* 1996. *MJS.* Ordinary people, costumed superheroes, and sinister villains all make their home in this postmodern metropolis. (Popular Paperbacks)

Busiek, Kurt, and Alex Ross. *Marvels.* 1994 (reissued in 2003). *MJS.* A photographer tries to document the feelings of normal people who interact with Marvel Comics' superheroes.

David, Peter. SpyBoy. *MJS.*

SpyBoy: The Deadly Gourmet Affair. 2001. Typical teen Alex Fleming discovers he is not really all that typical after all. (Quick Picks)

Trial and Terror. 2001. SpyBoy's adventures against Judge and Jury.

Bet Your Life. 2001. SpyBoy and Bombshell are on the trail of Madam Imadam, head of the Palindrome terrorist organization.

Bomb Appetite. 2003. Alex is on his deadliest mission ever, while Japan comes up with its own super spy—SpyGirl!

David, Peter, and D. Curtis Johnson. *Young Justice: A League of Their Own.* 2000. *JS.* Six teens, boys and girls, become the Justice League of America.

Dixon, Chuck, and Jordan Gorfinkel. *Birds of Prey.* 1999. *S.* Black Canary and Oracle are female superheroes in a world that is also home to Catwoman, Batgirl, and the late Green Arrow. (Popular Paperbacks)

Ellis, Warren. *StormWatch: Force of Nature.* 1998. *JS.* A team of superheroes sponsored by the United Nations battles evil. (Quick Picks)

Lee, Stan, and Christopher Priest. *Black Panther: The Client.* 2001. *S.* An African nation is led by an African superhero.

Loeb, Jeph. *Batman: The Long Halloween.* 1999. *S.* Early in Batman's career, he teamed up with Jim Gordon and Harvey Dent in an investigation of the murders of several members of Gotham City's crime families. (Popular Paperbacks)

Millar, Mark. *Ultimate X-Men: The Tomorrow People.* 2001. *S.* In a world much like ours, genetic mutations that give some young people unusual powers are beginning to appear and the government as well as Charles Xavier and the terrorist called Magneto are trying to recruit them. (Popular Paperbacks)

Miller, Frank. *Batman: The Dark Knight Returns.* 1988. *JS.* Batman comes out of retirement to fight the Joker once again and to save Gotham City.

Moore, Alan. *Tom Strong Book 1.* 2000. *JS.* A physical and mental superhuman, Tom Strong was born on a South Seas island, orphaned by his scientist parents, and raised by a steam-powered robot. He now fights evil alongside his beautiful wife and headstrong daughter. Tom quickly heads into battle against the Nazi superwoman Ingrid Weiss and a prehuman monster called the Pangean.

Morrison, Grant. *JLA: Earth 2.* 2001. *S.* The Justice League of America is called on by the good counterpart of Lex Luthor to combat the Crime Syndicate of Amerika, their parallel universe counterpart-opposites. (Quick Picks)

Smith, Kevin. *Daredevil Visionaries V.* 1999. *S.* (Film: *Daredevil*) Blind law partner by day, crime fighter by night, Daredevil must determine the true nature of a baby placed in his care. Is the baby a savior or the ultimate nightmare? (Popular Paperbacks) [Film]

Smith, Kevin, and Phil Hester. *Green Arrow: Quiver.* 2002. *JS.* When Oliver Queen, the Green Arrow, comes back to life, he discovers that the world moved. Now he must find out what happened in those missing years. (BBYA)

Fantasy and Science Fiction

With the popularity of books such as Harry Potter and movies such as *Lord of the Rings,* it is not surprising that fantasy and science fiction are currently popular in the graphic novel format.

Busiek, Kurt. *The Wizard's Tale.* 1997. *MJS.* Just how is a good wizard supposed to survive in an evil-dominated land?

Gaiman, Neil. *The Books of Magic.* 1993. *S.* Arthurian fantasy presented in graphic novel style, as Tim Hunter encounters magic in his search for identity.

Gaiman, Neil. *Death: The High Cost of Living.* 1994. *S.* Once every one hundred years, Death takes on human form to remember just what it is she is taking away. (Popular Paperbacks)

Gaiman, Neil. The Sandman. *S.* A fantasy series that many regard as the best examples of graphic novels, with a strong mythological foundation. Although a few of the titles in the series are appropriate for teens, many are not because of graphic violence and adult situations. But this is definitely a series to be aware of. The two titles listed here have appeared on YALSA lists.

> *Sandman: Dream Country.* 1999. Several tales, including one in which death tries to help an agoraphobic ex-superhero, are included in the third book in the Sandman series. (World Fantasy Award; Popular Paperbacks)

> *Sandman: World's End.* 1994. The eighth in the series, this collection of tales is told by travelers who seek shelter in a tavern from a reality storm. (Popular Paperbacks)

Kesel, Barbara, and Steve McNiven. *Meridian, Volume 1: Flying Solo.* 2002. *JS.* When Sephie inherits a sigil that has the power to create, she is thrust into the middle of a power struggle to keep her city safe.

Medley, Linda. *Castle Waiting: The Lucky Road.* 2000. *MJS.* A young woman seeks sanctuary for herself and her unusual newborn. (Popular Paperbacks)

Moench, Doug. *The Big Book of the Unexplained.* 1997. *S.* Graphic novel approach to the paranormal. (Popular Paperbacks)

Moore, Alan. *Promethea, Book One.* 2001. *S.* College student Sophie is swept into the realm of the ancient Greek gods. (Popular Paperbacks)

Petrie, Doug. *Buffy the Vampire Slayer: Ring of Fire.* 2000. *S.* Buffy faces the corpse of a demonic samurai who will bestow ultimate power upon whoever revives it. (Popular Paperbacks)

Pini, Wendy, and Richard Pini with others. Elfquest. *S.* Cutter and his tribe the Wolfriders are on a quest to unite the various elven tribes to fight their common enemies. A series of high-fantasy stories featuring elves and magic that has appeared as comic books, graphic novels, and even text novels. The first appearance was in 1978. Many libraries still have some of the volumes of the Complete Elfquest graphic novels. Although those are no longer in print, the stories are now available in the Elfquest Reader's Collection. The official Web site can be found at http://www.elfquest.com/.

1. Fire and Flight. 1988.

2. The Forbidden Grove. 1998.

3. Captives of Blue Mountain. 1997.

4. Quest's End. 1998.

5. Siege at Blue Mountain. 1998.

6. The Secret of Two-Edge. 1998.

7. The Cry from Beyond. 1998.

8. Kings of the Broken Wheel. 1998.

8a. Dreamtime. 1998.

9. Rogue's Curse. 2000.

9a. Wolfrider! 1999.

9b. Blood of Ten Chiefs. 1999.

9c. Kahvi. 2000.

9d. Chief's Howl. 1998.

10. Shards. 1998.

11. Legacy. 1998.

11a. Huntress. 1999.

11b. Wild Hunt. 2000.

11c. Shadowstalker. 2000.

12. Ascent. 1999.

12a. Reunion. 1999.

13. The Rebels. 1998.

13a. Skyward Shadow. 1999.

14. Jink! 1999.

14a. Mindcoil. 1999.

15. Forevergreen. 1999.

15a. Dream's End. 2001.

15b. Phoenix. 2002.

16. WaveDancers. 2002.

17. Worldpool. 2000.

Veitch, Tom, and Cam Kennedy. *Star Wars: Dark Empire*. 1993. *JS*. A graphic novel depiction of how Luke went over to the Dark Side. (Quick Picks)

Manga

Manga, the print equivalent of anime, which is also sometimes called Japanimation, is becoming more available in the United States, and it does have a strong teen following. The artwork for Teen Read Week 2002 featured a manga-style illustration. This work is known for its illustrations of big-eyed children and teens. When translated into English some publishers "flip" the book to make it easier for English, readers who read from left to right, but this can wreak havoc with the illustrations. Some publishers now translate only the text, so readers must start at what is usually thought of as the end of the book and read backward.

Crilley, Mark. *Akiko: The Menace of Alia Rellapor*. Volume 1. 1997. *MJS*. The adventures of fourth-grader Akiko, who is taken to a planet named Smoo.

Fujishima, Kosuke. *Oh My Goddess! 1-555-GODDESS*. 1996. *JS*. When Keiichi dials a wrong number, he reaches a goddess who will grant him one wish. Michele Gorman characterized it as "I Dream of Jeanie" meets "Dawson's Creek" in her article "What Teens Want: 30 Graphic Novels You Can't Live Without"—the cover story of the August 2002 issue of *School Library Journal*.

Kudo, Kazuya. *Mai the Psychic Girl.* 1995. *MJS.* When fourteen-year-old Mai finds out that her father is in trouble, she uses her psychic powers for something more than jokes. (Popular Paperbacks)

Miyazaki, Hayao. *Nausicaa of the Valley of Wind.* Perfect Collection Volume 1. 2001. *JS.* A young princess leads the battle for scarce natural resources in an ecologically devastated world. (Popular Paperbacks)

Nishiyama, Yuriko. *Harlem Beat.* Number 1. 1999. *S.* Nate enters the cut-throat subculture of street hoops. (Popular Paperbacks)

Sakai, Stan. *Usagi Yojimbo Grasscutter.* 1999. *S.* A ronin warrior rabbit finds himself in the care of Grasscutter, a legendary blade forged by the gods. Originally a black-and-white comic, this book has been issued by several publishers. (The Official Usagi Yojimbo Web site is at http://www.usagiyojimbo.com/) (Popular Paperbacks)

Soryo, Fuyumi. *Mars.* 2002. *JS.* Romance, Manga style, as Kira, a shy art student is rescued by Rei, a popular jock.

Takahashi, Rumiko. *Ranma 1/2.* Volume 1. 1993. *JS.* Cold water turns Ranma into a girl, while hot turns him back. (Popular Paperbacks)

Tamaki, Hisao. *Star Wars, a New Hope: Manga.* 2002. *MJS.* A novelization, in manga format, of the 2002 *Star Wars* movie.

Toriyama, Akira. *Dragonball.* 2000. *MJS.* Goku and Bulma are on a quest for the seven dragonballs, which when united, will grant one wish.

Tezuka, Osamu. *Black Jack.* 1999. *S.* The medical encounters of Doctor Black Jack, who can work miracles but doesn't have a license to practice —which puts him into some pretty dicey situations. (Quick Picks)

Watson, Andi. *Geisha.* 1993. *S.* An artist is blackballed because she is an android and so has to take work as a bodyguard for a high-fashion model.

Yune, Tommy. *Speed Racer: Born to Race.* 1999. *JS.* The origins of Speed Racer (an anime character) are detailed.

Humor

Once referred to as the "funnies" or "funny papers," humorous comics have been around for a long time. When published as graphic novels, they are often found in children's sections.

Groening, Matt. *Bart Simpson's Treehouse of Horror Spine-Tingling Spooktacular.* 2001. *MJS.* Humorous horror featuring the family from the longest-running animated television series.

Groening, Matt. *Simpsons Comics a Go-Go.* 2000. *MJS.* The adventures of the Simpson family, featuring Homer, Marge, Lisa, and Bart.

Groening, Matt. *Simpsons Comics Royale.* 2001. *MJS.* All the Simpson characters from the television series whom Americans know and love are here.

Scott, Jerry, and Jim Borgman. *Are We an "Us"?* **A Zits Collection Sketchbook.** Number 4. 2001. *MJS.* Fifteen-year-old Jeremy and his friends humorously work to survive adolescence and all that comes with it. (Quick Picks)

Smith, Jeff. *Bone: Out from Boneville.* 1995. *MJS.* Cousins, Fone Bone, Phoney Bone, and Smiley Bone are all on their own after being run out of Boneville. (Popular Paperbacks)

Spiegelman, Art, and Francoise Mouly. *Little Lit: Folklore and Fairy Tale Funnies.* 2001. *MJS.* Fractured fairy tales from some of the biggest names in graphic novels.

Spiegelman, Art, and Francoise Mouly. *Little Lit: Strange Stories for Strange Kids.* 2001. *MJS.* Bizarre stories in comic book format from great talents such as Maurice Sendak and Paul Auster.

Watterson, Bill. *The Indispensable Calvin and Hobbes: A Calvin and Hobbes Treasury.* 1992. *MJS.* An ornery six-year-old and his stuffed tiger have myriad adventures from many collections.

References

Rothschild, D. Aviva. *Graphic Novels: A Bibliographic Guide to Book-Length Comics.* Englewood, Colo.: Libraries Unlimited, 1995.

Weiner, Stephen. *The 101 Best Graphic Novels.* New York: NBM, 2001.

Chapter 12

Christian Fiction

Christian teens with strong religious convictions, particularly evangelical Christians, often enjoy reading stories that relate to their faith. Although some titles published in this genre are preachy and moralistic, which can be a turnoff to teen readers, others elegantly communicate a message of hope and redemption—a message many teens want to hear. Another aspect of this genre that attracts readers is the general absence of profanity and blatant sexual content, although there are now exceptions to this rule.

Christian fiction is another genre that blends well with others. In recent years, Christian publishing has flourished, and titles with a Christian orientation have been published in genres as diverse as science fiction, romance, and mystery. Especially plentiful and popular are Christian romances, which are often published in series, and usually pair Christian teens with unbelievers, forcing a moral dilemma.

Titles published as YA fiction in this area are generally aimed at younger readers. Many teen readers of Christian fiction also read adult Christian titles. Mort's *Christian Fiction* (2002) contains a chapter on YA Christian fiction and notes adult titles that are popular with teen readers.

The titles that follow represent a sampling of the diverse types of books that are being published in the area of Christian fiction. They share the qualities of other books in the stated genre, but with an added Christian orientation and message.

Subgenres

Contemporary Life

Brio Girls series. *MJS.* Teen romance with a Christian emphasis.

Stuck in the Sky. Lissa Halls Johnson. 2001. Artistic Jacie, a high school junior, falls for a boy who doesn't share her Christian worldview.

Fast Forward to Normal. Jane Vogel. 2001. Becca becomes resentful when her parents decide to adopt a Guatemalan refugee.

Opportunity Knocks Twice. Lissa Halls Johnson. 2001. Tyler runs into the girl of his dreams at a photo shoot. Now he must decide between two girls—one who shares his beliefs, and one who doesn't.

Double Exposure: Real Faith Meets Real Life. Kathy Wierenga. 2002. Hannah, who is committed to courtship, is confused after two boys kiss her.

Good-Bye to All That. Jeanette Hanscome. 2002. After Solana Luz decides to give up on romance and concentrate on science, she is sidetracked when Ramón, one of her uncle's ranch hands, starts pursuing her.

Grasping at Moonbeams. Jane Vogel. 2002. Becca is thrilled that her friend Solana seems to be ready to give her life to the Lord, but is she herself willing to do the same?

Baer, Judy. The Cedar River Daydreams series. *MJ.* Different teens experience a range of teen concerns and are influenced by their Christian beliefs.

New Girl in Town. 1988. Alexis "Lexi" Leighton desperately wants to make friends at her new high school, but where does she fit in?

Trouble with a Capital T. 1988. Lexi stands up to popular Minda and then tries to be her friend.

Jennifer's Secret. 1989. Lexi tries to figure out what's making Jennifer so unhappy.

Journey to Nowhere. 1989. When Minda starts hanging out with bad boy Matt, Lexi knows she must help.

Broken Promises. 1989. Peggy shares a terrible secret with Lexi.

The Intruder. 1989. Something's bothering Lexi's mom—what could it be?

Silent Tears No More. 1990. Binky makes a terrible discovery at her new baby-sitting job.

Fill My Empty Heart. 1990. A handsome new teacher, Mr. Cartwright, means trouble to Cedar River High.

Yesterday's Dream. 1990. Problems in her relationship with Todd bring Lexi down.

Tomorrow's Promise. 1990. Lexi's faith is shaken when her grandmother's condition worsens.

Something Old, Something New. 1991. Peggy returns to Cedar River High, and Lexi gets involved in an environmental campaign with Egg.

Vanishing Star. 1991. Horror movies, a purportedly haunted house, and a tennis player named Holly add up to big trouble.

No Turning Back. 1991. When Peggy breaks up with Chad, he's devastated.

Second Chance. 1991. Todd, a high school quarterback, sustains a serious injury while playing and may never walk again.

Lost and Found. 1992. Peggy makes it through a tough year, only to be faced with another problem.

Unheard Voices. 1992. Ruth, a new girl who has a hearing impairment, becomes the butt of cruel jokes at Cedar River High.

Lonely Girl. 1992. A lonely and mysterious new girl named Angela carries a secret.

More than Friends. 1992. When Lexi's friend Ashleigh comes to visit, her group turns on her.

Never Too Late. 1993. There's something strange about Ed, the new mechanic at Todd and Mike's body shop.

The Discovery. 1993. Nancy, the fiancée of Todd's older brother Mike, starts looking a little pale.

Special Kind of Love. 1993. When Jennifer stumbles upon an unpleasant secret about her parents, she withdraws from the group.

Three's a Crowd. 1994. Lexi and Todd were doing fine till Brock came to town.

Silent Thief. 1995. Lexi's mom has been acting strange, and now she's had a car accident.

The Suspect. 1996. Someone's been stealing from the school store.

Heartless Hero. 1997. Roger is a great football player, but he's a bully.

Worlds Apart. 1997. Dmitri, the new foreign exchange student from Greece, has Minda and Jennifer competing for his attention.

Never Look Back. 1997. Angela starts behaving strangely and then runs away.

Forever Friends. 1999. Egg is off to college, much to his sister Binky's chagrin, and Lexi's parents advise her to break up with Todd.

Lewis, Beverly. Holly's Heart series. *M.* Starting at age thirteen, Holly uses her Christian values to get through middle school and into high school. Originally published by Zondervan in the 1990s, the series is being reissued by Bethany House.

Good-Bye, Dressel Hills. 1994. Holly has to prepare to say good-bye to Dressel Hills when her stepfather takes a new job in Denver.

Second-Best Friend. 1994. Jealousy rears its ugly head when Andie's Austrian pen pal comes to visit.

Little White Lies. 1995. When Holly and Andie go to California for a two-week vacation, Andie flips for an older guy.

The "No Guys" Pact. 1995. Church camp descends into an all-out battle of the sexes.

Freshmen Frenzy. 1996. Holly isn't excited about starting high school, especially when it looks like Andie is developing a new set of friends.

Mystery Letters. 1996. Writing a Dear Holly column for the school newspaper turns out to be scary when some mysterious letters come to her.

Eight Is Enough. 1997. Oh no! Holly's mother is pregnant and the house already seems too small.

Best Friend, Worst Enemy. 2001. (Originally published as *Holly's First Love* in 1993.) Holly and her best friend, Andie, both have their hearts set on Jared.

Secret Summer Dreams. 2001. (Originally released in 1993.) Holly has been looking forward to visiting her dad in California, but it seems that nobody wants her to go.

Sealed with a Kiss. 2002. Holly has lied to her pen pal, who is college-aged and now wants to meet her in person.

The Trouble with Weddings. 2002. Holly tries to find the perfect bridesmaid dress for her mother's wedding.

California Christmas. Retitled *California Crazy*. 2002. Holly goes to southern California to spend Christmas with her dad and stepmom.

Straight A Teacher. 2002. Holly develops a crush on the new student teacher.

Mystery

Rushford, Patricia H. Jennie McGrady Mystery series. *MJ.* As Jennie McGrady tries to solve the mystery of her father's disappearance, she finds herself involved in all types of mysteries connected to her family, her school, and her Christian church.

Too Many Secrets. 1993. Jennie's grandmother, who has a connection to the FBI, has disappeared with a million dollars in stolen diamonds.

Silent Witness. 1993. Two years after her father's murder, Sarah Stanford starts remembering things that place her in danger.

Pursued. 1993. After Allison is crowned Princess of the Rose Festival, she starts receiving threats.

Deceived. 1994. Jennie accompanies her grandmother on a Caribbean cruise and finds danger.

Without a Trace. 1995. Jennie's five-year-old brother and his playmate have disappeared.

Dying to Win. 1995. After Courtney, the "Rainbow Girl," disappears, Jennie hunts to find out what's happened.

Betrayed. 1996. A bomb almost killed Jennie's uncle, so she heads to Montana to find out who is behind the violent act.

In Too Deep. 1996. Jennie is not convinced that her chemistry teacher committed suicide.

Over the Edge. 1997. When the mayor's daughter, Jessica, is murdered, her boyfriend Todd is accused. Todd also happens to be the best friend of Jennie's boyfriend Ryan, so she's on the case.

From the Ashes. 1997. Trinity Center, the home of Jennie's school and church, is destroyed by fire, and a family friend is injured.

Desperate Measures. 1998. At a Labor Day visit to a fur farm, Jennie encounters a crime that may have been perpetrated by animal rights activists.

Abandoned. 1999. Jennie discovers that her schoolmate Annie was found in a Dumpster when she was a baby.

Forgotten. 2000. On a mountain hike, Jennie is taken hostage by a wanted criminal.

Stranded. 2001. Flying lessons and a crash landing draw Jennie into a mysterious desert commune.

Grave Matters. 2002. Jennie plans a trip to Ireland with her grandmother to settle an estate and receives a threatening note.

Fantasy and Science Fiction

LaHaye, Tim, and Jerry B. Jenkins. Left Behind series. *S.* When the Rapture happens, the people left on Earth must work out what to do next as evil tries to manipulate events. This top-selling series of Christian thrillers has been a frequent readers' advisory request, with questions focusing on finding the book that features people disappearing from an airplane over the Atlantic, leaving behind all their clothing and possessions. It even has its own Web site: http://www.leftbehind.com. LaHaye and Jenkins also have written a Left Behind series for kids, but teen readers seem to gravitate to the series written for adults. **Adult**

Left Behind: A Novel of the Earth's Last Days. 1996. When passengers begin disappearing from pilot Ray Steele's plane, he begins to realize that something strange is happening, something big. In fact, Rapture has happened, and the apocalypse has begun.

Tribulation Force: The Continuing Drama of Those Left Behind. 1997. Ray Steele, one of those left behind, clings to his faith and establishes the Tribulation Force, a group of true believers, as Nicolae Carpathia, the antichrist, takes over the United Nations.

Nicolae: The Rise of Antichrist. 1998. The evil Nicolae creates a one-world religion and rules over the global community as Ray and his journalist friend Buck come to realize that Nicolae is the antichrist.

Soul Harvest: The World Takes Sides. 1999. After a devastating earthquake, Ray and Buck search the world for their families and struggle to survive.

Apollyon: The Destroyer Is Unleashed. 2000. As the Tribulation Force rallies in Jerusalem, Satan falls from heaven to open the bottomless pit and unleash a plague of locusts.

Assassins: The Great Tribulation Unfolds. 2000. Ray hatches a plan to assassinate the anitchrist.

The Indwelling: The Beast Takes Possession. 2001. The antichrist Nicolae has been assassinated—or has he? More prophecies come to pass as the second half of the tribulation period begins.

The Mark: The Beast Rules the World. 2001. The resurrection of the antichrist initiates a new world religion, Carpathianism. Followers are branded, and those who refuse will be killed.

Desecration: Antichrist Takes the Throne. 2002. Carpathia kills with bloody abandon and desecrates the temple in Jerusalem.

The Remnant: On the Brink of Armageddon. 2003. Nicolae Carpathia's bloodlust escalates, and when a million believers gather in Petra, the Global Community bombs the ancient city. Only a miracle can save them.

Armageddon: The Cosmic Battle of Ages. 2003. The Trib Force heads toward Armageddon, where the armies of the world are assembled on the eve of the second coming. The projected finale of the series is *Glorious Appearing,* planned for 2004.

Lewis, C. S. The Chronicles of Narnia. *MJS.* This classic series for all ages is often considered to be a Christian allegory. The magical land of Narnia is the setting of a wonder-filled fantasy adventure for all, where time moves at a different pace from that of our world. The series is listed here in order of internal chronology. *The Lion, the Witch, and the Wardrobe* was the first released. The books are annotated in the Alternate and Parallel Worlds section of Chapter 6, "Fantasy."

The Magician's Nephew. 1955.

The Lion, the Witch, and the Wardrobe. 1950.

The Horse and His Boy. 1954.

Prince Caspian. 1951.

The Voyage of the Dawn Treader. 1952.

The Silver Chair. 1953.

The Last Battle. 1956.

Historical

Morris, Lynn, and Gilbert Morris. Cheney Duvall MD series. This series is written for adults, but enjoyed by teens. Cheney Duvall graduates from medical school after the Civil War and ends up traveling all over the country when she can't find a position in a Pennsylvania hospital. **Adult**

> *The Stars for a Light*. 1994. Cheney is hired to accompany two hundred mail-order brides on their long sea voyage to Washington Territory.

> *Shadow of the Mountains*. 1994. Cheney journeys to the Ozarks to deliver the baby of a friend and encounters hostility and superstition.

> *A City Not Forsaken*. 1995. Cheney has an opportunity to practice in New York City. She arrives with her male nurse Shiloh Iron just before a deadly cholera epidemic erupts.

> *Toward the Sunrising*. 1996. On their way to New Orleans, Cheney and Shiloh become embroiled in the conflicts creating trouble in Charleston.

> *Secret Place of Thunder*. 1996. Cheney and Shiloh reach her great-aunts' plantation outside New Orleans to find them menaced by cult members.

> *In the Twilight, in the Evening*. 1997. Cheney takes a position in San Francisco at a hospital that refuses to treat the undesirables of the area, and then disaster strikes.

> *Island of the Innocent*. 1998. Cheney sails to Hawaii to try to convince Shiloh to return with her and ends up facing the dangers of Portuguese man-of-war, sharks, and an erupting volcano.

> *Driven with the Wind*. 2000. Shiloh proposes to Cheney on the long voyage back to New York, when she must defend herself from a revengeful plan.

Oke, Janette. Prairie Legacy. *MJS*. The story of Virginia, granddaughter of Marty and Clark Davis from Oke's Love Comes Softly series. **Adult**

> *The Tender Years*. 1997. Virginia, no longer a child and not yet a woman, finds much to admire in Jenny, the new girl at her school, and questions the restrictions her family places on her.

> *A Searching Heart*. 1999. Virginia graduates from high school as class valedictorian with college on the horizon.

> *A Quiet Strength*. 1999. Newlyweds Virginia and Jonathan take up residence with his grandmother while waiting for their own home to be built.

> *Like Gold Refined*. 2000. Virginia faces the possibility that daughter Mindy's birth mother may take her away and is saddened that her grandparents have grown too old to live on the farm.

Rivers, Francine. *The Last Sin Eater*. 1998. *S*. In 1850s Appalachia, ten-year-old Cadi becomes fascinated with the "sin eater," whom she encounters at her grandmother's gravesite.

Wick, Lori. Rocky Mountain Memories series. *JS.* Set in 1870s Colorado, this series is written for adults but enjoyed by teens.

> *Where the Wild Rose Blooms.* 1996. Clayton Taggart, a mine surveyor, yearns for life as a teacher when the strong-willed Jackie Fontaine enters his life.

> *Whispers of Moonlight.* 1996. To honor her dying father's last wish, Rebecca marries Travis.

> *To Know Her by Name.* 1997. Treasury Department agent McKay Harrington finds himself dependent on the mysterious Callie when he is wounded.

> *Promise Me Tomorrow.* 1997. Nineteen-year-old Katherine Taggart is hired by widower Chase McCandles to be a companion to his young son.

References

Mort, John. *Christian Fiction.* Westport, Conn.: Libraries Unlimited, 2002.

Appendix I

Resources

Since the 1997 publication of the first edition of *Teen Genreflecting,* many new resources have become available to help connect teens to books that they will enjoy. The following lists cover the more essential titles, with an asterisk (*) preceding the author name of "must-read" titles.

Working with Teens

Aronson, Marc. *Exploding the Myths: The Truth about Teenagers and Reading.* Scarecrow Press, 2001. A series of essays by a respected publishing authority on teens and reading.

*Chelton, Mary K. *Young Adult Services Professional Resources: A Selective Five-Year Retrospective Bibliography with Some "Classic" Exceptions.* 2001. Chelton's bibliography of resources (located at http://www.ala.org/yalsa/professional/index.html) is invaluable. It covers many resources useful to anyone providing library services to teens.

Edwards, Kirsten. *Teen Library Events: A Month by Month Guide.* Greenwood Press, 2001. Greenwood Professional Guides for Young Adult Librarians series.

*Jones, Patrick. *Connecting Young Adults and Libraries: A How to Do It Manual.* 2d ed. Neal Schuman, 1998.

Jones, Patrick. *New Directions for Library Service to Young Adults.* American Library Association, 2002.

Jones, Patrick, and Joel Shoemaker. *Do It Right: Best Practices for Serving Young Adults in School and Public Libraries.* Neal Schuman, 2001.

Kan, Katharine L. *Sizzling Summer Reading Programs for Young Adults.* American Library Association, 1998.

Leslie, Roger, and Patricia Potter Wilson. *Igniting the Spark: Library Programs that Inspire High School Patrons.* Libraries Unlimited, 2001.

Nichols, Mary Anne. *Merchandising Library Materials to Young Adults.* Libraries Unlimited, 2002. Libraries Unlimited Professional Guides for Young Adult Librarians series. A wealth of creative ideas for teen library areas, displays, and promoting library services and materials to teens.

Nichols, Mary Anne , and C. Allen Nichols, eds. *Young Adults and Public Libraries: A Handbook of Materials and Services.* Greenwood Press, 1998. A collection of thoughtful and inspiring essays written by such notable YA experts as Michael Cart, Lesley Farmer, Patrick Jones, and Tom Reynolds, covering topics that range from developing a core collection, YA nonfiction, and magazines, to merchandising, using technology, and homework assistance.

Sullivan, Edward T. *Reaching Reluctant Young Adult Readers: A Handbook for Librarians and Teachers.* Scarecrow Press, 2002. A brief look at reluctant readers and books for them.

Vaillancourt, Renee J. *Bare Bones: Young Adult Services Tips for Public Library Generalists.* Public Library Association/Young Adult Library Services Association, American Library Association, 2000.

Bibliographies of Books for Teens

Bodart, Joni Richards. *Radical Reads: 101 YA Novels on the Edge.* Scarecrow Press, 2002. The edgiest of the issue-related novels for teens are described and discussed with booktalks.

Bodart, Joni Richards. *The World's Best Thin Books: What to Read When Your Book Report Is Due Tomorrow.* Rev. ed. Scarecrow Press, 2000. Descriptions of one hundred novels for teens that are all less than two hundred pages. Indexed by subject, readability, author, title, and curriculum.

*Carter, Betty. *Best Books for Young Adults: The Selections, the History, the Romance.* 2d ed. American Library Association, 2000.

Holley, Pam Spencer. *What Do Young Adults Read Next: A Readers Guide to Fiction for Young Adults.* Volume 3. The Gale Group, 1999.

Makowski, Silk. *Serious about Series: Evaluations and Annotations of Teen Fiction in Paperback Series.* Scarecrow Press, 1998. More than fifty popular series from the 1990s are evaluated.

Online Resources

Web Sites

Center for Adolescent Reading http://www.teensread.org

Favorite Teen Angst Books http://www.grouchy.com/angst/

Genrefluent Page Reviews of Teen Books http://www.genrefluent.com/youngad.htm

Internet Public Library—Teen Space http://www.ipl.org/div/teen/

Reading Rants http://tln.lib.mi.us/~amutch/jen/

Richie's Picks http://www.richiespicks.com/

See Me 4 Books http://members.shaw.ca/betsyf/index.html

Teen Hoopla http://www.ala.org/teenhoopla/

Teenreads http://www.teenreads.com/

YALSA http://www.ala.org/yalsa/index.html

- **YALSA Winning Titles** http://www.ala.org/yalsa/booklists/index.html. The annual winners for the Alex Awards, Best Books for Young Adults, Margaret A. Edwards Award, Michael L. Printz Award, Outstanding Books for the College Bound, Popular Paperbacks, Quick Picks for Reluctant Young Adult Readers, Selected Audio Books, and Selected DVDs and Videos are listed.

- **Best of the Best Revisited: BoJo Jones and Beyond** http://www.ala.org/yalsa/booklists/bestofbest2000.html. Attendees of a YALSA preconference selected a list of the one hundred best books for teens published between 1966 and 2000.

- **Young Adult Librarians Homepage** http://yahelp.suffolk.lib.ny.us/

Discussion Groups

Adbooks is an online forum to discuss books written for teens. http://www.geocities.com/adbooks/

Alan, the Assembly on Literature for Adolescents, has an e-mail group that at the time of this writing is not very active. Subscription information and archives can be accessed at http://alan-ya.org/mailman/listinfo/alan-ya_alan-ya.org.

Teen Librarian is an online community for young adult librarians. It includes a slick online magazine, interviews, reviews, and articles of interest to librarians working with teens as well as discussion areas. http://www.teenlibrarian.com/

YALSA-BK is an e-mail discussion list: Send a message to listproc@ala.org. Leave the subject line blank. For the message, type "Subscribe YALSA-bk *first name last name*."

Other Professional Development Resources

ALAN (the Assembly on Literature for Adolescents) an NCTE (National Council of Teachers of English) special interest group holds a full-day workshop featuring numerous YA authors every year at the NCTE annual conference in November.

YALSA has a cadre of trainers available to assist those working with young adults in libraries. They are trained in seminars offered by YALSA as a part of the Serving the Underserved: Customer Services for Young Adults Project and have come to be known as the SUS trainers. The subjects they cover include adolescent development, reading interests, behavioral problems, youth participation, facilities, and computer services for teens.

The trainers have experience working with adult learners and are experts in the specialized field of young adult services.

YALSA offers a full slate of programs every year at the American Library Association annual conference. They also usually offer one or two preconferences lasting one to two days that cover a subject in depth. Recent preconferences have covered library services and materials for gay, lesbian, bisexual, and transsexual youth; science fiction and fantasy; poetry; and graphic novels.

Review Journals

ALAN Review. Produced by ALAN—the Assembly on Literature for Young Adults (http://www. alan-ya.org). Individual memberships for $20 annually include a subscription to the *ALAN* Review (three issues per year). Contact: ALAN Membership, National Council of Teachers of English, 1111 E. Kenyon, Urbana, Illinois 61801-1096

Booklist. Published twenty-two times a year. In addition to reviews of YA titles they do a short one-line annotation of why specific adult books will appeal to teens. Contact: P.O. Box 607, Mt. Morris, IL 61054-7564; Tel. (888) 350-0949

Bulletin of the Center for Children's Books. Published monthly except for August. Annual subscriptions are $70. Contact: University of Illinois Press, BCCB, 1325 S. Oak Street, Champaign, IL 61820

Horn Book. $29.95 for annual bimonthly subscription. Contact: http://www.hbook.com/index.shtml

Kirkus Children's Reviews. Contact: http://www.kirkusreviews.com/kirkusreviews/magazine/childrens.jsp

Kliatt. Reviews paperbacks and includes occasional short articles and bibliographies useful for working with teens. Six issues a year, each with approximately 250 reviews. Contact: kliatt@aol.com; 33 Bay State Road, Wellesley, MA 02121; Tel. (781) 237-7577

Library Journal. Contact: http://libraryjournal.reviewsnews.com/; P.O. Box 16027, North Hollywood, CA 91615-6027; Tel. (800) 588-1030

School Library Journal. Articles and reviews for librarians and media specialists, published monthly. Contact: http://slj.reviewsnews.com; P.O. Box 16388, North Hollywood, CA 91615-6388; Tel. (800) 595-1066 or (818) 487-4566

VOYA Voice of Youth Advocates. VOYA is an indispensable resource for reviews of YA titles and regularly reviews paperback originals. It also makes a distinct effort to provide good coverage of the adult science fiction and fantasy novels that teens read. Contact: http://www.voya.com/; e-mail voya@scarecrowpress.com; Scarecrow Press, 4720 Boston Way, Lanham, MD 20706; Tel. (888) 4VOYA97

Genre-Specific Resources

Alternative Formats

All the resources listed in this section pertain to graphic novels.

Comic Books for Young Adults http://ublib.buffalo.edu/libraries/units/lml/comics/pages/index.html

GNLIB – Graphic Novels in Libraries http://www.angelfire.com/comics/gnlib/

Graphic Novels in Libraries http://www.topica.com/lists/GNLIB-L

The Librarian's Guide to Anime and Manga http://www.koyagi.com/Libguide.html

No Flying, No Tights http://leep.lis.uiuc.edu/seworkspace/rebrennr/304LE/gn/index.html

Rothschild, D. Aviva. *Graphic Novels: A Bibliographic Guide to Book-Length Comics*. Englewood, Colo.: Libraries Unlimited, 1995.

Weiner, Stephen. *The 101 Best Graphic Novels*. New York: NBM Publishing, 2001.

Christian Fiction

Mort, John. *Christian Fiction: A Guide to the Genre*. Englewood, Colo.: Libraries Unlimited, 2002. A guide to Christian fiction arranged by subgenre and theme, with a chapter on young adult literature and adult titles that are popular with teens noted.

Fantasy

Herald, Diana Tixier. *Fluent in Fantasy*. Englewood, Colo.: Libraries Unlimited, 1999. A guide to fantasy arranged by subgenre. Teens read many of the same fantasy novels that adults do, making this is an invaluable tool to help teen fantasy readers.

Lynn, Ruth Nadelman. *Fantasy Literature for Children and Young Adults*. 4th ed. R. R. Bowker, 1995.

Historical Fiction

Adamson, Lynda. *Literature Connections to American History, 7–12: Resources to Enhance and Entice*. Englewood, Colo.: Libraries Unlimited, 1998.

Adamson, Lynda. *Literature Connections to World History, 7–12: Resources to Enhance and Entice*. Englewood, Colo.: Libraries Unlimited, 1998.

Multicultural

Barahona Center for the Study of Books in Spanish for Children and Adolescents http://www.csusm.edu/csb/english/center.htm

Helbig, Alethea K., and Agnes Regan Perkins. *Many Peoples, One Land: A Guide to New Multicultural Literature for Children and Young Adults*. Westport, Conn.: Greenwood Press, 2000. Covers five hundred of the multicultural books of fiction, oral tradition, and poetry dealing with African Americans, Asian Americans, Hispanic Americans, and Native Americans published for children and teens between 1994 and 1999.

Miller-Lachman, Lyn. *Global Voices, Global Visions: A Core Collection of Multicultural Books*. New Providence, N.J.: R. R. Bowker, 1995.

The Virginia Hamilton Conference focuses exclusively on multicultural literature for children and young adults. "Honoring author Virginia Hamilton, the conference reflects a commitment to promoting cultural awareness and affirming cultural pride while addressing the array of issues which surround the concept of culture." The conference is held each April at Kent State University in Kent, Ohio. http://dept.kent.edu/virginiahamiltonconf/

Science Fiction

Herald, Diana Tixier, and Bonnie Kunzel. *Strictly Science Fiction: A Guide to Reading Interests*. Westport, Conn.: Libraries Unlimited, 2002. A guide to science fiction arranged by genre with a chapter on science fiction published for teen readers.

Kunzel, Bonnie, and Suzanne Manczuk. *First Contact: A Reader's Selection of Science Fiction and Fantasy*. Lanham, Md.: Scarecrow Press, 2001. A readers' advisory tool to introduce teen readers to fantasy and science fiction with grade-related designations to help find appropriate books for middle school, junior high school, and senior high school readers.

YASFFA Young Adult Science Fiction and Fantasy discussion group: http://groups.yahoo.com/group/YASFFA/

Appendix II

Epic Fantasy

Many teens read and enjoy epic fantasy written for adults. This appendix lists series of interest to teen fantasy readers.

Brooks, Terry. Shannara series.

> *The Sword of Shannara.* 1977. (BBYA)
> *The Elfstones of Shannara.* 1982.
> *The Wishsong of Shannara.* 1985.

Heritage of Shannara series.

> *Scions of Shannara.* 1990.
> *Elfqueen of Shannara.* 1991.
> *Druid of Shannara.* 1992.
> *The Talismans of Shannara.* 1993.
> *First King of Shannara.* 1996.

Voyage of the Jerle Shannara series.

> *Ilse Witch.* 2000.
> *Antrax.* 2001
> *Morgawr.* 2002.

Dart-Thornton, Cecilia. Bitterbynde Chronicles.

> *The Ill-Made Mute.* 2001.
> *The Lady of the Sorrows.* 2002.
> *The Battle of Evernight.* 2003.

Douglass, Sara. The Wayfarer Redemption.

> *The Wayfarer Redemption.* 2001.
> *Enchanter.* 2001.
> *Starman.* 2002.

Eddings, David. The Belgariad series.

>*Pawn of Prophecy.* 1982.
>*Queen of Sorcery.* 1982.
>*Magician's Gambit.* 1983.
>*Castle of Wizardry.* 1984.
>*Enchanter's End Game.* 1984.

The Mallorean series. (Connected series to the Belgariad)

>*Guardians of the West.* 1987.
>*King of the Murgos.* 1988.
>*Demon Lord of Karanda.* 1988.
>*Sorceress of Darshiva.* 1989.
>*The Seeress of Kell.* 1991.

The Elenium series. (Connected series to the Belgariad)

>*Diamond Throne.* 1989.
>*Ruby Knight.* 1990.
>*Sapphire Rose.* 1992.

The Tamuli series. (Connected series to the Belgariad)

>*Domes of Fire.* 1992.
>*The Shining Ones.* 1993.
>*The Hidden City.* 1994.

Feist, Raymond. The Riftwar Saga. *S.*

>*Magician.* 1982. (Also released in two volumes as *Magician: Apprentice* and *Magician: Master*)
>*Silverthorn.* 1985.
>*A Darkness at Sethanon.* 1986.
>*Prince of the Blood.* 1989.

Riftwar Legacy.

>*Krondor, the Betrayal.* 1998.
>*Krondor, the Assassins.* 1999.
>*Krondor, Tear of the Gods.* 2001.

Haydon, Elizabeth. Rhapsody series.

>*Rhapsody: Child of Blood.* 2000.
>*Prophecy: Child of Earth.* 2001.
>*Destiny: Child of the Sky.* 2001.

Jordan, Robert. The Wheel of Time series. This series is so popular with teen readers that Tor has started reissuing some of the titles as part of their Starscape imprint, which is specifically targeted to children and younger young adult readers.

The Eye of the World. 1990. The reissue under Starscape imprint (2001) divided this into two books: *From the Two Rivers* and *To the Blight.* (BBYA)

The Great Hunt. 1990.

The Dragon Reborn. 1991.

The Shadow Rising. 1992.

The Fires of Heaven. 1992.

Lord of Chaos. 1994.

A Crown of Swords. 1996.

The Path of Daggers. 1998.

Winter's Heart. 2000.

Crossroads of Twilight. 2003.

Marillier, Juliet. Sevenwaters series.

Daughter of the Forest. 2000.

Son of the Shadows. 2001.

Child of the Prophecy. 2002.

Martin, George R. R. Song of Ice and Fire.

A Game of Thrones. 1996. (Locus Fantasy Award)

A Clash of Kings. 1999.

A Storm of Swords. 2000.

Weis, Margaret, and Tracy Hickman. The DragonLance Saga. A motley group of adventurers travels across the land to save it from evil. There are more than ninety titles in the DragonLance series, which was started by Margaret Weis and Tracy Hickman in 1985. There are many subseries written by a number of authors. The titles listed here are written by Weis and Hickman.

DragonLance Chronicle

Dragons of Autumn Twilight. 1984.

Dragons of Winter Night. 1985.

Dragons of Spring Dawning. 1985.

DragonLance Legends

Time of the Twins. 1986.

War of the Twins. 1986.

Test of the Twins. 1986.

War of Souls Trilogy

Dragons of a Fallen Sun. 2001.

Dragons of a Lost Star. 2002.

Dragons of a Vanished Moon. 2003.

Williams, Tad. Memory, Sorrow and Thorn.

The Dragonbone Chair. 1988.
The Stone of Farewell. 1990.
To Green Angel Tower. 1993.

Appendix III

Genre Fiction for Reluctant Readers

Many reluctant readers have adequate or even good reading skills, but for reasons of their own, they do not read. The titles listed here are novels (and a couple of short story collections) that are annotated in this book and that appeal to teen readers who do not consider reading a favorite activity. Most of them have appeared on YALSA's Quick Picks for Reluctant Young Adult Readers. They are arranged by genre, chronologically according to this guide's chapter arrangement. Some of the titles may be listed in more than one chapter. To locate annotations for specific titles, please consult the author and title indexes.

Many of the titles on the Quick Picks lists are nonfiction, and because this guide covers only fiction, those titles are not included here. Remember that not all reluctant readers enjoy reading fiction—many prefer nonfiction or magazines. To find nonfiction suggestions for reluctant readers please consult the Quick Picks lists at the YALSA Web site.

Issues

Alphin, Elaine Marie. *Counterfeit Son*

Anderson, Laurie Halse. *Speak*

Arnoldi, Katherine. *The Amazing True Story of a Teenage Single Mom*

Atkins, Catherine. *When Jeff Comes Home*

Bechard, Margaret. *Hanging on to Max*

Bennett, Cherie. *Life in the Fat Lane*

Block, Francesca Lia. *I Was a Teenage Fairy*; *Violet & Claire*

Bunting, Eve. *Blackwater*

Cart, Michael, ed. *Love & Sex*

Cole, Brock. *The Facts Speak for Themselves*

Cooney, Caroline B. *Burning Up*

Ferris, Jean. *Bad*

Flinn, Alex. *Breathing Underwater*

Frank, E. R. *Life Is Funny; America*

Fraustino, Lisa Rowe, ed. *Dirty Laundry: Stories about Family Secrets*

Giles, Gail. *Shattering Glass*

Glovach, Linda. *Beauty Queen*

Goobie, Beth. *Sticks and Stones*

Grant, Cynthia D. *The White Horse*

Griffin, Adele. *Amandine*

Haddix, Margaret Peterson. *Don't You Dare Read This, Mrs. Dunphrey*

Hobbs, Will. *The Maze*

Jenkins, A. M. *Breaking Boxes*

Koertge, Ron. *The Brimstone Journals; Stoner & Spaz: A Love Story*

Koss, Amy Goldman. *The Girls*

Lester, Julius. *When Dad Killed Mom*

McCormick, Patricia. *Cut*

McDaniel, Lurlene. *Till Death Do Us Part; Angel of Mercy; The Girl Death Left Behind*

McNamee, Graham. *Hate You*

Peck, Richard. *The Last Safe Place on Earth*

Rottman, S. L. *Rough Waters*

Sones, Sonya. *What My Mother Doesn't Know; Stop Pretending*

Soto, Gary. *Buried Onions*

Sparks, Beatrice, ed. *Go Ask Alice; Treacherous Love: The Diary of an Anonymous Teenager*

Stratton, Allan. *Leslie's Journal*

Trueman, Terry. *Stuck in Neutral*

Wallace, Rich. *Playing without a Ball*

Warner, Sally. *Sort of Forever*

Wersba, Barbara. *Whistle Me Home*

Williams, Carol Lynch. *The True Colors of Caitlynne Jackson*

Wittlinger, Ellen. *Hard Love*

Contemporary Life

Bauer, Joan. *Rules of the Road*

Black, Jonah. *Girls, Girls, Girls; Stop, Don't Stop*

Carter, Alden R. *Bull Catcher*

Chbosky, Stephen. *The Perks of Being a Wallflower*

Cohn, Rachel. *Gingerbread*

Craft, Elizabeth. *Show Me Love*

Dessen, Sarah. *Keeping the Moon*

Eberhardt, Thom. *Rat Boys: A Dating Experiment*

Korman, Gordon. *Son of the Mob*

Lynch, Chris. *Slot Machine*

MacDougal, Scarlett. *Start Here; Play*; *Popover; Score*

Mackler, Carolyn. *Love and Other Four-Letter Words*

McCants, William D. *Much Ado about Prom Night*

Noonan, Rosalind. *Any Guy You Want*

Qualey, Marsha. *Revolutions of the Heart*

Roberts, Christa. *For Real*

Staub, Wendy Corsi. *More than This*

Sweeney, Joyce. *Players*

Thomas, Rob. *Doing Time*; *Rats Saw God*

Adventure

Bell, William. *Death Wind*

Cooney, Caroline B. *The Terrorist*

Hoh, Diane. *Titanic: The Long Night*

Horowitz, Anthony. *Stormbreaker*

Lawrence, Iain. *Buccaneers*; *The Smugglers*

Paulsen, Gary. *Hatchet; Brian's Return; Brian's Winter*

Sacher, Louis. *Holes*

Smith, Roland. *Sasquatch*

Yolen, Jane, and Bruce Coville. *Armageddon Summer*

Mystery and Suspense

Avi. *Midnight Magic*

Chandler, Elizabeth. *Don't Tell; Legacy of Lies; No Time to Die*

Cooney, Caroline B. *Hush Little Baby; Wanted*

Cray, Jordan. *Gemini7*

Duncan, Lois. *Gallows Hill*

Golden, Christopher. *Meets the Eye*

Qualey, Marsha. *Close to a Killer; Thin Ice*

Smith, Roland. *Zach's Lie*

Werlin, Nancy. *The Killer's Cousin*

Fantasy

Applegate, K. A. *Search for Senna*; *Land of Loss*; *Enter the Enchanted*; *Realm of the Reaper*

Coville, Bruce. *Into the Land of the Unicorns*

Haddix, Margaret Peterson. *Just Ella*

Levine, Gail Carson. *Ella Enchanted*

Pierce, Tamora. *Tris's Book*

Pullman, Philip. *Clockwork*

Shusterman, Neal. *Downsiders*

Science Fiction

Gilmore, Kate. *The Exchange Student*

Haddix, Margaret Peterson. *Among the Imposters*

Hogan, James P. *Bug Park*

Kaye, Marilyn. *Amy, Number Seven*; *The Vanishing*

Logue, Mary. *Dancing with an Alien*

Lubar, David. *Hidden Talents*

Paulsen, Gary. *The Transall Saga*

Shusterman, Neal. *Scorpion Shards; The Dark Side of Nowhere*

Singleton, L. J. *Regeneration; The Search; The Truth*

Sleator, William. *Boltzmon!; Rewind; The Boxes*

Paranormal

Anderson, M. T. *Thirsty*

Atwater-Rhodes, Amelia. *Demon in My View; In the Forests of the Night; Shattered Mirror*

Bennett, Cherie. *Love Him Forever; The Haunted Heart*

Bird, Isobel. *So Mote It Be; Merry Meet; Second Sight; What the Cards Said; In the Dreaming; Ring of Light; Blue Moon*

Ewing, Lynne. *Party Girl; Goddess of the Night; Into the Cold Fire*

Klause, Annette Curtis. *Blood and Chocolate*

Metz, Melinda. *Gifted Touch; Haunted; Trust Me; Secrets*

Naylor, Phyllis Reynolds. *Jade Green*

Nixon, Joan Lowery. *The Haunting; Who Are You?*

Sleator, William. *The Beasties*

Tiernan, Cate. *The Coven; Blood Witch; Dark Magick; Awakening*

Vande Velde, Vivian. *Companions of the Night; Curses, Inc. and Other Stories; Ghost of a Hanged Man; Never Trust a Dead Man*

Windsor, Patricia. *The Blooding*

Zindel, Paul. *Night of the Bat; Rats; Reef of Death*

Historical

Cormier, Robert. *Heroes*

Hobbs, Will. *Jason's Gold*

Paulsen, Gary. *Soldier's Heart; Sarny*

Multicultural

Cofer, Judith Ortiz. *An Island Like You*

Flake, Sharon G. *The Skin I'm In*

Herrera, Juan Felipe. *Crashboomlove: A Novel in Verse*

Soto, Gary. *Buried Onions; Petty Crimes*

Williams-Garcia, Rita. *Like Sisters on the Homefront*

Alternative Formats

Appelt, Kathi. *Kissing Tennessee and Other Stories from the Stardust Dance*

Bendis, Brian-Michael. *Ultimate Spider-Man Power and Responsibility*

Cabot, Meg. *The Princess Diaries; Princess in the Spotlight*

Conford, Ellen. *Crush*

Danziger, Paula, and Ann P. Martin. *P.S. Longer Letter Later; Snail Mail No More*

David, Peter. *Spyboy: The Deadly Gourmet Affair*

Ellis, Warren. *StormWatch: Force of Nature*

Glenn, Mel. *Foreign Exchange: A Mystery in Poems; Who Killed Mr. Chippendale?*

Grimes, Nikki. *Bronx Masquerade*

Herrera, Juan Felipe. *Crashboomlove: A Novel in Verse*

Morrison, Grant. *JLA: Earth 2*

Myers, Walter Dean. *145th Street: Short Stories; Monster; Slam!*

Rennison, Louise. *Angus, Thongs, and Full-Frontal Snogging: Confessions of Georgia Nicolson; On the Bright Side, I'm Now the Girlfriend of a Sex God: Further Confessions of Georgia Nicholson*

Scott, Jerry, and Jim Borgman. *Are We an "Us"?*

Tezuka, Osamu. *Black Jack*

Veitch, Tom, and Cam Kennedy. *Star Wars: Dark Empire*

Title Index

A Is for AARRGH!, 153
Abandoned, 189
Abarat, 106
Abhorsen, 100
Absolutely Normal Chaos, 58, 173
Achingly Alice, 62
Acquaintance with Darkness, An, 144
Adventures of Barry Ween, Boy Genius, The, 177
Adventures of Blue Avenger, The, 59
Adventures of Midnight Son, The, 147, 163
After the War, 157
Aimee, 33
Ajeemah and His Son, 157
Akiko: The Menace of Alia Rellapor, 182
ALAN Review, 6, 196
Alex Rider series, 68
Alice Alone, 62
Alice on the Outside, 62
Alice Rose and Sam, 78
Alice series, 62
All about Andy, 126
All American Girl, 52, 58
All I Want Is Everything, 63
Am I Blue?, 23
Amanda/Miranda, 149
Amandine, 38, 204
Amazing Maurice and His Educated Rodents, The, 96, 104
Amazing True Story of a Teenage Single Mom, The, 34, 178, 203
Amber Spyglass, The, 108
America, 36, 40, 204
American Gods, 133
Among the Betrayed, 122
Among the Hidden, 122
Among the Imposters, 122, 206
Amy, Number Seven, 124, 206
Amy, on Her Own, 126
And It Harm None, 136
And the Two Shall Meet, 125
Angel Factory, The, 120
Angel of Mercy, 19, 204
Angel on the Square, 158
Angels on the Roof, 49
Angels Turn Their Backs, 20, 79, 128
Angus, Thongs, and Full-Frontal Snogging: Confessions of Georgia Nicolson, 174, 207
Anna of Byzantium, 153
Anne Frank and Me, 109

Annie on My Mind, 23, 52, 53
Another Amy, 124
Anthrax, 199
Any Guy You Want, 63, 205
Apollyon: The Destroyer Is Unleashed, 190
April and Mark Duet, 19
Aquamarine, 90
Arctic Incident, The, 89
Are We an "Us"? A Zits Collection Sketchbook, 184, 207
Aria of the Sea, 106
Armageddon: The Cosmic Battle of Ages, 190
Armageddon Summer, 71, 205
Art of Keeping Cool, The, 151
Artemis Fowl, 89
Artemis Fowl series, 89
Arthur Blessing series, 92
Arthur Trilogy, 92
Arthurian series, 92
Ascension, 106
Ascent, 182
Ashes of Roses, 149
Assassins: The Great Tribulation Unfolds, 190
At the Crossing Places, 92
At the Sign of the Star, 155
Athletic Shorts: Six Short Stories, 55
Austere Academy, The, 96
Avon True Romance series, 140
Awakening, 137, 206

Baby Be-Bop, 23, 90
Baby Help, 25, 35
Babylon Boyz, 29, 33
Backwater, 46
Bad, 30, 203
Bad Beginning, The, 96
Bad Intent, 80
Ballad of Sir Dinaden, The, 92
Bart Simpson's Treehouse of Horror Spine-Tingling Spooktacular, 183
Bat, 6, 151
Batman: The Dark Knight Returns, 180
Batman: The Long Halloween, 180
Battle of Evernight, The, 199
Beast, 94
Beasties, The, 130, 206
Beatnik Rutabagas from beyond the Stars, 116
Beauty, 94
Beauty Queen, 42, 204

Beetle and Me: A Love Story, The, 54
Before We Were Free, 164
Before Wings, 90
Beginning, The, 125
Beguilers, The, 121, 122
Behaving Bradley, 60
Being Dead, 138
Being with Henry, 40
Belgariad Series, 200
Bellmaker, The, 103
Best Books for Young Adults, 13
Best Friend, Worst Enemy, 188
Best of the Best, The, 125
Bet Your Life, 179
Betrayed, 132, 189
Better than Running at Night, 48
Beware, Princess Elizabeth, 155
Beyond the Western Sea series, 155
Big Book of the Unexplained, The, 133, 181
Big Burn, The, 149
Big Mouth & Ugly Girl, 39
Billion Dollar Boy, 113
Birchbark House, The, 141
Birds of Prey, 180
Bitterbynde Chronicles, 199
Black Book: Diary of a Teenage Stud, The, 12, 61,
         172, 173
Black Book, The, 12, 61, 172, 173
Black Jack, 183, 207
Black Mirror, 161
Black Panther: The Client, 180
Blackwater, 18, 203
Blood and Chocolate, 130, 206
Blood of Ten Chiefs, 182
Blood Trail, 75
Blood Witch, 137, 206
Blooding, The, 130, 207
Bloomability, 47
Blue Lawn, The, 24
Blue Moon, 136, 206
Blue Star Rapture, 55
Blue Sword, The, 99
Body of Christopher Creed, The, 77
Body of Evidence, 81
Boltzmon!, 115, 206
Bomb Appetite, 180
Bone: Out from Boneville, 184
Bone Dance, 46, 166
Bones in the Cliff, The, 72
Book of Enchantments, 98
Book of Fred, 40, 71
Book of Shadows, 137
Booklist, 6, 49, 196
Books of Magic, The, 181
Booktalker's Bible, The, 11, 14
Booktalking across the Curriculum, 11, 14
Borden Tragedy, The, 178
Born Blue, 32, 41
Born Confused, 163
Born in Sin, 55, 162

Borrowed Light, 25
Boston Jane: An Adventure, 144
Both Sides of Time, 109
Bouncing off the Moon, 113
Boxer, The, 144
Boxes series, 117
Boxes, The, 118, 206
Boy in the Burning House, The, 77
Brain Trust, 81
Brave the Betrayal, 105
Breadwinner, The, 167
Breaking Boxes, 23, 204
Breaking Point, 30, 31
Breaking Rank, 54
Breaking Through, 165
Breathing Underwater, 34, 204
Brian series, 68
Brian's Return, 68, 205
Brian's Winter, 68, 205
Briar Rose, 95
Briar's Book, 87
Brides of Eden, 149
Brimstone Journals, The, 39, 176, 204
Brio Girls series, 186
Broken Promises, 186
Broken Sword, The, 92
Bronx Masquerade, 207
Brothers, 71
Buccaneers, The, 67, 70, 205
Bud, Not Buddy, 40, 149
Buffalo Tree, 37
Buffy the Vampire Slayer: Ring of Fire, 181
Buffy the Vampire Slayer: The Origin, 177
Bug Park, 114, 206
Bull Catcher, 55, 204
Bulletin of the Center for Children's Books, 196
Bull Run, 146
Bulletin of the Center for Children's Books, 6, 196
Buried Onions, 33, 165, 204, 207
Burning Bones, 81
Burning for Revenge, 67
Burning Up, 26, 28, 203
"Buy More Books," 9, 13

Caged Eagles, 158
California Christmas, 188
California Crazy, 188
California Diaries series, 174
Call Me Francis Tucket, 147
Calling on Dragons, 97
Calling, The, 137
Camouflage, 71
Cannibals: Starring Tiffany Spratt, The, 59
Can't Let Go, 63
*Captain Nemo: The Fantastic History of a Dark
         Genius*, 155
Captives of Blue Mountain, 181
Carnivorous Carnival, The, 97

Cartoon History of the Universe II: From the Springtime of China to the Fall of Rome, The, 178
Case of the Goblin Pearls, The, 77, 164
Castle of Wizardry, 200
Castle Waiting: The Lucky Road, 181
Cat in Glass and Other Tales of the Unnatural, 138
Catalyst, 46
Catcher in the Rye, 37, 39
Catherine, Called Birdy, 172
Cedar River Daydreams series, 61, 186
Challenge Box, The, 136
Changeling, 137
Charlie's Run, 66
Charlie's Story, 38
Chasing Redbird, 47
Checkers, 37
Cheney Duvall MD series, 191
Cherokee Bat and the Goat Guys, 90
Chief's Howl, 182
Child of the Prophecy, 201
China Garden, The, 89
Chinese Handcuffs, 35
Choice, The, 131
Choosing Up Sides, 150
Christian Fiction, 4, 14, 185, 192, 197
Chronicles of Narnia, The, 107, 190
Chuck Farris and the Tower of Darkness, 114
Circle of Magic, 87, 88
Circle of Three series, 3, 135
Circle Opens, The, 88
Circuit: Stories from the Life of a Migrant Child, The, 165
Cirque Du Freak series, 135
City Not Forsaken, A, 191
City of the Beasts, 89
Clan Apis, 178
Clash of Kings, A, 201
Claws, 33
Clockwork, 95, 206
Clones, The, 114, 115, 126
Close to a Killer, 77, 205
Cockatrice Boys, The, 98
Code Name Cassandra, 80
Coffin Quilt: The Feud between the Hatfields and the McCoys, The, 144
Cold Fire, 88, 131, 205
Color of Magic, The, 96
Comfort, 31
Companions of the Night, 135, 206
Compass in the Blood, 77
Conditions of Love, 50
Confess-O-Rama, 59
Connecting Young Adults and Libraries, 2, 6, 11, 14, 193
Copper Elephant, 124
Coral Coffin, The, 81
Coraline, 133
"Cottage by the Sea, The," 138
Counterfeit Son, 42, 203

Court Duel, 100
Courtesan's Daughter, The, 153
Coven, The, 137, 206
Cowboy Ghost, 148
Crashboomlove: A Novel in Verse, 165, 207
Crazy Jack, 95
Crazy Loco, 165
Crossing Jordan, 28
Crossing the Panther's Path, 141, 161
Crossroads of Twilight, 201
Crown and the Court Duet, 99
Crown Duel, 99
Crown of Swords, A, 201
Crusader, 28, 38
Crush, 207
Cry from Beyond, The, 182
Crystal Cave, 93
Crystal Mask, 88
Crystal Prison, The, 104
Cuba 15, 165
Cure, The, 118
Curses, Inc. and Other Stories, 138, 206
Cut, 21, 204
Cyberspace series, 116
Cyborg from Earth, The, 114

Daja's Book, 87
Damage, 21, 57
Damar series, 98, 99
Dance for Three, A, 22, 25
Dancing in My Nuddypants: Even Further Confessions of Georgia Nicolson, 174
Dancing Naked, 25
Dancing on the Edge, 21
Dancing with an Alien, 120, 206
Danger Zone, 57, 69
Danger.Com series, 80
Dangerous Angels: The Weetzie Bat Books, 89
Daniel's Walk, 148
Dare, Truth, or Promise, 52
Daredevil Visionaries V, 180
Dark Garden, The, 128
Dark Light, The, 156
Dark Lord of Derkholm, 100
Dark Magick, 137, 206
Dark Portal, The, 104
Dark Secrets series, 80, 131
Dark Shade, 109, 142
Darkangel, The, 135
Darkness at Sethanon, A, 200
Darkness Be My Friend, 67
Darkness before Dawn, 35
Daughter of the Forest, 94, 201
Dave at Night, 41, 150
David Copperfield, 46
Dead Man's Hand, 80
Dead of Night, The, 67
Deadly Gourmet Affair, The, 179
Deal with a Ghost, 129, 132
Dealing with Dragons, 97

Dear America series, 140, 172
Dear Canada series, 172
Death: The High Cost of Living, 181
Death on the Amazon, 83
Death Wind, 71, 205
Deathwatch, 68
Deceived, 188
Deep Wizardry, 107
Demon in My View, 134, 206
Demon in the Teahouse, The, 78
Demon Lord of Karanda, 200
Deptford Mice Trilogy, 104
Derkholm series, 100
Desecration: Antichrist Takes the Throne, 190
Desire Lines, 23
Desperate Measures, 189
Destiny: Child of the Sky, 200
Detour for Emmy, 25
Devil and His Boy, The, 78, 155
Diamond in the Dust, A, 149
Diamond Throne, 200
Diary of a Teenage Stud, 61, 172, 173
Diary of a Young Girl, The, 156
Dinotopia: A Land apart from Time, 107
Dirty Laundry: Stories about Family Secrets, 32, 204
Disappearance, The, 76
Discover the Destroyer, 105
Discovery, The, 187
Discworld series, 96
Divine Wind, A Love Story, The, 157
Do It Right: Best Practices for Serving Young Adults in School and Public Libraries, 193
Dogland, 90, 152
Doing Time, 205
Dollmage, The, 100
Domes of Fire, 200
Don't Tell, 80, 131, 205
Don't You Dare Read This, Mrs. Dunphrey, 32, 173, 204
Door Near Here, A, 22
Double Exposure: Real Faith Meets Real Life, 186
Dovey Coe, 78
Down the Yukon, 72, 144
Downriver, 66
Downriver Duo, 66
Downsiders, 90, 206
Dr. Franklin's Island, 124
Dragon Reborn, The, 201
Dragonball, 183
Dragonbone Chair, The, 202
Dragondrums, 120
DragonLance Chronicles, 201
DragonLance Legends, 201
DragonLance Saga, 201
Dragons of a Fallen Sun, 201
Dragons of a Lost Star, 201
Dragons of Autumn Twilight, 201
Dragons of a Vanished Moon, 201
Dragons of Spring Dawning, 201

Dragons of Winter Night, 201
Dragon's Son, The, 93
Dragonsinger, 120
Dragonsong, 119
Dream Country, 181
Dreamcrusher, 125
Dreamland, 34
Dream's End, 182
Dreams of Mairhe Mehan, The, 143, 146
Dreamtime, 182
Drive, 51
Drive Me Crazy, 54
Driven with the Wind, 191
Druid of Shannara, 199
Dust Devils, 147
Dying to Win, 189

Eagles series, 158
Ear, the Eye and the Arm, The, 119
Earth Kitchen, The, 37
Earthshine, 19
"Echo-Boom May Keep U.S. Booming," 1, 6
Echorium Sequence, 88
Eclipse, 138
Eclipse of Moonbeam Dawson, The, 50
Edge, 20
Eight Is Enough, 188
Eight Seconds, 23
Electric Girl, 179
Elenium series, 200
Elfqueen of Shannara, 199
Elfquest, 181
Elfstones of Shannara, The, 199
Ella Enchanted, 94, 206
Elvenbane, 102
Elvenblood, 102
Elvenborn, 102
Elvin series, 59
E-Mail Murders, The, 82
Emma, 46
Empress of the World, 24
Enchanted Forest Chronicles, 97, 98
Enchanted Hearts series, 3, 128, 132
Enchanter, 199
Enchanter's End Game, 200
Enchantment, 93
Ender series, 112
Ender's Game, 112
Ender's Shadow, 112, 113
Enter the Enchanted, 105, 206
Entertain the End, 106
Ersatz Elevator, The, 97
Escape from Home, The, 155
Eternity Code, The, 89
Eugenides series, 88
Eva, 114
Everworld, 105
Every Time a Rainbow Dies, 51, 161
Evvy's Civil War, 146

*Excellence in Library Services to Young Adults:
    The Nation's Top Programs*, 9, 13
Exchange Student, The, 120, 206
*Exploding the Myths: The Truth about Teenagers
    and Reading*, 193
Extreme Elvin, 60
Eye of the World, The, 201

Face on the Milk Carton series, 43
Face on the Milk Carton, The, 43, 47
Facts Speak for Themselves, The, 35, 203
Fade, 119
Faerie Wars, 106
Falcon and Egg series, 102
Falcon and the Charles Street Witch, 102
Falcon's Egg, 102
Fallen Angels, 152, 163
Fallout, 63
Fantasy Literature for Children and Young Adults, 197
Far North, 66
Fast Forward, 126
Fast Forward to Normal, 186
Faster, Faster, Faster, 61
Fear the Fantastic, 105
Feed, 122
Feeling Sorry for Celia, 60, 175
Fever, 1793, 142
Fever, The, 125, 142
Fighting Ruben Wolfe, 33
Fill My Empty Heart, 186
Final Reckoning, The, 104
Finding Hattie, 145
Fingerprints, 132
Finnegan Zwake Mysteries, 80
Fire and Flight, 181
Fire and Fog, 149
Fire Arrow, 87
Fire, Bed & Bone, 154
Fire Bringer, 103
Firegold, 106
Fires of Heaven, The, 201
Firesong, 87
Firestorm, 80
Fire-Us Trilogy, 122
*First Contact: A Reader's Selection of Science
    Fiction and Fantasy*, 198
First King of Shannara, 199
First Part Last, The, 25
First Test, 99
Five Paths, The, 136
Flight of the Raven, 69, 71, 120
Flipped, 51
Flood, 32
Fluent in Fantasy, 86, 110, 197
Flyers, 59
Focus, 121
Following Fake Man, 76
For All Time, 109
For Better, for Worse, Forever, 19
For Mike, 43

For Real, 63, 205
For the Love of Venice, 27
Forbidden Forest, 91
Forbidden Grove, The, 181
Force Majeure, 113
Foreign Exchange, 207
Foreign Exchange: A Mystery in Poems, 76, 175
Forever, 52
Forever Friends, 187
Forever King, The, 92
Forevergreen, 182
Forged by Fire, 31, 162
Forgotten, 189
Forgotten Fire, 157
Fortune, 6
Freak the Mighty, 17, 72
Freewill, 49
Frenchtown Summer, 175
Fresh Girl, 36, 167
Freshmen Frenzy, 188
Frog Princess of Pelham, The, 58, 96
*From Romance to Realism: 50 Years of Growth and
    Change in Young Adult Literature*, 2, 13
From the Ashes, 189
From the Dust Returned, 132
From the Two Rivers, 201
Full Circle, 138

Gabriel's Story, 147
Gadget, The, 151
Gallows Hill, 79, 131, 205
Game, The, 22
Game of Thrones, A, 201
Garden, The, 157
Gateway to the Gods, 105
Gathering Blue, 122
Geisha, 183
Gemini7, 80, 205
*Gentleman Outlaw and Me-Eli: A Story of the Old
    West*, 148
Geography Club, 39
Georgia Nicholson series, 60, 172
Get It While It's Hot. Or Not, 25
Getting Near to Baby, 18
Ghost Boy, 41
Ghost Canoe, 72, 144
Ghost in the Tokaido Inn, 78
Ghost of a Chance, 129
Ghost of a Hanged Man, 129, 206
Ghost Soldier, 128
Ghostworld, 178
Gifted Touch, 132, 206
Gingerbread, 47, 90, 204
Girl Death Left Behind, The, 19, 204
Girl Gives Birth to Own Prom Date, 54
Girl in a Cage, 155
Girl in Blue, 146
Girl of Kosovo, 70, 167
Girl with a Pearl Earring, 155
GirlHearts, 19

Girls, The, 39, 204
Girls, Girls, Girls, 61, 204
Girls Got Game: Sports Stories and Poems, 56
Girls in Love, 54, 63
Girls out Late, 64
Girls Trilogy, 54, 63
Girls under Pressure, 64
Give a Boy a Gun, 39, 170
Giver, The, 122
*Global Voices, Global Visions: A Core Collection
    of Multicultural Books,* 198
Go!, 62
Go and Come Back, 166
Go Ask Alice, 42, 170, 174, 204
Goblin Wood, The, 98
God of Beer, 27
Goddess of the Night, 206
Goddess of the Night series, 3
Goddess of Yesterday, 91
Gold Dust, 152, 161
Golden Compass, The, 108
*Gonick's the Cartoon History of the Universe III:
    From the Rise of Arabia to the Renaissance,*
    178
Good Moon Rising, 53
Good Night, Mr. Tom, 156
Good-Bye Chunky Rice, 177
Good-Bye, Dressel Hills, 188
Good-Bye to All That, 186
Goose Chase, 94
Gospel According to Larry, 27
Gossip Girl, 63
Gourmet Zombie, The, 83
Graduation of Jake Moon, The, 19
*Graphic Novels: A Bibliographic Guide to
    Book-Length Comics,* 177, 184, 197
Grasping at Moonbeams, 186
Grave, The, 109
Grave Matters, 189
Great Hunt, The, 201
Great Interactive Dream Machine, The, 116
Great Turkey Walk, The, 148
Greater than Angels, 156
Green Angel, 123
Green Arrow: Quiver, 180
Green Man: Tales from the Mythic Forest, The, 97
Groo and Rufferto, 177
Grooming of Alice, The, 62
Growler's Horn, 81
Guardians of the West, 200
Gypsy Rizka, 96

Habibi, 161
Halfblood Chronicles, 102
Half-Human, 91, 97
Halfway to the Sky, 18
Handbook for Boys: A Novel, 50
*Hang a Thousand Trees with Ribbons: The Story of
    Phillis Wheatley,* 143
Hanging on to Max, 25, 203

Happy Birthday, Dear Amy, 125
Hard Love, 24, 204
Harlem Beat, 183
Harper Hall Trilogy, 119
Harry Potter and the Chamber of Secrets, 101
Harry Potter and the Goblet of Fire, 101
Harry Potter and the Order of the Phoenix, 101
Harry Potter and the Philosopher's Stone, 101
Harry Potter and the Prisoner of Azkaban, 101
Harry Potter and the Sorcerer's Stone,
Harry Potter series, 85, 100
Hatchet, 65, 68, 205
Hate You, 34, 204
Haunted, 132, 206
Haunted Heart, The, 128, 206
Haunting, The, 79, 129, 206
Have a Nice Life series, 62
Haveli, 28, 168
Head above Water, 36, 57
Head Games, 81
Heart & Soul, 22
Heartless Hero, 187
Heaven Eyes, 89
"Hello," I Lied, 24
Here There Be Ghosts, 129
Heritage of Shannara series, 199
Hermit Thrush Sings, The, 123
Hero, 41
Hero Ain't Nothin' but a Sandwich, A, 42
Hero and the Crown, The, 99
Heroes, 150, 207
Hero's Song, 87
Hidden City, The, 200
Hidden Secrets, 68
Hidden series, 122
Hidden Talents, 119, 131, 206
High Seas Trilogy, 69
High Wizardry, 107
Higher Education, 114
His Dark Materials, 108
History of the Universe, 178
Hitchhikers, The, 138
Hitchhiker's Guide to the Galaxy, The, 115
Hitchhiker's Trilogy, 115
Holding up the Earth, 170
Hole in the Sky, 123
Hole in the World, A, 48
Holes, 37, 60, 72, 205
Hollow Hills, The, 93
Holly's First Love, 188
Holly's Heart series, 62, 187
Homeless Bird, 168
Hooked on Horror, 128, 138
Hoot, 59
Hope Was Here, 58
Hope's Crossing, 142
Horizontal Man, The, 80
Horn Book, 6, 196
Horse and His Boy, The, 108, 190
Hostage, 74

Hostile Hospital, The, 97
Hot Picks, 8
Hot Pursuit, 80
House of Stairs, 75
House of the Scorpion, The, 124
House of Winter, The, 136
House You Pass on the Way, The, 162
How I Created My Perfect Prom Date, 54
How I Spent My Last Night on Earth, 60
How to Be a Real Person (in Just One Day), 22
Howl's Moving Castle, 85, 96
Hunting of the Last Dragon, The, 99
Huntress, 182
Hush, 39
Hush Little Baby, 75, 205

I.D., 117
I Am Mordred: A Tale from Camelot, 93
I Am Morgan le Fay, 93
I Am series, 93
I Hadn't Meant to Tell You This, 36
I Want to Buy a Vowel: A Novel of Illegal Alienation, 61
I Was a Teenage Fairy, 35, 93, 203
Ice Cold, 125
If Rock and Roll Were a Machine, 4, 48
Ill-Made Mute, The, 199
Ilse Witch, 199
Imposter, The, 126
In a Dark Wood, 91
In Search of Andy, 125
In the Dreaming, 136, 206
In the Forests of the Night, 134, 206
In the Stone Circle, 129
In the Twilight, in the Evening, 191
In Too Deep, 189
Indispensable Calvin and Hobbes: A Calvin and Hobbes Treasury, The, 184
Indwelling: The Beast Takes Possession, The, 190
Initiation, 136
Inside Out, 22
Inside the Illusion, 105
Inside the Walls of Troy, 154
Into the Land of the Unicorns, 102, 206
Intruder, The, 186
Ironman, 56
Island, 117
Island Like You, An, 164, 207
Island of the Innocent, 191
Islander, The, 134

Jack the Ripper: A Journal of the Whitechapel Murders 1888–1889, 178
Jackie's Wild Seattle, 26
Jacob Have I Loved, 151
Jade Green, 79, 133, 134, 206
Jake's Orphan, 40, 149
James Printer: A Novel of Rebellion, 142
Janey's Girl, 48
Jason series, 72, 144

Jason's Gold, 72, 144, 207
Jennie McGrady Mystery series, 82, 188
Jennifer's Secret, 186
Jessica Darling series, 60
Jink!, 182
JLA: Earth 2, 180, 207
Joey Pigza Loses Control, 21
Johnny Voodoo, 53
Journal of Douglas Allen Deeds: The Donner Party Expedition, 1846, The, 68
Journal of Jesse Smoke: A Cherokee Boy, Trail of Tears, 1838, The, 141
Journal of Joshua Loper: A Black Cowboy, The, 147, 172
Journal of William Thomas Emerson: A Revolutionary War Patriot, The, 172
Journey to Nowhere, 186
Jubilee Journey, 49, 161
Julie, 66
Julie of the Wolves, 66
Julie series, 66
Julie's Wolf Pack, 66
Jump Ball: A Basketball Season in Poems, 56
Jumper, 119
Jumping off the Planet, 113
Jumping Tree, The, 50, 165
Junk, 40
Just Ella, 94, 206
Just Trust Me, 63

Kahvi, 182
Kaiulani: The People's Princess: Hawaii, 1889, 173
Keepers of the Flame, 122
Keeping the Moon, 48, 52, 205
Keeping You a Secret, 24
Killer, The, 126
Killer's Cousin, The, 75, 205
Killing Frost, A, 67
Kim: Empty Inside: The Diary of an Anonymous Teenager, 22, 174
Kin series, 153
Kindling, The, 122
King of Shadows, 109
King of the Murgos, 200
Kingfisher's Tale, The, 81
Kings of the Broken Wheel, 182
King's Shadow, 154
King's Swift Rider: A Novel on Robert the Bruce, The, 154
Kinship, 152
Kinship series, 152
Kirkus Children's Reviews, 6, 196
Kiss the Dust, 27, 167
Kissing Tennessee and Other Stories from the Stardust Dance, 207
Kite Rider, The, 157
Kit's Wilderness, 132
Kliatt, 6, 196

Knocked Out by My Nunga-Nungas: Further,
    Further Confessions of Georgia Nicolson,
    174
Kotuku, 50
Krondor, Tear of the Gods, 200
Krondor, the Assassins, 200
Krondor, the Betrayal, 200
Kurt Busiek's Astro City: Life in the Big City. What
    It's Like to Live in the City of Superheroes,
    179

Lab 6, 117
Lady Knight, 99
Lady of the Sorrows, The, 199
Lake of Secrets, 133
Lamb, the Gospel According to Biff, Christ's
    Childhood Pal, 60
Land, The, 146
Land Girls, 156
Land of Loss, 105, 206
Larry Gonick's The Cartoon History of the
    Universe, 178
Last Battle, The, 108, 190
Last Book in the Universe, The, 123
Last Enchantment, The, 93
Last Grail Keeper, The, 110, 131
Last Rainmaker, The, 147
Last Safe Place on Earth, The, 28, 204
Last Sin Eater, The, 191
Last Stop, 117
Laws of Nature, 130
"Leading the Horse to Water," 4
Leave It to Chance: Shaman's Rain, 177
Leaving Fishers, 38
Left Behind: A Novel of the Earth's Last Days,
    189–190
Left Behind series, 189
Legacy, 182
Legacy of Lies, 80, 131, 205
Leonardo's Hand, 40, 128
Leslie's Journal, 35, 204
Lethal Gorilla, The, 82
Letters, The, 168
Library Journal, 6, 7, 13, 177, 182, 196
Life History of a Star, The, 152
Life in the Fat Lane, 16, 37, 203
Life Is Funny, 32, 171, 204
Life, the Universe and Everything, 115
Lightkeeper's Daughter, The, 49
Like Father, Like Son, 125
Like Gold Refined, 191
Like Sisters on the Homefront, 26, 163, 207
Lion, the Witch, and the Wardrobe, The, 107, 108,
    190
Lionclaw, 92
Lirael, 100
Literature Connections to American History, 197
Literature Connections to World History, 197
Little Chicago, 36
Little House on the Prairie books, 142

Little Lit: Folklore and Fairy Tale Funnies, 184
Little Lit: Strange Stories for Strange Kids, 184
Little Soldier, 40
Little White Lies, 188
Lives of Our Own, 28, 160
Living Nightmare, A, 135
Lonely Girl, 187
Long Patrol, The, 103
Longtusk, 152
Looking for Alibrandi, 49
Looking for Red, 18, 129
Lord Brocktree, 104
Lord Kirkle's Money, 156
Lord of Chaos, 201
Lord of the Nutcracker Men, 156
Lord of the Rings Trilogy, 3, 10, 85, 86, 87, 180
Losing Joe's Place, 59
Lost and Found, 187
Lost in Cyberspace, 116
Lost One, The, 131
Lottery, The, 38
Love among the Walnuts, 58
Love and Other Four-Letter Words, 49, 53, 205
Love & Sex, 23, 52, 203
Love Him Forever, 132, 206
Love Rules, 24
Love, Sara, 36
Love That Dog, 175
Love Trilogy, 62
Lovely Bones, The, 134
Loves Me, Loves Me Not, 52, 164
Lucky Thirteen, 125
Lucy the Giant, 70
Lyddie, 144

Magic Can Be Murder, 101
Magic Kingdom for Sale. Sold!, 106
Magic Steps, 88
Magician, 200
Magician: Apprentice, 200
Magician: Master, 200
Magicians Gambit, 200
Magician's Nephew, The, 108, 190
Magician's Ward, 101
Mai the Psychic Girl, 183
Mairelon and Kim Duet, 101
Mairelon the Magician, 85, 101
Mairhe Mehan series, 143
Make Lemonade series, 33, 176
Making the Saint, 136
Making Up Megaboy, 39, 170
Mallorean series, 200
Mana's Story, 153
Maniac Magee, 29
Many Peoples, One Land: A Guide to New
    Multicultural Literature for Children and
    Young Adults, 198
MapHead, 117
MapHead: The Return, 117
MapHead series, 117

Marco's Millions, 118
Mariel of Redwall, 103
Mark: The Beast Rules the World, The, 190
Marlfox, 104
Mars, 183
Martin the Warrior, 103
Martyn Pig, 38
Marvels, 179
Mary, Bloody Mary, 155
Mary Mehan Awake, 143
Mary Newbury series, 137
Matilda Bone, 154
Matter of Profit, A, 120
Mattimeo, 103
Maus, 178
*Maus II: A Survivor's Tale: And Here My Troubles
        Began*, 179
Max the Mighty, 34, 72
Maze, The, 30, 66, 204
"Meet the Future," 1
Meets the Eye, 81, 130, 205
Memories of Summer, 22
Memory Boy, 124
Memory, Sorrow and Thorn, 202
Meridian, Volume 1: Flying Solo, 181
Merlin Conspiracy, The, 107
Merlin series, 93
Merriam-Webster's Collegiate Dictionary, 1
Merry Meet, 136, 206
Midnight Magic, 77, 154, 205
Midnight Predator, 134
Midnight's Choice, 104
Midsummer Night's Dream, A, 109
Midwife's Apprentice, The, 154
Mighty series, 72
Mind Riot, 178
Mind Riot: Coming of Age in Comix, 48
Mindcoil, 182
Miracle's Boys, 31, 163
Miserable Mill, The, 96
Misfits, The, 27, 81
Misfits series, 81
Missing Angel Juan, 90
Missing Pieces, 125
Mississippi Trial, 1955, 151
Money Hungry, 40, 162
Monster, 31, 169, 170, 207
Moon Demon, 131
Moonstones, The, 54
More than Friends, 187
More than This, 63, 205
Morgawr, 199
Mossflower, 103
Most Wanted, 80
Mostly Harmless, 116
Motherland, 164
Motorcycle Ride on the Sea of Tranquility, 165
Moves Make the Man, The, 55
Mr. Tucket, 147
Mr. Was, 118

Much Ado about Prom Night, 60, 205
Murdered, My Sweet, 76
My Angelica, 54, 61
My Father's Scar, 23
My Heartbeat, 23
My Life and Death, by Alexandra Canarsie, 21
My Life as a Girl, 53
My Louisiana Sky, 32
My Name Is America series, 140, 172
My Sister's Bones, 21
Mystery Letters, 188
Mystery Mother, 125
Mystery of Errors, A, 78
Mystery of Mary Rogers, The, 178
Mystify the Magician, 106

Name Me Nobody, 24, 164
Nathan's Run, 76
Nausicaa of the Valley of Wind, 183
Never Look Back, 187
Never Too Late, 187
Never Trust a Dead Man, 129, 206
*New Directions for Library Service to Young
        Adults*, 193
New Girl in Town, 186
New Tales for Old, 110
Nicolae: The Rise of Antichrist, 190
Night Flying, 133
Night Hoops, 56
Night Is for Hunting, The, 67
Night of the Bat, 130, 207
Night Shade, 131
Night Watch, 96
Nightjohn, 145
9-11: Artists Respond, 178
No Condition Is Permanent, 32, 167
"No Guys" Pact, The, 188
No Lack of Lonesome, 165
No Time to Die, 80, 205
No Turning Back, 41, 167, 187
Nobody's There, 76
Noli's Story, 153
*North by Night: A Story of the Underground
        Railroad*, 145, 172
Nory Ryan's Song, 156
Notes from a Liar and Her Dog, 20
Nothing but the Truth, 26
Nowhere to Call Home, 150

Ocean Apart, a World Away, An, 157
Of Heroes and Villains, 81
Of Sound Mind, 53
Oh My Goddess! 1-555-GODDESS, 182
Old Kingdom Trilogy, 100
*On the Bright Side, I'm Now the Girlfriend of a Sex
        God: Further Confessions of Georgia
        Nicolson*, 174, 207
On the Devil's Court, 56
On the Fringe, 37
Once upon a Marigold, 94

1-800-WHERE-R-YOU series, 79, 80
101 Best Graphic Novels, The, 177, 184, 197
145th Street, 207
Opportunity Knocks Twice, 186
Origins, 138
Other Side of Dawn, The, 67
Other Side of Truth, The, 167
Out of the Dust, 150
Out of the Fire, 17
Out of Time, 109
Outcast of Redwall, 103
Outlaws of Sherwood, 91
Outrageously Alice, 62
Outsiders, The, 29, 37
Outsmart, 63
Outward Bound, 113
Over the Edge, 189
Over the Wall, 19, 57
Overboard, 66
Owl in Love, 104
Oy, Joy!, 53

P. C. Hawke Mysteries, 82
P.S. Longer Letter Later, 175, 207
Page, 99
Painting the Black, 56
Pankration: The Ultimate Game, 153
Paper Trail, 71
Paperback Advance, 8
Parallel Universe of Liars, The, 53
Parrot in the Oven, 165
Parsifal's Page, 92
Party Girl, 29, 206
Parvana's Journey, 70, 167
*Pastwatch: The Redemption of Christopher
    Columbus,* 118
Path of Daggers, The, 201
Pawn of Prophecy, 200
Pay It Forward, 27
Payback, 132
Pearls of Lutra, 103
*Pedro and Me: Friendship, Loss and What I
    Learned,* 179
Peeling the Onion, 17
Perfect Girls, 124
Perks of Being a Wallflower, The, 47, 174, 204
Petty Crimes, 166, 207
Phantom of 86th Street, The, 83
Pharaoh's Daughter, 153
Phoenix, 182
Phoning a Dead Man, 75
Pictures of Hollis Woods, 37
Plague Trilogy, 125, 126
Play, 62, 126, 205
Players, 57, 205
Playing for Keeps, 77
Playing with Fire, 131
Playing without a Ball, 33, 39, 57, 204
Plunking Reggie Jackson, 55
Po's Story, 153

Point Blank, 69
Popover, 62, 205
Popular Paperbacks, 13
Possession, 131
Postcards from No Man's Land, 23
Prairie Legacy, 191
Predator and Prey, 130
*Primrose Past: The 1848 Journal of Young Lady
    Primrose,* 172
Prince Caspian, 108, 190
Prince of the Blood, 200
Princess Diaries, The, 47, 58, 61, 173, 207
Princess Diaries series, 2, 47, 172
Princess in Love, 173
Princess in the Spotlight, 173, 207
Princess in Waiting, 173
Prisoner of Time, 109
Promethea, Book One, 181
Promise Me Tomorrow, 192
Prophecy: Child of Earth, 200
Protector of the Small series, 99
Protester's Song, The, 81
Prowlers, 130
Prowlers series, 82, 130
Publishers Weekly, 6, 17
Pursued, 188
Pursuing Amy: Who Can You Trust?, 124

Queen of Attolia, The, 69, 88
Queen of Sorcery, 200
Quest's End, 181
Quick Picks, 13
Quiet Strength, A, 191

Rag and Bone Shop, The, 30
Raging Quiet, The, 17
Rain Is Not My Indian Name, 166
Rainbow Boys, 54
Ranma 1/2, 183
Ransom of Mercy Carter, The, 142
RanVan: The Magic Nation, 79, 132
Rat Boys: A Dating Experiment, 58, 205
Rats, 130
Rats Saw God, 51, 205
Raven of the Waves, 153
Ready?, 62
Realm of the Reaper, 105, 206
Rebels, The, 182
Reckoning, 138
Red Midnight, 27, 67
Redhanded, 30
Redwall, 103
Redwall series, 103
Reef of Death, 70, 207
Regeneration, 126, 206
Regeneration series, 126
Remembrance, 156
Remnant: On the Brink of Armageddon, The, 190
Replica series, 124, 126
Reptile Room, The, 96

Responsive Public Library: How to Develop and Market a Winning Collection, The, 13
Restaurant at the End of the Universe, The, 115
Restless, 129
Return of the Perfect Girls, 125
Reunion, 107, 182
Revelations, 132
Revolutions of the Heart, 29, 53, 161, 205
Rewind, 117, 119, 125, 206
Rhapsody: Child of Blood, 200
Rhapsody series, 200
Riftwar Legacy, 200
Riftwar Saga, 200
Ring of Light, 136, 206
River, The, 68
River Boy, 18
River Thunder, 66
Road Home, The, 152
Robin Hood series, 91
Rocky Mountain Memories series, 192
Rogue's Curse, 182
Romiette and Julio, 52, 160
Rooster, 152
Ropemaker, The, 99
Rose Daughter, 94
Rosemary's Baby, 127
Rosey in the Present Tense, 18, 128
Rough Waters, 41, 204
Roughnecks, 55
Rowan Hood: Outlaw Girl of Sherwood Forest, 91
Royal Diaries series, 140, 172
Royals, The, 155
Ruby in the Smoke, The, 78
Ruby Knight, 200
Ruby Raven, 81
Rules of the Road, 58, 204
Run If You Dare, 57
Run, Jonah, Run, 61
Running Loose, 47, 56
Ruth series, 157

Sabriel, 100
Sacrifice, The, 67, 131
Safe House, 80
Salamandastron, 103
Sally Lockhart series, 78
Sammy Keyes and the Curse of Moustache Mary, 82
Sammy Keyes and the Hollywood Mummy, 82
Sammy Keyes and the Hotel Thief, 82
Sammy Keyes and the Runaway Elf, 82
Sammy Keyes and the Search for Snake Eyes, 82
Sammy Keyes and the Sisters of Mercy, 82
Sammy Keyes and the Skeleton Man, 82
Sammy Keyes series, 82
Samurai series, 78
Sandman, The, 181
Sandman: Dream Country, 181
Sandman: World's End, 181
Sandry's Book, 87

Sapphire Rose, 200
Sarny, 145, 207
Sarny series, 145
Sasquatch, 72, 205
Savage Damsel and the Dwarf, The, 92
Saying It Out Loud, 18
Schernoff Discoveries, The, 60
School Library Journal, 6
Scions of Shannara, 199
Score, 62, 205
Scorpion Shards, 120, 206
Scorpions, 29
Scream Museum, The, 82
Screen Test, 49
Sealed with a Kiss, 188
Search, The, 126, *206*
Search for Senna, 105, 206
Search of the Moon King's Daughter, 156
Searching for Dragons, 97
Searching Heart, A, 191
Second Bend in the River, The, 143
Second-Best Friend, 188
Second Chance, 187
Second Helpings, 60
Second Sight, 136, 206
Second Stringer, 56
Secret Clique, 124
Secret Life of Bees, The, 152
Secret of Two-Edge, The, 181
Secret Place of Thunder, 191
Secret Sacrament, 107
Secret Scroll, The, 131
Secret Star, 41
Secret Summer Dreams, 188
Secrets, 132, 206
Secrets and Lies, 63
SeedFolks, 160
Seeing Stone, The, 92
Seek, 170
Seeker, 138
Seeress of Kell, The, 200
Send Me Down a Miracle, 50
Send One Angel Down, 145
Series of Unfortunate Events, A, 96
Services and Resources for Children and Young Adults in Public Libraries, 6
Seven for a Secret, 151
Seven Wild Sisters, 89
Sevenwaters series, 201
Sex, 62
Shabanu: Daughter of the Wind, 28, 168
Shabanu series, 28, 168
Shade's Children, 123
Shades of Simon Gray, 133
Shadow Club, The, 30
Shadow Club Duo, 30
Shadow Club Rising, The, 30
Shadow in the North, The, 78
Shadow Man, 80
Shadow of the Hegemon, 113

Shadow of the Mountains, 191
Shadow People, 30, 74
Shadow Puppets, 113
Shadow Rising, The, 201
Shadow Spinner, 153
Shadowstalker, 182
Shakeress, The, 144
Shakespeare series, 155
Shakespeare Stealer, The, 155
Shakespeare's Scribe, 155
Shakespeare's Spy, 155
Shannara series, 199
Shards, 182
Shark Bait, 31, 50
Shattered Mirror, 134, 206
Shattered Sky, 120
Shatterglass, 88
Shattering Glass, 38, 204
Shayla series, 36
Shayla's Double Brown Baby Blues, 36, 42
Shining Ones, The, 200
Shiva's Fire, 168
Shots on Goal, 57
Show Me Love, 63, 205
Siege at Blue Mountain, 181
Sight, The, 103
Sights, 110
Silent Tears No More, 186
Silent Thief, 187
Silent to the Bone, 37
Silent Witness, 188
Silver Chair, The, 108, 189
Silver Eyes, 126
Silver Kiss, The, 134
Silverthorn, 200
Silverwing, 104
Simply Alice, 62
Simpsons Comics a Go-Go, 183
Simpsons Comics Royale, 183
Single Shard, A, 157
Sirena, 91
Sisterhood of the Traveling Pants, The, 174
*Sizzling Summer Reading Programs for Young
       Adults,* 193
Skeleton Key, 69
Skeleton Man, 133
Skellig, 18, 89
Skin Deep, 81
Skin I'm In, The, 162, 207
Skyward Shadow, 182
Slam!, 57, 207
Slap Your Sides, 151
Slave Day, 27, 29, 172
Slaves of the Mastery, 87
Slaying of the Shrew, The, 78
Sloppy Firsts, 60
Slot Machine, 59, 205
Smack, 40, 42
Smugglers, The, 67, 70, 205
Smythe and Shakespeare series, 78

Snail Mail No More, 175, 207
So Long and Thanks for All the Fish, 116
So Mote It Be, 135, 206
So You Want to Be a Wizard, 107
Soldier Boy, 147
Soldier Boys, 156
Soldier X, 70
Soldier's Heart, 146, 207
Someone Like You, 25
Something Old, Something New, 187
Somewhere in the Darkness, 33, 163
Son of the Mob, 53, 59, 205
Son of the Shadows, 201
Song of Ice and Fire, 201
Song of the Wanderer, 102
Song Quest, 88
Songs of Eirren, *The,* 87
Songs of Power, 123
Sorceress of Darshiva, 200
Sorceress, 137
Sort of Forever, 20, 204
Soul Harvest: The World Takes Sides, 190
Soul Survivor, 81
Soulmate, 135
Speak, 20, 203
Special Kind of Love, 187
Speed Racer: Born to Race, 183
Spellbound, 25, 137
Spider Boy, 48
Spinners, 95
Spite Fences, 28, 152
Split Image, 21, 175
SpyBoy, 179
SpyBoy: The Deadly Gourmet Affair, 179, 207
Square Root of Murder, The, 83
Squared Circle, 55
Squire, 99
Squire, His Knight, and His Lady, The, 92
Squire's Tale, The, 92
Stained Glass Rose, 149
Stalker, 80
Star Shards Trilogy, 120
Star Split, 126
Star Wars: Dark Empire, 182, 207
Star Wars, a New Hope: Manga, 183
Stargirl, 54
Starman, 199
Stars for a Light, The, 191
Starsiders Trilogy, 113
Start Here, 62, 205
Staying Fat for Sarah Byrnes, 56
*Stealing South: A Story of the Underground
       Railroad,* 145
Step from Heaven, A, 34, 164
Stephen Fair, 43
Sterkarm Handshake, The, 119
Stetson, 33
Stick and Whittle, 148
Sticks and Stones, 26, 204
St. Michael's Scales, 20

Stone of Farewell, The, 202
Stoner & Spaz: A Love Story, 49, 204
Stones of Mourning Creek, The, 28
Stop, Don't Stop, 61, 203
Stop Pretending: What Happened When My Big Sister Went Crazy, 22, 204
Storm of Swords, A, 201
Storm Warriors, 143
Stormbreaker, 69, 205
StormWatch: Force of Nature, 180, 207
Storyteller's Beads, 167
Storyteller's Daughter, The, 150
Stowaway, 69, 157
Straight A Teacher, 188
Stranded, 189
Stranded in Harmony, 51
Strange Stories for Strange Kids, 184
Strangers and Beggars, 98
Strangers in Paradise High School!, 178
Straw into Gold, 95
Straydog, 21
Street Magic, 88
Strictly Science Fiction, 112, 126, 198
Strife, 137
Strike Two, 57
Stuck in Neutral, 17, 204
Stuck in the Sky, 186
Substitute, The, 125
Subtle Knife, The, 108
Summerland, 106
Sunshine Rider: The First Vegetarian Western, 148
Surfing Corpse, The, 82
Surviving the Applewhites, 60
Suspect, The, 187
Suth's Story, 153
Swallowing Stones, 32
Sweep series, 63, 137
Sweet-Blood, 17
Switch, 74
Switchers, 104
Switchers series, 104
Sword of Shannara, The, 199
Sword of the Rightful King, 93

Taggerung, 104
Take It Easy, 66
Taking of Room 114, The, 175
Tale of One Bad Rat, The, 41, 179
Talismans of Shannara, The, 199
Tamuli series, 200
Tangerine, 17, 55
Tara and Star series, 175
Tartabull's Throw, 109, 130
Taste of Salt: A Story of Modern Haiti, 28
Tears of a Tiger, 18
Teen Genreflecting, 15, 193
Teen Library Events: A Month by Month Guide, 193
Teen People, 1, 2
Tender, 48

Tender Years, The, 191
Tenderness, 30, 74
Terrific Connections with Authors, Illustrators, and Storytellers, 10, 13
Terrorist, The, 68, 205
Test of the Twins, 201
That Summer, 48
There and Back Again, 116
There's a Dead Person Following My Sister Around, 129
Thicker than Water: Coming of Age Stories by Irish and Irish-American Writers, 168
Thief, The, 88
Thief of Souls, 120
Thin Ice, 74, 205
Things Not Seen, 119
Third Day, the Frost, 67
Thirsty, 134, 206
This Boy Is Mine, 63
This Lullaby, 48, 52
Three Clams and an Oyster, 57
Three Days, 74
Three's a Crowd, 187
Through the Veil, 136
Thursday's Child, 32
Ties that Bind, Ties that Break, 157
Tiger in the Well, The, 78
Tightrope, 29
Till Death Do Us Part, 19, 204
Time Apart, A, 51
Time for Dancing, 18
Time of the Twins, 201
Timeline, 118
Titanic: The Long Night, 69, 205
Tithe, a Modern Faerie Tale, 88
To Green Angel Tower, 202
To Know Her by Name, 192
To Say Nothing of the Dog, 116
To the Blight, 201
"Today's Kids Meet the Future," 6
Tom Jones, 46
Tom Sawyer, 46
Tom Strong Book 1, 180
Tomorrow series, 67, 70
Tomorrow, When the War Began, 67
Tomorrowland: Ten Stories about the Future, 112, 126
Tomorrow's Promise, 186
Toning the Sweep, 19, 163
Too Many Secrets, 188
Too Soon for Jeff, 25, 26
Torn Thread, 156
"Totara Hill," 138
Touching Spirit Bear, 31
Toward the Sunrising, 191
Tower High series, 175
Transall Saga, The, 117, 206
Transformation, 125
Transformation: The Quest Is Fulfilled at Last, 107
Transworld Skateboarding, 2

Treacherous Love: The Diary of an Anonymous Teenager, 36, 174, 204
Treasure at the Heart of the Tanglewood, 95
Treasury of Victorian Murder, 178
Tree Girl, 88
Trial and Terror, 179
Trials of Death, 135
Tribulation Force: The Continuing Drama of Those Left Behind, 189
Tribute to Another Dead Rock Star, 50
Trino series, 164
Trino's Choice, 164
Trino's Time, 46, 164
Tris's Book, 87, 206
Triss, 104
Trouble with a Capital T, 186
Trouble with Weddings, The, 188
Trouble's Daughter: The Story of Susanna Hutchinson, Indian Captive, 142
Troy, 91, 153
True Colors of Caitlynne Jackson, The, 22, 204
True-to-Life from Hamilton High series, 25
Trust Falls, 62
Trust Me, 132, 206
Truth, The, 126, 206
Truth or Dairy, 52
Tucket series, 147
Tucket's Gold, 147
Tucket's Home, 148
Tucket's Ride, 147
Tunnels of Blood, 135
Turnabout, 124
Turning Seventeen, 63
Twelve Impossible Things before Breakfast, 98
Twilight Boy, 76
Twilight in Grace Falls, 49
Twilight Zone, 127
Twisted Summer, 77
Two Princess of Bamarre, The, 94
Two Suns in the Sky, 150

Ultimate Spider-Man Power and Responsibility, 179, 207
Ultimate X-Men: The Tomorrow People, 180
Ulysses, 46
Under a War-Torn Sky, 70
Under the Mermaid Angel, 50
Understand the Unknown, 106
Unheard Voices, 187
Unicorn Chronicles, 102
Unprotected Witness, 72
Usagi Yojimbo Grasscutter, 183

Vampire Mountain, 135
Vampire's Assistant, The, 135
Vampire's Beautiful Daughter, The, 135
Vanishing, The, 20, 123, 206
Vanishing Chip, The, 81
Vanishing Star, 187
Victoria May Blossom of Britannia, 172

Viking Claw, The, 81
Vile Village, The, 97
Violet & Claire, 38, 203
Virtual Amy, 125
Virtual War, 114, 115
Vision Quest: A Wrestling Story, 4, 48, 56,
Voice on the Radio, The, 43, 47
Voices of Youth Advocates (VOYA), 5, 6, 196
Voyage of the Dawn Treader, *The*, 108, 190
Voyage of the Jerle Shannara series, 199

Waifs and Strays, 98
Walk across the Sea, 144
Walker's Crossing, 71
Walking up a Rainbow, 145
Walks Alone, 141
Wanderer, The, 47, 69
Wannabe, 42
Wanted, 75, 205
War, 117
War Dog, 156
War of Souls Trilogy, 201
War of the Clones, 126
War of the Eagles, 158, 161
War of the Twins, 201
War Within: A Novel of the Civil War, The, 146
Warrior Angel, 21
Watcher, The, 34, 106
Watchers series, 117
Water: Tales of Elemental Spirits, 98, 99
Water series, 106
Watership Down, 103
WaveDancers, 182
Wayfarer Redemption, The, 199
We Have to Talk, 63
Wee Free Men, The, 96
Weekly World News, 2
Weetzie Bat, 90
Welcome to the Ark, 120
Wessex Papers, The, 62
Whale Talk, 38, 56
What Child Is This?, 40
What Daddy Did, 20
What Every Girl (Except Me) Knows, 46
What Girls Learn, 18
What Happened to Lani Garver, 74
What Janie Found, 43
What Kind of Love? The Diary of a Pregnant Teenager, 173
What My Mother Doesn't Know, 54, 204
"What Teens Want," 177
What the Cards Said, 136, 206
Whatever Happened to Janie?, 43, 47
Wheel of Time series, 200
When Dad Killed Mom, 19, 204
When Jeff Comes Home, 35, 42, 203
When Kambia Elaine Flew in from Neptune, 36, 42, 163
When Lightning Strikes, 80

When My Name Was Keoko: A Novel of Korea in World War II, 158, 167
When She Was Good, 34
Where the Wild Rose Blooms, 192
Whirligig, 20
Whispers of Moonlight, 192
Whistle Me Home, 24, 204
White Bread Competition, 165
White Horse, The, 41, 42, 204
White Wolf, 72
Whitechurch, 32
Who Are You?, 77, 206
Who Killed Mr. Chippendale?, 76, 175, 207
Who Will Tell My Brother?, 26, 166
Wicked Day, 93
Wide Window, The, 96
Wild Blood, 105
Wild Ginger, 167
Wild Hunt, 182
Wild Man Island, 67
Wild Things, 130
Wildside, 116
Williwaw!, 72
Wind on Fire Trilogy, 87
Wind Singer, The, 87
Window, The, 17
Winter People, 141
Winter's Heart, 201
Wise Up to Teens: Insights into Marketing and Advertising to Teenagers, 1, 6
Wishsong of Shannara, The, 199
Witch Baby, 90
Witch Child, 137, 143
Witches' Chillers series, 3, 136
Witches' Key to Terror, 137
Witches' Night of Fear, 137
Witches' Night Out, 136
Without a Trace, 189

Witness, 150
Wizard Abroad, A, 107
Wizard's Dilemma, The, 107
Wizard's Tale, The, 180
Wizardry series, 107
Wizards of the Game, 108
Wolfrider!, 182
Woman in the Wall, The, 90
World and I, 6
Worldpool, 182
World's End, 181
Worm Tunnel, The, 81
Wrango, 147
Wreckers, The, 67, 69
Wrestling Sturbridge, 57
Wrinkle in Time, A, 117
Written in the Stars, 136
WWF, 2

Xenocide Mission, The, 113

Year Down Yonder, A, 150
Year of the Griffin, 100
Year of the Hangman, 142
Year of Wonders, 154
Yesterday's Child, 76
Yesterday's Dream, 186
You Don't Know Me, 34
You Know You Love Me, 63
Young Adult Services Professional Resources: A Selective Five-Year Retrospective Bibliography with Some "Classic" Exceptions, 193
Young Justice: A League of Their Own, 180

Z for Zachariah, 123
Zach's Lie, 75, 205
Zazoo, 161
Zel, 95

Subject Index

AA. *See* Alcoholics Anonymous
Abandonment, 22, 33, 38, 40, 109, 123, 144
Abarat, 106
Abenaki, 141
Abilene, Kansas, 172
Abolition, 143
Aboriginal, 70
Abortion, 26
Abuse, 15, 16, 22, 23, 31, 32, 34–36, 41, 54, 57,
    110, 145, 149, 152, 167, 171.
    See also Sexual abuse
Accidents, 16, 17, 33, 41, 55, 56, 128, 133, 151
Acid rain, 124
Acronyms, 111
Action, xii, 28, 29, 30, 35, 54, 61, 65–68, 70, 86,
    101, 111, 112, 140, 146
Activism, 15, 26–27
Adbooks, 195
Addictions and addicts, 15, 33, 40–42
Admiralty Island, 67
Adolescent development, 195
Adoption, 42, 69, 78, 80, 109, 119, 142, 153, 154,
    161, 162, 166, 186
Adrenaline, 128
Adult fiction, 3, 7
Adventure, 3, 17, 27, 34, 37, 41, 46, 59, 60, 65–71,
    77, 86–90, 94, 104, 107, 109, 111–18, 120,
    122, 126, 139, 142, 144, 146, 148, 149,
    152, 156, 158, 167, 179, 189, 204
Advertising, xi, xvi
Advising teen readers, 4–6. *See also* Readers'
    advisory
Affairs, 19, 33
Afghanistan/Afghani, 70, 167
Africa/African, 7, 19, 40, 41, 43, 81, 157, 180
African American, 18, 19, 28, 29, 32, 35, 36, 52,
    76, 81, 147, 149, 152, 159–63, 198
Age of Exploration, 140
Aging, 30, 124
Agoraphobia, 20, 25, 79, 181
AIDS, 15, 19, 151, 179
Airplanes, 102, 190
ALA. *See* American Library Association
Alabama, 29
ALAN. *See* the Assembly on Literature for
    Adolescents
Alaska, 66, 67, 70, 72

Albania/Albanian, 70
Alberta, 79
Alberta Institute of Technology, 79
Albino, 41
Alcoholic, 16, 20, 22, 24, 33, 42, 46, 165
Alcoholics Anonymous, 31
Alex Awards, xi, 7, 195
Alienation, 17, 30, 74
Aliens, 98, 105, 106, 112, 116, 117, 120–22
Allegory, 189
Allergies, 121
Alternate and parallel worlds, 85, 105–8, 116–18,
    130, 189
Alternate history, 142
Alternative formats, 2–4, 26, 33, 34, 39, 41, 42, 48,
    58, 60, 61, 133, 146, 147, 150, 169–84,
    197, 206
Alternative high school, 25
Alzheimer's, 19
Amateurs, 73
Amazon, 9, 68, 83, 89
American history, 141–52
American Library Association, 5, 7
American Red Cross, 177
American Revolution, 142
Américas Award, 8, 165, 176
Amputation, 69, 88
Ancestors, 146, 160
Ancient civilizations, 153, 154
Ancient Egypt, 109
Androgyny, 38
Androids, 183
Aneurysm, 90
Angels, 20, 49, 79, 89, 120, 128, 152, 156, 163
Anger, 19, 20, 21, 33, 46, 56, 167
Anglo-Saxon, 153
Angst, xii, 15, 59, 63, 88, 134, 174, 178, 194
Animal rights activists, 189
Animals, 21, 27, 95, 100, 102–5, 124, 129, 174
Anime, 182, 183
Annette, Texas, 171
Annotations, xv, 194
Anorexia, 21, 50
Anthologies, 23, 32, 91
Anthropologist, 32, 167
Antichrist, 190
Anticonsumerism, 27

Antigay feelings, 24
Antigovernment position, 71
Apache, 141
Apartments, 20, 24, 53, 59, 79, 82, 97, 168
Apocalypse, 190
Appalachia, 22, 191
Appalachian Trail, 18
Appeal factors, xiv, 5
Appendixes, xiv, 193–205
Apprentice, 78, 88
Arab American, 161
Aramanth, 87
Arcade, 28, 38
Archaeological dig, 81
Archaeologists, 51
Archetypal, 86
Architects, 33
Ark, 43
Arkansas, 41, 163
Arkansas River, 41
Armageddon, 190
Armed, 39, 170
Armenian, 157
Armor, 154
Army, 103, 146, 152, 163, 167
Army of the West, 147
Arrows, 87
Arsonists, 88
Art and artists, 1, 4, 19, 29, 33, 48, 50, 77, 151,
     161, 168, 173, 176, 183
Art school, 48
Arteria, 115
Arthur Ellis Award, 8
Arthurian legend, 92, 93, 131, 181
Articles, 195, 196
Artificial intelligence, 117
Ashes, 132
Asian Americans, 163, 164, 198
Asians, 163
Assassination, 106, 120, 134, 144, 164, 190
Assembly on Literature for Adolescents (ALAN),
     6, 7, 195, 196
   ALAN Award, 7
   ALAN Review, 6, 196
Asteroid, 60, 114, 116
Astrology, 136
Astronauts, 51
Astrophysics, 25
At sea, 47, 67, 69–70
Atlanta, 18
Atlantic Ocean, 190
Atlantis, 106, 107
At-risk children, 55, 162
Attention-deficit disorders, 20
Auctions, 29, 145
Audience, xiii
Aunts, 18, 31, 32, 33, 46, 47, 48, 50, 58, 63, 77, 80,
     89, 90, 96, 107, 133, 149, 164, 166, 167,
     191
Auras, 129, 131

Auschwitz, 178
Australia/Australian, 32, 33, 49, 67, 70, 157
Australian Aurealis Award, 120
Austria/Austrian, 188
Author visits, 10
Autobiography, 165, 170
Avon True Romance, 140
Awards, xi, xii, xv, xvi, 7, 8, 111
Azatlan, 124
Aztecs, 105

Babies, 19, 25, 26, 35, 37, 58, 75, 82, 88, 91, 102,
     109, 149, 166, 180, 189, 191
Babylon, 29, 33
Baby-sitting, 28, 176, 186
Baker and Taylor, 8
Barnes & Noble, xi, 9
Baseball, 19, 21, 55, 56, 77, 106, 130, 150, 152, 160
Basketball, 39, 55, 56, 57, 69
Bats, 130
Battle of Bull Run, 171
Battle school, 113
Battles, 26, 58, 70, 90, 94, 100, 103, 107, 112, 113,
     126, 130, 150, 152, 156, 166, 180, 183
BBYA. *See* Best Books for Young Authors
Beaches, 34, 72, 90, 121, 144
Bears, 31, 94, 108, 179
Beasts, 89, 94, 105, 130
Beatings, 28, 31, 34
Beauty and the Beast, 94
Beauty pageant, 16, 37
Beauty queen, 58
Beauty salon, 77
Bee fairies, 89
Bees, 89, 152, 178
Beguilers, 121
Behavioral issues, 119, 195. *See also* Mental,
     emotional, and behavioral issues
Belgium/Belgian, 156
Bellmaker, 103
Best Books for Young Adults (BBYA), xv, 7, 9, 13,
     16–43, 46–62, 66–72, 74, 76–78, 88–92,
     94–101, 103, 104, 106–10, 113–24, 129,
     130, 132–35, 137, 138, 142–46, 149–58,
     161–68, 170–76, 178–80, 195, 199, 201
Bestiary, 102–5
Best-selling books, 3, 111
Betelgeuse, 115
Bethany House, 4, 62, 140, 187
Bibliogoth, 120
Bibliographies, 194, 196
Bigfoot, 72, 89
Bildungsroman, 46
Bio Union, 126
Biology, 69
Biracial, 50, 102, 161
Bird Stump, 116
Birthdays, 20, 25, 32, 39, 54, 58, 59, 105, 125, 133,
     151, 166
Bisexuality, 22, 196

Bishop's Bird Stump, 116
Bison, 117
Black holes, 114
Black Plague, 118
Blackmail, 63
Blacks, 28, 38, 55, 143, 147, 160
Bleak books, 15, 31
Blindness, 17, 95167, 180
Blood, 88, 97, 115, 127, 137, 153
Blood and Bone alley, 154
Boarding school, 62, 69, 100, 119, 145
Boats/boating, 55, 70, 72
Bodyguard, 121, 173, 183
Boltzmon, 115, 205
Bomb shelter, 123
Bombs, 68, 69, 150, 189, 190
Bonesetter, 154
Boneville, 184
Book appearance, 5, 12, 91
Book club, 11
Book discussion groups, 5, 6, 9, 11
Book jobbers, 13
Book lists, xvi
Book of the Year for Children Award, 8, 104
Booksellers, xiii, 9, 12
Bookstores, xi, 2, 9, 10, 12, 24, 66, 77, 111, 136,
        164
Booktalking, 11, 12, 14, 194
Boot camp, 113
Boston, 75, 81, 130, 144, 152, 160, 172
Boxes, 117, 118
Boxing, 21, 30, 144
Boyfriends, 17, 24, 25, 34, 35, 36, 41, 52, 53, 54,
        57, 59, 62, 63, 64, 76, 79, 81, 125, 132,
        136, 164, 166, 189
Boys, 12, 21, 22, 24, 30, 31, 35, 36, 38, 40, 41, 47,
        49, 53, 54, 55, 59, 60, 68, 69, 72, 74, 76,
        77, 78, 88, 89, 96, 108, 109, 112, 122, 129,
        135, 144, 146, 148, 150, 151, 152, 156,
        157, 161, 163, 165, 166, 167, 173, 177, 186
Brain, 18, 19, 31, 90, 107
Brain damage, 31
Brain rotting, 123
Brain tumor, 18, 19
Bram Stoker Award, 8
Brand names, xii
Brazil, 68
Breakups, 61
Breast cancer, 18
Brides, 78
Britain/British, 23, 63, 68, 69, 93, 108, 156, 158,
        161
Britons, 94
Bronx, 82, 176
Brooklyn, 32, 161, 171
Brothers, 17, 18, 23, 24, 26, 29, 32, 34–37, 40–43,
        46, 48–51, 53, 55, 57, 59, 68, 71, 72, 74,
        75, 87, 94, 96, 99, 102, 113, 123, 129, 133,
        144, 146, 147, 149, 151, 152, 156, 161–63,
        165–67, 171, 187, 189. *See also* Siblings

Brown University, 63
Browsing, xii
Bryn Mawr, 53
Bubonic plague, 154
Buchenwald, 157
Buck, 103
Buckey City, Illinois, 149
Buffalo, 147, 197
Buggers, 112
Bull riding, 23
Bull Run, 146, 171
Bulldozers, 115
Bullies, 59, 60, 107, 164, 187
Burglars, 74
Burrowing, 32, 59
Byzantine Empire, 153

Cabins, 31, 77, 82
California, 41, 48, 60, 68, 144, 145, 151, 165, 166,
        174, 188
Camera, 28, 79, 117
Camp, 19, 23, 25, 55, 59, 71, 80, 90, 96, 125, 150,
        151, 156, 158, 161, 162, 166, 167, 174, 188
Campaigns, 27, 58, 67, 187
Camper, 66
Camping, 67, 117
Campus, 48, 81, 131, 162
Canada, 8, 43, 66, 68, 71, 90, 142, 158, 161, 172,
        175
Canadian awards, 8
Canadian Children's Book Centre, 8
Canadian Library Association, 8, 43, 104
Cancer, 20, 51, 74, 107, 173
Canyonlands National Park, 30
Canyons, 30, 67
Cape Flattery, 144
Captives, 74, 98, 103, 109, 113, 142
Captivity, 117, 152
Car accidents, 18, 114, 164, 187
Car chases, 75
Car jacking, 20
Carbondale Ranch, 41
Cardiopulmonary resuscitation, 109
Careers, 79, 121, 180
Caribbean, 8, 70, 77, 188
Carnegie Medal, 18, 23, 108
Carnival, 79, 97, 128
Carpathian Mountains, 93
Castles, 77, 92, 94, 96, 100, 154
Catalogs, xv, 6, 8, 9, 13
Catering, 53
Catholics, 49, 141, 150
Cats, 96, 138, 174, 178
Cattalo, 148
Cattle, 172
Cattle drive, 147, 148
Cayuco, 27
Cedar River, 61, 186, 187
Celebrations, 136, 161
Celebrity, 27, 82

Celts/Celtic, 87, 88
Cemetery, 38, 129, 132
Censorship, 28
Centaurs, 99
Center for Adolescent Reading, 159, 194
Central America, 81
Central Park, 19, 102
Cerebral palsy, 17, 49
Channeling, 136
Chantilly, Virginia, 159
Characters, xv, 3, 5, 15, 16, 25–27, 34, 35, 40,
        45–47, 49, 51, 58, 61, 62, 65, 66, 71, 75,
        77, 79, 86, 88, 90–94, 97, 102, 108, 112,
        115, 118, 139, 141, 142, 146, 149, 154,
        156, 157, 159–61, 172, 174, 183
Cheating, 53, 165
Cheerleaders, 34, 59, 80
Chefs, 83
Chela, 120
Chemical elements, 46
Cherokee, 90, 141
Chesapeake, 151
Chicago, 36, 147, 171
Chickentown, 106
Child Welfare League of America, 39
Children, xii, xvi, 6–8, 10–12, 35, 42, 61, 62, 66,
        70, 80, 85, 86, 96, 100–102, 107, 108, 112,
        119, 121, 122, 129, 133, 145, 153, 154,
        157, 166, 173, 176, 179, 182, 183, 198
Children's Book Awards, 8
Chimpanzee, 114
China/Chinese, 35, 89, 144, 157, 163, 178
Chinatown, 77
Chinese American, 175
Chinese Cultural Revolution, 167
Chisholm Trail, 172
Chivalry, 92
Cholera epidemic, 191
Christ, 60
Christian beliefs, 186
Christian fiction, xiii, 3, 4, 14, 61, 62, 82, 185–92,
        197
    contemporary life, 186–88
    fantasy and science fiction, 189, 190
    historical, 191, 192
    mystery, 188, 189
Christmas, 40, 63, 81, 173, 188
Churches, 28, 39, 82, 108, 188, 189
Cinderella, 58, 94
Circle of justice, 31
Circumcision, 32
Cirrus Coven, 137
City of Chammur, 88
Civil rights movement, 140
Civil War, 78, 117, 128, 140, 143, 144, 146–48,
        191
Civilization, 27, 68
Clairvoyance, 131
Clans, 104, 106, 119, 135

CLASP. See Consortium of Latin American Studies
        Programs
Class trips, 63, 125
Classroom, 123, 175
Claudette Colbert High School, 135
Clayr, 100
Cliques, 39, 54, 60, 124
Clones, 114, 116, 124, 125, 126
Clubs, 11, 42, 71, 90, 121
Coaches, 21, 35, 47, 57
Cocaine, 33, 42
Coffeehouse, 47
Collection development, xii, xvi, 6–9
College, 19, 21, 23, 25, 26, 42, 47, 52, 55, 68, 69,
        81, 108, 176, 181, 187, 188, 191
Collie, 21
Colonial times, 104, 142, 143, 178
Colorado, 34, 41, 66, 149, 161, 192
Colorado River, 66
Columbine High School, 34, 176
Comancheros, 147
Comas, 37, 58, 133
Comic books, 39, 59, 81, 169, 170, 176, 184
Coming of age, xii, 41, 45–53, 56, 86, 90, 160, 164,
        166, 167, 168
Commercials, 61
Commoners, 106
Commonwealth, 113
Communes, 50, 144, 189
Community, xii, 10, 11, 12, 13, 20, 27–29, 31, 50,
        82, 87, 89, 90, 103, 134, 151, 152, 160,
        161, 162, 190
Community service, 50, 82
Competition, 17, 31, 54, 62
Computer geeks, 38
Computer services, 195
Computer-generated graphics, 39, 170
Computers, 38, 39, 69, 75, 81, 107, 114, 122, 123,
        133, 170
Confessions, 30
Confess-O-Rama, 59
Conformity, 118
Connected short stories, 4, 32, 164, 169–72
Conscientious objector, 151
Conspiracies, 71, 79, 114, 121, 124, 137, 138
Contemporary, xiii, 4, 15, 16, 28, 31, 43, 45, 46,
        54, 61, 69, 74, 75, 90, 98, 118, 137, 138,
        140, 141, 148, 160, 166, 168, 172, 173,
        175, 177, 203
Contemporary life, 16, 45–64, 161, 162, 186–88,
        203
Contemporary mysteries, 164–66, 175
Core collections, 194
Coretta Scott King Award, 7, 19, 31, 57, 146, 152,
        162, 163, 176
Coretta Scott King Honor, 26, 31, 33, 36, 40, 162,
        163, 170
Coretta Scott King Task Force, 7
Correctional facilities, 36
Correspondence, 161, 174

Corruption, 166
Corvettes, 23, 75
Consortium of Latin American Studies Programs, 8
Counselors, 25, 51
Countryside, 74, 130, 156
Courage, 65, 98, 120, 153
Court magicians, 107
Cousins, 26, 33, 51, 57, 69, 75, 106, 108, 121, 133,
    145, 147, 151, 162, 163, 164, 171
Covens, 136, 137
Cover art, xiv
Cowboys, 46, 146, 147, 163
Cows, 147, 163
Craft, the, 136, 137
Crafts, 87
Creative Academy, 60
Creature, 18, 89, 102, 118
Cree, 29, 161
Crime and criminals, 30, 31, 35, 72, 74, 75, 80–82,
    89, 103, 130, 136, 147, 164, 170, 179, 180,
    189
Crime Syndicate of Amerika, 180
Crime Writers of Canada, 8
Crones, 94, 96
Crows, 97
Cruises, 77, 188
Crushes, 23, 52, 60, 137, 164, 176, 188
Crying girls, 18
Cuba/Cuban, 52, 77, 164, 165, 167
Cuban American, 52, 164
Cults, 38, 65, 69, 71, 122, 149, 191
Cults and militias, 120
Cultural groups, 159, 160
Culture and cultures, 2, 3, 27, 40, 90, 107, 141,
    157, 159–64, 166–68, 198
Cutting. See Self-mutilation
Cyborgs, 114

Dachau, 178
Daemons, 108
Dancers, 18, 168
Dances, 26, 39, 68, 170, 171
Dark fantasy, 86
Dark magick, 137, 138
Dating, 23, 28, 47, 124, 161, 174
Daughters, 21, 46, 49, 50, 53, 61, 63, 71, 76, 79,
    90, 95, 99, 100, 116, 123, 131, 144, 150,
    153, 155, 158, 180, 189, 191
Dawson, 50, 144, 182
Deafness, 17, 53, 156
Death, 15, 18–21, 30, 31, 33, 47, 49, 50, 53, 57, 66,
    67, 72, 76, 79, 98, 100, 102, 106, 115, 119,
    120, 124, 125, 128, 132, 136, 143, 156,
    162, 170, 179, 181
Debate, 26, 112
Debt, 145
Deerfield, Massachusetts, 142
Delft, Holland, 155
Demolition expert, 75
Demons, 108

Demonstrations, 108
Dene Indian, 66
Denver, 148, 161, 188
Depression, 17, 22, 32, 57, 149
Depression era, 149
Desert, 68, 102, 189
Detectives, 30, 119
Detention facility, 31
Developmentally disabled, 32, 38, 50
Diabetes, 17
Dialogue, 2, 4, 26, 51, 58, 176
Diaries, 3, 4, 26, 32, 42, 58, 137, 140, 152, 154,
    169, 170, 172–74
Diary format, 3, 172–74
    contemporary, 173
    historical, 172, 173
Dinosaurs, 102, 107
Disabilities, 17, 20
Disappearance, 43, 77, 82, 188, 189
Discworld, 96
Disease, 15, 16, 18, 19. 20
Disfigurement, 41, 56
Dismemberment, 134
Distributors, 8
Divorces, 18, 51, 66, 113
Doctors without Borders, 26
Dogland, 90, 152
Dogs, 21, 26, 37, 48, 49, 58, 62, 67, 70, 72, 82, 90,
    102, 106, 152, 154, 156, 166
Dogwood Junior High, 171
Dollmage, 100
Dolls, 47, 90
Dolphins, 116
Domestic abuse, 34
Dominican Republic, 164
Dos and Don'ts for Teen Reader Advisory, 4
Downsider, 90
Down's syndrome, 36, 57
Dragonballs, 183
Dragons, 85, 94, 97, 98, 99, 102, 105, 111, 119
Dreams, 21, 34, 46, 47, 79, 80, 107, 131, 133, 135,
    136, 138, 149, 153, 154
Drinking, 17, 20, 21, 27, 33, 38, 55, 70, 113, 164
Drones, 124
Dropouts, 20, 39, 51, 53
Drug abuse, 20, 41, 170
Drug dealing, 30
Drugs, 20, 30, 31, 33, 34, 40, 41, 42, 47, 54, 124,
    162, 174
Drunk driving, 18
Dusky Devastators of the Depression, 149
Dust Bowl, 149, 150, 176
Dwarfism, 16
Dying, 18, 19, 20, 27, 49, 106, 123, 134, 144, 163,
    192
Dysfunction, 16, 41, 88, 113
Dystopian, 122

Earth, 21, 28, 37, 60, 102, 113, 114, 115, 116, 118,
    120, 121, 123, 152, 170, 180, 190

Earthquake, 148, 190
Eating disorders, 22, 64. *See also* Anorexia
Echoes Island, 88
Edgar Allan Poe Award. *See* Edgar Award
Edgar Award, 8, 42, 68, 73, 77, 78, 82
Edgeview Alternative School, 119
Editorials, 108
Educational associations, xiv
Educators, xii, xiii, 139, 141
Egypt/Egyptian, 69, 109, 153
1880s, 144, 145
Eighteenth century, 67, 141–45, 155, 156, 172
Eire, 106
Eisner Award, 179
Elderly persons, 35, 38, 39, 40, 49, 51, 58, 66, 74,
        76, 82, 106, 156
Electronic resources, 11
Elephants, 96
Eleventh century, 154
Elizabethan times, 78, 155
Ellis Island, 149
Elves, 88, 102, 181
E-mail, 21, 71, 75, 80, 174, 175,
E-mail discussion groups, 11, 195
Emelan, 88
Emotions, 20, 22, 74, 128. *See also* Mental,
        emotional, and behavioral issues
Endangered species, 120
Enemies, 34, 48, 70, 99, 107, 125, 153
England/English, 8, 51, 61, 67–69, 78, 92, 98, 101,
        109, 130, 142, 148, 153–56, 172, 173, 179,
        182
Environmental issues, 59, 187
Epic fantasy, 69, 86–88, 199–201
Epidemics, 142, 191
Epilepsy, 74, 123
Epistolary novels, 4, 174, 175
Equinox, 136
Espionage and terrorism, 65, 68, 69, 70
Essays, 21, 193, 194
Ethiopia, 167
Ethnic hate, 123
Ethnic war, 70
Ethnicity, 70, 123, 159, 160, 162, 167
Europe/European, 48, 50, 141, 142, 154, 156, 173
Evangelical Christians, 185
Evil, 17, 29, 57, 67, 76, 86–89, 94, 96, 99, 103,
        104, 107, 108, 124, 131, 134, 137, 180,
        190, 201
Ex-cons, 77
Execution, 118
Exploration, 112
Expository reading, 140
Expressways, 115
Extinct species, 117
Extraordinary powers, 3, 126, 179
Extrasensory powers, 125

Faerie, 85, 88, 89,106
Fairfax County Public Library, 159

Fairies, 35, 38, 62, 72, 88, 94, 95, 106, 138
Fairy godmothers, 58, 62
Fairy tales, 93–95, 184
Families, xii, 16–19, 22, 23, 26–28, 32, 34, 35,
        37–43, 46, 49–51, 53, 58, 59, 66, 68,
        70–72, 75, 82, 87, 89, 90, 94, 96, 99, 100,
        103, 104, 106, 107, 109, 112, 113, 120–24,
        128–30, 132, 136–38, 141–46, 149–54,
        156–58, 161, 163–67, 174, 183, 188, 189,
        191
Famines, 109, 156, 167
Fans, 3, 4, 55, 74, 85, 86, 100, 112, 114, 116, 119,
        139, 148, 172
Fantasy, xii, xiv, 2, 3, 6, 36, 40, 58, 65, 69, 77,
        85–112, 115, 116, 118, 130, 131, 139, 142,
        153, 154, 177, 180, 181, 189, 196–99, 205
Farms, 40, 48, 142, 144, 149, 150, 156, 170, 176,
        189, 191
Fat. *See* Overweight
Fathers, 16, 17, 19–26, 30–42, 46–53, 56, 57, 59,
        63, 66, 67, 70–72, 74–79, 82, 87, 89, 91,
        93–95, 99, 100, 103, 104, 110, 113, 117,
        120, 121, 125, 129, 130, 132, 136, 138,
        142, 144–52, 155–57, 160, 163, 165–68,
        170, 171, 173, 174, 176, 178, 179, 183,
        188, 192
Favorite Teen Angst Books, 194
FBI, 53, 71, 188
Fear, 93, 109, 128, 167
Female circumcision, 167
Ferrets, 103
Ferry, 66, 72
Fiancées and fiancés, 75, 144, 166, 187
Field trips, 109
Field workers, 151
Fifth century, 93
Fights, 20, 23, 26, 28, 33, 40, 49, 50, 59, 67, 88, 93,
        99, 100, 102, 103, 105, 112, 120, 142, 144,
        146, 156, 157, 161, 168, 179, 180, 181
Filipinas, 25
Film, 3, 17, 27, 29, 43, 48, 49, 54, 56, 59, 60, 72,
        101, 114, 118, 127, 173, 178, 179, 180
Filmmaker, 38
Fire lizards, 119
Firebird, 85
Fires, 17, 28, 46, 49, 88, 96, 109, 144, 189
First Nations. *See* Native Americans
First Peoples, 141
Fish Frat, 74
Fishbowls, 116
Fisherman, 48
Flat, 133. *See also* Apartments
Flight skills, 117
Flint, Michigan, 22
Flirting, 64
Floods, 32, 66, 123
Florida, 17, 38, 81, 90, 122, 142, 147, 152, 164,
        173
Flowers, 95
Flying, 133, 157, 197

Flying car, 101
Flying lessons, 189
Focus group, 6
Folk, 121
Folklore, 8, 88, 133
Folktales, 46, 93
Football, 17, 29, 31, 47, 51, 55, 56, 57, 75, 187
Forests, 37, 88, 91, 97, 99, 149
Formats, xii, 2–6, 10, 31, 32, 39, 60, 71, 76, 97,
     129, 135, 140, 150, 165, 169–72, 175, 176,
     177–80, 183, 184
Foster care, 36, 39, 40, 42, 71, 102, 109, 149, 167
Foster children, 12, 32, 36
Fourteenth century, 154
France/French, 69, 70, 94, 141, 142, 155, 156, 161,
     175
Franklin Middle School, 159
Freak show, 135
Freaks, 97
Free Mountain Militia, 71
Freedom, 87, 88, 102, 103, 108, 145, 149
Freedomtown, 161
French Alps, 69
Frenchtown, 150, 175
Fresno, 33, 165
Friends, xii, xiii, 11, 12, 16, 18, 20, 22–26, 28–30,
     32–38, 41–43, 45, 47–50, 53–57, 59–64,
     67, 71, 72, 74, 75, 79, 80, 82, 87, 88, 90,
     97, 99, 101, 107, 110, 114, 115, 117, 121,
     122, 124, 129–33, 135, 137, 142, 144, 147,
     149, 150, 153, 155–58, 161–63, 166, 167,
     171, 173–75, 178, 179, 184, 186–91
Friendship, 17, 21, 23, 25, 29, 32, 38, 43, 56, 61,
     66, 149, 160, 163, 167, 175, 179
Frogs, 96
Frying Pan of Doom, 98
Fund-raiser, 29, 108

Gambling, 53
Game shows, 61
Games, 4, 9, 10, 28, 39, 54, 55, 61, 108, 114, 115,
     121, 125, 132, 151
Gangs, 29, 30, 33, 40, 41, 72, 88, 107, 131, 165,
     167
Gangsters, 42
Gay, 22, 23, 24, 33, 39, 54, 90, 196
Geese, 94
Gemstone, 88
Gender, 5, 23, 86
Genetic engineering, 112, 114, 119, 124–26
Genetics, 16
Genius, 89, 112, 113, 177
Genocide, 157
Genovia, 173
Genre fiction, xii–xvi, 1, 2, 3, 5, 6, 8, 9, 12, 13
Genre Fiction for Reluctant Readers, 202
Genre writer's organizations, xiv
Genreblending, 3, 135
Genrefluent Page Reviews of Teen Books, 195

Genres, xii–xiv, xvi, 6, 1, 2, 3, 4, 5, 6, 12, 16, 52,
     65, 73, 112, 127, 139, 170, 177, 185
Geoffrey Bilson Award, 8, 67
Georgia, 26, 28, 152, 163,
Germany/Germans, 70, 151, 178
Get Graphic@ Your Library, 10
Ghostlands, 130
Ghosts, 36, 40, 61, 69, 75, 77, 79, 117, 127–29,
     132, 138, 154
Girlfriends, 21, 25, 32, 34, 35, 53, 60, 63, 76, 80,
     132, 174
Glaciers, 99
Glen Canyon Dam, 123
Global Community, 190
Globe Theatre, 109
Goat Guys, 90
Goats, 98
Goblin Pearls, 77, 164
Goblins, 89, 98
Goddesses, 91, 131, 182
Gods, 91, 105, 133, 179, 181, 183
Good and evil, xii, 86
Gore, 115, 127
Gorgon, 91, 97
Goth, 17, 48
Gotham City, 180
Graduation, 109, 163, 171
Graffiti, 26, 29
Grail Keepers, 110
Grand Canyon, 66, 123
Granddaughters, 40, 161, 191
Grandfathers, 18, 19, 23, 32, 56, 69, 76, 81, 99,
     151, 161
Grandmothers, 19, 21, 22, 38, 47–50, 54, 72, 77,
     80, 99, 102, 106, 116, 118, 131–33, 147,
     150, 151, 163–65, 171, 173, 186, 188, 189,
     191
Grandparents, 28, 49, 148, 151, 174, 191
Graphic novels, xiv, 2, 4, 10, 34, 41, 48, 133, 169,
     170, 176–84, 196, 197
     fantasy and science fiction, 180–82
     humor, 183, 184
     manga, 182, 183
     real-life themes, 177–79
     superheroes, 179, 180
Graphics, 176
Grave robbing, 144
Graves, 109
Gray Death, 94
Graymoss, 79, 129
Great Plains, 67, 142
Great Quake of 1906, 149
Greater Dunitsa, 96
Greece, 105, 153, 174, 187
Greed, 95
Greek gods, 181
Greenwich Village, 173
Gremlins, 179
Grief, 18, 121
Griffins, 99, 100

Group home, 120
Growing up, 45, 90, 166, 171
Gryphons, 99, 100
Guardians, 89, 96, 103, 137, 143
Guatemala/Guatemalan, 27, 186
Guerrilla warfare, 67
Guides, xiii, xiv, xvi, 1, 2, 4, 7, 8, 10, 13, 66, 68,
    85, 86, 98, 108, 111, 128, 139, 140, 162,
    170, 177, 197, 198, 202
Gunmen, 22, 72
Guns, 20, 50, 71, 109
Gyms, 21, 56

Haida, 50
Hair, 95, 101, 123, 148
Haiti/Haitian, 28, 51, 161, 167
Half-breed, 102
Half Circle Hold, 119
Hang gliding, 30
Happy endings, 46, 52, 94
Hardcover books, 5, 111
Hard science fiction, 114, 115
Hares, 103
Harlem, 21, 41, 150, 152, 163, 171, 183
Harlem Renaissance, 41, 150
Harley-Davidson, 165
Harmony, 51
Harper, 32, 119, 120
Hatchet, 68
Haunted, 80, 83, 88, 128, 131, 136
Haunted house, 187
Hawaii, 24, 50, 164, 173, 191
Hazelwood High, 36
Headaches, 95
Healer, 95, 107, 144
Hearing impairment, 187. *See also* Deafness
Heart attack, 19, 51
Heaven, 190
Hebrew Home for Boys, 41, 150
Hedgehogs, 104
Hedgewitch, 98
Herbal remedies, 95
Heritage, 49, 106, 147
Heroes and heroines, 17, 18, 22, 28, 34, 37, 41, 58,
    65, 68, 71, 72, 86, 87, 90, 91, 98–100, 112,
    114, 116, 139, 145–48, 179
Heroin, 33, 40, 42
Hiding, xvi, 65, 93, 97, 122, 138, 167
High school, xv, 12, 18–22, 24–26, 29, 30, 33, 35,
    38, 39, 48, 49, 51, 52, 54–57, 59, 60, 62,
    63, 74–76, 79, 81, 82, 109, 110, 123, 130,
    134, 135, 137, 163, 165, 170–76, 178, 179,
    186–88, 191, 198
Hiking, 18, 189
Hilarity, 96, 115, 138, 148, 173, 177
Hippies, 72, 151, 176
Hispanic Americans, 52, 160, 164–66, 176, 198
Historians, 116
Historic trail, 47

Historical books, 3, 4, 16, 50–52, 54, 61, 65, 67,
    70, 73, 74, 109, 118, 133, 139, 140–42,
    146, 151, 153, 154, 156, 157, 160, 172, 206
Historical fiction, 3, 8, 67, 72, 109, 139–58, 160,
    161, 167, 172, 197
Historical mysteries, 77–79
History, 2, 17, 45, 46, 49, 118, 122, 133, 138–42,
    145, 148, 151, 154, 157, 170, 172, 178
Hitchhiking, 115
Hogwarts School, 101
Holland, 155
Holocaust, 95, 109, 156, 157, 178
Holy Grail, 92
Home schools, 30
Homecoming, 29, 37
Homecoming queen, 16
Homeland, 157, 158, 160, 161
Homelessness and foster living, 15, 31, 36, 39–42,
    71, 74, 147, 157, 168, 179
Homesteads, 40, 147, 149
Homework, 18, 194
Honor student, 60
Hood ornaments, 37
Horn Book, 196
Horror, xiii, 6, 21, 98, 127, 128, 138, 146, 177, 183,
    187
Horror Writers Association, 8
Horse, 76, 95, 108
Hospitals and hospitalization, 17, 19–22, 55, 76,
    97, 124, 132, 156, 191
Hostages, 22, 39, 74, 89, 170, 175, 189
Hotels, 32, 76
Housekeepers, 133, 149, 152
Housemates, 87
Housing projects, 25, 162, 165, 176
Hudson River, 178
Hugo Award, 8, 101, 111, 112, 116, 133
Humanity, 98, 120, 135
Humanoids, 117
Humor, 16, 18, 20, 45, 46, 51, 53, 56, 58–63, 82,
    91–95, 97, 98, 104, 115, 116, 127, 148,
    154, 163, 165, 171, 178, 183
Humorous fantasy, 95–98
Humorous science fiction, 115, 116
Humorous westerns, 148
Hunger strike, 20
Hunting, 68, 123

Iceland, 81
Ida, Texas, 50
Identity, xii, 23, 42, 43, 46, 75, 100, 122, 149, 159,
    161, 163, 164, 181
Illegal immigrant, 61
Illinois, 55, 149, 150, 171, 196
Illustrated stories, 4
Illustrations, 13, 89, 182
Imagination, 11, 59, 85, 98, 127, 129
Immigrants and immigration, 3, 78, 143, 148, 159,
    163, 171
Immortality, 105, 132

Imprints, 85, 200
India, 163, 164, 168
Indian heritage, 26, 166
Industrialization, 143, 148
Infants, 25, 33
Inheritance, 16, 46, 104, 116, 119, 124, 145
Injury, 187
Insane asylum, 109. *See also* Mental hospitals
Inspiration, 4, 19
Institutions, 20
Integration, 90, 152
Intelligence agency, 68, 69
Interest in reading, xiii
International Reading Association, xv, 8
    Young Adult Choice list, xv, 8, 17, 19–22, 24,
        25, 28–30, 32–37, 39, 42, 43, 47–49,
        51–58, 60, 66, 68–70, 72, 76–79,
        90–92, 94, 100–4, 106, 109, 122,
        128–31, 134, 137, 138, 145–47, 150,
        151, 155–57, 160–62, 170–76
International Reading Association Award (IRA),
    xv, 8, 28, 32, 40, 135, 149, 150, 152, 173
Internet, 10, 11, 80
Internet Public Library—Teen Space, 195
Interracial issues, 28, 81, 161
Interrogators, 30
Interviews, 195
Inuit, 66
Invasion, 67, 70, 108, 132
Inventors, 40, 124
Invisibility, 20, 119, 131, 179
Iowa, 145
IRA. *See* International Reading Association Award
    (IRA)
Iraq, 27
IRAYAC. *See* International Reading Association
Ireland/Irish, 38, 94, 106, 107, 109, 141, 143, 149,
    155, 156, 159, 161, 168, 189
Irish Americans, 168
Iron Age, 51
Islands, 26, 31, 49, 50, 66, 74, 91, 106, 107, 114,
    117, 124, 125, 134, 142, 149, 151, 180
Issues, xii, xiii, 3, 5, 6, 15–45, 47, 52, 53, 55–57,
    61, 62, 66, 67, 71, 74, 93, 95, 128, 139,
    146, 151, 152, 160–67, 170–74, 176, 194,
    196, 198, 202
Italy/Italian, 49, 74, 149

Jamaica/Jamaican, 51, 157, 161
Jane Addams Award, 28
Japanese Americans, 18, 164
Japanimation, 182
Japan/Japanese, 18, 38, 78, 157, 158, 161, 163,
    164, 167, 168, 180
Jazz, 41, 81, 150
Jerusalem, 161, 190
Jesuits, 141
Jews, 78 109, 135, 146, 150, 157, 161, 178
Jobs, xii, 6, 30, 32, 33, 39, 42, 47, 48, 52, 68, 81,
    114, 121, 122, 130, 150, 176, 179, 186, 188

Jocks, 54, 183
Johannesburg, South Africa, 41, 167
Jokes, 183
Journalist, 167, 190
Journals, 6, 18, 34, 35, 107, 129, 169, 170, 172,
    174, 177. *See also* Diary format
Journeys, 33, 67, 69, 104, 106, 118, 121, 123, 143,
    156, 160
Judges, 12, 78
Juneteenth, 161
Jungles, 27, 68, 166
Junior high school, xiii, xv, 175, 198
Junk shop, 58
Junkyard, 33
Justice League of America, 180
Juvenile behavioral center, 37
Juvenile correctional facilities, 12, 30, 37, 72
Juvenile delinquents, 113

Kansas, 147, 148, 166, 172
Karate, 17
Kent State University, 81, 198
Kentucky, 144
Kidnappings, 33, 35, 42, 43, 72, 75, 76, 80, 89, 96,
    99, 103, 113, 121, 126, 133, 136, 141, 142,
    147, 153
Kids in the system, 36, 37
Killer bees, 59
Killers, 17, 20, 30, 33, 78, 126, 131
Killings, 18, 20, 39, 48, 68, 150, 190. *See also*
    Murder
Kilts, 96
King Philip's war, 142
Kings, 41, 91, 92, 94, 95, 97, 99, 106, 107, 127,
    154, 155
Kinship, 28
Kirkus Children's Reviews, 196
Kissing, 35, 94, 96, 131, 173, 186
Kitchens, 37, 108
Kites, 157
Kittens, 106
Klan. *See* Ku Klux Klan
Kliatt, 6, 196
Knights, 79, 88, 92, 99, 154
Knives, 105
Korea/Korean, 34, 157, 158, 163, 164, 167
Ku Klux Klan, 145, 150, 176
Kugisko, 88
Kurds, 27

Labor camps, 113, 156
Labor Day, 189
Labrador retriever, 156
Lakes, 76, 77, 105, 133
Lambda Award, 53, 162
Land of Oz, 86
Land mine, 161
Language, 2, 8, 53, 153, 158, 175
Latino Literary Hall of Fame, 165
Latinos, 2, 8, 164, 165, 166

Law, 33, 117, 122
Lawyers, 46, 59
Leadership, 29
Learning disabilities, 55
Legal protection, 117
Legends, 56, 57, 72, 89, 90–93, 134, 153, 154
Lenape Indians, 109, 142
LEP-recon, 89
Lesbians, 22–24, 39, 162, 196
Letters, 60, 168, 170, 174, 175, 188
Leukemia, 58
Liars, 20
Librarians, xii, xiii, 6, 7, 10, 13, 18, 40, 100, 120,
        195, 196
Libraries, xi, xii, xiv, 6, 1, 6, 9, 10, 11, 12, 100,
        111, 159, 177, 181, 195, 197
Library associations, xiv
Library books, 107
Library catalogs, xv
Library services, promoting, 194
Life Is Hard books, 16, 29, 31–43, 57, 161, 162,
        163, 165
Lifeguards, 32, 34
Lighthouse keeper, 144
Lightning, 80, 125
Lights, 117
Linguist, 119
Lion Salve, 77
Lions, 153
Lirgonians, 116
Listservs, 9
Little Italy, 42
Liverpool, 109
Living dead, 81, 130
Locus, 101, 112, 116, 201
London, 38, 40, 70, 78, 101, 109, 151, 154, 155,
        156, 167
Loners, 39. See also Outsiders
Long Island, 18, 34
Los Angeles, 90, 159, 165
Los Angeles Public Library, 159
Lotteries, 38
Louisiana, 32, 53, 55
Love, xii, 5, 10, 13, 18, 19, 21–24, 34, 42, 45, 46,
        51–54, 61, 62, 66, 87, 88, 91, 96, 99, 102,
        104, 106, 107, 109, 116, 118–20, 122, 129,
        130, 132, 134, 143, 144, 147, 150, 151,
        159–62, 164, 170, 173–76, 183
Lowell, Massachusetts, 144
Luftwaffe, 70
Lying, 48, 115
Lynching, 151, 152

Macabre, 127
Mad scientist, 124
Magazines, xi, xii, 194, 195, 202
Mages and magicians, 77, 87, 99, 107, 154. See
        also Sorcerers; Wizards
Magic, 22, 37, 45, 58, 85–88, 90, 94, 95, 98,
        100–102, 106, 107, 116, 152, 174, 181, 189

Magical creatures, 102
Magical powers, 58
Maids, 155. See also Servants
Mail-order brides, 191
Mainstream fiction, 2
Malapropisms, 93
Male readers, 172
Mammoths, 152
Manga, 169, 177, 182, 183, 197
Manhattan, 63, 83
Manitoba, 47, 166
Manners, 101
Maori, 50
Maps, 116, 117
Margaret A. Edwards Award, 7, 195
Marketing, xi, xii, 1, 3. 6, 11–13
Marriage, 66, 94, 163, 164, 168
Maryland, 130
Massachusetts, 46, 142, 144
Massachusetts Institute of Technology, 46
Massacre, 121, 141
Master race, 126
Masters, 77, 93, 98, 116, 121, 129, 135, 154, 155,
        158
Mathematics, 46
Mechanics, 118 187
Mechs, 114
Media, 16, 31, 135, 169
Media specialists, 196
Medical school, 55, 191
Medical treatment, 40
Medicines, 95
Mementos, 67
Memories, 19, 41, 91, 95, 117, 122, 128, 133, 163,
        174
Mental capabilities, 20, 112
Mental, emotional, and behavioral issues, 16,
        20–22, 132,176
Mental hospitals, 25, 36, 37, 55, 132
Mental illness, 20, 22, 34, 71
Mental patients, 21
Mentors, 88, 120, 125
Merchandising, 194
Merchants, 94, 155
Mermaids, 90, 91, 97, 107, 134
Messages, 78, 98, 102, 116, 185, 195
Messiah, 60
Meteor, 123
Mexican American, 50, 165
Mexico/Mexican, 50, 124, 151, 165, 174
Miami, Florida, 164
Mice, 104, 178
Michael L. Printz Award, 1, 7, 23, 31, 34, 132, 164,
        169, 170
Michael L. Printz-Honor, 17, 18, 20, 23, 24, 49, 60,
        77, 89, 99, 124, 174, 176
Michigan, 22, 71, 149
Middle ages, 17, 91, 118, 154, 155, 172
Middle class, 27, 36
Middle Earth, 86

Middle Passage, 143
Middle school, xiii, xv, 11, 17, 18, 39, 59, 60, 62, 65, 108, 129, 142, 187, 198
Midnight (city), 134
Migrant, 165
Military, 68, 70, 112
Military scientists, 68
Militias, 65, 69, 71
Mill, 49
Millard Central Middle School, 159
Miller, 95
Millionaire, 69
Mind probe, 123
Miners, 116, 121, 149
Mining, 113, 114, 132, 192
Ministers, 46, 61
Minneapolis, 124
Minnesota, 40, 106, 149
Minorities, 3, 159, 160, 162, 164
Minstrels, 92
Misfits, 50, 119. *See also* Outsiders
Missing children, 15, 42, 43, 108
Missionary, 19
Missions, 21, 67, 108, 153, 180
Mississippi, 146, 151
Missouri, 68, 148
Mixed formats, 170
Mixed heritage, 49, 160, 161, 162
Mobsters, 42, 53
Models, 35, 53, 59, 64, 126, 183
Mohawk, 133, 141, 161
Monarch, 155
Monastery, 87
Money, 30, 37, 40, 42, 51, 79, 96, 117, 162, 167
Money, Mississippi, 151
Monsters, 42, 59, 98, 127–30, 180
Montana, 149, 189
Moon, 113, 126, 131, 136
Moonhawk Kin tribe, 153
Moral, 112, 145
Mormon, 144
Mossflower, 103
Motherlessness, 46, 48, 62, 63, 78, 152
Mothers, 18–22, 24–26, 28, 30–38, 40, 41, 47–51, 53–55, 57, 59, 63, 71, 75–80, 82, 88–91, 94, 95, 98, 101, 102, 106, 107, 110, 115, 117, 119–22, 124, 125, 129–34, 137, 141, 143, 144, 147, 150, 151, 156, 157, 162, 163, 166–68, 170, 173, 176, 178, 186–88, 191
Motorcycles, 48, 165
Mountain Patriots Association, 71
Mountains, 68, 71, 81, 93, 99, 109
Mousemaid, 103
Movements, 27, 139, 140, 143, 148, 151
Movies, 4, 48, 49, 54, 56, 59, 85, 87, 100, 180, 183, 187
Mulande, 167
Mulhoney, Wisconsin, 58

Multicultural fiction, xiii, 36, 46, 49, 70, 141, 159–68, 176
Multiculturalism, 160–66, 198, 206
Multiple issues, 31, 34, 41, 173
Multiple viewpoints, 172
Multiple voices, 39, 170
Mummy, 83
Murder, 19, 21, 30, 31, 33, 42, 71, 72, 75–82, 91, 97, 129, 130, 134, 137, 149, 155, 167, 170, 175, 178, 180, 188, 189
Museum of Natural History, 82
Music, 1, 22, 51, 118, 119, 120
Musicians, 22, 48, 81
Musk-oxen, 66
Mutism, 20, 21
Mystery and suspense, xii, 3, 4, 16, 20, 28, 29, 36, 38, 42, 43, 65, 70, 73–83, 90, 108, 120, 124, 128, 129, 132, 137, 139, 140, 161, 164, 175, 177, 178, 185, 188, 204
Mystery series, 79–83
Mystery Writers of America, 8, 73
Mythic reality, 89, 90
Mythical creatures, 105
Mythopoeic Award, 93, 100
Myths and legends, 89–93, 98, 179, 181

Nanotechnology, 114
Narnia, 107, 108, 189
National Anthem, 26
National Book Award, 21, 165, 176
National Coalition for the Homeless, 39
National Consortium of Latin American Studies Programs, 8
National Council of Teachers of English, 7, 195, 196
National forest, 81
National Honor Society, 10
National Merit, 51
Native Americans, 26,, 53, 67, 98, 137, 139–42, 166, 198
Natives, 121
Natural resources, 183
Natural world, 89
Navy, 50
Nazis, 70, 151, 156, 180
Nebraska, 159
Nebula Award, 8, 111, 112, 133
Necromancy, 100
Neighborhoods, 33, 104, 174
Neighbors, 24, 28, 36, 43, 49, 51, 54, 56, 58, 74, 82, 106, 121, 134, 144, 152, 156, 176
Nevada, 24, 78
New Jersey, 49, 88, 163, 164, 171
New Mexico, 114, 165
New Orleans, 145, 191
New World, 118
New Year's Eve, 82
New York, xvi, 13, 14, 19, 41, 42, 47, 49, 51, 53, 72, 90, 102, 123, 126, 130, 137, 143–45, 150, 173, 184, 191, 197

New York Public Library (NYPL) Books for the
    Teen Age, 165
New York University, 163
New Zealand, 50, 52, 66, 67, 122, 149–51, 154,
    176
Newbery Award, 29, 66, 72
Newbery Honor, 18, 21, 29, 33, 37, 55, 58–60, 68,
    88, 94, 99, 119, 124, 171
Newborn, 181
Newfoundland, 151
News clippings, 26, 170
Newsletter, 11
Newspapers, 18, 28, 50, 57, 78, 161, 166, 188
Nightmares, 34, 35, 43, 121, 180
Nike, xi, xii
9-1-1, 20, 82
1920s, 40, 41, 131, 150, 157, 176
1930s, 40, 127, 150, 176
1960s, 127, 139, 151, 152, 165, 167
Nineteenth century, 69, 109, 142, 143–45, 148,
    155, 156, 163, 178
Noctumbos, 121
Nomadic, 28, 168
Nonagenarians, 124
Nonfiction, 8, 66, 68, 140, 177, 194, 202
Norbit, 116
North Africa, 81
North America, 8, 16, 141
North Carolina, 78, 128
North Dakota, 40, 149
Northern slope, 66
Nuclear bomb, 69
Nurses, 143, 145, 152, 191
Nursing home, 47, 50

Oakland, California, 33
Objibwa, 141
Obsessions, 30, 122
Obsessive-compulsiveness, 21
Obsidian, 92
Oceans, 69
O'Dell Award. See Scott O'Dell Award
Ogres and ogresses, 94
Ohio, 143, 150, 172, 198
Oklahoma, 150, 176
Olympics, 55, 105, 153
Omaha, Nebraska, 159
Online community, 195
Online forum, 195
Online resources, 194, 195
Oppression, 166
Oral tradition, 198
Orchards, 137
Oregon, 144, 148, 149
Oregon Trail, 147
Orphanages, 40, 89, 149
Orphans, 17, 29, 40, 41, 49, 67, 75, 89, 96, 97, 99,
    100, 109, 124, 133, 134, 145, 150, 153,
    154, 157, 167, 179, 180
Oscar Wilde Middle School, 108

Ostara, 136
Ostracism, 29
Otters, 104
Outcasts, 27, 33, 39, 41, 46, 49, 56, 72, 87, 102,
    120, 178
Outlaws, 148
Out-of-home placements, 39
Outsiders, 28, 29, 31, 33, 34, 36–39, 56, 162, 170,
    178
Outstanding books for middle school, xv
Outstanding Books for the College Bound, 195
Overdose, 50
Overlords, 123
Overseas, 151
Overweight, 16, 24, 33, 34, 37, 38, 48, 53, 56, 164,
    166
Owls, 59, 104
Ozarks, 191

Painter, 151, 155
Paintings, 18
Pakistan/Pakastani, 26, 28, 163, 168
Palestine, 157
Pankration, 153
Paperbacks, 5, 6, 12, 111, 196
Parallel universes, 105, 108, 115, 117, 118, 180
Paralysis, 16
Paranormal, xiii, 40, 52, 61, 63, 73, 74, 79, 82, 85,
    98, 109, 100, 110, 117, 119, 127–38, 177,
    181, 205
Parasites, 121, 134
Parental responsibility, 28
Parents, 4, 18, 20, 22, 24–26, 31, 32, 34, 36, 38,
    40–42, 46, 48–51, 59, 65, 66, 69, 75, 80,
    88, 90, 96, 100, 101, 104, 109, 113, 117,
    119, 122, 123, 131 133, 134, 137, 144, 148,
    161, 163, 164, 174, 176, 178, 180, 186, 187
Pariahs, 38
Paris, 109, 125
Parkside Middle School, 125
Parody, 95, 148
Parsonage, 46
Party, 17, 20, 50, 86, 115, 145
Pastors, 26, 77, 163
Patterson, New Jersey, 164, 171
Pawnee, 147
Pea Island, 143
Pearls, 103
Peasants, 155
Peddlers, 145
Pen pal, 188
Penguin Putnam, 85
Pennsylvania, 57, 61, 109, 191
Penthouse, 97
Pern, 86, 119
Persecution, 109
Persia, 94, 153
Personalities, 86, 121
Perspectives, 93, 139, 160, 171
Petra, 190

Philadelphian, 142
Philanthropy, 162
Philosophy, 112, 168
Phoenix, 104
Photo shoot, 186
Photographers, 35, 163, 179
Physical abuse, 31, 34
Physical challenges, 16, 17, 31, 55
Physicians, 26
Picaresque, 148
Pictsies, 96
Pictures, 132
Pied Piper, 96
Pigeons, 51
Pigs, 82, 178
Pilgrim parties, 100
Pilot, 190
Pine marten, 103
Pinkerton agency, 146
Pirates, 67, 69, 70, 81, 87, 103, 116
Pitchers (baseball), 21, 55, 56
Plagues, 122, 125, 126, 154, 190
Plane crash, 66, 68, 124
Planets, 111, 112, 114, 119, 120, 121, 182
Plantations, 79, 129, 131, 145, 146, 164, 191
Plants, 95, 124, 160
Playwright, 78
Plot, xiii, xv, xvi, 5, 49, 58, 62, 66, 89, 96, 102
Poems and poetry, 8, 10, 31, 56, 76, 97, 129, 175,
    176, 196, 198
Poets, 22, 143
Poles, 178
Police, 30, 39, 42, 50, 59, 74, 75, 80
Political activism, 26
Political asylum, 77
Political situations, 27
Politics, 27–28, 67, 68, 167
Pollution, 118
Pompano Beach, 61, 173
Pools, 32, 62, 90
Poppies, 124
Popular Paperbacks, 7, 9, 13, 17–19, 22–24, 26,
    28–31, 33, 36, 40, 42, 47, 51–53, 55–61,
    66, 68, 69, 72, 76, 78, 89, 90, 94, 95, 104,
    109, 115, 118–20, 123, 128, 130, 133–35,
    143, 144, 146–48, 152, 154, 156, 157,
    160–65, 168, 169, 171–81, 183, 184, 195
Popularity, xiv, xvi, 3, 4, 7, 8, 9, 11, 12, 15, 16, 18,
    23, 30, 37, 38, 39, 41, 48, 65, 68, 73, 74,
    77, 86, 90, 98, 103, 112, 114, 115, 116,
    118, 124, 127, 131, 134, 140, 142, 154,
    159, 173, 177, 180, 183, 185, 186, 197
Population, xi, 3, 12, 123
Population Police, 122
Portuguese man-of-war, 191
Possession, 17, 125
Postapocalypse, 122–24
Postcards, 161
Posttraumatic stress disorder (PTSD), 36
Post-Vietnam, 152

Potato famine, 156
Practical jokes, 30
Prairie du Sac, 18
Prairie romance, 140
Preachers, 23, 50, 149, 150
Precognition, 79, 100, 110, 119, 130
Preconferences, 196
Predators, 130
Pregnancy, 22, 24–26, 40, 41, 52, 71, 119, 163,
    167, 173, 188
Prehistory, 115, 152, 153
Prejudice, 161
Prep school, 39, 61, 96, 161
President, 52
Prey, 68
Priests, 88, 107, 154
Princes, 88, 94, 106, 108, 120, 173
Princesses, 77, 87, 93, 97, 99, 154, 155, 173, 183,
    188
Printers, 142
Prison, 29, 33, 78, 88, 106, 133, 144, 162, 163
Prisoners, 21, 89, 155
Private schools, 22, 30, 122
Problem novels, xiii, 15
Professional development, 195, 196
Programs, 9, 10, 11, 13, 196
Prohibition, 150
Project Crescent, 125, 126
Prom, 54, 60, 62
Promiscuity, 60
Prophecy, 103, 107, 190
Protagonists, xv, xvi, 2, 5, 15, 16, 24, 26, 28, 37,
    39, 42, 45, 46, 58, 66, 68, 71, 73, 74, 79,
    86, 92, 98, 104, 112, 141, 146, 160, 166,
    171, 172, 177
Provincetown, 50
Prowlers, 130
Pseudonyms, 2
Psionic powers, 98, 110, 119, 120, 129–32
Psychiatric facility, 40. See also Mental hospitals
Psychic powers, 80, 106, 110, 123, 183
Psycho, 39
Psychological abuse, 34
Psychological thriller, 75
Psychologist, 19
PTSD. See Posttraumatic stress disorder
Puberty, 120, 124, 152
Publishers, xiv, 2, 4, 5, 8, 85, 111, 172, 182, 183
Publishers' catalogs, 6, 9
Publishing industry, xiv, 2–4, 111, 159
Puerto Rico/Puerto Rican, 164, 171
Punks, 33, 90
Puns, 61, 95
Puppet show, 119
Pura Belpre, 151, 164, 165, 171

Queens, 42, 69, 87, 88, 96, 97, 102, 103, 172, 180
Quests, 43, 49, 57, 86, 87, 89, 90, 95, 97, 105, 106,
    114, 117, 121, 123, 124, 126, 137, 148,
    181, 183

Quick Picks, 7, 9, 13, 17–26, 28–42, 47–49, 51–55,
    57–63, 66–72, 74–77, 79–81, 87, 90, 94,
    95, 102, 105, 114, 115, 117–24, 126,
    128–32, 134–38, 144–46, 150, 154,
    161–66, 170, 171, 173–76, 178–80,
    182–84, 195, 202
Quidditch, 101
Quinceanera, 165

Rabbits, 103, 183
Racism, 26–29, 31, 36, 71, 145, 152, 172
Radio, 10, 47, 75, 79, 170
Rafting, 41, 89
Rainbow forces, 24
Ranch, 126
Ranch hands, 186
Rap, 169
Rape, 35, 51, 134
Rapture, 190
Rapunzel, 95
Rats, 58, 96, 103, 104, 130, 179
Ravensmere, 89
Read for the Fun of It, 10
Readers, xi–xvi, 1–13, 15, 16, 18, 26, 29, 36,
    45–47, 49, 52, 60–62, 65, 66, 71, 73–75,
    77, 79, 85–87, 89–92, 95, 97, 98, 100, 102,
    111, 112, 115, 116, 120, 127, 128, 130,
    133, 134, 138–42, 145, 146, 148, 152, 154,
    156, 159, 160, 162, 166, 169–72, 176, 178,
    182, 185, 190, 197, 198, 200, 202
Readers' advisors, xii–xiv, xvi, 1, 2, 4, 7, 9,55, 140,
    198
Reading habits, 1
Reading interests, 195
Reading promotion, xii
Reading Rants, 195
Reading tastes, xii
Rebellion, 51, 154
Rebels, 95, 146
Reconstruction, 143, 145, 147
Recovery, 123
Recruiters, 55
Red Valley, 49
Redemption, 185
Redwall Abbey, 103, 104
Regency era, 101
Regency romances, 139
Rehabilitation center, 30
Reincarnation, 132
Relationships, xii, 3, 5, 6, 7, 10, 17, 23, 29, 32, 35,
    46, 47, 48, 51, 52, 53, 62, 70, 81, 90, 134,
    145, 152, 160, 161, 174, 186
Relatives, 17, 19, 26, 101, 132, 153, 164, 166, 171
Religion, 28, 40, 50, 135, 168, 185, 190
Religious beliefs, 28, 40
Relocation camp, 151
Reluctant readers, xii, 11, 12, 54, 146, 194, 202
Reporters, 126, 166
Research, 28, 50, 66, 130, 133, 140, 144

Resources, xvi, 8, 9, 11, 12, 13, 93, 139, 177, 193,
    194, 195, 197
Respect, 4
Resurrection, 190
Review journals, 196
Reviews, xii, xv, 6, 8, 195, 196
Rhythm, 170, 176
Richie's Picks, 195
Riddles, 95
Rifles, 32
Rituals, 81, 134, 136
Rivets, 111
Roaring Twenties, 149
Robberies, 22
Robert the Bruce, 154, 155
Robots, 114
Rock band, 90
Rock stars, 24, 50
Rodent, 80
Rogers' Rangers, 141
Roman Empire, 140
Romance, xii, 3, 13, 29, 45, 46, 49, 51–54, 58, 59,
    61, 62, 71, 73, 77, 79, 80, 81, 88, 109, 127,
    128, 134, 135, 137, 139, 140, 150, 154,
    156, 160, 171, 173, 183, 185, 186
Rome, 153, 178
Romeo and Juliet, 53, 144
Royal Bay, 54
Royalty, 173
Rumors, 26, 60, 61
Rumplestiltskin, 95
Runaways, 20, 30, 40, 66, 70, 71, 74, 119, 146,
    147, 187
Running, 28
Russia, 69, 70
Russian Revolution, 158
Rusties, 113

Sabbat, 136
Saber-toothed tigers, 117
Sabotage, 123
Sacrifice, 88, 98, 118
Sadness, 128, 138
Sailors, 69
Saints, 154
Salem, 79, 135, 136, 137, 142, 143
Samurai, 181
San Diego, 51, 165
San Francisco, 148, 149, 179, 191
Sangman, 89
Sasquatch, 72, 89
Satan, 108, 136
Satanist, 61
Satire, 95, 115, 153
Sauk Prairie High School, 18
Sawmill, 96
Saxons, 93
Scandals, 37, 61
Schizophrenia, 22
Scholarships, 25, 26, 36, 49, 55, 57, 161

School, xi, xiii, 7, 9, 10, 12, 13, 15, 17, 18, 20–26, 28, 30–32, 35, 36, 38–40, 46–55, 57, 59, 61, 68, 69, 72, 74, 76, 79, 82, 85, 96, 100, 108, 109, 112–15, 119, 121, 124, 132–35, 137, 139,
School violence, 15, 170
Science, 68, 111, 112, 114, 166, 178, 186,
Science fiction, xii, 2, 3, 4, 6, 52, 65, 71, 85, 98, 110, 111–26, 130, 177, 185, 196, 198, 205
Science Fiction and Fantasy Writers of America, 8
Science teacher, 166
Scientific discovery, 114
Scientific experiment, 117
Scientific research, 144
Scientific terms, 46
Scientific theory, 111
Scientists, 23, 82, 123, 124, 126, 180
Scope, xiv
Scotland/Scottish, 119, 154, 155, 166
Scott O'Dell Award, 150, 151, 176
Scottish-English border wars, 119
Screenplays, 31, 169, 170
Scripts, 155
Sculpture, 21, 49, 138
Sea, 65, 67, 69, 74, 104, 106, 157, 177, 191
Seattle, 26, 50, 150
Secrets, 10, 18, 32, 38, 49, 67, 90, 92, 100, 102, 113, 137, 138, 145, 161, 167, 173, 186, 187
Security agent, 126
See Me 4 Books, 195
Seeing stone, 92
Segregation, 29, 53, 161
Selection criteria, xiv
Self-esteem, 34, 48
Self-mutilation, 20, 21
Selkies, 97
Seminars, 195
Senior citizens, 82
September 11, 177
Serfs, 154
Serial killers, 30, 82, 126
Series, xiv, xv, 2–4, 6, 9, 11, 12, 25, 28, 33, 36, 43, 45, 47, 54, 59–64, 66–70, 72–74, 78–82, 85–89, 91–93, 96–104, 106, 107, 109, 112, 113, 115–17, 119, 121, 122, 124, 126, 128, 130–32, 134–37, 140, 141, 143–45, 147, 152, 153, 155, 157, 158, 164, 168, 172–76, 181, 183, 185–92, 194, 199–201
Service learning, 10
Serving the Underserved, 195
Setting, xv, xvi, 4, 30, 45, 52, 55, 61, 69, 74, 75, 77, 86, 91, 98, 100, 101, 105, 107, 109, 118, 116, 121, 134, 139, 140, 142, 146, 148, 151, 152, 154, 159, 175, 189
Seventeenth century, 142, 143, 155
Sex, 34, 52
Sexual abuse, 31, 35, 36, 42, 47, 93, 174, 179
Sexual advances, 57,
Sexual content, 185
Sexual identity, 22–24, 53, 164, 171

Sexual orientation, 23
Sexual relationships, 62
Sexuality, 23, 52
SF. See Science fiction
Shakers, 144
Shaman, 123
Shantytown, 149
Shapeshifters, 104, 105
Sharks, 191
Sheep, 145
Shelter, 12, 108
Shipbuilder, 155
Ships, 47, 69, 70, 157
Shipwreck, 72, 144
Shirts, 38, 59, 94
Shootings, 19, 32, 39, 81
Shootout, 42
Shopping carts, 21
Short stories, 23, 32, 37, 52, 55, 56, 97–99, 112, 128, 132, 138, 164, 165, 166, 168, 170, 171, 202
Shorthand, 155
Shyness, 90, 92, 183
Siblings, 20, 33, 42, 67, 97, 144, 165. See also Brothers; Sisters
Sidhe, 88
Sierra Leone, 32, 167
Sigils, 181
Singers, 88
Sisters, 18, 19, 21, 22, 27, 28, 31, 33, 34, 36, 37, 40, 48, 52, 68, 75, 80, 87, 89, 91, 94, 99, 107, 109, 115, 120, 121, 123, 126, 129, 130, 131, 141, 145, 147, 149, 151, 152, 156, 157, 167, 171, 187. See also Siblings
Sitka, Alaska, 70
Sixteenth century, 119, 155
Skateboarding, 71
Skeleton, 82
Skinhead, 79
Slammin'!@ Your Library, 10
Slapstick, 60, 95
Slasher movie, 59
Slasher stories, 127
Slaves and slavery, 29, 87, 102, 104, 108, 117, 118, 143, 145–47, 152, 157, 163, 172
Sleeping Beauty, 94, 95
Sleuths and sleuthing, 73, 76, 82, 114
Sluts, 26, 32, 48
Small towns, 29, 32, 38, 48, 59, 61, 76, 79, 110, 133, 152, 165, 171
Smallpox, 69
Smiths, 95
Smoo, 182
Snake bite, 28
Snakes, 59, 96
Snobbery, 62
Snow, 68
Soap opera, 62
Soap star, 58
Soccer, 17, 55, 57, 59, 174

Social concerns, 26–31, 151, 163
Social reformer, 28
Social Responsibilities Round Table, 7
Social satire, 61
Society, xii, 3, 7, 26, 30, 32, 41, 101, 121, 122, 159, 167
Sociopaths, 38
Sociopolitical issues, 28, 166
Softball, 57, 151
Software, 107
Soldiers, 27, 67, 171
Soldiers of God, 71
Somerset University, 81
Songs, 48, 88
Songwriters, 34
Sons, 25, 42, 53, 78, 87, 91, 92, 94, 97, 103, 114, 142, 146, 153, 154, 155, 157, 158, 161, 172, 192
Sons of Liberty Two, 71
Sopranos, 120
Sorcerers, 85, 87
Soul eaters, 120
Sound effects, 2, 170
Soup kitchen, 108
South, 28, 47, 61, 79, 90, 145, 146, 152, 188
South Seas, 69, 81, 157, 180
Southern Illinois University, 55
Southwest, 142
Space, 113
Space exploration, 114
Space opera, 116
Space travel, 114
Spain/Spanish, 8, 76, 142, 197
Speakers, 13, 35
Special effects, 100, 114
Specimens, 124
Speculation, 112
Spelling bees, 25, 165
Spiders, 98, 179
Spirits, 46, 90, 128, 130
Spiritualism, 46, 86, 131
Splatterpunk, 127
Spontaneous human combustion, 81
Sports, 3, 45, 48, 54–57, 162
Spur Award, 8, 66
Spy, 58, 69, 146, 151, 180
Squires, 92, 99
Squirrels, 104
St. Louis, 149
St. Mary's Church, 82
St. Thomas, 141
Stabbings, 75
Stalkers, 27, 29, 30
Stampede, 147
Starscape, 200
Starvation, 109
Starwort, 94
Stealing, 37, 76, 187
Stepbrothers, 40

Stepfathers, 20, 31, 32, 35, 40, 41, 46, 72, 147, 167, 188
Stepgrandfather, 46
Stepmothers, 53, 75, 94, 114, 136, 188
Stepsisters, 94
Stereotypes, 161
Stock market crash, 150
Stoners, 49, 51, 63
Storms, 67, 69, 72, 181
Story line, xv, 2, 86, 112
Storytellers, 129, 138, 154
Stowaways, 69, 157
Strategists, 113
Street kids, 167
Stress, xii, 25, 58, 175
Stress reliever, 95
Student councils, 29
Students, 8, 18, 19, 22, 25, 29, 30, 36, 38, 48, 55, 59, 68, 81, 98, 100, 108, 125, 133, 161, 175, 176, 179, 181, 183, 187, 188
Subdivisions, 40
Subgenres, xiii, xiv, 2, 3, 65, 74, 86, 97, 112, 170, 177
Substance abuse, 31, 41, 42, 57, 174,
Substitute teachers, 36
Subterranean, 90, 130
Suburbia, 134
Subways, 90, 117
Suicide, 20, 35, 38, 40, 49, 134, 161, 189
Sultan, 153
Sumatra, 66
Summer, 9, 10, 21, 22, 24, 27, 47, 48, 55, 56, 58, 59, 62, 71, 77, 90, 101, 125, 129, 131, 149, 151, 160, 162, 163, 164, 173, 174, 175
Summer reading games, 9, 10, 193
Super powers, 126
Superheroes, 177, 179, 180
Superhuman, 124, 180
Supernatural. See Paranormal
Supernatural powers, 117, 127, 131, 135
Superstition, 191
Surfing, 47, 60
Surrealism, 17, 90
Survival, xii, 27, 65–70, 105, 117, 122, 125, 139, 142, 147, 152, 153, 156, 157, 167, 178
Survival camp, 96
Suspense, 28, 29, 30, 37, 42, 43, 66–69, 71, 73–75, 77, 79, 80, 93, 118, 128, 134, 135, 169
Suspension (school), 23, 26
Swans, 94
Swashbucklers, 86
Swim team, 38, 56
Swimmers, 18, 36, 56, 57
Swimming, 38, 55, 90
Swimming hole, 75
Swordplay, 86
Swords, 93, 107
Sydney, 49

Tabloids, 125, 126
Talent, 33, 56, 57, 69, 87, 119
Taliban, 167
Tallness, 29, 48, 58, 70, 120
Tamil Tigers, 164
Tangerine, Florida, 17
Tanglewood, 95
Tarantula, 48
Tarot cards, 136
Tarrytown, New York, 145
Tattoos, 50, 96, 123
T'Chin, 120
Teachers, 16, 17, 29, 32, 35, 36, 41, 48, 83, 88, 98,
     104, 114, 125, 145, 166, 173, 175, 186,
     188, 189, 192
Technology, 68, 89, 105, 112, 114, 118, 194
Teen advisory boards and groups, 6, 9, 10
Teen Hoopla, 195
Teen parents, 24–26, 28, 168, 176
Teen participation councils, 9
Teen Read Week, xi, 10, 169, 177, 182
Teen reading programs, 10
Teenreads, 195
Telekinesis, 110, 119
Telepathy, 47, 90, 110, 118, 119, 130
Teleportation, 110, 118, 119, 130
Television, xi, 10, 61, 79, 115, 127, 135, 179, 183
Tennis player, 187
Termites, 17
Terror, 128, 145
Terrorists and terrorism, 39, 57, 65, 68, 69, 71, 123,
     177, 179, 180
Texas, 17, 49, 50, 58, 148, 161, 164, 165, 171, 172
Theater, 78, 80
Theatrical troupe, 155
Theft, 30, 77
Theme attraction, 90
Themes, xiv, xvi, 1–4, 6, 10, 15, 16, 20, 31, 34, 41,
     42, 52, 54, 58, 65, 70, 71, 86, 90, 92, 97,
     98, 112, 114, 116, 122, 124, 128–30, 134,
     140–43, 146, 152, 154, 159, 169, 177, 197
Thieves, 147
Thirteenth century, 157
Thorns, 123
Thought bubbles, 176
Thrillers, 190
Tigers, 36, 117, 184
Time, 88, 107, 108
Time machine, 116
Time travel, 85, 101, 108–12, 116, 118, 119, 125,
     130, 131, 139, 142
Time Tube, 119
Titanic, 69, 148, 149
Topeka, Kansas, 7
Tor Books, 13
Tor Teen, 85
Tornadoes, 72, 113
Toronto, 32, 59
Torture, 35
Tourism, 27

Tourists, 100
Tower High School, 56, 76, 175
Towns, 17, 21, 23, 27, 28, 48, 49, 50, 57, 60, 67,
     76, 77, 80, 95, 107, 122, 123, 129, 133,
     149, 150, 157, 161, 166, 176, 187
Traders, 87, 123
Tragedy, 15, 18, 23, 31, 33, 34, 39, 46, 47, 56, 160,
     173, 179
Trail of Tears, 141
Transmutation, 58
Transvestites, 32
Transylvania, 103
Travels, 18, 19, 54, 58, 75, 76, 80, 88, 96, 107, 109,
     118, 119, 125, 142, 144, 145, 147, 201
Treason, 95, 107
Treasures, 70
Treasury Department agent, 192
Trees, 37, 40, 88, 133
Trends, xii, xiii, 1, 2, 3, 4, 73, 97, 169
Trials, 31, 33, 170, 178
Triangle Shirtwaist Company, 149
Tribes, 40, 153, 181
Tribulation Force, 190
Tricksters, 96
Trinity Center, 189
Triwizard Tournament, 101
Trojan War, 91
Trolls, 93, 94, 98, 105
Troy, 91, 140, 153, 154
Truth, 30, 39, 40, 74, 132, 162, 165, 167
Tsimshian Indian, 158, 161
Tulsa, 29
Turkeys, 148
Turks, 157
Turtles, 96, 177
Tutoring, 11, 54, 88
Twelfth century, 92, 157
Twentieth century, 148–50, 156
Twenty-first century, 119
Twins, 20, 57, 87, 88, 117

U.S. history, 140
Ukulele, 54
Uncles, 26, 27, 32, 38, 40, 41, 47, 50, 53, 58, 66,
     69, 70, 80, 81, 118, 123, 133, 144, 149,
     151, 157, 163, 164, 167, 186, 189
Uncommon common animals, 102–4
Undead, 129, 134
Underground, 75, 98
Underground Railroad, 129, 145, 172
Underland, 108
Underseas, 123
Unexplained phenomena, 132–34
Unicorns, 85, 102
Union forces, 146
Unique issues, 31
Unique settings, 157, 158
Unitarian, 25
United Kingdom, 40
United Nations, 180, 190

United States, 3, 8, 10, 27, 39, 77, 118, 124, 141, 143, 149, 150, 157, 162, 163, 164, 165, 182
Universities, 89
University of Illinois Press, 196
Upheaval, 146, 166
Urban fantasy, 86, 98
Urban Institute, 39
Urchin, 88, 101
Utopian/dystopian, 121, 122

Vacation, 50, 101, 121, 188
Valedictorian, 191
Valentine's Day, 171
Valley, 67, 99, 106, 123
Value of reading, xii
Vampire Mountain, 135
Vampires, 61, 98, 127, 128, 134, 135
Vancouver, 32, 158
Vectors, 120
Vegetarianism, 148
Venice, 27
Vermont, 27, 130, 150, 176
Verse novels, 4, 33, 129, 169, 170, 175, 176
Veterans, 148
Victims, 15, 42, 72, 134, 145
Victorian times, 78, 109, 116, 172, 178
Vietnam, 139, 161, 163, 165,
Vietnam War, 139, 148, 151, 152, 171
Vikings, 81, 153
Villages, 27, 51, 66, 97, 123, 132, 141, 142, 151, 154, 156–58, 166
Villains, 96
Violence, 29, 33, 35, 54, 88, 127, 165, 181
Virginia, 22, 33, 39, 146, 159
Virtual reality, 114, 115
Virtual war, 114
Virus, 122, 123
Visions, 79, 131, 136, 154
Visual learners, 169
Vivitare, 120
Vogon, 116
Voice, 2, 29, 33, 34, 42, 87, 117, 120, 154, 165, 172
Voice of Youth Advocates (VOYA), xv, 6, 18, 19, 21, 28, 31, 36, 39, 40, 53, 66, 71, 78, 92, 149, 152, 155, 163, 168, 170, 171, 176, 177, 196
Volcanic activity, 124, 191
Volunteers, 9–11, 26, 29, 97, 120, 171
VOYA. See Voice of Youth Advocates (VOYA)

Wales, 93, 129, 154
War, 32, 41, 65, 67, 69–71 78, 91, 99, 114, 115, 119, 120, 122, 123, 133, 142, 143, 146, 147, 154, 156–58, 161, 163, 166
Warriors, 21, 104, 183
Washington, 144
Washington, D.C., xvi, 125, 143
Washington Territory, 191
Water, 64, 66, 98, 101, 161, 183

Water People, 121
Wealth, 13, 23, 29, 30, 34, 54, 58, 63, 69, 72, 76–78, 89, 96, 109, 116, 122, 124, 140, 145, 151, 152, 154, 155, 163, 164
Weapons, 78, 88, 98, 105
Weasels, 103
Weather, 87, 150
Web sites, xi, 10, 11, 27, 181, 183, 190, 194, 202
Weddings, 48, 78, 173, 188
Weeding, 6
Werewolves, 127, 129, 130, 135
Wessex Academy, 62
West, 129, 143, 146, 147
West Virginia, 144
Western Europe, 154–56
Western Writers of America, 8
Westerns, 8, 140, 143, 146, 148, 154, 155, 156
Westward expansion, 140, 143, 146–48
What if, 47, 91, 111
Whitbread Award, 18, 89, 101
Whitechurch, 32
White supremacist, 71
Whites, 21, 28, 29, 36, 55, 147, 151, 157, 160, 161, 162, 166
Wicca, 135, 136, 137
Widows and widowers, 25, 36, 40, 46, 141, 145, 149, 154, 168, 192
Wild West show, 147
Wilderness, 65, 66, 67, 68, 132
Wilderness Adventure camp, 125
Wildfire, 149
Wildlife biologist, 30
Wildlife refuges, 26
Wildlife rescue, 27
Winding Circle, 87
Windows, 76, 122, 124
Wings, 38, 97
Winter, 68, 142
Winter solstice, 136
Wisconsin, 18, 29, 53, 55, 58, 161
Witches and witchcraft, 3, 17, 63, 79, 96, 99, 101, 102, 108, 128, 129, 131, 135–38, 142, 143
Witches' Night Out coven, 136
Witness Protection Program, 39, 65, 72, 75
Witnesses, 39, 72, 78, 82, 171
Wizards and wizardry, 95, 96, 100, 101, 102, 107, 108, 180
Wizards of the Warrior World, 108
Wolfriders, 181
Wolves, 66, 72, 103, 105, 129, 130
Woodbane conspiracy, 137, 138
Woods, 49, 88, 89, 108, 109
Working class, 33, 160
Working with teens, 193–94
Workshop on Adolescent Literacy, xiii
World Fantasy Award, 181
World history, 140, 152–58
World Science Fiction Convention, 8
World War I, 148, 156
World War II, 23, 70,, 150, 151, 156, 158, 167

Wormholes, 116
Wotwots, 116
Wrestlers and wrestling, 20, 56, 57
Writing, 7, 24, 46, 54, 58, 61, 80, 124, 140, 145, 195

Xenocides, 113

YALSA. *See* Young Adult Library Services Association (YALSA)
YALSA 100 Best Books, xv, 17–19, 21, 23, 26–28, 33, 35, 37, 42, 47, 53, 55–58, 60, 66–68, 72, 75, 76, 78, 93–95, 97, 99, 100, 103, 104, 106, 107, 108, 112, 114, 115, 119, 120, 122, 123, 134, 144, 146, 151, 152, 154, 156, 163, 168, 171, 172, 174, 176, 178, 195
YALSA-BK, 10, 195
YALSA-L, 10

YASFFA. *See.* Young Adult Science Fiction and Fantasy Association discussion group
Yellow fever, 142
Yeti, 72, 89
Young Adult Canadian Book Award, 8, 90
Young Adult Choices Poll, xv, 8
Young Adult Library Services Association (YALSA), xi, xv, 7, 9, 13, 195, 196
Young Adult Science Fiction and Fantasy discussion group, 198
Younger audience, 142
Youth groups, 25
Youth participation, 195
Yukon, 72, 144

Zimbabwe, 119
Zombies, 81, 127, 129, 130
Zondervan, 4, 62, 187
Zoos, 82, 104, 120

Author Index

Abelove, Joan, 18, 166
Adams, Douglas, 115
Adams, Richard, 103
Adamson, Lynda, 197
Adler, Elizabeth, 141, 161
Aiken, Joan, 98
Alch, Mark L., 1, 6
Alder, Elizabeth, 154
Alexander, Lloyd, 96
Allende, Isabel, 89
Almond, David, 18, 89, 132
Alphin, Elaine Marie, 42, 128, 203
Altmann, Anna, 93, 110
Alvarez, Julia, 164
Anderson, K. J., 155
Anderson, Laurie Halse, 20, 46, 142, 203
Anderson, M. T., 122, 134, 206
Appelt, Kathi, 171, 207
Applegate, K. A., 105, 206
Aragonés, Sergio, 177
Armstrong, Jennifer, 122, 143, 146
Arnoldi, Katherine, 34, 178, 203
Aronson, Marc, 193
Ashley, Bernard, 40
Atkins, Catherine, 35, 42, 203
Atwater-Rhodes, Amelia, 134, 206
Auch, Mary Jane, 149
Austen, Jane, 101, 148
Avi, 26, 77, 154–55, 205
Ayres, Katherine, 145, 172

Baer, Judy, 61, 186
Baker, Sharon, 12, 13
Bardi, Abby, 40, 71
Barker, Clive, 106
Barrett, Tracy, 153
Barron, T. A., 88
Baskin, Nora Raleigh, 46
Bat-Ami, Miriam, 150
Bauer, Joan, 37, 46, 58, 204
Bauer, Marion Dane, 23
Baum, L. Frank, 86
Baxter, Stephen, 152
Bechard, Margaret, 24–25, 203
Bell, Hilari, 98, 120, 123
Bell, William, 71, 205
Bendis, Brian-Michael, 179, 207
Bennett, Cherie, 16, 37, 109, 128, 132, 203, 206
Bennett, James W., 55
Bernardo, Anilu, 52, 164

Berry, James, 157
Berry, Liz, 89
Bertrand, Diane Gonzales, 46, 164
Bird, Isobel, 3, 135, 206
Black, Holly, 88
Black, Jonah, 12, 61, 172–73, 204
Blacker, Terence, 120
Blacklock, Dyan, 153
Blackwood, Gary, 142, 155
Block, Francesca Lia, 23, 35, 38, 89, 93, 203
Bloor, Edward, 17, 28, 38, 55
Blume, Judy, 52
Bodart, Joni Richards, 11, 194
Bodett, Tom, 72
Boock, Paula, 52
Booth, Martin, 156
Borgman, Jim, 184, 207
Bowler, Tim, 18
Bradburn, Frances, 169
Bradbury, Ray, 132
Bradley, Kimberly Brubaker, 18
Branford, Henrietta, 72, 154
Brashares, Ann, 174
Brenaman, Miriam, 146
Brennan, Herbie, 106
Brennan, Michael, 179
Breslin, Theresa, 156
Brockett, D. A., 149
Brooke, Peggy, 40, 149
Brooke, William J., 153
Brooks, Bruce, 20, 55
Brooks, Geraldine, 154
Brooks, Kevin, 38
Brooks, Martha, 40, 46, 166
Brooks, Terry, 106, 199
Bruchac, Joseph, 133, 141
Bryant, Sharon, 37
Buffie, Margaret, 20, 79, 106, 128
Bunting, Eve, 18, 203
Burgess, Melvin, 40, 42
Burks, Brian, 141, 147
Busiek, Kurt, 179, 180
Butcher, Nancy, 122
Butler, Susan, 123
Buzzeo, Toni, 10, 13
Cabot, Meg, 2, 47, 52, 58, 61, 172–73, 207
Cadnum, Michael, 20, 30, 91, 153
Calhoun, Dia, 106
Cann, Kate, 62
Carbone, Elisa, 143

Card, Orson Scott, 93, 111, 112, 118
Carroll, Jenny, 79, 80
Cart, Michael, 2, 3, 13, 23, 52, 112, 126, 194, 203
Carter, Alden R., 55, 204
Carter, Betty, 194
Carvell, Marlene, 26, 166
Chabon, Michael, 106
Chambers, Aidan, 23
Chandler, Elizabeth, 80, 131, 205
Chbosky, Stephen, 47, 174, 204
Chelton, Mary K., 9, 13, 193
Chevalier, Tracy, 155
Childress, Alice, 42
Choldenko, Gennifer, 20
Clark, Catherine, 52
Clement-Davies, David, 103
Clements, Andrew, 119
Clowes, Daniel, 178
Cochran, Molly, 92
Cochran, Thomas, 55
Cofer, Judith Ortiz, 164, 171, 207
Cohn, Rachel, 47, 90, 204
Cole, Brock, 35, 203
Cole, Sheila, 173
Coleman, Evelyn, 55, 162
Coles, William E., Jr., 77
Colfer, Eoin, 89
Conford, Ellen, 58, 96, 171, 207
Connelly, Neil, 20
Cook, Karin, 18
Cooney, Caroline B., 26, 28, 40, 43, 47, 68, 75, 91,
    109, 142, 203, 205
Cooper, Susan, 109
Cormier, Robert, 30, 74, 119, 150, 175, 207
Couloumbis, Audrey, 18
Coville, Bruce, 32, 71, 91, 97, 102, 205–206
Cowley, Joy, 138
Craft, Elizabeth, 205
Cray, Jordan, 80, 205
Creech, Sharon, 47, 58, 69, 173, 175
Crew, Linda, 149
Crichton, Michael, 118
Crilley, Mark, 182
Cross, Gillian, 29, 75
Crossley-Holland, Kevin, 92
Crutcher, Chris, 7, 32, 35, 37, 38, 47, 55, 56
Curry, Jane Louise, 109, 142
Curtis, Christopher Paul, 40, 149
Cushman, Karen, 154, 172
Cusick, Richie Tankersley, 73

Dahl, Michael, 80
Dalkey, Kara, 106
Danziger, Paula, 175, 207
Dart-Thornton, Cecilia, 199
Datlow, Ellen, 97
David, Peter, 179, 180, 207
Davis, Terry, 4, 48, 56
Day, Dianne, 149
Dean, Carolee, 31

DeFelice, Cynthia, 150
Delaney, Mark, 3, 81
de Lint, Charles, 89, 98
Denenberg, Barry, 172
Desai Hidier,Tanuja, 163
Dessen, Sarah, 25, 34, 48, 52, 205
Deuker, Carl, 56
de Vos, Gail, 93, 110
Dickinson, Peter, 99, 114, 153
Disher, Garry, 157
Dixon, Chuck, 180
Dodd, Quentin, 116
Douglass, Sara, 199
Dowell, Frances O'Roark, 78
Downing, Wick, 40, 128
Draper, Sharon M, 18, 31, 35, 52, 160, 162
Duane, Diane, 107
Duncan, Lois, 79, 131, 205
Durham, David Anthony, 147
Dygard, Thomas J., 56

Easton, Kelly, 152
Eberhardt, Thom, 58, 205
Eddings, David, 200
Edwards, Kirsten, 193
Elliott, L. M., 70
Ellis, Deborah, 70, 167
Ellis, Warren, 180, 207
Erdrich, Louise, 141
Etchemendy, Nancy, 138
Ewing, Lynne, 3, 29, 131, 206

Fama, Elizabeth, 66
Farmer, Lesley, 194
Farmer, Nancy, 119, 124
Ferris, Jean, 23, 30, 53, 58, 93, 94, 203
Fienberg, Anna, 25
Flake, Sharon G., 40, 162, 207
Fleischman, Paul, 20, 146, 160, 170, 171
Fletcher, Ralph, 48
Fletcher, Susan, 144, 153
Flinn, Alex, 30, 31, 34, 204
Fogelin, Adrian, 28
Fonseca, Anthony, 128, 138
Frank, Anne, 156
Frank, E. R., 32, 36, 40, 171, 204
Frank, Hillary, 48
Frank, Lucy, 53
Fraustino, Lisa Rowe, 32, 204
Freymann-Weyr, Garret, 23
Friel, Maeve, 38
Friesen, Gayle, 48
Froese, Deborah, 17
Fujishima, Kosuke, 182

Gaiman, Neil, 133, 181
Gallo, Don, 37
Galloway, Priscilla, 153
Gantos, Jack, 21, 23
Garden, Nancy, 23, 53

Garfield, Henry, 109, 130
Garland, Sherry, 147
Geary, Rick, 178
George, Jean Craighead, 66
Geras, Adele, 91, 153
Gerrold, David, 113
Giblin, James Cross, 112
Giff, Patricia Reilly, 37, 156
Gilbert, Barbara Snow, 71
Giles, Gail, 38, 204
Gilmore, Kate, 120, 206
Gilstrap, John, 76
Glenn, Mel, 21, 56, 76, 175, 207
Glovach, Linda, 42, 204
Golden, Christopher, 81, 82, 113, 130, 177, 205
Gonick, Larry, 178
Gonzales, Albino, 165
Goobie, Beth, 26, 38, 90, 204
Goodman, Alison, 120
Goodman, Joan Elizabeth, 142
Gorfinkel, Jordan, 180
Gorman, Michele, 177, 182
Gottesfeld, Jeff, 109
Gould, Steven C., 116, 119
Grant, Cynthia D., 41, 42, 59, 204
Gray, Dianne E, 170
Gray, Luli, 102
Green, Timothy, 76
Gresh, Danny, 114
Gresh, Lois, 114
Griffin, Adele, 38, 204
Grimes, Nikki, 176, 207
Groening, Matt, 183
Gurney, James, 107
Guy, Rosa, 76

Haddix, Margaret Peterson, 32, 38, 94, 122, 124,
    173, 204, 206
Hahn, Mary Downing, 148
Halam, Ann, 124
Hanauer, Cathi, 21
Hanscome, Jeanette, 186
Hardman, Ric Lynden, 148
Harris, Robert J., 155
Harrison, Michael, 76
Hartinger, Brent, 39
Hartnett, Sonya, 32
Hautman, Pete, 17, 118, 123
Hawes, Louise, 18, 128
Hawke, Simon, 78
Haydon, Elizabeth, 200
Hayes, Daniel, 59
Helbig, Alethea K., 198
Heneghan, James, 32, 109
Herald, Diana Tixier, 9, 13, 110, 112, 126, 197, 198
Hernandez, Jo Ann Yolanda, 165
Herrera, Juan Felipe, 165, 176, 207
Hesse, Karen, 69, 150, 157, 176
Heuston, Kimberley, 144
Hewett, Lorri, 28, 160

Hiaasen, Carl, 59
Hill, David, 66
Hill, Pamela Smith, 110, 131
Hinton, S. E., 29
Hirsch, Karen, 48, 178
Hite, Sid, 48, 148
Hobbs, Valerie, 25, 48, 66
Hobbs, Will, 26, 30, 65–67, 72, 144, 204, 207
Hoffman, Alice, 90, 123
Hogan, James P., 113, 114, 206
Hoh, Diane, 69, 205
Holeman, Linda, 156
Holley, Pam Spencer, 194
Holm, Jennifer L., 144
Holmes, Barbara Ware, 76
Holt, Kimberly Willis, 32
Homer, 46
Honeycutt, Natalie, 49
Hoobler, Dorothy, 3, 78
Hoobler, Thomas, 3, 78
Horowitz, Anthony, 68, 78, 155, 205
Hosler, Jay, 178
Howarth, Lesley, 117
Howe, James, 27, 34
Howe, Norma, 59
Hrdlitschka, Shelley, 25
Hughes, Dean, 156
Hunt, Caroline Rose, 172
Hunter, Mollie, 154
Hurwin, Davida Wills, 18
Huth, Angela, 156
Hyde, Catherine R., 27

Ingold, Jeanette, 17, 149
Isaacs, Anne, 156

Jacobs, Paul Samuel, 142
Jacques, Brian, 103
Janeczko, Paul, 176
Jarvis, Robin, 104
Jeapes, Ben, 113
Jenkins, A. M., 21, 23, 57, 204
Jenkins, Jerry B., 190
Jimenez, Francisco, 165
Johnson, Angela, 18, 19, 25, 129, 163
Johnson, D. Curtis, 180
Johnson, Kathleen Jeffrie, 53
Johnson, Lissa Halls, 186
Joinson, Carla, 149
Jones, Diana Wynne, 4, 85, 96, 100, 107
Jones, Patrick, 2, 6, 10, 11, 14, 193, 194
Jordan, Robert, 200
Jordan, Sherryl, 17, 99, 107

Kan, Katharine L., 177, 193
Karr, Kathleen, 131, 144, 148
Kaye, Marilyn, 123, 124, 206
Keane, Nancy, 11, 14
Keizer, Garret, 27

Kennedy, Cam, 182, 207
Kerr, M. E., 24, 151
Kessler, Cristina, 32, 167
Kidd, Sue Monk, 152
Kimmel, Elizabeth Cody, 129
Kindl, Patrice, 90, 94, 104
King, Stephen, 127
Kirkpatrick, Katherine, 142
Kirwan, Anna, 172
Klass, David, 34, 49, 57, 69
Klause, Annette Curtis, 130, 134, 206
Koertge, Ron, 37, 39, 49, 59, 112, 176, 204
Koja, Kathe, 21
Konigsburg, E. L., 37
Korman, Gordon, 53, 59, 205
Koss, Amy Goldman, 39, 57, 204
Krisher, Trudy, 28, 152
Kudo, Kazuya, 183
Kunzel, Bonnie, 112, 126, 198
Kurtz, Jane, 10, 13, 167

Lackey, Mercedes, 102
LaHaye, Tim, 189–190
L'Amour, Louis, 146
Laird, Elizabeth, 27, 167
Lane, Dakota, 53
Langemack, Chapple, 11, 14
Lasky, Kathryn, 78, 126
Lawrence, Iain, 41, 49, 67, 69, 156, 205
Laxalt, Robert, 147
Leavitt, Martine, 100
Lee, Stan, 180
L'Engle, Madeleine, 117
Lerangis, Peter, 117
Les Becquets, Diane, 28
Leslie, Roger, 194
Lester, Julius, 19, 153, 204
Levine, Gail Carson, 41, 94, 150, 206
Levitin, Sonia, 76, 118
Lewis, Beverly, 62, 187
Lewis, C. S., 107, 189–190
Lipsyte, Robert, 21
Lisle, Janet Taylor, 151
Littke, Lael, 133
Loeb, Jeph, 180
Logue, Mary, 120, 206
Lovecraft, H. P., 127
Lowenstein, Sallie, 121
Lowry, Lois, 112, 122
Lubar, David, 108, 119, 131, 206
Luiken, Nicole, 126
Lundgren, Mary Beth, 36
Lynch, Chris, 32, 49, 59, 152, 161, 205
Lynn, Ruth Nadelman, 197
Lynne Evarts, 18

MacDougal, Scarlett, 62, 205
Mackler, Carolyn, 49, 53, 205
Macy, Sue, 56
Magorian, Michelle, 156

Makowski, Silk, 194
Manczuk, Suzanne, 198
Marchetta, Melina, 49
Marillier, Juliet, 94, 201
Marsden, John, 37, 67, 70
Martin, Ann M., 174, 175, 207
Martin, George R. R., 201
Martínez, Victor, 165
Matas, Carol, 146, 156, 157
Matcheck, Diane, 67, 142
Mazer, Norma Fox, 19, 34
McCafferty, Megan, 60
McCaffrey, Anne, 86, 111, 119
McCants, William D., 60, 205
McCaughrean, Geraldine, 157
McColley, Kevin, 74
McCormick, Patricia, 21, 204
McDaniel, Lurlene, 19, 204
McDonald, Janet, 25
McDonald, Joyce, 30, 32, 74, 133
McKinley, Robin, 91, 93, 94, 98, 99
McLaren, Clemence, 154
McNamee, Graham, 34, 204
McNiven, Steve, 181
Mead, Alice, 70, 167
Medley, Linda, 181
Metz, Melinda, 132, 206
Meyer, Carolyn, 49, 155, 161
Mikaelsen, Ben, 27, 31, 67
Miklowitz, Gloria D., 71
Millar, Mark, 180
Miller, Frank, 180
Miller, Mary Beth, 33
Miller-Lachman, Lyn, 198
Min, Anchee, 167
Miyazaki, Hayao, 183
Moench, Doug, 133, 181
Moore, Alan, 180, 181
Moore, Christopher, 60
Moore, Martha, 49, 50
Moore, Terry, 178
Moriarty, Jaclyn, 60, 175
Morris, Gerald, 92
Morris, Gilbert, 4, 191
Morris, Lynn, 191
Morrison, Grant, 180, 207
Mort, John, 4, 14, 185, 192, 197
Mosher, Richard, 161
Mosier, Elizabeth, 53
Mouly, Francoise, 184
Mowry, Jess, 29, 33
Murphy, Pat, 116
Murphy, Rita, 133
Murphy, Warren, 92
Myers, Walter Dean, 7, 29, 31, 33, 50, 57, 147, 152, 162, 163, 169–172, 175, 207

Na, An, 34, 164
Naidoo, Beverley, 41, 167
Namioka, Lensey, 157

Napoli, Donna Jo, 27, 74, 91, 94, 95
Naylor, Phyllis Reynolds, 62, 71, 79, 133
Nelson, Theresa, 19
Newth, Mette, 156
Nichols, C. Allen, 194
Nichols, Mary Anne, 194
Nicholson, William, 87
Nishiyama, Yuriko, 183
Nix, Garth, 100, 123
Nixon, Joan Lowery, 76, 77, 79, 129, 206
Nodelman. Perry, 60
Nolan, Han, 21, 32, 41, 50
Noonan, Rosalind, 205
Norton, Andre, 102
Nye, Namoi, 161

Oates, Joyce Carol, 39
O'Brien, Robert C., 123
Oke, Janette, 191
O'Keefe, Susan Heyboer, 21
Okimoto, Jean Davis, 50
Oppel, Kenneth, 104
O'Reilly, Brian, 6
Orr, Wendy, 17
Osa, Nancy, 165

Park, Barbara, 19
Park, Linda Sue, 157, 158, 167
Parker, Daniel, 62
Paterson, Katherine, 112, 144, 151
Patrick, Denise Lewis, 147, 163
Pattou, Edith, 87
Paulsen, Gary, 2, 7, 60, 65, 68, 117, 145, 146, 147,
    205, 206, 207
Peck, Richard, 28, 116, 148, 150, 171, 204
Peck, Robert Newton, 147
Pennebaker, Ruth, 50
Perkins, Agnes Regan, 198
Peters, Julie Anne, 24
Petrie, Doug, 181
Philbrick, Rodman, 17, 34, 68, 72, 112, 123
Pierce, Meredith Ann, 95, 135
Pierce, Tamora, 87, 88, 99, 206
Pike, Christopher, 73
Pini, Richard, 181
Pini, Wendy, 181
Placide, Jaira, 36, 167
Plummer, Louise, 22, 25
Plum-Ucci, Carol, 74, 77
Powell, Randy, 50, 57
Pratchett, Terry, 96, 104
Price, Susan, 119
Priest, Christopher, 180
Pulliam, June, 128, 138
Pullman, Philip, 78, 95, 108, 206

Qualey, Marsha, 29, 53, 74, 77, 161, 205
Quarles, Heather, 22

Randle, Kristen D, 54
Rapp, Adam, 36, 37, 124
Ravenwolf, Silver, 3, 136
Rees, Celia, 137, 143
Rennison, Louise, 11, 60, 172, 174, 207
Reynolds, Marilyn, 24, 25, 35
Reynolds, Tom, 194
Rice, Anne, 134
Rice, David, 165
Rinaldi, Ann, 143, 144, 146
Ritter, John, 19, 57, 150
Rivers, Francine, 191
Roberts, Christa, 205
Roberts, Katherine, 88
Roberts, Laura Peyton, 129
Roberts, Willo Davis, 74, 77
Robinson, James, 177
Rosenberg, Liz, 22
Rothschild, D. Aviva, 177, 184, 197
Rottman, S. L., 33, 36, 41, 57, 204
Rowling, J. K., 4, 85, 100
Rushford, Patricia H., 82, 188
Ryan, Pam Munoz, 151
Ryan, Sara, 24
Rylant, Cynthia, 134

Sacher, Louis, 37, 60, 72, 205
Sakai, Stan, 183
Saldana, Rene, Jr., 50, 165
Salinger, J. D., 39
Salisbury, Graham, 31, 32, 37, 50
Sanchez, Alex, 54
Santana, Patricia, 165
Savage, Deborah, 50
Schmidt, Gary D., 95
Schwartz, Virginia, 145
Scieszka, Jon, 112
Scott, Jerry, 184, 207
Sebold, Alice, 134
Seidler, Tor, 112
Shan, Darren, 135
Sheffield, Charles, 113, 114
Shelley, Mary, 129
Sheppard, Mary C., 151
Shetterly, Will, 90, 152
Shoemaker, Joel, 193
Shoup, Barbara, 51
Shusterman, Neal, 20, 30, 90, 120, 121, 206
Silverberg, Robert, 121
Singer, Marilyn, 129, 132
Singleton, L. J., 126, 206
Skurzynski, Gloria, 112, 114, 115, 126
Sleator, William, 75, 115, 117, 119, 121, 130, 206
Smith, Cynthia Leitich, 166
Smith, Jeff, 184
Smith, Kevin, 180
Smith, L. J., 135
Smith, Paul, 177
Smith, Roland, 72, 75, 205
Smith, Sherri L., 70

Smith, Sherwood, 99
Snell, Gordon, 168
Snicket, Lemony, 4, 96
Sniegoski, Thomas E., 113
Somtow, S. P., 135
Sones, Sonya, 22, 54, 176, 204
Soryo, Fuyumi, 183
Soto, Gary, 33, 165, 166, 204, 207
Sparks, Beatrice, 22, 36, 42, 174, 204
Spiegelman, Art, 178, 179, 184
Spinelli, Jerry, 29, 54
Spooner, Michael, 148
Springer, Nancy, 41, 75, 91, 93
Staples, Suzanne Fischer, 28, 168
Staub, Wendy Corsi, 205
Stevenson, James, 72
Stewart, Mary, 93
Stine, R. L., 73
Stoehr, Shelley, 42
Stoker, Bram, 8, 133, 134
Stolz, Karen, 171
Strasser, Todd, 39, 54, 60, 170
Stratton, Allan, 35, 204
Sturtevant, Katherine, 155
Sullivan, Edward T., 194
Sweeney, Joyce, 57, 205
Sykes, Shelley, 43

Takahashi, Rumiko, 183
Talbot, Bryan, 41, 179
Tamaki, Hisao, 183
Tashjian, Janet, 27
Taylor, Mildred D., 146
Taylor, Theodore, 145
Taylor, William, 24
Tchen, Richard, 95
Temple, Frances, 28
Tezuka, Osamu, 183, 207
Thesman, Jean, 54, 150
Thoene, Bodie, 4
Thoene, Brock, 4
Thomas, Rob, 27, 29, 51, 68, 171, 172, 205
Thompson, Craig, 177
Thompson, Julian F., 71
Thompson, Kate, 104, 121, 122
Thomson, Sarah L., 93
Tiernan, Cate, 63, 137, 206
Tolan, Stephanie S., 60, 69, 71, 120
Tolkien, J.R.R., 86
Toriyama, Akira, 183
Toten, Teresa, 22
Tracy Hickman, 201
Trueman, Terry, 17, 22, 204
Turner, Megan Whalen, 69, 88

Vaillancourt, Renee J., 194
Van Draanen, Wendelin, 51, 82
Van Pelt, James, 98

Vance, Susanna, 110
Vande Velde, Vivian, 101, 129, 135, 138, 206
Veitch, Tom, 182, 207
Vella-Zarb, Karen, 6
Verne, Jules, 112, 155
Vijayaraghavan, Vineeta, 164
Vogel, Jane, 186
Von Ziegesar, Cecily, 63

Wallace, Karen, 13
Wallace, Rich, 33, 39, 57, 129, 204
Walter, Virginia, 39, 170
Walters, Eric, 158, 161
Warner, Sally, 20, 22, 145
Watson, Andi, 183
Watterson, Bill, 184
Weaver, Beth Nixon, 152
Weaver, Will, 33, 37, 124
Weiner, Stephen, 177, 184, 197
Weis, Margaret, 201
Wells, H. G., 112
Welter, John, 61
Werlin, Nancy, 37, 75, 161, 205
Wersba, Barbara, 24, 204
Whelan, Gloria, 158, 168
White, Ellen Emerson, 152, 173
White, Robb, 68
White, Ruth, 22
Wick, Lori, 192
Wieler, Diana, 51, 79, 132
Wierenga, Kathy, 186
Williams, Carol Lynch, 22, 54, 61, 204
Williams, Lori Aurelia, 36, 42, 163
Williams, Tad, 202
Williams-Garcia, Rita, 26, 51, 161–163, 207
Willis, Connie, 116
Wilson, Jacqueline, 54, 63
Wilson, Patricia Potter, 194
Windling, Terri, 97
Windsor, Patricia, 130, 207
Winick, Judd, 177, 179
Wittlinger, Ellen, 24, 204
Wolff, Virginia Euwer, 33, 151, 176
Woodson, Jacqueline, 31, 36, 39, 112, 162, 163
Wrede, Patricia C., 85, 97, 98, 101
Wulffson, Don, 70
Wynne-Jones, Tim, 43, 77

Yamanaka, Lois-Ann, 24, 164
Yep, Laurence, 77, 164
Yolen, Jane, 71, 93, 95, 98, 129, 155, 205
Young, Karen Romano, 54
Yumoto, Kazumi, 168
Yune, Tommy, 183

Zindel, Paul, 3, 70, 82, 130, 151, 207
Zollo, Peter, 1, 6
Zusak, Markus, 33

About the Author

DIANA TIXIER HERALD, a former readers' advisory librarian, is a consultant and lecturer from Grand Junction, Colorado, who specializes in genre fiction. She currently serves as Chair of the ALA Young Adult Services Association Quick Picks for Reluctant Young Adult Readers Committee and has been elected to the Margaret A. Edwards Committee.